DOG DAYS

DOG DAYS

The New York Yankees' Fall from Grace and Return to Glory

1964-1976

PHILIP BASHE

R A N D O M   H O U S E   /   N E W   Y O R K

All statistics referred to are from *The Baseball Encyclopedia*,
Joseph L. Reichler, editor, sixth edition (1985),
published by Macmillan Publishing Company.

Grateful acknowledgment is made to the following for permission
to reprint previously published material:

GEORGE D. WOLF: Excerpts from *Yankees by the Number* by George D. Wolf.
This work was privately published and is available from George D. Wolf,
2323 Delanoy Avenue, Bronx, New York, 10469-6305.
Reprinted by permission.

Library of Congress Cataloging-in-Publication Data

Bashe, Philip.
Dog days: the New York Yankees' fall from grace and return to glory,
1964–1976 / by Philip Bashe.
p.   cm.
Includes bibliographical references.
ISBN 0-679-41310-3
1. New York Yankees (Baseball team)—History.   I. Title.
GV875.N4B37   1994   796.357'64'097471—dc20   93-45894

Manufactured in the United States of America
2   4   6   8   9   7   5   3
First Edition
Book design by JoAnne Metsch

To Justin Eric Romanowski Bashe,
the biggest hit in our lives

ACKNOWLEDGMENTS

MY SINCERE THANKS to the following for their kind assistance. From the New York Yankees: Jeff Idelson, Rob Butcher, Linda Reiner, Jim Ogle, Marty Naughton, Kirk Randazzo, and Jeff Pfeifer. Also the media- or public-relations departments of the New York Mets, Atlanta Braves, Baltimore Orioles, Cleveland Indians, San Francisco Giants, St. Louis Cardinals, and Pittsburgh Pirates.

Special thanks to those players, managers, coaches, batboys, front-office personnel, broadcasters, and sportswriters who consented to speak with me. Alphabetically they are: Jack Aker, Bernie Allen, Maury Allen, Sandy Alomar, Ruben Amaro, Stan Bahnsen, Frank Baker, Steve Barber, Ray Barker, Fred Beene, Vern Benson, Howard Berk, Curt Blefary, Ron Blomberg, Bobby Bonds, Jim Bouton, Clete Boyer, Billy Bryan, Bill Burbach, Danny Cater, Chris Chambliss, Horace Clarke, Lou Clinton, Rocky Colavito, Bob Costas, Bobby Cox, John Cumberland, Joe D'Ambrosio, Pat Dobson, Joe Donnelly, Al Downing, Doc Edwards, Dock Ellis, John Ellis, Mike Ferraro, Ed Figueroa, Rob Gardner, Jake Gibbs, Dick Groat, Larry Gura, Steve Hamilton, Fran Healy, Mike Hegan, Ralph Houk, Arlene Howard, Catfish Hunter, Stan Isaacs, Steve Jacobson, Mike Kekich, John Kennedy, Jerry Kenney, Ron Klimkowski, Steve Kline, Andy Kosco, Hal Lanier, Phil Linz, Hector Lopez, Jim Lyttle, Lee MacPhail, Rudy May, Lindy McDaniel, Sam McDowell, George "Doc" Medich, Frank Messer, Gene Michael, Pete Mikkelsen, Bill Monbouquette, Archie Moore, Ross Moschitto, Jerry Moses, Thad Mumford, Bobby Murcer, Dave Pagan, Gabe Paul, Phil Pepe, Fritz Peterson, Lou Piniella, Pedro Ramos, Hal Reniff, Roger Repoz, Bobby Richardson, Bill Robinson, Rollie Sheldon, Tom Shopay, Duke Sims, Joe Soares, Bill Stafford, Fred Stanley, Ron Swoboda, Ralph Terry, Dick Tidrow, Tom Tresh, George Vecsey, Frank Verdi, Bill Virdon, Pete Ward, Gary Waslewski, Steve Whitaker, Roy White, Stan Williams, Dooley Womack, and Vic Ziegel.

Finally, very special thanks to my editor, David Rosenthal; his assistant, Tad Floridis; copy editor Ed Cohen; proofreader Eva Young; art director Andy Carpenter; designer JoAnne Metsch; production editor Dennis Ambrose; my agent, Jed Mattes; his assistant, Robert Grogan; Robert and Rochelle Bashe; the late Evelyn Bashe; and, as always, Patty Romanowski Bashe.

CONTENTS

PROLOGUE

WITH SPARKLING OCTOBER sunshine glinting off its white horsehide, the ball seemed to hang in midair, yielding a moment of infinite possibilities. Enough distance for a bloop hit? A sure final out? Thirty thousand necks craned skyward.

Then the sphere descended to the infield, and with it plummeted the New York Yankees' hopes for a come-from-behind victory in the seventh game of the World Series. Hitter Bobby Richardson flung his bat aside and with head bowed trotted stoically toward first base, while Roger Maris, crouched in the on-deck circle and representing the tying run, dropped his chin to his chest.

St. Louis second baseman Dal Maxvill gleefully camped under the ball. Even before he'd secured it in his glove, joyful bleachers fans were dropping down onto the warning track like paratroopers at Normandy, and teammates were swarming to the mound to mob pitcher Bob Gibson.

The Cardinals were baseball's 1964 World Champions.

Fireworks exploded, bugles blared, and exultant fans patrolled Busch Stadium in a then rare act of (condoned) civil disobedience. Meanwhile the Yankees retired glumly to the visitors' clubhouse, shut the steel door behind them, and slowly peeled off their gray flannel road uniforms.

Over muffled chants of "We want Gibson!" manager Yogi Berra quietly told his team, "You guys played good. We'll get 'em next year." Trailing 6–0 after five innings, they had battled back to within two runs.

Though disappointed, Mickey Mantle, Elston Howard, Tom Tresh, and the others by no means cloaked themselves in mourning. As always, optimism prevailed. Scarcely anyone in the room doubted that the American League pennant winners for thirteen of the past fifteen seasons wouldn't return to the World Series a sixth consecutive time in 1965, the Bronx Bombers and the Fall Classic being then as synonymous as *The Ed Sullivan Show* and Sunday night.

But twelve painful years were to pass before New York made it back, during which time the game of baseball and America itself would undergo profound changes destined to rattle the foundations of both. On that balmy afternoon in St. Louis, few foresaw that this baseball dynasty, once compared to U.S. Steel, was badly tarnished. The team that had long tyrannized the national pastime was about to begin a humiliating odyssey—from Damned Yankees to Yankees of the Damned.

PART I

A Lot of Guys Got Old at Once

1964

STARTERS	Joe Pepitone (1B)	RELIEVERS
Whitey Ford	Bobby Richardson (2B)	Pete Mikkelsen
Jim Bouton	Tony Kubek/Phil Linz	Hal Reniff
Al Downing	(SS)	Bill Stafford
Mel Stottlemyre	Clete Boyer (3B)	Steve Hamilton
Ralph Terry	Tom Tresh (LF)	Pedro Ramos
Rollie Sheldon	Mickey Mantle (CF)	
	Roger Maris (RF)	
	Elston Howard (C)	

I

THE YANKEES ANNOUNCED a press conference for the next afternoon at the Crystal Suite of the Savoy Hilton Hotel. There, it was presumed, they would stage Yogi Berra's rehiring. In his managerial debut, New York's star catcher-turned-skipper had helmed the club to the best won-loss record in baseball that year.

With a grand flourish he would ink a contract, clap on the navy-blue Yankees cap with its distinctive intertwined white *N* and *Y*, then pose grinning with general manager Ralph Houk while flashbulbs lit up the room. It promised to be a brief, uneventful photo opportunity, for which the media, still fatigued from covering the World Series, were grateful.

They sat stunned, then, in their metal folding chairs when Houk stated from the podium with a terse, cryptic "It was better for all concerned" that the Yankees had let Yogi go. The day had already brought the stunning news of Soviet premier Nikita Khrushchev's abrupt ouster. Berra's firing, while less momentous globally, came as no less of a shock to the baseball world.

Prior to the press conference, club co-owner Dan Topping summoned Berra to his Fifth Avenue office, where he and Houk informed him of their decision. Yogi, who'd worn Yankees pinstripes in more games than anyone except the legendary Iron Horse, Lou Gehrig, returned home to Montclair, New Jersey, in tears. Although the future Hall of Famer publicly professed no bitterness, the club quarantined him from reporters, anxious to avoid the public-relations debacle of 1960, when management forced its seventy-year-old manager, the effusive Casey Stengel, into retirement following a World Series loss to the Pittsburgh Pirates. In twelve seasons the Old Professor had brought an extraordinary ten pennants to the Bronx but was then deemed too old.

After Stengel stiffly read a statement prepared for him by the Yankees, a writer asked if he had in fact been fired.

"You're goddamn right I was fired!" Casey shot back, while embarrassed club officials exchanged pained looks. The incident aroused public sentiment that baseball's most storied team was also its most heartless. Terminating the ever-popular Yogi would only solidify the front office's villainous image.

As those in the Crystal Suite listened cynically, Houk stressed that the team was merely moving its former manager elsewhere within the organization. At the mention of Berra's ambiguous new title, "field consultant," one scribe inquired acerbically if that meant he would now be assisting the grounds crew. The job as described by Houk— scouting and "most anything I want him to do"—sounded little better.

In another astonishing development, and a truly bizarre confluence of events, word circulated throughout the room that in St. Louis, Johnny Keane had stepped down as manager of the World Champion Cardinals, dousing the lights on that city's celebration.

"It was shocking," recalls Maury Allen, then a sportswriter for the *New York Post*. "Suddenly both of the managers who'd just competed in this great World Series were gone." For the moment, the twin incidents seemed unrelated.

Pressed by reporters to name Berra's successor, Houk reeled off several candidates.

"What about Keane?" a voice piped up.

"He's not available, is he?" asked Houk.

Informed that Keane had quit less than twenty-four hours after clutching the World Series trophy to his chest, Houk nodded thoughtfully and replied, "If that's so, then I would add him to the list. He would certainly be considered."

II

ONLY A YEAR BEFORE, in that same room, the Yankees had proudly displayed their eighteenth field general in team history. The appointment of Berra, age thirty-nine, drew snickers from at least three sportswriters who had indirectly set in motion the Rube Goldberg–like mechanism that had catapulted Yogi to the status of major-league pilot without so much as a day's training maneuvers.

Around World Series time it was customary for the two major wire services to fabricate preposterous trades, to stir the imaginations of the off-season hot-stove league. The more preposterous the deal, the better. "They would just throw it out onto the wires, even though more often than not there was nothing to it," explains Stan Isaacs, a reporter and later a columnist for Long Island's *Newsday*. "To me it seemed like false journalism."

During a lull in the 1960 World Series, he and two colleagues who also frowned on this practice conspired to entrap the Associated Press's Joe Reichler, one of the most flagrant transgressors. The trio jokingly decided to circulate its own rumor.

"So what was the most outlandish, ridiculous thought in the world at that time?" Isaacs asks rhetorically. "*Yogi Berra as manager.*" Berra may have been the preeminent catcher of his era, and quite possibly the best receiver in baseball annals, but few in or out of the game considered the eighth-grade dropout, who was nearly as famous for mangling the English language as for mangling balls into the seats, managerial material.

In the writers' purported scenario, San Francisco Giants owner Horace Stoneham was contemplating filling the vacancy in his own dugout with Yogi. "We threw it out there," says Isaacs, "and sure enough it went around." The threesome watched in amusement as reporters converged upon Berra at the batting cage, asking him whether or not he would take the job.

Although Berra lacked a formal education, he was a laureate of self-promotion when it came to parlaying his immense popularity into product endorsements and other income-generating ventures. He shrewdly responded to queries with a noncommittal "I haven't spoken to Stoneham yet," further fueling the rumors, which gained momentum like a ground ball skittering over artificial turf. When Isaacs cautioned a colleague not to run the story, confessing, "We made it up!" the editor replied, "I don't care. It's going around, and I'm going to print it."

In an instance of fantasy shaping reality, the Boston Red Sox courted Berra two years later when they were in the market for a manager. Then the Washington Senators. Both were perennial also-rans, and so Berra turned them down. But the Yankees worried they might lose Number 8, one of their few stars with true marquee value, to another organization.

So at spring training in 1963, the club propositioned Berra about succeeding Ralph Houk at year's end. Houk, who had two World Series rings to show for two seasons as manager, was to take over the general managership being vacated by Roy Hamey, allegedly for reasons of health.

"I didn't have any training in that type of work and had no intentions of becoming general manager," admits Houk. "Didn't really want it." After a frustrating career as a third-string New York catcher from 1947 to 1954, Houk managed three years at the Yankees' Denver minor-league affiliate. He then coached another three seasons under Casey Stengel before co-owners Topping and Del Webb swept baseball's most senior citizen aside to make room for his highly touted heir apparent.

Upon being named manager, Houk rhapsodized, "This is the goal I've been shooting for all my life." But now, in 1963, the tobacco-chawing Kansan was being asked to exchange pinstripes for a pin-striped suit. A loyal company man since he signed for a whopping $200 bonus in 1939, Houk capitulated, albeit reluctantly. "I told them, 'Well, if that's what you want, I really have no reason not to do it.' "

Berra was sworn to secrecy, made a player-coach, and advised to spurn future suitors. During the 1963 World Series, Baltimore asked New York permission to speak to him about managing the Orioles, a bona fide contender. But by then Berra was just weeks away from being giddily presented to the media like a debutante at the fall cotillion.

Lovable, comical Yogi, the Yankees were convinced, would not only help humanize the franchise and atone for their callous firing of Stengel, he would also counter the pandemonium on the other side of the Harlem River. In 1962 Casey materialized in the abandoned Polo Grounds as manager of the infant New York Mets, an expansion team conceived to woo the wounded hearts of fans still mourning the traitorous New York Giants and Brooklyn Dodgers, who in 1958 deserted the Big Apple for San Francisco and Los Angeles, respectively.

Never mind that the Old Professor occasionally took siestas on the Mets bench during games and presided over a last-place maiden season in which the team posted the third-worst winning percentage (40–120, .250) in modern baseball history. Stengel and his crew of castaways captured New York's fancy. Inventor of an arcane language known as Stengelese, colorful Casey monopolized the papers even as the Bronx Bombers continued to routinely dominate the American League. Yankees management could only scratch its heads in wonderment. Wasn't winning box office enough?

It was believed that Berra would return the Bronx Bombers to the top of the sports page and fill Yankee Stadium's increasingly empty seats. In their sophomore season the lowly Mets drew 1.1 million to the decaying Polo Grounds. Meanwhile the first-place Yankees watched their attendance tumble by more than 200,000 for the second straight year to just over 1.3 million. With Stengel's club moving into a stylish new stadium in Flushing, Queens, in 1964, the Yankees had further cause for alarm. Hopefully Berra's presence would stem the emigration of fans to these National League upstarts.

At the same time, naming him manager represented the height of conceit, insofar as it implied that even a novice could lead New York's roster of superstars to a pennant—or, rather, that he would be swept up in its greatness like a stone in the surf and surge toward first place.

"Yogi was put in there as a figurehead," relief pitcher Hal Reniff says, "to keep one of the Yankees greats a part of the game. They still thought that anybody could manage us and win." In the past, he adds wryly, that might have been true. "I don't know that we played under managers so much as we were good caretakers. Who had to *manage* those Yankees teams?"

But the club that assembled in Fort Lauderdale for spring training revolved around an aging axis: catcher Elston Howard, the 1963 American League MVP, was thirty-five, the same age as 24-game winner Whitey Ford. And Mickey Mantle, the slugging centerpiece of the lineup and its once-fleet center fielder, was a rickety thirty-two, still recuperating from the broken foot that had restricted him to just 65 games.

An aura of instability pervaded camp. The players uniformly adored Houk and hated to see him go. Along with elevating Houk to GM, the club dismissed popular coach Johnny Sain, a guru of pitching theory, and demoted to the minors batting coach Wally Moses, who, according to his disciples, could part the Red Sea. "What are they trying to do?" left fielder Tom Tresh griped privately. "How do they expect us to win?"

Berra's abrupt metamorphosis from peer to authority figure stirred uneasiness. At the time, not everyone appreciated his predicament. "There was a lot of pressure on Yogi taking over the club," Tresh says in retrospect. "Here's a guy who's been a teammate of most of the players for a number of years; he's on the labor side of the fence. Then all of a sudden he's promoted to management's side, and there's this line between the two. Yogi feels a loyalty to his teammates and feels close to these guys as friends, but he also has to set policy, discipline, and do things that might not be pleasant for him. It was tough for the veterans to differentiate between Yogi the teammate and Yogi the manager."

On the first day of spring training, when the new manager stood up to address his charges, he inspired mostly giggles and wisecracks. "I'm quitting!" someone shouted. In particular, several of the younger players couldn't look beyond Berra's unpolished exterior, which belied a keen baseball mind. They saw only a squat, inarticulate man tentatively trying on the vestments of leadership and finding them an awkward fit. Bobby Richardson, New York's taciturn, steady second baseman, recalls, with a note of regret, "There was probably not the respect there should have been."

As Opening Day approached, the team set aside its disquiet and focused on a fifth consecutive flag. Ultimately, management could have drafted a peanut vendor from the mezzanine to write out the lineup card. As far as the players were concerned, says pitcher Stan Williams, "It really didn't matter much."

A World Series sweep by the overpowering Sandy Koufax and the Los Angeles Dodgers the previous fall hadn't dented New York's confidence. "Even though they beat us four in a row," points out Tresh, "those ball games were close, every one of them. Going into '64, we still felt we had the best ball club."

With good reason. The lineup that had rolled to 104 wins was returning intact, from the infield of Joe Pepitone, Richardson, Tony Kubek, and Clete Boyer, to Tresh, Mantle, and Maris roving the outfield, to the battery of Howard coupled with the finest starting foursome in baseball: 20-game victors Ford and Jim Bouton; Ralph Terry, winner of 40 games in 1962 and 1963 combined; and young Al Downing, who in a half-season posted a 13–5 record and a 2.56 ERA while averaging one strikeout per inning. The bench, too, brimmed with depth and talent. Had Hector Lopez, Phil Linz, John Blanchard, and their fellow utility men seceded to form a rebel club, they undoubtedly could have placed in the first division.

III

THE BERRA ERA opened ominously: three straight one-run defeats in extra innings. Two of them, to the Baltimore Orioles, crumbled in the hands of Pete Mikkelsen, the rookie reliever whom the rookie manager had lobbied for in spring training. Ralph Houk wanted to keep prospect Tom Metcalf, but Berra insisted on the unimpressive-looking Mikkelsen, a poker-faced, bespectacled right-hander who'd been languishing in the minors since 1958.

"Slim and none" is what he'd thought of his chances to make the club that spring. "I was playing class-A ball, and, heck, that's all I thought I was ever going to do," says Mikkelsen, now a vineyard owner in Washington. "In the Yankees' system back then, we just played for fun. No one ever figured on playing in New York, because they didn't replace anyone very often, and when they did, they usually got them elsewhere."

Berra astutely recognized that a sinkerballer able to induce ground balls to the Bombers' airtight infield would serve the team well. Mikkelsen soon justified that confidence, logging a 7–4 record with a bullpen-high 12 saves, while Metcalf never pitched another game in the bigs. Considering that New York would have to claw its way to the pennant that year, nosing out the Chicago White Sox by just one game, Berra's lone roster move ultimately spelled the difference between winning and losing.

Along with Mikkelsen, the listing Yankees righted themselves and steamed into contention despite an epidemic of nagging injuries to Mantle, Maris, Tresh, Terry, and Kubek. Yogi couldn't field his regular eight until a May 11th doubleheader against Cleveland, and just three innings into game one, Yankees began to drop from the lineup like ducks in a shooting gallery.

Shortstop Kubek checked his swing on a pitch and strained his back; enter Phil Linz. Then left fielder Tresh jammed a finger sliding and had to be replaced by Hector Lopez. Several innings later, right fielder Maris slammed into a wire fence while swiping an Indians home run and raised an ugly knot on his head; Pedro Gonzalez took his spot. Two weeks passed before everyone was healthy enough for Berra to try again.

In 1963 the team had sailed to the pennant, leaving second-place Chicago ten and a half games back. This year's campaign, however, pitted them against not one but two legitimate contenders. When the

White Sox strutted into Yankee Stadium in mid-June for five games in three days, New York was sitting five games back, and two and a half behind second-place Baltimore.

"It was competition we'd never had to face before," says Hal Reniff. "Normally the Yankees just won the pennant every year and then played whichever team got lucky in the National League. Now *we* were in that position. We weren't at full strength, and the other teams were better than before. So it wasn't just a matter of playing a hundred and sixty-two games and finishing on top. We actually had to grind it out like normal teams and win the pennant."

Grind they did, at Chicago's expense. The Sox's savvy manager, inveterate Yankees-hater Al Lopez, held the distinction of being the only opposing pilot since 1949 to break New York's stranglehold on the AL: with the 1954 Cleveland Indians, who needed a league record 111 wins to stave off the Bombers, and with the 1959 Chisox. Eight other Lopez clubs wound up bridesmaids, three of them boasting winning percentages of .600 or better.

Recent numerology showed the Yankees to be vulnerable every five years: 1954, 1959, . . . 1964? Though the season was still young, a Chicago sweep—or taking four of five—could badly stagger New York, a prospect that had Lopez rubbing his ex-catcher's hands together until he nearly started a fire. Instead, over the next seventy-two hours, baseball's Job would watch in agony as Berra's club slashed his lead to ribbons.

Reliever Steve Hamilton, pressed into starting game one of a Friday-night doubleheader, starched the Sox, 6–1; Whitey Ford followed with a dazzling 3–0 shutout, raising his season record to 8–1. Then on Saturday afternoon Bill Stafford picked up a 6–3 win in middle relief.

In the first game of Sunday's twin bill, Phil Linz, rarely mentioned in the same breath as the rest of the Yankees wrecking crew, stunned everyone in the ballpark by smacking two Ballantine blasts, only the fifth and six home runs of his career. Bud Daley and Reniff combined to stall the White Sox bats as the home team handily took yet another, 8–3.

During the cruel bottom of the ninth of Sunday's second game, destiny seemed to conspire overtime against Al Lopez. The Yankees, behind 3–1, had two men on and one out when Pedro Gonzalez slapped a sure double-play ball to the left side. Shortstop Ron Hansen gloved it and flipped the ball to second baseman Al Weis.

"*Safe!*"

Second-base umpire Bill McKinley thrust his arms outward. Hansen's toss, he claimed, pulled Weis off the bag. The normally reserved

Lopez hustled out to argue, waving, pointing, and ranting, but to no avail. As "E6" blinked on the scoreboard, 37,000 fans taunted the Yankees' perennial shadows.

No sooner had he trudged back to the visitors' dugout than Clete Boyer lined a single to load the bases. Bobby Richardson then greeted knuckleballer Hoyt Wilhelm with a game-tying sacrifice fly. In the tenth, as the stadium rocked, Joe Pepitone singled home rookie Archie Moore to complete the five-game sweep, 4–3.

Afterward, a beleaguered Lopez, reflecting on the disputed call, remarked ruefully: "They shot the wrong McKinley."

One week later the scene repeated itself in Chicago's Comiskey Park. The Yankees edged the White Sox in four straight (2–0 twice, 2–1 in seventeen innings, and 6–5), depositing them in third place, three and a half games back. By the time Bill Stafford chalked up the final out of a grueling Father's Day doubleheader that dragged on for twenty-six innings and seven and a half hours, weary White Sox fans had changed the customary chant of "Yankees, Go Home!" to "Yankees, *Let Us* Go Home!"

New York, sole possessors of first place for the first time all year, left the Windy City flying high but encountered sudden turbulence in Baltimore. The imposing Orioles hammered New York pitching for 9–8 and 7–4 victories. Then, in game three, Baltimore ace Steve Barber struck out nine in the course of a 3–1 win to send Yogi Berra's team home in second place, not to mention second-guessing its manager's strategy.

Since early June, infield understudy Phil Linz, a natural shortstop, had been guarding the hot corner in place of slumping third baseman Clete Boyer. When injury-prone Tony Kubek pulled a groin muscle in Chicago that would sideline him through the All-Star break, Berra, instead of simply replacing him at short with Linz, elected to shift Boyer to Kubek's spot, thus playing two men out of position.

Boyer, a sponge at third, didn't have Linz's range at short. And Linz, by his own admission, was a "terrible" third baseman. "I hated playing there," he says. "I'd lose sleep over it. The team was pretty upset about the move; all the guys were complaining." Especially the pitchers. In the 9–8 trimming by Baltimore, the Yankees had squandered a 7–2 lead, giving away seven runs in the eighth. Two grounders eluded Linz—balls that Boyer almost certainly would have smothered to shut off the rally.

And the pitcher responsible for the lead unraveling was none other than Berra's pet, Pete Mikkelsen. Several of his bullpen colleagues felt the manager was wearing out the rookie while rusting out the other firemen. Mikkelsen himself says, "In those days, if one guy was hot, they'd stay with him until he wasn't. I think maybe they should have used Hal Reniff more."

Reniff, whose 18 saves led the relief corps in 1963, expected to be Berra's number-one saver. Instead, he complains, "I couldn't get into a ball game; I was like a mop-up man. That broke me down, because I lost a lot from sitting around and not throwing properly." In addition to Reniff, Bill Stafford and Steve Hamilton also developed sore or stiff arms from erratic work.

Some of the starters also grumbled about misuse. "Yogi, of course, had a great deal to learn," says Rollie Sheldon, who chipped in five wins in six decisions after being recalled from the minors in June. "Early in the season he was taking out pitchers a little too soon. Then he was leaving them in too long." It was Sheldon, in fact, whom Berra lifted for Mikkelsen in the Baltimore opener, despite seven strong innings and no sign of tiring.

Upon reflection, Berra's players take pains to acknowledge the difficulties their manager faced: forced to learn by trial and error while under the scrutiny of the most demanding fans and media (and ballplayers?) in baseball. But at the time, recalls Steve Hamilton, "Most of the season, people were critical of the way Yogi managed."

Nevertheless, the club stampeded through July, winding up the month at 61–37, .623. But it was a deceptive record, more indicative of New York's ability to stretch for the clutch run rather than overwhelm opponents as in years past. Only Mickey Mantle's .325 batting average ranked among the league's leading hitters, a category that historically resembled the Yankees' starting lineup. The infielders, especially, were stirring up air at the plate: Pepitone was batting .256, Richardson .242, Kubek .232, and Boyer .224.

A late-July doubleheader against the Indians provided a sobering reminder of the sputtering attack. On a blisteringly hot Sunday in the Bronx, the young left-hander Sam McDowell and Luis Tiant, a Cuban-born right-hander making his major-league debut, fanned eighteen Yankees between them.

"Until then, teams were afraid of us," says pitcher Al Downing, "especially our left-handed batters." Yankee Stadium, opened in 1923, had been designed to facilitate its left-handed-hitting home-run machine, the mighty Babe Ruth. Ever since, the club traditionally stocked its lineup with lefties able to poke balls over the enticingly close right-field fence, just 296 feet away.

"The theory in baseball had always been: You can't overpower power hitters," says Downing. "But McDowell and Tiant blew the ball right past us." He remembers thinking, "Wait a minute, we're in trouble here. Teams are going to take a different approach to playing us and start doing this to us."

"That whole season," Downing reflects, "was like an omen of what was to come."

IV

DOWNING AND JIM Bouton revived after sluggish starts, upping their records from 2–2 and 5–7 to 8–4 and 12–8. But as New York entered a crucial span in early August—fifteen games in a row against Baltimore and Chicago—Berra was scrounging to fill the other two slots in his four-man rotation.

All season long, Whitey Ford, the Chairman of the Board, had been bothered by calcium deposits in his right hip. Originally diagnosed as a minor nuisance, the chronic soreness eventually forced the left-hander to miss ten days. An August 4th outing against Kansas City in which he pitched well but lost 5–1 left Ford discouraged and uncharacteristically downcast.

As for Ralph Terry, the FBI might have conducted a missing-persons investigation. The strapping six-foot-three Oklahoman had amassed 567 innings the previous two seasons, more than any American League hurler; yet in 1964 he plummeted, in his own words, "from the penthouse to the outhouse.

"I pulled a muscle in my lower right side the first exhibition game of spring training," explains Terry. "It took me three or four weeks to come around. Yogi was the new manager, and he wanted me to throw hard. We were playing another exhibition game, and he kept saying, 'Throw hard, throw hard.' So I aggravated it again, and I really wasn't very effective the first part of the year."

Bounced to the bullpen by June, Terry surrendered game-winning hits in extra innings twice in two days, sinking his record to 2–8 by the All-Star break. Asked by reporters about his plans for the three-day sabbatical, he quipped, "I'm going to take three days of shock treatment."

Ford's injury granted Terry a reprieve during a two-week swing west in late July and early August. The right-hander won all three starts. "The greatest road trip I ever had," he recalls. "Then we come home, and I'm back in the bullpen." Unusually independent-minded for a ballplayer of his generation, Terry remains candid. "I was really pitching good, so it was hard for me to understand. Although," he adds, without rancor, "I was never one of Yogi's favorites."

As Baltimore and New York opened a four-game set at Yankee Stadium on August 7, the two clubs sat deadlocked for the junior-circuit lead, with Chicago lurking one and a half games behind. On Friday night, Steve Barber blanked Jim Bouton, 2–0, the deciding margin coming on a first-inning RBI single by third baseman Brooks Robinson.

The next afternoon, an Old Timers' Day crowd of over 52,000 kept a wary eye on Ford, who temporarily eased their minds with two scoreless innings. But when the Yankees spilled back onto the field to start the third, Rollie Sheldon came strolling in from the bullpen as Ford lay in agony on the trainer's table. Baltimore's ten-inning 6–5 triumph concerned Berra less than the prospect of a pennant drive minus his top pitcher.

In front of the majors' largest crowd all year, Al Downing nipped Dave McNally 2–1 and hoisted the Yankees to within a game of first. But in the Sunday nightcap, the Orioles quickly staked a 4–1 lead against surprise starter Stan Williams. Williams, who had been struggling since Opening Day, got the hook in the fourth inning. Meanwhile, a lonely Ralph Terry viewed all four games from a hard bench in the bullpen. The Birds hung on to win, 4–2, and drop New York into third.

Arriving in Baltimore on August 14 to launch an eleven-game road trip, the Bombers were feeling a bit frayed, and not only from perusing the standings. That afternoon the Columbia Broadcasting System announced that it had purchased 80 percent of the team for $13.2 million. Dan Topping and Del Webb each took home 10 percent of the club's stock and a hefty windfall, with an option to eventually divest their remaining holdings. It was the most ever paid for a sports franchise.

Eight of the league's ten team owners immediately approved the transaction, exceeding the required three-fourths majority. Dissenting were Kansas City's contentious Charlie Finley, a past and future cleat in the Yankees' side, and Chicago's Arthur C. Allyn.

Word of the CBS-Yankees union elicited almost as piercing an outcry as Richard Burton and Elizabeth Taylor's scandalous nuptials earlier that year. Several politicians actually threatened to investigate the sale, while the purists in the bleachers and the press all sounded a similar, if vague and unsubstantiated, refrain: that the passage of baseball's most renowned club from loving private ownership into the hands of an entertainment-industry Goliath would somehow compromise the integrity of the game. That two other Big Apple sports teams, basketball's Knicks and hockey's Rangers, belonged to the Madison Square Garden Corporation, a blooming commodity on the New York Stock Exchange, seemed to get overlooked amid all the keening.

Finley and Allyn, protesting the suspect hastiness of the whole affair, managed to force another vote several weeks later. But despite much politicking on their part, the transaction was upheld. It was only the third time the franchise had changed ownership since 1903, the year a struggling Baltimore club set up shop in Manhattan as the Highlanders.

New York's pennant hopes sagged along with CBS stock as the Birds pecked away at an ineffective Yankees bullpen to win 5–4. Berra, in a move that sent heads shaking up and down the dugout, had summoned ailing Steve Hamilton to protect a 2–1 lead for Rollie Sheldon in the sixth inning, with two outs and a runner on. A walk to Boog Powell, a home run to Brooks Robinson, and the Orioles were out front to stay, as nemesis Steve Barber upped his lifetime mark against New York to 11–8.

Although the Bombers rebounded in games two and three, Baltimore still held a two-and-a-half-game advantage. "We really figured we had a shot at the pennant," recalls Barber. "In fact, if I'd had any kind of year, we probably would have won it." After going 20–9 the year before, the Birds' staff leader hobbled through a strange 1964, slumping to 9–13. "I went 4–1 against the Yankees," says Barber, "2–1 against the White Sox, and 3–11 against the rest of the league, teams I should have cleaned house on. I carried quite a load of guilt that whole winter."

The Yankees, understandably, looked forward to moving on to Chicago, which they had already victimized twelve of fourteen times. Should New York rouse itself and go on to finish first, certainly Al Lopez's patsies would deserve a share of their World Series money.

But these were not the same fatalistic White Sox the Bombers had humiliated back in June. Nor were these the same swaggering Yankees. Besides losing Mickey Mantle to a jammed knee for the series, they found themselves in a rare state of desperation. "In the past when we were winning, it was always a big series for the opposition," explains Clete Boyer. "Now, in '64, it was a big series for us."

The avenging Chisox tormented New York with three narrow defeats in a row. First, Juan Pizarro outdueled Ralph Terry, who was on temporary parole from the bullpen, 2–1. Then, in game two, Al Downing, prone to lapses of concentration, uncorked a mistake that outfielder Floyd Robinson muscled just inside the foul pole, puncturing an eighth-inning New York 3–0 lead.

A trio of White Sox bounded across home plate to the booming accompaniment of the Hallelujah Chorus from Handel's *Messiah* together with bursts of rockets and Roman candles. With New York's own injured messiah physically unable to deliver salvation, the slumping Bombers wasted a scoring opportunity in the tenth before Chicago pushed across the winning run. Sitting slumped in his office after the painful 4–3 loss, the normally impassive Berra was on the verge of tears.

Victorious Baltimore having opened up a four-game lead, the following night's contest loomed large. "It was a game we had to have," says Jim Bouton, nicknamed Bulldog for his fierce competitiveness. Nursing a 1–0 lead in the third with the bases loaded, he got Sox third baseman Pete Ward to ground easily to Joe Pepitone and hustled to first to take the toss. The pitcher's heel scraped the bag just ahead of the runner, ending the threat.

But not in umpire Lou DiMuro's eyes, which managers had questioned on occasion for their proficiency. When Bouton spun around to see the ump's arms extended, he exploded like the Comiskey Park scoreboard and flung the ball to the ground. The Bulldog snarled and barked while the runner on second alertly dashed home ahead of Pepitone's frantic throw for a 2–1 Chicago lead.

"I was so caught up in the team's struggle, I lost my head," admits Bouton, who lost on unearned runs, 4–2. "It was very uncharacteristic of me," he adds. "I wasn't one to argue with the umpires. In fact, I never got thrown out of a game in my career. But I definitely felt and heard my spikes hit the bag. I just couldn't convince anybody of it."

Bouton's blunder and the funereal clubhouse scene afterward suggested a team unraveling like the stitching on a worn-out ball. The early-season murmurs of discontent with the manager had by now swelled into a deafening chorus, tainting the club's play. Bouton, surprised at the griping aimed Berra's way, remarks, "That was the first time I saw athletes play differently under different managers."

The 1961-to-1963 Yankees had thrived under Ralph Houk, a brilliant motivator of men who in times of struggle knew how to rally them with clubhouse pep talks. "Yogi didn't give the rah-rah speeches like Ralph did," says Bouton. "Also, Ralph would coddle guys: pat them on the fanny and tell them they were really nice fellas and not to worry about things. The players were spoiled. Yogi didn't do that."

Like other diamond standouts who'd graduated to the dugout, the three-time MVP failed to comprehend why any professional would require periodic psychological maintenance. *He'd* never needed his ego massaged in seventeen seasons. After a 10–1 thumping by the lowly Athletics, writers asked Berra if he planned to take the team to task for its sloppy play. The manager shook his head and replied in his blunt style, "They don't have to be told. They know how bad they're going. Why can't they come out on their own?"

The players could forgive Yogi his occasional oversights and strategic miscues. What they could not overlook was his penchant for second-guessing players in front of the others, something Houk scrupulously avoided. "If Ralph had a beef with you," says Rollie Sheldon, "he'd have the clubhouse guy call you into his office, then shut the door and talk to you alone. But Yogi would criticize a certain pitch thrown by a pitcher where some of his teammates could overhear. And that's never a good situation."

Sometimes, though, a keen observation by Berra incited unjustified indignation. "Yogi knew more baseball than people gave him credit for," Al Downing says in his defense. "He may have known more baseball than Houk. But the guys didn't respect Yogi's knowledge. Their feeling was, 'Here's a guy who just came off the field. How could he know so much about baseball?' Yet he did."

Downing offers an analogy: "It's like ten guys who go to school together and join the same company, and then one day one of them becomes the CEO. The other nine are going to say, 'He's no smarter than us.' Yogi would tell Pepitone, 'Joe, why'd you do that? That was a dumb play.' If Houk says it: 'Gee, you're right, Ralph.' But if Yogi says it: 'Aw, c'mon, Yogi.' Guys resented it."

Things deteriorated to where Berra's slightest gaffe—like his repeatedly mispronouncing Boston star Carl Yastrzemski's last name, a challenge even for Polish-Americans—became grist for locker-room jokes. "Guys were always whispering about it," recalls Bouton. " 'Today Yogi did this.' Or the latest Yogi joke."

"Then guys were going behind his back and complaining to the front office." Joe Trimble, writing in the *Daily News*, later insinuated that Tony Kubek and Bobby Richardson had tried to instigate a midseason mutiny. Distressed over Berra's ebbing authority, the Yankees' heralded double-play combo reportedly had threatened to quit if he returned as manager in 1965, something the two of them vigorously denied then, and which they deny still.

"You probably didn't see, about six days later, a two-sentence correction that there was nothing to that story," points out Richardson. "In fact, I really enjoyed playing for Yogi." After the *Daily News* story appeared, following Berra's firing on October 16, "I got hundreds of angry letters from all over the country," says Richardson. "Terrible letters. If ever I should have sued somebody, that would have been the time. The article had no basis whatsoever."

Major-league retirees who regularly make the rounds of baseball-card shows and fantasy camps are understandably reluctant to criticize one another, however. The stream of Yankees in and out of Ralph

Houk's office—Kubek and Richardson among them—certainly indicated a problem with club morale.

Rather than defend the manager, Houk undermined Berra's authority by absorbing without comment the complaints and the pleas for him to come back. It was also no secret that the man who'd spent his playing days laboring in obscurity behind Berra was not his biggest admirer.

"We all knew that they didn't get along," says Clete Boyer, "although I don't know why." Long-festering resentment lurking in the heart of a bullpen catcher? "Ralph should have been happy to be Yogi's backup," Boyer says with a laugh, "because he never had a good arm, he couldn't hit, and he couldn't run."

Now Number 8 once again occupied the position Houk coveted. Personal conflicts aside, Houk privately disagreed with his superiors' decision to make Berra manager. And, wanting to put his own stamp on the club, he probably planned to replace Yogi at the earliest opportunity with someone of his own choosing.

Ironically, Berra's own diligence backfired. He never grew into the role the club intended for him—that of the convivial, quotable raconteur. Apparently Yankees management had always believed what it read. The local press corps could have told them that certain writers had been contriving Berra bons mots for years, compressing his spoken lumps of coal into diamonds on the printed page.

"Leonard Koppett of the *New York Post* [and later *The New York Times*] was particularly good at changing one of Yogi's comments to make it sound funnier," says *Newsday*'s Stan Isaacs, "though there is a malaprop quality to him. On occasion he *would* say things in a funny way."

Such as Berra's skewed observation that year about a popular Minneapolis restaurant called Charlie's: "Nobody goes there anymore; it's too crowded." But most of the time, "Yogi was a serious guy," says Isaacs, adding, "I think his lack of formal education made him very suspicious of reporters."

As a result, the press didn't always give Berra his due as rookie manager. Despite locker-room unrest he'd kept a club tattered by injuries in contention. "I think the print media resented Yogi," contends Al Downing. "Remember, for years they'd portrayed him as a buffoon. Now this guy was managing a club that was in the pennant race. Their first inclination was to say, 'He has great players.' But some of those players weren't having good years."

The lackluster image of Berra as drawn by the press did not enhance his standing with Ralph Houk, who accompanied the team on its Baltimore-Chicago road trip and was appalled by the off-field behavior:

players reveling until the wee hours, then staggering to the ballpark in less than peak condition.

The guilty included superstars and longtime Berra pals like Mickey Mantle. "He ran wild on Yogi," says sportswriter Maury Allen, "staying out late and carrying on." Clearly the manager could not control his players. Team discipline had broken down.

But had it really?

Houk himself had never imposed a curfew as manager. After racking up yet another win under the lights, his clubs were known to wind up under tables. "Ralph treated everybody like men," explains Rollie Sheldon. " 'You guys know what it takes to win ball games and stay in shape, so I'll leave you on your own. But if I find out you're punishing your body and you're not going to be good for the team, then I'll take action.' " Given the Yankees' perpetual perch atop the American League, he rarely had to.

Berra followed the same lenient philosophy. Phil Pepe, then a scribe for the *New York World Telegram and Sun*, observes wryly that the 1964 Yankees "weren't doing anything differently than before—except not winning."

In his reticent way, Berra did attempt to correct certain players' work habits. His benching of Clete Boyer hardly endeared him to the nine-year veteran, who admits, "Our relationship at that time wasn't too good." But in hindsight, says Boyer, himself a coach after finishing his playing career, "Yogi probably thought I was too much of a carouser. He may have been trying to teach me something. I never knocked him for it."

Berra's chief shortcoming wasn't so much an inability to instill order but a *perceived* lack of leadership, a dilemma partly beyond his control. At times, though, the rookie skipper's inexperience showed conspicuously. "Yogi was not a real confident manager," says Steve Hamilton, recalling instances of Berra wondering aloud on the bench, "Should we hit-and-run now?" "Should we steal?"

"I like Yogi," the reliever emphasizes, "but he didn't verbalize well. He didn't lead us well."

V

ON AUGUST 20, CHICAGO handed the lifeless Yankees their tenth loss in fifteen games, 5–0. Whitey Ford, winless in over a month, felt no discomfort in his hip, only the pain of getting rocked for all five runs in three innings. The White Sox vaulted past Baltimore into first, while New York dropped to four and a half games back. "It looked like we were out of it," remembers Clete Boyer. "We figured Chicago and Baltimore couldn't both go into slumps."

The players grimly tramped onto the bus for the ride to O'Hare Airport. As they sat in rush-hour traffic for two hours, cursing the sweltering heat, tempers soared. Phil Linz's especially.

He'd expected to see action against Chicago, a club the twenty-five-year-old had pummeled all season. "If there was any team you would play me against," he says, "it would be the White Sox. But Yogi started getting pressure to put Tony Kubek back in. Somebody—maybe Whitey Ford—said, 'You've got to get Phil out of there.'"

Sitting in the back of the hot bus, Linz was, he admits, "still simmering about not playing." To calm himself, he took out the harmonica he'd bought the day before, put it to his lips, and attempted the first song on the learner's sheet: "Mary Had a Little Lamb." Taps would have been more appropriate.

The tale of what happened next has grown so distorted over the years that Linz himself confesses to incorporating other versions for dramatic effect. To the best of his recollection, Yogi Berra, who was sitting up front, heard the halting bleats and bellowed over his shoulder, "Linz, shut that thing up!"

Linz mumbled, "*I* didn't lose the game," and resumed wheezing into the mouth organ until his manager stormed up the aisle and glared down at him, a hand raised menacingly.

"Hey, Linz! I said take that harmonica and shove it up your ass! You'd think you just won four straight!"

"Here, you take it." Linz nonchalantly tossed the instrument to Berra, who swatted it away, sending it ricocheting off Joe Pepitone's knee. The Yankees' playful first baseman began yelping, "Ow, Jesus, my knee! My knee!"

"I jumped up from my seat," Linz remembers, "and really started to blast off. 'What are you getting on me for? I give one hundred percent. Why don't you talk to some of these guys who *aren't* hustling?'" He laughs. "I was really an asshole."

Berra turned and lurched back to his seat, grumbling, "I'll take care of you." That's when Frank Crosetti, the officious third-base coach, stood up and in his shrill voice screamed at Linz, "Shut your ass!"

"Fuck you, Crow!"

By now most of the bus was convulsed with laughter, snapping the tension.

The Harmonica Incident, as it came to be known, helped to anchor and unify a team adrift. Perhaps, theorizes Linz, his resentful words about teammates' complacency "may have hit home with some of those guys." Most important, the episode established newfound respect for the manager.

"Out of that came the realization that Yogi was in charge," says Bobby Richardson.

The Yankees bus brouhaha released a media deluge that obscured an equally significant development: in Boston, on that same afternoon, the mountainous Oriole Boog Powell plowed into the left-field wall, chipping a bone in his left wrist. Losing their cleanup hitter for three weeks slowed down the torrid Birds, whose 10–9 record in that period enabled Yogi Berra's team to once again force a three-way contest for the AL crown.

Rejuvenation didn't come right away. The second-division Red Sox extended New York's losing streak to six with 7–0 and 5–3 wins that butted the Bombers to six games back with thirty-nine left to play. But then a lanky rookie right-hander named Mel Stottlemyre blanked Boston 8–0, aided by home runs from Roger Maris, John Blanchard, and a limping Mickey Mantle.

Stottlemyre was just three games into his major-league career and, already, putting the brakes on Yankees slumps was becoming a habit for him. Called up on August 11 from Richmond, where he was 13–3, the remarkably poised twenty-two-year-old had ended a three-game slide by beating the White Sox 7–3 behind another Mantle home run, this one a towering 502-foot blast that put center fielder Gene Stephens flat up against the Yankee Stadium bleachers wall, peering skyward in astonishment. Next, Stottlemyre stifled Baltimore 3–1. The auspicious debut drew comparisons to Whitey Ford's rookie season of 1950, when his nine wins against one defeat in July, August, and September enabled the Yankees to fend off the fast-gaining Detroit Tigers.

One day after helping Stottlemyre to victory number three, Mantle homered again as Jim Bouton foiled the Bosox 4–3 and salvaged a split. Not exactly an exhibition to generate pennant fever, but, fortunately for New York, the Orioles helped by taking three out of four from the White Sox.

Gratefully returning to the Bronx, the Bombers knocked off Boston three games to one the following weekend while Baltimore and Chicago skirmished to a four-game draw. A landslide by either team could have put the flag irrevocably beyond the Yankees' reach. But as August slipped into September, the Birds' edge over New York had dwindled to three.

"That's when we knew we had a chance," says Clete Boyer, recalling the eve of the Boston series. "Guys started commenting, 'With Yogi's luck'—we all believed Yogi was lucky—'they'll split and we'll win.' And that's what happened. We got hot, and everybody came together."

VI

THE PINSTRIPED CONVERGENCE occurred in Kansas City, for decades home to the Blues, a New York farm team that, like a wartime factory, used to ship the Yankees one awesome player after another: Whitey Ford, Elston Howard, Hank Bauer. In the three-game set that Yogi Berra termed a must-win, his team played like it still owned the K.C. club.

Friday night New York outlasted the Athletics 9–7 in ten innings. At the time it hardly seemed the start of a 17–3 streak—just another troubling reminder of a bullpen in shambles.

With two gone in the ninth, Pete Mikkelsen yielded a game-tying home run to Ken Harrelson. Since midsummer, the relief corps had been putting on more gory spectacles than a drive-in movie, blowing countless games in the late frames. More and more, starters were playing that dubious role as Berra grew increasingly leery of entrusting leads to firemen who seemed to have a penchant for arson.

Desperate for support, on September 5 the Yankees wrote the Cleveland Indians a $75,000 check and promised two players later in exchange for Pedro Ramos, a well-traveled right-hander. This seemingly minor transaction would prove a coup for New York.

Ramos was a most unlikely savior. For four consecutive seasons the losingest pitcher in the American League, he touched bottom in 1961 with an 11–20 mark. Mickey Mantle routinely pummeled the Cuban exile so unmercifully that he once told him, "You're the closest I ever came to feeling sorry for a pitcher." An abundance of hitters fattened their figures against Ramos, who led the junior circuit in gopher balls three times.

To be fair, the blue-eyed six-footer had pitched six seasons for Washington, a city whose unofficial motto, "First in war, first in peace, last in the American League," summed up its ball club's inglorious history. Few in the nation's capital mourned the Senators' exodus to Minneapolis in 1961, the year the league expanded from eight to ten teams by establishing a new franchise in Los Angeles and awarding D.C. another, equally bad, assortment of fledgling Senators.

In 1962, just as the Minneapolis club was turning respectable, it unloaded Ramos to homely Cleveland. The next entry on his résumé would almost surely be—yikes!—Kansas City.

Informed of the trade to the Yankees, Ramos just about kicked up the heels of his cowboy boots and flung his wide-brimmed black Stetson for joy. In addition to his clash with Indians manager Birdie Tebbetts, who'd molded him into a reliever, he says that "All my career I really wanted to pitch for the Yankees." When Casey Stengel was manager, Ramos used to sidle over to the New York dugout and implore, "When are you gonna trade for me?"

One day after finally getting his wish, Ramos stood on the mound seeking to protect Rollie Sheldon's 3–0 lead with one on and none out in the bottom of the ninth. Fearsome Rocky Colavito and Jim Gentile both singled, scoring a run and giving Berra an uneasy déjà vu ("all over again," as he once said). Billy Bryan then whacked a hard grounder toward right field, but Joe Pepitone stabbed it and turned a seamless double play.

This sure isn't like the Washington Senators, Ramos marveled as he faced Ed Charles. A pop-up, and the Yankees' new closer notched his first save. He was to record six more, plus a win, in thirteen appearances over the Bombers' final twenty-eight games. No longer did Yogi Berra practically have to summon ballpark security to forcibly remove his starters from the rubber.

"Boy, Pedro," Mel Stottlemyre kidded after yet another sparkling Ramos performance, "I'm getting tired of shaking your hand every day." Down the stretch the two newcomers came to the Yankees' rescue like the U.S. Cavalry. "If we didn't get Pedro and Mel," Al Downing says plainly, "we wouldn't have won the pennant."

On September 17, Stottlemyre bedeviled the Angels, 6–2, giving New York a one-third share of first place with Baltimore and Chicago. Once again Mickey Mantle contributed to Stottlemyre's cause with his 450th lifetime home run. Mantle, one of several offensive standouts during New York's September surge, lashed the ball at a .400-plus clip to end the season at .303, with 35 home runs and 111 RBIs.

Elston Howard, Joe Pepitone, and Roger Maris all went on tears of their own that month. Howard (.313 BA, 15 HR, 84 RBI) batted just under .400; Pepitone (.251 BA, 28 HR, 100 RBI) clubbed 12 home runs and knocked in 30 runs. And Maris (.281 BA, 26 HR, 71 RBI) sent home one clutch run after another. Against Washington on September 25 he unloaded his twenty-fifth and twenty-sixth home runs, the latter to break a 5–5 tie in the ninth.

Of all of New York's late-season heroes, no one enjoyed more notoriety than Phil Linz. A sprained wrist ended Tony Kubek's season two weeks prematurely. Linz, signed as a shortstop out of high school, earned the nickname "Supersub" by filling in more than capably. He sprayed key hits, ran the bases with authority, and, in an 8–1 taming of Cleveland, belted a two-run homer. His teammates jokingly dubbed him "MVM," for Most Valuable Musician.

The famed Harmonica Incident probably did more for the Baltimore native's image than a .400 season. "After that, every town we came into, the people in the stands were singing 'Mary Had a Little Lamb,' " he remembers. "In Boston they threw harmonicas onto the field." While no virtuoso on the instrument, Linz grew proficient enough so that in the off-season "I went to a lot of banquets and made a lot of money. My agent said that if we'd won the World Series that year, he could have gotten me a week out in Las Vegas." As it was, the curly-headed utility man received a $20,000 contract from Hohner Harmonicas to promote its product.

From mid- to late September the Yankees reeled off eleven consecutive wins to stay a hairsbreadth ahead of stubborn Baltimore and Chicago. Over the final two and a half weeks, the Orioles went 9–4, and the White Sox 10–3, including nine straight to close in a blaze. The Yankees, however, vanquished thirteen of their last seventeen opponents. Due to a fluke in scheduling, after mid-August neither team faced New York, leaving Hank Bauer's and Al Lopez's outfits seething in frustration.

Roger Repoz, a rookie outfielder employed as a late-inning defensive replacement for Mickey Mantle during the last few weeks, recalls with awe the methodical calm of the Yankees juggernaut as it roared toward the championship.

"It was amazing to watch guys of their caliber," he says. "They were in the midst of a pennant race, yet it didn't bother them at all. They just went to work. And they knew they were going to win." After all, winning was part of a Yankee's job description.

The pennant clincher, against Cleveland, attracted fewer than 15,000 rooters to Yankee Stadium. Despite the team's dramatic resurrection, attendance crept up by less than 4,000 in 1964. The Mets, meanwhile, though burrowed in the National League cellar for a third straight time, drew 650,000 more than the year before.

"The fans during that era took the Yankees for granted," says Bobby Richardson. "They pretty much thought we were going to win every year. Of course," he concedes, "we did." The second baseman recalls the frosty reception from New York partisans following the bitterly fought 1960 World Series: "When we flew back home from Pittsburgh, only two people were there to greet us at the airport. And they were a couple of girls after the single guys on the club."

As the crowd sprinkled about the cavernous ballpark yawned, New York broke a 3–3 stalemate with five runs in the bottom of the eighth. Berra then called on Pedro Ramos to preserve the victory. After recording two quick outs, the reliever faced the Indians' dugout and gestured vulgarly at his former manager, Birdie Tebbetts.

"I couldn't give him the finger," Ramos explains, "so I say, 'Take that!' and give him some *arm* instead." An easy pop-up behind the plate, and Ramos braced himself for the mob of jubilant players about to come hurtling onto the mound.

Instead, his teammates ambled out of the dugout, pumped his hand, and pounded his back—such was the extent of Yankees rejoicing. "I guess we all excited that we won the pennant and everything," he says in heavily accented English, still sounding slightly unsure, "but it was almost like it was just another game."

Well, yes. Mickey Mantle, for example, could add this fifth consecutive crown to his collection, making for twelve in fourteen seasons. He retired to the trainer's room, leaving the younger players to spray champagne in one another's hair and cavort about the clubhouse. The relatively subdued scene belied a collective pride in the team's September rally. Of the franchise's previous twenty-eight title winners, none had been so far down so late in the year.

"I think we did a hell of a thing, being six games out and fighting back the way we did," says Phil Linz, 3-for-5 in the clincher. "Truthfully," adds Clete Boyer, "I felt Baltimore and Chicago both had better clubs than we did."

An elated Yogi Berra basked in a feeling of personal vindication. Whatever his flaws, the rookie manager never panicked, even when it appeared the Yankees' dynasty would end with his reign. In the aftermath of one of the crushing defeats in Chicago light-years ago, Berra considered the Yankees' plight and said evenly, "The world didn't end yet."

"Yogi's strength was that he was low-key, easygoing, and played down controversies," praises Jim Bouton. "If you've got a good team, you mostly want a manager who gets out of the way and just lets the guys play ball, and Yogi did that. I thought he did a very good job."

VII

REGARDLESS OF THE season's outcome, Berra's fate had been sealed as far back as mid-August. Ralph Houk, convinced that the team would not rebound, decided then that a managerial change had to be made at once. The replacement he had in mind, San Francisco's pilot, Alvin Dark, was reportedly on thin ice and about to take a plunge.

Two events swiftly derailed Houk's plan. First, Dark disqualified himself by allegedly spouting white-supremacist remarks to *Newsday*, something he later denied. Though a local favorite, the former New York Giants shortstop now seemed a poor choice to manage in a cauldron of racial unrest like the Big Apple. Only days before Dark's comments appeared in print, fierce rioting erupted in Harlem. Houk scratched that name off his list.

Then the relatively sudden sale of the team to CBS made any move inadvisable until after the season. And so Yogi Berra had William S. Paley and the corporate bigwigs at acquisitive Black Rock to thank for unwittingly preserving his job another two months.

Houk next zeroed in on St. Louis's Johnny Keane. In the mid-1950s the two had managed against each other in the minor leagues, Houk at Denver and Keane at Omaha. The Yankees' GM admired Keane's firm hand—precisely what he felt his club needed. "I was a strong believer in Johnny," Houk says.

Keane wouldn't have to be pried away from the Cardinals. Virtually everyone in baseball, including Keane himself, knew that the guillotine was being readied for him for the end of the season. After a strong second-place showing the year before, Keane's club floundered in 1964, matching the Yankees for internal strife. On September 5, the Cardinals slumbered a distant third, seven and a half games behind Philadelphia. That afternoon, with the third-place Bombers appearing in nearby Kansas City, Houk allegedly dispatched a secret emissary to St. Louis—most likely traveling secretary Bill Bergesch, Keane's former general manager at Omaha—to offer him the New York job for 1965.

Soliciting another club's manager during the season violated baseball rules, and both Houk and Bergesch have denied that any such meeting took place. Keane's wife and daughter, however, did later confirm that the Yankees made overtures while Keane was still in the Redbirds' employ. A handshake deal was supposedly consummated in Chicago the following week.

Houk envisioned the immediate future like this: (1) the Yankees and Cardinals both limp to disappointing finishes; (2) St. Louis lets Keane go in favor of feisty Leo Durocher, while New York dismisses Yogi Berra for the audacity of failing to win the pennant; and (3) New York promptly hires Keane. Not a happy denouement to the season, perhaps, but a tidy one.

Then came one of the most jarring turnabouts in sports history. Not only did the Yankees stir to life in the American League, but the complexion of the National League race changed as abruptly as skies before a tornado. Philadelphia, six and a half games up with twelve to go, went into a tailspin.

Gene Mauch's club lost one game, then another, then another, until ten defeats had piled up, the last three coming against the fast-gaining Redbirds. An 8–5 spanking of the Phillies on September 30 in their series finale gave St. Louis sole possession of first place.

As Johnny Keane entertained reporters in his ramshackle office, front-office consultant Branch Rickey burst in through a back door to pump his hand. The legendary eighty-two-year-old "Mahatma" had been pushing for the manager's removal since midseason.

"Johnny Keane," Rickey rumbled, his heavy eyebrows twitching, "you're a gosh-dang good manager!" Contritely he hastened from the room.

Neither Rickey nor any of the Cardinals knew that Keane already had specific plans to bail out. He tucked away his secret—as well as a letter of resignation, dated September 28—in his back pocket. Only third-base coach Vern Benson had an inkling that something was up.

In Pittsburgh, Keane invited him to breakfast at Stouffer's, away from the team hotel. "If I take another job next year," the manager asked cryptically, "will you go with me?"

"John, you brought me here," said Benson, Keane's first appointee. "I'll go anyplace with you except Korea."

Looking back, Benson says he assumed Keane was referring to the Pirates. "I knew Danny Murtaugh was retiring, and it seemed a logical place for John to go. I didn't give the Yankees a single thought. He told me, 'Well, if I make a move, I'll be back in touch with you,' and nothing more was said the rest of the year."

The Cardinals' pennant express temporarily lost speed; they dropped their next two contests to the dismal Mets, so that on Sunday, October 5, only one game separated St. Louis, Philadelphia, and Cincinnati. The mathematical possibilities for a two- or three-team tie, forcing either a playoff or a round-robin tournament, caused more head-scratching than a tax return.

But the National League pennant race would see a simpler resolution: The Cards routed the Mets 11–5 at Busch Stadium while Philadelphia awoke from its nightmare to beat Cincinnati for the second day in a row. St. Louis, celebrating its 200th birthday, would host its first Fall Classic in eighteen years. And Johnny Keane was about to take on the team he knew he'd be managing once the Series ended.

VIII

ODDSMAKERS PICKED NEW York to win as decisively as incumbent Lyndon Johnson was expected to whip challenger Barry Goldwater in the upcoming presidential election. In the first inning of game four, a twenty-first Yankees World Championship seemed all but assured.

After fielding blunders handed St. Louis the opener, 9–5, New York regrouped to win games two and three, 8–3 behind Mel Stottlemyre, and 2–1 on Mickey Mantle's dramatic ninth-inning clout into Yankee Stadium's upper-right deck. The home run, his sixteenth in Series competition, broke Babe Ruth's long-standing record and appeared to crush the Cardinals' spirit.

The next afternoon, Mantle's shadow again darkened home plate in the sort of situation that makes cleanup hitters salivate: one run in, runners at the corners, and nobody out. Mantle cracked a single to right-center, scoring Bobby Richardson and sending Roger Maris streaking to third. When right fielder Mike Shannon bobbled the ball, Mantle forgot momentarily about his aching legs and limped toward second. Dal Maxvill applied the tag for the inning's first out.

Johnny Keane had seen enough of Ray Sadecki, 20–11 in regular play but woeful thus far in the postseason, and he signaled for Roger Craig, a two-time 20-game loser. "It was almost like John was conceding we were beat," says Dick Groat, the Cardinals' all-star shortstop. "Roger was in his doghouse about as deep as you can possibly be."

Craig allowed an RBI single to Elston Howard but escaped without further damage. When lifted for pinch hitter Carl Warwick in the top of the sixth, he'd compiled eight strikeouts and kept the score at 3–0. Warwick knocked a base hit to left; Curt Flood then singled to right.

With one out, Groat rapped an apparent double-play ball to sure-handed Bobby Richardson. In a chaotic sequence of events, played out in mere seconds, the ball stuck in the webbing of his glove, making him double-clutch his toss to second. Phil Linz, already airborne to avoid the incoming base runner, grasped at the phantom throw. The ball, when it came, trickled off Linz's glove and landed on the ground, along with Linz, who was violently upended by the speedy Flood. Richardson drew the error.

"I just didn't field it cleanly," says the second baseman, accustomed throughout his career to performing that intricate ballet around the bag with Tony Kubek.

"Had Tony been at shortstop"—instead of watching the action from

the bench in street clothes—"we'd at least have gotten the one out."
The inference that Kubek, at six-foot-three, two inches taller than
Linz, could have stretched for the ball, remains a sore point with Linz,
whose two Series home runs tend to be forgotten.

"I wasn't in the same class at shortstop as Tony," he admits, "but I
played great those last thirty games of the season. I'm going to tell
Bobby someday: If Tony had been playing, we might not have been
in the World Series to start with."

With the bases now loaded, up stepped Cardinals third baseman
Ken Boyer, the National League's RBI leader. Elston Howard con-
ferred on the mound with Al Downing, who, after fading down the
stretch, had originally been assigned to the bullpen. But then Whitey
Ford injured himself in game one, exiting with what the Yankees
claimed was a sore heel. Only after the Series ended did they reveal
their ace left-hander was actually suffering from a serious circulation
problem in his pitching arm. Ford could barely raise a comb to his
hair, and missed the remaining games.

Downing shook off Howard's call for a second low-outside fastball
and came in with a 1–0 change-up that Boyer swatted toward the left-
field corner, a mere 312 feet away. It was a thoroughly ordinary line
drive, nothing like Mantle's climbing blast the day before, but it fought
through the air and made the seats for a grand slam.

The parade of runners crossed home plate in front of a dejected
Elston Howard. Clete Boyer, however, couldn't restrain a smile.
Brother Ken had six years on him, as well as superior stats in every
offensive category. But while Yankee Clete attended the Fall Classic
with the regularity of a Fortune 500 CEO, Cardinal Ken had never
been there before.

"When he hit the home run," says Boyer, "I was probably as happy
as he was." Although, he adds quickly, "You don't think that's the one
that's going to beat you."

Boyer's grand slam indeed turned the series around. The 4–3 score
stood, evening the series at two games apiece. "We had them down
and were just gonna whomp 'em," reflects Rollie Sheldon, "and all of
a sudden we let them back in. And then Bob Gibson got hot."

Gibson, the Cardinals' ferocious 19-game winner, fanned thirteen
in contest number five. He was one out away from a 2–0 shutout when
Tom Tresh made contact with an incandescent fastball. It disappeared
over the scoreboard in right-center to send the game into extra innings.

In addition to having lost Kubek and Ford to injuries, the Yankees
were without Pedro Ramos, ineligible for postseason play because he
arrived after the trading deadline. Ramos, never to have a second
opportunity, watched on TV as left-handed Tim McCarver weighed in

against right-hander Pete Mikkelsen in the top of the tenth. Two Redbirds edged away from the bases.

Percentages suggest—some might say dictate—that a manager should counter a lefty bat with a lefty arm whenever possible, yet Yogi Berra left Mikkelsen on the mound, while southpaw Steve Hamilton, wickedly effective against lefties, remained in the bullpen. The Cardinals' catcher ripped a three-run homer.

"Yogi received a *tremendous* amount of criticism for leaving Mikkelsen in," says Hamilton.

The series returned to Busch Stadium, St. Louis holding a 3–2 lead and a psychological edge from two stunning back-to-back victories. Boyer's and McCarver's game-winning wallops brought to mind the late-inning assaults of the Bronx Bombers. "Five o'clock lightning," they called it. Now time was running out for the Yankees.

Jim Bouton, game three's winning pitcher, set up a seventh contest by muzzling the opposition while benefiting from three home runs. Roger Maris's shot onto the pavilion roof fractured a 1–1 sixth-inning tie. Mickey Mantle put the next pitch *over* the roof. Two frames later, Joe Pepitone deposited four runs in the Yankees' coffers with a grand slam, for an 8–3 final.

The odds-defying developments of the past month had landed Ralph Houk and Johnny Keane in equally precarious positions. After orbiting closer and closer together, their two teams were now about to collide, insuring the glare of unwanted attention on what would have been a pair of routine managerial shifts carried out as two other World Series opponents gloried in the limelight.

Should the Yankees win, the noose around Houk's neck would tighten. Can you really fire the manager of the World Champions without outraged fans torching your office? (Or, more likely in those still civil times, bombarding newspapers with nasty epistles?) Conversely, should the Cardinals win, could Keane walk away without public debate over his sanity? It's doubtful either man slept too soundly that night.

Johnny Keane tapped Bob Gibson to start game seven on only two days' rest. Yogi Berra, for his part, rushed back his fifth-game starter, young Mel Stottlemyre, 9–3 on the season. Some Yankees, among them Whitey Ford and Mickey Mantle, privately questioned why Ralph Terry, a veteran of four Fall Classics, wasn't called upon. He'd hurled two shutout innings in game four and was certainly well rested. According to Terry, the reason was that he technically belonged to the Cleveland Indians, as partial compensation for Pedro Ramos. Like the Yankees' alleged tampering with Johnny Keane, this too skirted baseball rules.

For trades conducted after September 1, no players-to-be-named-later could exchange hands until the season's completion. To acquire Ramos, New York gave Cleveland two choices from a list of a half-dozen pitchers to be "named later"—and the Indians claimed Terry immediately.

"I found out during the Series I was on that list," Terry explains. "One of the other players got it from Yogi and told me. I asked Houk about it in St. Louis, before the last two games, and he said, 'No, no, no. I'll talk to you about it on the plane going back,' and all this other bullshit. I told him, 'Hey, I feel good, I'm throwing good. *You'd better get me off that list.*'

"I could have gone public with it and maybe had the deal voided," says Terry, who was officially sent packing a week later. "But that's why they hardly even let me go near the bullpen. Because suppose Yogi or Houk, knowing they've put me in an irrevocable trade, pitch me in the seventh game and I win it? They're going to look bad trading me, aren't they?

"I knew I wasn't getting anywhere near that mound in the last game."

Gibson pitched as if he'd just returned from a month's vacation, exploding the ball in a shower of sparks. But Stottlemyre was having no such fortune. As they'd done throughout the Series, the Cardinals ran the bases fearlessly, rattling the Yankees. In the fourth inning, with first and second occupied, Joe Pepitone nabbed a grounder wide of first and started the 3–6–1 double play. But Dick Groat barreled into Phil Linz at second, forcing a wide throw that sailed past Stottlemyre. Ken Boyer came home with the game's first run.

Mike Shannon then singled McCarver to third. On the first pitch to meek-hitting Dal Maxvill, Johnny Keane sent both runners. The strategy caught New York napping. Elston Howard whipped a throw to Bobby Richardson, who swiped in vain at Shannon, then pegged home, attempting to cut off the run. "Tim was out from here to Times Square," recalls Dick Groat.

But Shannon had clipped Richardson as he slid by. The errant relay skittered past Howard, and McCarver hurtled across home plate. A double steal, from a pair that between them filched two bases all year.

"St. Louis just outhustled us in that seventh game," says Linz. "We'd never faced a team so aggressive on the basepaths. Double stealing? I don't think anybody double-stole on us the entire season! They were going from first to third, doing all kinds of things. We weren't used to it, and we made a lot of mistakes in the infield."

After four innings, with the score 3–0, Al Downing replaced Stottlemyre. Four batters and no outs later he too was taking a shower, saddled with a Series ERA of 8.44. At the end of five, St. Louis held a daunting 6–0 lead.

Mickey Mantle halved that margin with a three-run homer in the sixth. The Cardinals got one back the following inning when Ken Boyer homered off Steve Hamilton, nudging brother Clete as he rounded third. Heading into the top of the ninth, the Yankees trailed 7–3.

Gibson, working his twenty-seventh inning in seven days, reared back and whiffed both Tom Tresh and pinch hitter John Blanchard, giving him 31 K's, a new Series record. In between, Clete Boyer and Phil Linz touched him for solo shots, to bring New York within two. Putting the home runs in perspective, Boyer laughs and says, "Gibson just didn't want to walk us. If it had been a close game, Phil and I probably wouldn't have gotten a foul off him."

The Yankees bench came alive. Richardson, the next batter, already had 13 hits, another World Series mark. "If Bobby got on," remembers Linz, "we felt we had a good chance to tie the game. Gibson was tiring, and it was a real short porch in right field." Roger Maris was crouched on deck.

Keane visited Gibson on the mound but never considered the hook. After the game the Cardinals manager endeared himself to sportswriters with the poetic explanation, "I had a commitment to his heart." One ball and one strike later, the shirt-sleeved crowd stood cheering and chanting as Gibson went into his windup. Richardson brought the bat around, and the ball arced benignly into the balmy blue sky . . .

The flight back to New York gave the players ample time to reflect on the franchise's first successive World Series losses since the inception of the dynasty, in 1921 and 1922. "It was disheartening, because we should have won that Series," says Rollie Sheldon. "We were the better team."

Yogi Berra dropped into the seat next to Bobby and Betsy Richardson. "Tomorrow I go in to the Yankees about my contract," he said cheerfully. "Do you think I should ask for one year or two?"

IX

THE RICHARDSONS LEARNED of Berra's firing over the car radio on the drive home to South Carolina the next day. "I was totally surprised," says the second baseman. Others had expected the ax to fall. "Christ, everybody knew that would happen a month before," says Hal Reniff. "It was pretty cut-and-dry."

After outplaying the Yankees on the diamond, the Cardinals sur-

passed them in newspaper headlines. Just thirty minutes before an
11:00 A.M. news conference to announce Johnny Keane's rehiring on
October 16, the diminutive manager handed team owner August
Busch, Jr., his neatly typewritten letter.

Up until two weeks ago, the beer baron would have gratefully
accepted Keane's resignation. Now he virtually begged him to reconsider, hoping to entice him with a substantial increase for two years.
He'd made the offer before, humbly, with one game left in the regular
season. The Redbirds' lofty place in the standings didn't leave him
much choice.

Keane had turned Busch down then, saying he preferred to wait
until after the final game, and he rebuffed him again. Sitting next to
Keane in the Anheuser-Busch boardroom, the Cardinals' grim-faced
owner looked as if he'd sampled too many suds down at the brewery.

The St. Louis press conference may have been as much a charade
as the one about to begin in New York. Gussie Busch called Keane's
decision "a complete bombshell." Yet rumors persist that the team
owner had made up his mind to fire Keane around the same time that
Ralph Houk decided to ditch Yogi Berra, and that he had quietly
granted the Yankees permission to sound out his field general about
future employment. Who could blame Busch if he conveniently omit-
ted mention of his role in paving the way for Keane's departure? Irate
fans would have run him out of St. Louis on a Budweiser Clydesdale.

Keane could simply have torn up the letter he'd composed with his
wife's help three weeks earlier. But he resented the embarrassing leaks
about his impending firing. A baseball Willy Loman who'd labored
diligently in the organization for thirty-five years, the St. Louis native
felt betrayed.

"I think there was some bitterness over feeling unwanted in his
own town," observes George Vecsey, then a *Newsday* reporter who
befriended Keane during the waning days of the National League race.
"A sense of 'I'll show them. I'll go to the Yankees.' "

By resigning, Keane became only the third manager in history to
jilt a World Championship club. His stand made him a national hero
in the eyes of every working stiff who'd ever fantasized about marching
into the boss's office, pounding a fist on the desk, and declaring, "I
quit!" No one yet realized that Keane made his leap secure in the
knowledge that he'd parachute gently into a Yankees uniform.

Asked by reporters if he had any job prospects, Johnny Keane lied:
"Nobody has contacted me."

On Tuesday, October 20, Keane, in a Yankees cap, stood shoulder to shoulder with Ralph Houk on the same rostrum where Yogi
Berra's blood had been spilled four days earlier. If Houk ever recon-

sidered his decision of early September and privately asked, or implored, Keane to graciously bow out of their agreement, he's never said so.

The commissioner of baseball, Ford Frick, considered Houk's claim that he didn't contact Keane until after the World Series suspect enough to demand an accounting of the affair over the weekend. But Frick adjudged the Yankees general manager innocent of tampering.

To a mostly skeptical room, Houk reiterated that he'd first learned of Keane's availability the day of Berra's firing. "An outrageous lie," sportswriter Maury Allen scoffs. Besides sullying Houk's credibility, the deception tarnished somewhat Keane's previously sterling reputation. "He was brought in with a terrible cloud over his head," says Allen. "The whole environment was very uncomfortable all winter."

The Mets, whose public-relations acumen far outdistanced their baseball ability, swiftly took advantage of the Yankees' latest bungle. With a minimum of persuasion, in November they lured Berra away from the Yankees and appointed him first-base coach.

At a press conference, Berra somewhat sheepishly unveiled his new uniform, emblazoned with the familiar number 8 on its back, but with the Mets' blue-and-orange script logo on the front. He'd never worn anything other than Yankee pinstripes since coming to the big leagues in 1946. By this time next year, Berra would be relieved to have escaped the Bronx.

1965

STARTERS
Mel Stottlemyre
Whitey Ford
Al Downing
Jim Bouton

Joe Pepitone (1B)
Bobby Richardson (2B)
Tony Kubek/Phil Linz
(SS)
Clete Boyer (3B)
Tom Tresh (LF)
Mickey Mantle (CF)
Hector Lopez/Roger
Maris (RF)
Elston Howard (C)

RELIEVERS
Pedro Ramos
Hal Reniff
Pete Mikkelsen
Steve Hamilton

I

POOR JOHNNY KEANE will forever be remembered as the Herbert Hoover of baseball: the wrong man in the wrong place at the wrong time. When the opportunity to manage the Yankees came along, he couldn't believe his good fortune. Not long into the 1965 season, he couldn't believe his bad luck.

Or perhaps he could, for Johnny Keane knew misfortune and disappointment as thoroughly as he knew the game of baseball. An Irishman from South St. Louis, John Joseph Keane signed with the hometown Cardinals in 1929 at the age of seventeen. The scrappy shortstop hit well enough to allay concerns about his slight build and seemed destined for the majors.

Playing for the Houston Buffalos in 1935, Keane rapped a game-winning home run off a hulking Galveston right-hander named Sig Jakucki. His next at-bat against Jakucki he took a fastball on the side of the head. For seven days Keane lay comatose with a severely fractured skull, hovering between life and death. He didn't get out of the hospital until six weeks later, which put an end to his season.

Keane came back the following spring, determined not to let the incident unnerve him at the plate. Despite a respectable .272 average, his manager and coaches insisted the fire had gone out in his pale blue eyes.

They all, however, saw in Keane the makings of a manager. In 1938 the organization assigned him to its class-D team in Albany, Georgia. His winding journey through the St. Louis farm system began with two pennants in a row. Along the way Keane won three more championships, yet apparently didn't impress the front office enough to merit consideration for the big-league job at a time when it seemed everyone but the batboy was submitting résumés: in the 1950s, the Cardinals consumed seven skippers, yet repeatedly overlooked the humble Keane.

Realizing he needed to make himself more visible, in 1959 he accepted a coaching job with St. Louis under manager du jour Solly Hemus. Two years later Hemus bowed to the inevitable, and the Redbirds tapped Keane as his successor—if only because by then they had depleted the field. The rookie skipper was just months shy of his fiftieth birthday.

When Keane arrived at the Yankees' 1965 spring-training camp, his leathery, lined face testified to the years spent crisscrossing the Midwest on hot, dusty buses and wolfing down greasy-spoon chow. Having worn Cardinals white and red all his life, donning Yankees white and blue felt peculiar, he admitted. In the eyes of his new players, Keane looked more than a little out of place. Johnny Keane, managing the Yankees? For Japan to have made Douglas MacArthur emperor might have seemed less absurd.

Understandably, the players anxiously questioned how a team gunning for its sixth straight pennant could be on its fourth manager since 1960. For all their complaints about Yogi Berra, many Yankees deplored his humiliating mistreatment. "Yogi got the shaft pretty good," says Clete Boyer. "To me that was the start of the organization's decline, because it took away a lot of the players' respect.

"The Yankees had been so close and stable for so many years. You had guys who knew they were going to have a job. When they went and fired Yogi, I think we just understood then, 'This ain't the way things are supposed to be.' "

Jim Bouton, however, finds the notion of widespread indignation over Berra's dismissal amusing. "I don't remember anyone getting too outraged over the way Yogi was fired," he scoffs, adding pointedly, "The same guys who were going behind his back and complaining to the front office are probably the same guys now saying he shouldn't have been fired. But they were the ones who got him fired."

Hindsight, of course, frequently distorts memory. After just a few weeks under Johnny Keane, says Bouton, "The guys suddenly realized, 'Hey, Yogi was pretty good!' "

Early that spring, when days still consisted of calisthenics, drills, and suntans in the outfield, Keane inspected his awesome new crew and remarked, "They're all professionals, these boys. A man would be a fool if he started to change things around." Yet the new manager immediately set about overhauling the patented New York attack with all the subtlety of a wrecking crew. Truly a product of the team and league he'd left behind, Keane believed in scraping for runs through bunts, hit-and-runs, stolen bases. Finesse.

By contrast, the brutish Yankees approached baseball rather like a warring Stone Age tribe. Wield big stick, club foe to death, ugh. Squeeze the runner home? Swipe a base? Tom Tresh, New York's most prolific base stealer in 1964 with a mere thirteen thefts, expresses the pervading attitude toward the running game: "Why risk getting thrown out, when somebody else is going to hit one?"

From the day they joined the organization, Yankees learned to rely on the long ball. "However they did it at the top was the way they did it on down through the whole system," explains Hal Reniff. "So Johnny Keane's concept on managing was altogether different from what I'd dealt with. It was kind of like, 'I'll put on the plays, and you guys execute 'em.' "

Reniff, the bullpen's scathing wit, recalls his teammates' scornful reaction: " 'Execute? We don't execute plays. What are you talking about? Even a pitcher ain't supposed to bunt. The guy in front of him's supposed to knock everybody in!' "

It was a distinct minority of players who glanced around camp and, like Johnny Keane, saw a spluttering, one-dimensional offense in dire need of a tuneup. "Changing the approach to playing the game was the right idea," Al Downing contends, "because we were no longer a ballclub that could sit back and hit three-run homers." As for the team's resistance to Keane's methods, Downing says, "The players didn't resent it because it wasn't the Yankees Way. They resented it because *they couldn't do it.*"

Right though he may have been, the autocratic Keane undermined his own cause by trying to impose his will "like a general," as Hector Lopez puts it. "He insisted we do things his way. And he wouldn't compromise at all."

Ultimately, a manager must adapt his style to his personnel, not the other way around. Just as important as evaluating ballplayers' capabilities, he must analyze a team's collective personality. Keane, whose ideas about managing were formed a generation before, wasn't naturally predisposed to studying athletes' psychological makeups. Neither was Yogi Berra, for that matter. But Berra had been around his teammates long enough to have at least gleaned some insight into each.

As an outsider, there was much Johnny Keane didn't understand about the most unique organization in baseball. Had he risen through the ranks like Ralph Houk, he'd have known that Yankees adhered to an unconventional system of rules: namely, none at all. Call it one of the perks of winning.

Just days after taking the reins in St. Louis, Keane forged a reputation for firmness by firing a habitual curfew violator in front of the entire team. The culprit, Mickey McDermott, may have been a notorious "night rider," in ballplayers' lingo, but on the 1965 Yankees he could have been a hall monitor.

"We had established a style of living," Jim Bouton explains, "which was to stay out late at night. We'd never had to follow any rules before, and we always won." The Bronx Bombers did, however, observe a certain bottom-line work ethic. Anyone slacking off quickly snapped to after being warned, *"Don't mess with my World Series money."*

"Now," says Bouton, "here was Johnny Keane trying to make us follow rules." The new manager established a midnight curfew, a concept as foreign to the Yankees as finishing out of first. The players, already upset with the front office for the constant shake-ups, rebelled by piling into Fort Lauderdale bars night after night like sailors on leave. Their conduct disturbed the austere Keane, who had once studied for the priesthood.

"To have a religious man managing the Yankees was like having the pope run the Mafia," Bouton says sympathetically. "In his naïveté, John thought that ballplayers who had practice the next day should get some sleep. He couldn't believe that they weren't just coming back to the hotel late—some of them weren't coming back at all! Guys would head over to the ballpark right from somebody's apartment or hotel room, or from a bar or nightclub, hung over. It was blatant. You'd sit around the lobby at midnight, and you wouldn't see any of the players."

Distressed, Keane held a team meeting. "You guys are World Champions, and I'm not going to tell you how to live," he began in a quiet voice sharpened by a midwestern twang. "But a few of you fellows are becoming a little bit"—he searched for a euphemism—*"careless."* As a ballplayer who'd made the most of his moderate ability through diligence and hard work, Keane couldn't tolerate these gifted athletes abusing their talent.

"A week or two later he told us that more than a few of us were being 'careless.' And by the end of spring training, about twenty-two out of twenty-five guys were being 'careless,' " says Bouton, including himself among the overwhelming majority. Two conspicuous exceptions were roommates Bobby Richardson and Tony Kubek, known affectionately as the Milkshake Twins. "The rest of us," chuckles Phil Linz, "were up to no good."

Keane's admonitions had little effect. "He'd been used to disciplining people in the minor leagues, which you have to do," says Clete Boyer. "But in the major leagues, it's hard to discipline grown men. We know this is our job, but we also know that if we want to have a cocktail, we're going to."

Shortly before the exhibition season ended, Boyer and Roger Maris were arraigned on charges of assaulting a male model outside a local watering hole. The victim required eleven stitches and lost a tooth, earning Maris the clubhouse nickname Rocky. The widely reported incident confirmed that Johnny Keane would prove a no more effective disciplinarian than Yogi Berra.

In desperation over his waning authority, the manager chose to make an example of ringleader Mickey Mantle. On days when the Yankees star sleepwalked into the clubhouse wearing a nightclub tan, Keane ordered him to center field, hefted a bag of balls and a bat, and proceeded to exorcise the demon alcohol by making Mantle pant in pursuit of line drives. After fuming through several sessions of this punishment, Mantle revolted. Fielding a short hop, he sent it whistling past Keane's ear. The two glared at each other and thereafter observed an uneasy truce.

On any other team, with any other player, Keane's actions would have been appropriate. But he failed to appreciate Mantle's exalted status among his teammates. Reserve outfielder Archie Moore offers an example: "When it came time to divide up the World Series money, I asked Steve Hamilton how the vote worked. 'It's real simple,' he said. 'Just watch number seven. When he raises his hand to vote someone a full share, you raise your hand.' "

By refusing to defer to Mantle, Keane alienated the others, who watched disapprovingly as the two also clashed over where Mantle would play. The manager felt Mickey's fragile knees made him a defensive liability in Yankee Stadium's lone prairie of a center field. Even Mantle's admiring teammates admitted privately that he could no longer command the territory. Yogi Berra saw this in 1964, when he tried him briefly in left and then hid him in right from September on.

So the fact that Keane had Mantle and Tom Tresh swap positions in a spring-training experiment was hardly news. Except that late one evening, reporter Joe King of the dying *World Telegram and Sun* needed to file a story before retiring to his favorite pastime at the hotel bar. "Joe King was not always sober," colleague Steve Jacobson of *Newsday* says kindly.

With a deadline looming, King reflected on Whitey Ford's atrocious outing that afternoon against the Dodgers: eleven runs in five innings. The simple case of a thirty-six-year-old pitcher on the mend from major surgery getting knocked around? Oh no. King deduced that Ford had deliberately sabotaged the game as a protest against his buddy Mantle's ill-treatment.

The next day, King approached Johnny Keane and mumbled apologetically, "I think I was a bad boy last night. I may have caused you some trouble." By then New Yorkers were riveted by the shrieking headline FEUD OVER MANTLE SPLITS YANKS. King soon dreamed up yet another spring report that accused Mantle of threatening to ignore balls hit in his direction until *his* buddy Ford was restored to the top of the starting rotation ahead of Mel Stottlemyre. King's flights of fancy only exacerbated the very real tension festering in the Yankees' camp.

The players had already coined a bushel of derisive epithets for the manager, among them "Squeaky" and "Midget." "We got off on the wrong foot right off the bat," Phil Linz says. "We didn't like him, and he didn't like us. That's the way it was."

Nothing dispels turmoil like winning, however. Five games into the grapefruit-league schedule, New York had yet to lose. Johnny Keane beamed while entertaining reporters' joking predictions of a perfect season. Then the defeats like the one to the Dodgers started racking up, dampening his confidence in the team he'd proclaimed "the greatest I've ever managed."

Time for another meeting. "You guys aren't as bad as your record indicates," Keane consoled his players, who looked at one another and laughed.

"We never won a lot of games in spring training," says Rollie Sheldon. "We just tried to get in shape for Opening Day. When the bell rang, we knew we'd be ready."

Johnny Keane wasn't so sure. Late in the exhibition season he committed blasphemy by calling a practice on an off-day; the baseball equivalent of breaking the sabbath. "Everybody was P.O.'d," says Steve Hamilton, "especially some of the big guys. It really didn't help matters a lot."

II

OPENING DAY AGAINST Minnesota in wintry Metropolitan Stadium set the tone for the year. New York, which had gone 12–15 in exhibition, errored five times and dispensed runs like coffee at an AA meeting. Johnny Keane's men pecked away at the Twins' 4–0 lead, tying the score in the ninth, only to break down in the eleventh. Defensive replacement Arturo Lopez, in his major-league debut, misplayed Bob Allison's leadoff pop fly to left into a triple.

After intentionally walking the next two hitters to load the bases, Pedro Ramos came within one strike of squeezing out of the jam. Then Twins rookie Cesar Tovar hacked a line drive that a charging Tom Tresh trapped on the frozen surface as the winning run scored. Far more disappointing than the 5–4 setback was the postgame news that Elston Howard would be lost indefinitely.

The sturdy receiver smacked a double and a home run, but afterward couldn't uncrook his right arm. Howard shouldn't have been behind the plate in the first place, still wincing from an injury suffered in an April 3rd exhibition game. Twenty-four hours before Opening Day, a worried Howard was telling reporters he didn't expect to be in the lineup.

"He'll play," snapped Johnny Keane. "I need his bat." He got it, for all of nine innings.

John Blanchard did the catching in game two, a 4–3 loss to the Los Angeles Angels that revealed a disturbing detail about the new skipper: "He wasn't a Yankees-type manager," says Bobby Richardson, "and we found out in a hurry." Ahead 2–1 in the sixth, Whitey Ford yielded his second flimsy single of the inning. Out of the dugout hastened stone-faced Johnny Keane, signaling to the bullpen for Hal Reniff.

"You just don't do that," Richardson says. Past New York managers probably would have left Ford in, anticipating the inevitable eleventh-hour offensive barrage. "But Johnny Keane had never managed a team that could go into the seventh or eighth inning behind and *know* it was going to win," Richardson points out. "His moves weren't typical Yankees moves."

Keane, conservative as a brown suit, managed strictly by the book. "I remember one time Mickey was up with a count of 3-and-0," says Clete Boyer, "and they gave him the take sign. You don't give Mickey Mantle the take sign! I don't care if you're down seven to nothing.

Because he might pop one out. Mickey had been here fourteen years by then. He knew whether or not to swing."

Perhaps, Boyer suggests, the need to prove himself in his new surroundings compelled Keane to overmanage "instead of just letting guys play."

The Bronx Bombers looked down their noses at such hyperactive maneuvering, bristling whenever flashed a sign. *A bunt—in this situation? Is he kidding?* They'd carry out the manager's orders half-heartedly, popping up into a double play, then trudge back to the dugout, more convinced than ever that Johnny Keane's strategy did not work.

"The guys said they were trying just as hard," Jim Bouton remarks. "Like hell they were."

On the dismal 4–7 opening homestand, run production dried up, while earned run averages mushroomed along with the team's medical bills. Against Kansas City, Roger Maris strained his right hamstring muscle in pursuit of a fly ball, sidelining him for nearly a month. A few days later Mickey Mantle complained of a sore right leg and had to sit out a week. And Tony Kubek, once again a magnet for injuries, was to miss three weeks with shoulder damage.

Most crippling of all, Elston Howard's condition was diagnosed as bone chips, requiring immediate surgery. Instead of a catcher's mitt, he would be wearing a plaster cast from wrist to bicep through early June.

"That was a great loss," says Hector Lopez, "because Ellie was the key to the ball club." In recent years the Yankees had weathered extended absences of Maris, Mantle, and Kubek by shifting a Joe Pepitone to the outfield or inserting a Phil Linz at short. But Howard was their pillar, averaging more than 120 games behind the plate annually since stepping into Yogi Berra's shoes in 1960.

The season's first confrontation with Baltimore produced one win against three losses, including both ends of a May 2nd Sunday double-header. Backup catchers John Blanchard and Bob Schmidt combined for no hits in six trips to the plate in the 4–2 and 5–0 defeats, which left New York in eighth place with a 7–9 record. Yogi Berra would have consulted his calendar and with a grunt dismissed claims of a Yankees collapse as laughably premature.

Johnny Keane, already wilting from the pressures of managing in the media capital of the world, sent eyeballs rolling by calling yet another meeting. "For Chrissake," says Hal Reniff, "the only team meetings we used to have were at the end of the year: 'Congratulations, we won another one.' "

The normally reserved manager addressed his players with a sneering "New York Yankees *my ass!*"

"He started bawling us out for not winning, not hustling," recalls Phil Linz. "We thought, *What the hell is he talking about? It's only the third week of the season!*

"Keane thought we were all spoiled. We did have kind of a cavalier attitude toward winning," Linz concedes. "But we always used to start off the year around .500, three or four games behind. We knew we'd get into a streak at some point and begin pulling ahead, especially later in the season, because we had a lot of money players.

"But Johnny Keane really pushed the panic button," he says. "He'd point to players and ask accusing questions. 'Why did you make that play?' 'Why did you make that throw?' We'd never experienced that before. To put us down like that? He was walking into a team that had won five pennants in a row! It was ridiculous."

And enough to make a number of Yankees pine for their ex-manager. When the Mets bused up to the Bronx for the annual Mayor's Trophy Game the next day, Yogi Berra's "What, me worry?" grin must have seemed a saintly vision.

Before the exhibition, management announced a trade to bolster the catching: John Blanchard and Rollie Sheldon to the Athletics for Doc Edwards, a .244 hitter after three years in the majors. Sheldon, who'd fallen into disuse, was glad to go. But Blanchard, after fourteen seasons in the organization, broke down in front of his locker. "It was awful," remembers Linz. "He cried like a baby."

Sheldon paced the last-place A's with a 10–8 record in 1965. Edwards, though solid with the glove, batted a meager .190 in pinstripes and was farmed out by midseason. "The trade just didn't make any sense," says Sheldon, who now lives in Kansas City, selling insurance. Why break up a lefty-righty platoon by swapping the left-handed Blanchard for a weak-hitting right-handed receiver, he asks, when you already have one in journeyman Schmidt? On top of which giving up a capable pitcher. "And that was one of Ralph Houk's first moves as general manager."

Unfortunately, it was typical of his tenure. Few deals that year or next materialized into anything more than opportunities for some marginal major-league players to experience the thrill of playing for the Yankees.

Their armor pierced by injuries, the Bombers looked to the front office to plug the holes until Howard, Maris, *et al.*, returned. Most believed they could still make a run for the pennant. "We weren't a bad ball club," says Al Downing, "we just needed help.

"We got the wrong help."

Such as thirty-five-year-old Bobby Tiefenauer, an itinerant knuckle-baller still looking for his first winning season in the bigs. The frequent sight of Yankees receivers scurrying after passed balls made it quickly apparent that they could no more handle Tiefenauer's specialty than catch butterflies bare-handed. Within weeks he was sent on to Cleveland, his third stop that summer.

A week after trading Blanchard and Sheldon, Houk exchanged infielder Pedro Gonzalez for a jackstraw by the name of Ray "Buddy" Barker, hitless in twelve big-league at-bats. Hearing of the deal with the Indians, reporter Jim Ogle of the Newhouse papers huffed, "Can you believe it? The Yankees, reduced to ragpickers."

Fact was, New York had always adopted other clubs' castoffs, often trading bright prospects for lackluster veterans to lend a hand nailing down pennants come September. Amid the mighty Yankees lineup, many of those sow's ears suddenly resembled silk purses.

Case in point: Dale Long, a thirty-four-year-old first baseman picked up late in 1960 from San Francisco, where he hit just .167. In New York, however, the ghost of Babe Ruth seemed to possess him. Long pounded out a .366 average during the pennant drive, only to be handed to the expansion Senators that winter. When the Yankees needed seasonal help two years later, they obtained him again.

Ray Barker didn't have the good fortune to join the 1960 Yankees, but the trade turned out to be a break for a career that hadn't seen many. The crew-cut twenty-nine-year-old was in his eleventh season of pro ball, and unless something drastic happened, it was going to be his last. A sales job awaited him back home in Martinsburg, West Virginia.

He'd come close to quitting the game long ago, in 1955, his first year in the Baltimore chain. "I would tend to get down on myself when I wasn't hitting, and consequently my defense would suffer at times," Barker reflects. "That probably cost me any kind of a major-league career."

As a nineteen-year-old playing in Thetford, Canada, where the groundskeepers regularly burned the infield with gasoline to melt the snowdrifts, Barker struck out with the bases loaded for the second time in a night. He was still brooding about it the next inning when with two outs an opposing batter bunted up the third-base line.

"The third baseman barehands it and makes a beautiful throw to me at first base," recalls Barker. "Instead of stretching, I caught the ball standing up straight, and the guy was safe. Would've been the third out." With Thetford leading, 4–0.

"About the next eight or nine guys get on by errors, base hits, walks;

we come out of the inning behind, 7–4. I wanted to dig a hole and crawl into it. I get to the dugout, and of course the players are upset with me. Not to mention the manager, Barney Lutz.

"He grabs me by the back of the uniform and pushes me up the runway. I was mad at myself anyway, and I jerked away from him. He yelled, 'Go ahead, take a punch at me!' I said, 'Barney, I'm not mad at you, I'm mad at myself.' He stood there for a couple of minutes, then said, 'I have just one question to ask you, son. Do you think that if your mother or father was in the stands tonight they would have been proud of you?'

"Well, I busted out crying like a baby. All the guys on the bench thought Barney was beating the hell out of me, and they were all tickled to death about it. While I was trying to get myself straightened out, someone hollered, 'Barker, you're up!'

" 'Barney,' I said, 'send me home. I'm done. I quit. I just wanna get out of here. Can't handle it.'

" 'No,' he said. 'I'm gonna make a ballplayer out of you or knock the hell out of you, one of the two. Get your ass up there and hit!'

" 'Barney, I don't want to.' So he pushed me out of the dugout. I was still wiping the tears out of my eyes as I grabbed a bat and walked up to the plate. Lo and behold, the bases are loaded, and we're still losing, 7–4.

"Well," says Barker, "I tattooed one over the right-center-field fence and cried all the way around the bases. I just didn't deserve it. I still get choked up just talking about it."

Barker graduated to triple-A ball, then remained stranded there despite quality numbers. In 1960 he batted .311 with 101 RBIs, but the Orioles had big Jim Gentile at first and dealt him to Cleveland. Barker knocked in 92 runs for its Jacksonville club; the Tribe picked up veteran Joe Adcock. In all, seven "very frustrating" years just one rung below the majors.

"To see all the pitchers I'd played against and handled pretty good," says the first baseman, "and they'd all made it to the big leagues, and there I was still down in triple-A."

In his first major-league start—just one day after reporting to New York—Barker doubled home the tying run off Boston's Earl Wilson, one of those pitchers he'd owned back in the minors. As Barker pulled up at second, Wilson turned and shouted, "Same old shit up here, huh?" Barker came around to score on a Tony Kubek single and later contributed another hit to the Yankees' 5–3 victory, only their tenth in twenty-four games.

In June he smashed three home runs in three straight games, two of them as a pinch hitter, to tie the major-league record. His club-leading .289 average off the bench won Barker one of the team's few pay raises that winter, and he returned home a local celebrity.

Ironically, an off-season of area speaking engagements led to a weight gain that nearly cost Barker a spot on the 1966 roster. Playing sporadically, he never recaptured his stroke and the following season wound up back where he started, in Baltimore's farm system. Ray Barker's career ended without his qualifying for a big-league pension. But during a gloomy summer in the Bronx, he flickered brightly, if briefly. He still lives in Martinsburg, where he works as a security guard.

Barker's May–June offensive spark couldn't ignite the rest of the Yankees' bats. As they prepared to host Chicago on June 4, the team batting average defied belief: .216. Pepitone, Kubek, and Boyer— that's three quarters of the infield—were all south of .200.

In the Friday-night opener, ninth-place New York wasted ten score-less innings courtesy of Bill Stafford. With one out in the fifteenth and New York trailing 2–0, Johnny Keane cast an eye down the bench for a pinch hitter until he found his man.

Whitey Ford?

Keane had run out of batters. But with a .183 average that season, Ford's chances of landing a hit equaled nearly anyone else's. He didn't, and the Yankees went down to defeat. Contemplating the draining loss, Keane muttered bravely, "You can't let it discourage you," while looking about as discouraged as a man could be. First place now was eleven and a half games uptown. Even .500 was beginning to recede in the distance, New York's record sinking to 19–27.

Three quick wins over Chicago raised hopes, however, as did the prospect of an impending series in always hospitable Kansas City. Following a 6–1, 12–0 Sunday sweep, the latter a dazzling Al Downing three-hitter, the Yankees headed for Newark Airport in a rare festive mood.

There the team learned that its chartered jet was temporarily grounded by mechanical difficulties. About a dozen restless players peeled off from the group and wandered into a cocktail lounge. As the anticipated fifteen-minute delay stretched into two and a half hours, one for the road turned into one more for the road, give or take a couple of mores. It wasn't until midnight that the boarding announcement sounded and the Yankees headed gratefully for the gate, some less steadily than others.

Mickey Mantle, Hal Reniff, and Pedro Ramos weaved past Keane and wife Lela, his constant companion. "He don't say nothing," recalls Ramos, "he just look." Glowered is probably more like it. The next day the manager announced to a largely bemused clubhouse that he was fining the trio $250 each and that other offenders would receive reprimands.

"Two hundred fifty dollars?" Mantle cracked. "Hell, I drink that much in a day!"

Several reporters on the Yankees beat witnessed the goings-on in the airport bar. Some might have even charged a round or two to their expense accounts. But none intended to write about the trifling incident. That is, until the ham-handed New York front office inflated it into a major story by publicizing the fines. For that, blame Ralph Houk. The players, however, tended to reproach only Johnny Keane.

"The whole thing was blown out of proportion," protests Ramos. "We not drunk or anything. We just have a couple of drinks. But I guess because Mickey was in there," he adds, "Keane wanted to make a big shit out of it."

Keane's reaction made him seem petty, more chaperone than manager, and irrevocably shattered relations between him and his men. Whereas the 1964 Harmonica Incident united the club and renewed Yogi Berra's authority, the Newark Nightcap had the opposite effect.

When Keane ordered slumping Joe Pepitone to report early for extra batting practice, the defiant first baseman "walked into the clubhouse the same time he always did," Clete Boyer recalls. "Johnny said right there, 'You're fined fifty dollars!' "

Pepitone retorted, "I don't give a shit! Take it all!"

Fifty dollars poorer, "Joe didn't come out early the next day either," Boyer adds, laughing. Pepitone's habitual tardiness may have concerned Keane less than the fact that he had begun dating the manager's daughter, Pat, an attractive divorcée and mother of two. Keane would rather have seen his only child abducted by pirates than going out with Pepitone, then temporarily between marriages.

Contributing to Keane's woes was a recently published book by Bill Veeck, Jr., which alleged that he'd encountered similar discord on the World Champion Cardinals. According to *The Hustler's Handbook*, a stinging examination of the national pastime, a number of St. Louis players were openly critical of their manager all summer, star shortstop Dick Groat in particular.

Veeck, the maverick team owner and promoter, wrote that the Redbirds' general manager, Bing Devine, eventually put down the insurrection by pressuring Groat to apologize to Keane in front of the team. Groat, now a broadcaster for the University of Pittsburgh Panthers basketball team, has no desire to reentangle himself in the controversy, saying diplomatically, "I don't want to knock Johnny

Keane." But he does concede the club "had problems" and that friction between him and the manager undoubtedly influenced Keane's decision to resign.

Veeck's revelations did not come as a total shock to the Yankees, who'd heard whispers of trouble in St. Louis long before the '64 Series. "There was probably more disarray on the Cardinals at that time than on the Yankees," notes Steve Hamilton. As players' representative, he occasionally chatted with his Redbirds counterpart, Tim McCarver.

"Johnny Keane," says Hamilton, "was going through all kinds of bad times."

The bad times would not let up, and in June another wave of injuries all but capsized the Yankees. In the space of a week, Keane lost his 3-4 combination. First Mickey Mantle pulled his left hamstring trying to score from second base against Kansas City. Six days later, Roger Maris, only recently recovered from his torn hamstring, hurt his hand sliding during a sweep of the Senators. Mantle was expected to take two weeks or more to heal, while Maris was listed as day-to-day.

Replacements like youngsters Roger Repoz (.220 BA), Ross Moschitto (.185), and Art Lopez (.143) did not exactly strike fear in opposing pitchers' hearts. Nor did two other rookie additions, infielder Horace Clarke (.259) and catcher Jake Gibbs (.221). A vengeful league of Davids now rose up to slay Goliath.

"The first time I had to pitch against the Yankees," says Rollie Sheldon, "I worried, *Boy, they're going to knock my brains out.* But I found out they had weaknesses just like any other team." Facing Mel Stottlemyre on June 24, Sheldon stymied New York 3–2, and in August blanked them 4–0.

"They weren't the same ball club," observes Ralph Terry, who in one game that season required a mere 70 pitches to shut out his former teammates 4–0. Terry, 11–6 for Cleveland, quit pitching two years later for an even more solitary pursuit, golf. Since the mid-1980s he's been a touring pro on the senior circuit.

"The Yankees didn't have the awesome players anymore," Terry adds, "and those young guys couldn't quite carry it."

III

REALIZING HE'D BEEN handed the wheel of the *Titanic*, Johnny Keane scrambled for the lifeboats. The Yankees skipper took to managing every game as if it were the World Series, prodding injured players back into the lineup prematurely.

Only days after Maris damaged his hand, Keane collared the two-time MVP during a squeaker against the A's. "Can you hit?" he implored.

"Sure, I can," Maris grumbled, "one-handed." He couldn't even turn a doorknob, and the pain occasionally brought him to tears, but Keane appeared skeptical.

Through late September, Maris alternated between the bench and his Kansas City home, limited to rare pinch-hit appearances when not shuttling from doctor to doctor. None could seem to agree on the nature of his injury. With a week remaining in the season, the Yankees sheepishly admitted their orthopedic surgeon had erred: Maris's hand was fractured, not merely bruised. He underwent surgery at once, having produced a mere 8 homers and 27 RBIs in only 46 games.

Word of the latest casualty sent Johnny Keane's shoulders sagging and his temper soaring. Trainer Joe Soares, responsible for delivering the distressing news, came to expect an earful every time he knocked timidly on the manager's door, which Keane opened like a man expecting the Grim Reaper.

"Poor Johnny," recalls Soares. "It got so that when you told him somebody was hurt, he didn't believe it. He thought the players were reneging on him." Before a game against the Tigers on May 27, scheduled starter Whitey Ford reported total numbness in his left hand, the same condition that had driven him from the 1964 World Series opener. Dr. Denton Cooley, the noted Houston heart surgeon, diagnosed the problem as a blocked artery and that winter operated to enhance blood flow to Ford's valuable left arm.

One side effect of the surgery was that the ruddy-complexioned southpaw no longer perspired on the upper-left side of his body. Naturally this resulted in a plethora of locker-room wisecracks, such as: "Whitey is the only guy who gets ten days out of a Five-Day Deodorant Pad."

Catcher Doc Edwards recalls in amazement how after a few innings, "The right side of his jersey would be soaking wet, while the other side was dry as a bone." Despite the surgery, diminished circulation continued to plague Ford periodically, especially in temperatures under seventy degrees. At times he could barely feel the baseball in his hand.

Johnny Keane listened appreciatively to the veteran's complaint, but nevertheless sent him to the mound that chilly Detroit night. Ford lasted a single inning, during which he was constantly wetting his fingers, blowing on them—anything to coax back some sensation.

After thirteen seasons Ford appeared to have reached the end of the road. But then, beginning in June, he rebounded miraculously, snapping up seven straight victories en route to a fine 16–13, 3.24 ERA year. In the season finale Ford notched career victory number 232 to surpass Red Ruffing as the winningest pitcher in Yankees history.

Warmer weather contributed to Number 16's rejuvenation. So did supplementing his slider, curve, and fastball with an array of doctored pitches. As would befit a street-smart kid from Astoria, Queens, in the twilight of his career Ford employed everything from saliva, to mud, to a gluey concoction of turpentine, resin, and baby oil, which he mixed like a pharmacist, then concealed in a roll-on deodorant applicator. One time Yogi Berra, a notorious mooch, was rummaging the clubhouse for deodorant and spotted one in Ford's locker. Minutes later he could be heard yelping in pain, "*Son of a bitch! What the hell is this stuff?*" frantically flapping his arms, which were adhered at the pits.

Ford's most effective weapon was a custom-made ring that featured a tiny rasp for gouging the horsehide. When a ground ball was needed to get him out of a fix, the impish-faced pitcher innocently rubbed up the baseball. A few passes back and forth over the ring's serrated teeth and the next pitch tangoed its way toward home plate.

After games, Ford slipped his accessory to Joe Soares, who stashed it at the bottom of a trunk filled with medical supplies. The ring then accompanied the Yankees from city to city as if it were the president's nuclear-code briefcase. "It scared me a little bit, having to take care of the thing," says Soares, a reluctant accomplice. "As soon as Whitey retired, I threw it away."

Compared to Pedro Ramos, Ford was a mere apprentice at serving up illicit pitches. The Cuban's repertoire included tobacco-juice ball, Vaseline ball, and spitball—sorry, *Cuban palmball.*

"Spitball illegal. Cuban palmball legal," Ramos explains straightfaced. Even when he wasn't wetting the ball, the prospect that he might be kept suspicious batters off balance.

"I threw a sinkerball, which a lot of times they say was a spitball," he says. "If they want to believe it was a spitball, I never tell them differently; it give me an extra pitch." Facing Baltimore one day, Ramos had the Orioles screaming at the home-plate umpire to strip-search him on the mound for illegal substances. Three times he was sent to the clubhouse for a change of shirts.

The pitcher didn't confine his illegal activities to the baseball diamond. In 1979, four years after retiring from the Mexican League at age forty, Ramos was arrested on charges of cocaine possession, drug trafficking, and weapon possession, and later served eighteen months in prison for violating probation. He got into scrapes as a Yankee too, once tussling with five men outside a Bronx bar and landing in the hospital with knife wounds. A dashing figure in his flamboyant western outfits, the reliever was a favorite with the ladies. Anyone thinking of rooming with him on the road was warned, "Room with Pedro, and you'll wind up sleeping in a tree."

"He always had some activity going," says Ray Barker. "He'd call and say, 'Hey, Rooms, I need the room for a couple of hours.' So I'd go out, have a couple of drinks and something to eat. When I got back to the hotel I'd call him from the lobby, and he'd always say, 'Give me another hour!'

"I used to tell him, 'Nope, Pete, I've got to play tomorrow, and I'm going to bed. Do whatever you have to do, or keep on doing what you're doing, but I'm coming up.' "

Phil Linz, another roommate, remembers, "He always carried a pistol, which he put under his pillow at night. I'd say to him, 'Hey, Pedro, make sure that barrel is pointed the other way!' " According to Linz, Ramos feared that as he was a Cuban expatriate, agents of Fidel Castro might try to kidnap him and bundle him home to Pinar del Río.

Nonsense, says Ramos. "Why Castro want me in Cuba?" he protests playfully. "He can't hit me anyway." A California Angels scout since 1991, the Florida resident pitches batting practice to the Miami-Dade Community College baseball team and claims to still throw seventy miles per hour. "And it's no wet, it's dry," he vows. "A natural sinker."

Johnny Keane frowned on Ramos's personal habits but called him into 65 games, tying Luis Arroyo's club high. Although not as overwhelming as the year before, Number 14 posted a career-low 2.92 ERA, a 5–5 won-loss ratio, and 19 saves. Some victories were hardearned, like a 10–6 win over Cleveland in game one of a televised Sunday doubleheader.

Indians third baseman Max Alvis led off the ninth by ripping a single past the mound. Ramos, rarely seen without tobacco tucked in his cheek, lunged for the ball and in doing so swallowed his chaw. While the reliever was retching on the mound, a laughing Clete Boyer reminded him, "Turn around, Pete. You're on TV!"

With the exception of Ramos and seldom-used Steve Hamilton (3–1, 5 SV, 1.39 ERA), the Yankees bullpen foundered all year. Hal Reniff and Pete Mikkelsen protected only four games between them while slumping to 3–4 and 4–9, respectively.

The starting rotation, considered a strong point in spring training, collapsed as well. Al Downing, the American League's top strikeout artist a year ago, turned in a disappointing 12–14, with a 3.40 ERA. The once promising Bill Stafford finished 3–8, with a 3.56 ERA, on his slide out of the game. Going into 1963, the twenty-three-year-old right-hander had a 31–19, .613 record in two and a half seasons. Then he damaged the rotator cuff in his shoulder, an injury that at the time almost automatically spelled the end of a pitcher's career. "From then on I was barely hanging on," says Stafford, who now lives in Michigan, where he works in sports promotion.

Most mystifying of all was the sudden decline of Jim Bouton, 4–15, 4.82 ERA, whose arm corroded like an abandoned car alongside the Cross Bronx Expressway. X rays turned up nothing. All Bouton knew was that his bicep just ached. He'd experienced arm trouble the first half of 1964, then hurled 13–6 ball the rest of the way to finish 18–13, 3.02 ERA.

"It was the best stretch of pitching I'd ever done in my life," he says. "I was really rolling. I thought I was going to win twenty games in 1965."

Robbed of his velocity, Bouton wouldn't win that many over the remaining seven years of his career. He quickly came to learn the distances of outfield fences around the league after watching balls disappear behind them with disturbing regularity. On April 30, Baltimore's Boog Powell and Curt Blefary each socked two-run homers during a 10–4 shellacking. Despite lugging around a 7.11 ERA, the ever-loquacious Bouton could still joke, "My little boy knows four words, and three of them are 'Daddy's washed up.' "

The six-foot right-hander searched in vain for a win the entire second half while his loss ledger mounted. "I lost my mechanics and rhythm," he explains, "and I could never find them again." For athletes, driven equally by ego and insecurity, the line between self-confidence and self-delusion is perilously thin. Bouton's stratospheric ERA notwithstanding, "I always thought that the next game my arm would feel good and I would win," he says. And when that happened? "Then the other guys would start to play well, and we'd get hot."

The realization that the pennant race had passed them by began to seep in during the last stop of a discouraging 8–9 road trip leading up to the All-Star break. Sixth-place New York straggled into Minneapolis twelve and a half games behind the league-leading Twins. Nothing less than a sweep would keep them in contention.

Minnesota's offensive armada of Tony Oliva, Harmon Killebrew, Zoilo Versalles, Jimmie Hall, Bob Allison, and Don Mincher pummeled Bouton in the opener 8–3, then showed some restraint in taking game one of a Saturday doubleheader 4–1. The Bombers were trailing in the nightcap 5–4 when Clete Boyer clubbed an eighth-inning grand slam off reliever Johnny Klippstein to delay their burial one more day.

Sunday's skirmish seesawed back and forth for three and a half hours, jangling Johnny Keane's already frayed nerves. The manager lost his composure at one point, suffering what doctors described later as a mild attack of nervous exhaustion. After receiving oxygen, he calmed down and remained on the bench as the two teams went into the ninth inning tied at 4–4.

With two gone, New York had Elston Howard and Joe Pepitone at the corners. Roger Repoz chopped a bouncer up the first-base line that reliever Jerry Fosnow speared. But in lunging to make the tag, he let the ball squirt from his glove as Howard steamed across home.

"Interference! Batter out!" barked Ed Hurley. The ruling brought Johnny Keane and a contingent of enraged Yankees rushing to home plate, where they heatedly questioned the ump's competence, as well as his ancestry. Upon consultation with first-base umpire John Flaherty, Hurley reversed his decision. The run stood; 5–4, New York. Now Minnesota skipper Sam Mele came charging out to raise dust around the batter's box while boos thundered down from the stands.

This time Hurley remained firm, and the Twins sulked back onto the field to play under protest—an unnecessary action, it would turn out.

Keane, feeling lucky for a change, summoned yesterday's winning pitcher, Pete Mikkelsen, to guard the lead. The sinkerballer disposed of dangerous shortstop Zoilo Versalles, walked third baseman Rich Rollins, and retired 1964 batting titlist Tony Oliva on a fly to center. Up lumbered Harmon Killebrew, 2-for-3 on the afternoon.

Baseball's premier home-run hitter the past three years ran the count to 3-and-2. Two foul balls heightened the tension until the air seemed to vibrate with electricity. Killebrew then jacknifed Mikkelsen's eighth pitch into the bleachers for a 6–5 Minnesota victory.

"That was the one that did us in," says Phil Linz. "It was all over after that."

IV

MICKEY MANTLE, WHITEY Ford, Elston Howard, Tony Kubek, Bobby Richardson, and other lifelong Yankees were as unaccustomed to losing as Perry Mason. Consider that since Richardson's arrival as a twenty-year-old rookie in 1955, Yankee Stadium had hosted the World Series every fall with the exception of 1959.

Not only that, but, as the second baseman points out, "We were also winners my two years in the minor leagues, at Binghamton and Denver." The organization's proud tradition was sown down on the farm, so that its young players graduated to the parent club with a taste for first place.

Playing outside the bustle of the pennant race hit the Yankees hard. It felt . . . *unnatural.* "You just couldn't believe that you weren't a contender," Clete Boyer, a veteran of five World Series, says with a shake of his head.

Management appeared equally shell-shocked. Sportswriter George Vecsey recalls, "I can still hear Ralph Houk saying, over and over, 'Well, you *know* Mantle's gonna hit. And you *know* Maris is gonna hit. And Howard? You just *know* Ellie's gonna hit.' Then you added it all up, and all of these guys had gone down the drain together." None of them hit. Mantle, then a .309 lifetime batter, slumped to .255, his poorest performance by far; Maris, .239; Howard, .233; Pepitone, .247; Richardson, .247; Kubek, .218.

From midseason on, "we were down, going through the motions," says Phil Linz (.207 BA, 2 HR, 16 RBI on the year). "At the end we played like a second-division team, where you get beat so easily. It was awful."

Steve Hamilton remembers Mantle hotdogging a fly ball by swiping his glove at it and botching the play. After the inning, "Mickey apologized, 'Sorry I dropped it, but I've always wanted to do that!' It's something he never would have done had we been in a pennant race."

Of all the Yankees, Mantle seemed the least able to cope with the team's failure in addition to his own eroding skills. As the club's unequivocal leader, he could have tried rallying his teammates, praising, consoling, or cajoling where necessary. Instead Mantle withdrew into a shell that only close friends such as Whitey Ford could penetrate. At meetings he'd roll his eyes and drawl, "What the fuck are we doing here?"

Vecsey reflects, "Mickey was not a person who could reach out to anybody, because he was so preoccupied with himself. You had him sulking over money problems, women problems, not taking care of his body, showing up hung over with scratches up and down his back, bragging, 'I got laid last night.'

"That sent the wrong signals to the young players: 'Look at Mick. He gets laid, he comes in late, hung over. It's okay.' "

One time that summer Mantle partied deep into the night, expecting to sit out the next game due to a minor ailment. The following day, when he made his way gingerly up the dugout and checked the lineup card, he was stunned to find himself batting third and playing left field.

"Nobody had ever done that in the past," explains Steve Hamilton. Unlike his predecessors, stern Johnny Keane would not brook Mantle's reckless behavior. Adds Hamilton, "Mickey wasn't in very good shape that day—he was pie-eyed—but he did hit a home run."

Mantle, who turned sixty in 1991, has said many times that if he'd known he was going to live so long, he'd have taken better care of himself. Sadly, throughout eighteen illustrious seasons that included the 1956 AL Triple Crown, the fear that he wouldn't live much past forty shadowed baseball's golden boy.

In 1952 his father, Elvin Mantle, a lead miner who'd trained the eldest of his five children to switch hit, died of Hodgkin's disease at age thirty-nine. Two uncles and his paternal grandfather had also lost their lives to the cancer, leading young Mantle to believe a similar fate lay in store for him. Alcohol, in immense quantities, not only intensified the brilliance of the moment but numbed dark thoughts of the future.

Carousing and self-absorption aside, Mantle provided leadership simply by taking his position day after day and playing through terrible pain. Sports injuries had been a part of his life from the time he was a star athlete at Oklahoma's Commerce High School. As a result of a kick in the left shin during football practice, Mantle developed a chronic bone infection, osteomyelitis, that required five surgeries.

In 1951 the nineteen-year-old phenom shattered precedent by vaulting from class-C ball into the Yankees' starting lineup. That October, while digging for a fly ball during the second game of the World Series, he caught his cleats on a drainage hole, tearing the cartilage in his right knee and setting the tragic undertone of a remarkable career.

Four operations over the years couldn't strengthen the joint to adequately support his muscular 195-pound body. Yet Mantle displayed surprising speed. The Commerce Comet, they used to call him. On a team that considered the stolen base a moving violation, he abducted 21 in 1959, accounting for nearly half the Yankees' total.

Age, arthritis, and the pounding of some 2,000 games gradually crippled Mantle to the point where by 1965 he had to hoist himself up the stairs and prepare his legs for more than an hour before games: whirlpool and massage to improve circulation, then binding himself from ankle to thigh with elastic bandage.

The elaborate pregame ritual reduced his discomfort only so much. "Mickey'd swing a bat," remembers Doc Edwards, "and when he'd land on his foot, you'd see the grimace on his face from the pain. But he never complained." Fear of taking a fastball on the knees kept him off the plate, and pitches now snuck past that a younger Mantle would have punished for trying to outfox him. His power output dimmed in 1965 to 19 home runs and 46 RBIs.

In center he went after balls stiffly, as if on stilts. Twenty-year-old

Ross Moschitto, a redheaded gazelle who frequently spelled Mantle defensively, recalls that "Mickey could run straight fairly well, but he really felt the pain whenever he had to make a turn." Even throwing gave him difficulty. By August, tendinitis in his right shoulder prevented Number 7 from reaching the infield, so that Tony Kubek had to travel halfway into the outfield to relay Mantle's withering lobs.

A less beloved veteran might have generated clubhouse resentment. "Can't cut it anymore." "He's hurting the team." "Get him out of there." Not Mantle. Not from the Yankees. Catcher Jake Gibbs, speaking for many, reflects, "We didn't care if Mickey hit nineteen home runs or none. It was still an inspiration to us just to have him in the lineup."

Mantle's ongoing feud with the manager did not escape his teammates' attention. "Mickey was a superstar, but Johnny Keane didn't give him that much respect," Pedro Ramos says. "Instead of asking, 'Mickey, how do you feel today? You think you can play today?' now Mickey had to find out if he was in the lineup." The thirty-three-year-old Mantle was so unhappy under Keane that he later admitted, "If I had been financially set, I would've retired at the end of the season."

Tom Tresh remembers bitterly, "Keane would sometimes put Ross Moschitto in for Mickey in the middle of an inning. So here's Mickey Mantle running out to the outfield. Then all of a sudden here comes Ross Moschitto, and Mickey has to make the long run back in, more or less saying to everybody in the stands that he's not as good defensively as this young guy.

"I know how embarrassing that had to be for Mickey. Of course he never said anything, but it was breaking my heart. And I'm sure it did the same to a lot of the other players. We all respected Mickey so much," says Tresh, "that when somebody appears to be against him . . . I don't want to say you don't play as hard, but do you care as much about what happens?"

Tresh did appear to care, deeply. In spite of his feelings toward Johnny Keane, Number 15 stepped forward to carry the team. While one star after another toppled around him, Tresh led New York in every offensive category except stolen bases.

A .279 batting average with 27 home runs and 74 RBIs reversed the declining graph on Tresh, who put up his best numbers since capturing Rookie of the Year honors in 1962. The switch-hitting shortstop filled in for army-reservist Tony Kubek that year and nearly gave Kubek cause to reenlist: .286 with 20 homers and 93 RBIs.

Although merely grazed by the sophomore jinx, Tresh, by then an outfielder, slumped badly the second half of 1964 to wind up a worrisome .246. Over the winter, he says, "I felt that after playing in New York for three years"—that is, alongside Mantle, Maris, and Howard—"it was my time to produce at those guys' levels."

Foremost behind the Bronx empire's unparalleled longevity was its ability to develop heirs at virtually every position: having a Joe DiMaggio waiting in the wings as a Babe Ruth faded; then, a Mickey Mantle, poised to receive Joltin' Joe's baton fifteen years later. During 1965, handsome Tom Tresh arose as Mantle's likely successor.

Against Chicago in the second game of a June doubleheader, the twenty-seven-year-old slugged three consecutive home runs, just missing a fourth. Six weeks later he again tormented the Sox. In the tenth inning of a 6–6 tie, Danny Cater hooked a ball toward the left-field corner of Yankee Stadium. Tresh, racing to his right, reached across his body to snare it at the low wall and toppled head first into the stands. The crowd roared as he emerged holding his catch aloft. One out later, with Yankee Stadium still abuzz, Tresh vaporized an Eddie Fisher pitch over the right-field fence to win the game, the best performance of his nine-year career. "It was almost like an Ozark Ike feat," he jokes, referring to the preposterously gifted cartoon character Tresh followed as a boy.

On August 24, he clubbed his seventh deciding blow of the season. The two-run shot off Minnesota's Jim Perry in the eighth inning pulled out a 2–1 victory for Mel Stottlemyre who, in just his first full season, displaced Whitey Ford as the team's stopper.

Stottlemyre (20-9, 2.63 ERA) led the league in complete games (18) and innings pitched (291). Ironically, until 1964 New York had been grooming him for the bullpen. Because he relied on a natural sinker, he didn't impress instantly, not like a Sam McDowell, a Sandy Koufax, or some other flamethrowers who could turn the air around home plate infrared. The Yankees signed him without having to shell out a penny in bonus money.

Composed on the mound, reserved off it, Stottlemyre's chief asset was his nerve. Even when up against the league's top low-ball hitters, the poker-faced right-hander went to the sinker, matching strength for strength.

"Mel wasn't afraid of the bat," says Doc Edwards, later a coach with Stottlemyre on the New York Mets. "He came into the strike zone with all his pitches, and he was going to make you hit him to beat him." In a two-hit whitewashing of the Senators, "He threw something like eighty-six pitches," the catcher recalls. "Eighty sinkers and six sliders."

V

ON SEPTEMBER 8, New York announced Johnny Keane's rehiring for
1966. The low-key news conference represented a break with tradition,
for the Yankees normally waited until after the season to confirm any
decisions involving the manager. But the front office wanted to give
Keane a public vote of confidence and simultaneously blunt the rumors
of his impending move to Shea Stadium. (A broken hip had recently
forced Casey Stengel into retirement.)

"We cannot blame our present position on the manager," Ralph
Houk underscored, hoping to drive the point home with his players
as well as the fans. Not that this show of solidarity was likely to improve
the atmosphere in the dugout a great deal.

A mimeographed statement posted on the clubhouse bulletin board
informed the Yankees of their manager's return. Few seemed surprised. "Who's going to admit their mistake?" Hal Reniff asks rhetorically. "Especially when they win a pennant the year before, bring in
another manager, and he loses. There's no way in hell these people
are going to admit their mistake that fast."

Keane appeared relaxed at the Yankee Stadium press event. But it
was not so easy to tell if he was truly smiling or gritting his teeth at
the prospect of enduring another year of hostility from players and
fans alike. Lately the sight of Number 21 prompted a symphony of
boos in the Bronx; at least the sparse attendance kept the volume
down.

In all his years in uniform, Keane never spent a lonelier season than
1965. He and his wife lived secluded above Manhattan in a suite at
the Hilton Hotel, a far cry from the rolling fifty-six-acre ranch outside
Houston they called home in the off-season. Every game found loyal
Lela Keane behind the Yankees dugout, rooting and keeping score as
she had through twenty-eight years of devoted marriage.

Keane felt his players' disdain. "If he didn't," Bill Stafford comments, "there was something wrong with him." And according to
Tom Tresh, the manager's suspicions of malingering weren't entirely
paranoid. "When we had a lot of injuries," he says candidly, "I questioned how quickly we wanted to heal."

It seemed like Keane was always disappearing into his paneled office
to chew on his small cigars and perhaps rue the day he ever left St.
Louis. He rarely communicated with his team, particularly with the

fill-ins, who needed occasional pep talks to know where they stood and what was expected of them.

Isolated from his club, Keane confided only in Vern Benson, one of two coaches who accompanied him from St. Louis. "The players didn't like him either," says Hector Lopez, recalling the nickname they'd coined for Benson: "Radar." "He'd listen in to conversations and report it back to Johnny Keane. That wasn't the Yankees' style."

Untrue, says Benson. "I was not a spy for Johnny Keane," he insists. "I never reported anything to him, including things I saw that probably *should* have been reported."

Surprisingly, despite the turmoil raging below, Ralph Houk never came down from his office to intervene. "I've always felt that it's the general manager's job not to interfere with the manager," is his explanation. "I know I wouldn't want one interfering with me.

"Johnny was a strong man and a great individual," Houk continues. "I wouldn't have felt right telling him what he should and shouldn't do."

Not all the players made Keane a scapegoat for the New York collapse. "It wasn't John's fault," says Clete Boyer. "It was age. But he was the guy that wound up getting crucified because the Yankees were falling apart."

The day he signed his new contract, Johnny Keane's lineup included nineteen-year-old Bobby Murcer at short, Ray Barker at first, and outfielders Roger Repoz, Arturo Lopez, and Archie Moore. "It felt like a spring-training game," recalls Moore, today a professor of physical education at Indiana University of Pennsylvania, "but in a major-league park." A near-empty one at that: Fewer than 7,000 spectators—probably the same folks who stand around at car accidents—turned out. Between the minuscule crowds and a citywide newspaper strike, the Yankees stumbled through the season's final weeks in relative privacy, finishing in sixth place, twenty-five games back.

Yankee Stadium sat eerily deserted that October, as the Fall Classic alternated between Minneapolis and Los Angeles. "It was a strange feeling," remembers Hector Lopez. "Being in the Series five years in a row, then having to listen to it." Most Yankees couldn't bring themselves to switch on the radio or TV. "I went to Puerto Rico," says Phil Linz. "I didn't want to watch it."

1966

STARTERS
Mel Stottlemyre
Fritz Peterson
Al Downing
Fred Talbot
Whitey Ford
Jim Bouton

Joe Pepitone (1B)
Bobby Richardson (2B)
Horace Clarke/Clete
Boyer (SS)
Clete Boyer/Tom Tresh
(3B)
Tom Tresh/Roy White
(LF)
Mickey Mantle (CF)
Roger Maris (RF)
Elston Howard (C)

RELIEVERS
Hal Reniff
Pedro Ramos
Steve Hamilton
Dooley Womack

I

NEW YORK CONDUCTED no major trades in the off-season, apparently convinced that the debacle of 1965 had been an aberration. Or, given Ralph Houk's contention "We think we can win the pennant," perhaps a figment of others' imaginations.

The Yankees' only activity was to deal Doc Edwards to the Indians for outfielder Lou Clinton; Pete Mikkelsen to the Pirates for thirty-five-year-old right-hander Bob Friend; and Phil Linz to the Phillies for another shortstop, Ruben Amaro.

Linz knew he was bound elsewhere. "I found out through Houk that Johnny Keane insisted on trading me," he says. Yet word of the swap stung nonetheless. "I cried for a full day." True, the Bronx Bombers no longer exhibited supremacy on the field, but like penniless tycoons awaiting the repossessor, they still enjoyed the trappings of success. Yankee Stadium boasted baseball's most luxurious locker room, with sauna, spacious lounge, and plush carpeting the hue of a dollar bill. Reporting to Philadelphia's charmless Connie Mack Stadium "was like going to Iwo Jima," Linz moans. "The clubhouse there was all cement. It was awful."

The Yankees coveted Amaro, a former Gold Glove winner, as insurance for Tony Kubek, whose playing future was in doubt. Physicians at the Mayo Clinic linked his chronic neck and shoulder pain to a damaged nerve at the top of the spine. When Kubek was informed that a single jolt could leave him permanently paralyzed, he retired, at age twenty-nine.

Recurrent injuries had not only dulled the luster of a once shining career but sapped some of his passion for the game. In 1965, Kubek batted just .218, far below the .297 BA of his 1957 rookie-of-the-year season. Looking back, he says, "I probably should have quit after '64." Befitting one of baseball's more articulate and perceptive athletes, Number 10 stepped right into a job on NBC's *Game of the Week*, and since 1990 has lent his candor to Yankees cablecasts.

Despite Kubek's sagging statistics, a number of Yankees consider his premature departure central to the club's downfall. "That really hurt us," says Steve Hamilton, "because Tony was the team leader— not Mantle, not Maris, not Richardson."

Bobby Richardson had nearly left baseball himself in 1964, worn out from the travel and wanting to be with his family. At that time, Ralph Houk, realizing that Kubek might also not be long for the game, extracted from the pair a gentleman's agreement that they would not quit together. The arrangement called for Richardson to play through 1965, and Kubek, at least through 1966. New York's second baseman, at the age of thirty, started home on the final day of the 1965 season looking forward to civilian life.

Once Houk learned of Kubek's irreversible medical problems, he invoked the promise of a year ago. "I called Bobby and Betsy," he says, "and asked if they could just give me one more year, to let me see if I couldn't get someone else."

Former owner Del Webb, who'd sold CBS his 10-percent share in the club in March 1965, had a solution. "If you want Bobby back," he told Houk, "just give him a blank contract." Richardson laughs while retelling the story. "He didn't understand that money was not involved in my decision. I told Ralph I would play, but at the same salary I made the year before"—$40,000.

II

IF JOHNNY KEANE thought he was due a reprieve in 1966 from the bad breaks and bad blood of the year before, he swiftly learned otherwise, walking into a virtual replay. Mickey Mantle showed up in Fort Lauderdale bearing a fresh serpent-shaped surgical scar on his right shoulder, still unable to throw; Roger Maris showed up complaining of numbness in his right hand, still unable to swing properly; and Joe Pepitone showed up when he felt like it.

In March, the twenty-five-year-old first baseman missed the team bus to Orlando for an exhibition game against Minnesota. He had his new wife, an actress, phone the clubhouse with a story about a sore leg that prevented him from making the trip. Keane, too exasperated to pursue the matter further, reprimanded Pepitone the next day in a private powwow but stopped short of fining him.

A 17–11 grapefruit-league record that spring didn't fool anybody. "I knew '66 was going to be a disaster," says Al Downing, "worse than '65. We didn't have the dominant players anymore who could go out and do the job on a daily basis."

Before they'd even gotten their bearings, the Yankees were 0–3 and profoundly demoralized. On April 12, the Bronx's largest Opening Day crowd in fourteen years watched Detroit's Mickey Lolich outgun his boyhood hero, Whitey Ford, 2–1. In the first inning, opposing manager Charlie Dressen incurred Ford's eternal wrath by complaining to the umpires about the hot-water bottle stashed in the pitcher's back pocket. Deprived of his hand warmer in the chilly spring weather, Ford couldn't feel the ball and had to forgo breaking pitches in favor of an all-fastball diet.

Nevertheless, the cagey veteran kept the Tigers at bay until Norm Cash's ninth-inning rope to center sent home the deciding run. Next the Yankees knuckled under in both ends of a doubleheader, 3–2 and 5–2. In the nightcap, Detroit batters welcomed aging Bob Friend to the American League by tattooing his pitches around and out of the ballpark. Just two months later, Ralph Houk was quietly moving the 1–4 veteran to the Mets in return for cash. Jokes abounded that CBS must have entrusted Yankees deal-making to Jackie Gleason and Art Carney of its far more successful property, *The Jackie Gleason Show*.

Rookie southpaw Fred "Fritz" Peterson temporarily stemmed the tide, nosing out Baltimore 3–2 in his big-league debut at age twenty-four. "I thought they'd carry me off the field," remembers Peterson.

But so deep was the gloom already enveloping the Yankees that "Everybody just walked into the clubhouse and went on as if nothing had happened."

Game five, against the Orioles, was enough to bring Johnny Keane to his knees, as New York lost its second starting shortstop of 1966. Graceful Ruben Amaro was floating back into left to haul in a dying swan off the bat of Curt Blefary when, in Amaro's words, "Tom Tresh tried a diving catch and took my right knee with him," tearing the ligaments.

As teammates carted him off on a stretcher, the thirty-year-old Mexican bemoaned his *mala suerte*, his bad luck. He'd looked forward all winter to teaming up with Bobby Richardson. In spring training the two developed such a fluent rhythm on the double play that Amaro recalls: "Bobby told me, 'If playing with you at shortstop is this easy, I may stick around one more year. This is going to be fun.' " Visiting Amaro in Lenox Hill Hospital a few weeks later, Richardson joked, "Well, Ruben, you made it easier for me to retire after all."

"I thought getting traded to the Yankees was the break of my career," sighs the son of Santos "Kungaro" Amaro, a Latin and Caribbean star outfielder enshrined in the Cuban Baseball Hall of Fame. (His mother also played, on the first women's softball team in Veracruz, Mexico. "They met on the baseball field," explains Amaro, himself the father of a major-leaguer, outfielder Ruben, Jr., when their teams competed against each other in a publicity stunt.)

Amaro's collision with Tresh kept him on the disabled list virtually all year. In 1967 he surprised many by playing 123 games at shortstop and turning in a .973 fielding percentage, the second best in the league. But, he admits, "I did not play as I had before. Something was missing." According to other Yankees, that "something" was a few crucial steps to either side. Amaro ended his playing days with California in 1969, but has remained in baseball ever since, most recently as a Detroit Tigers Latin America scout.

With Amaro incapacitated, Johnny Keane penciled in Bobby Murcer against Baltimore. The nervous teenager promptly committed three errors, including a throw to the wrong base that greased the Orioles' winning rally in a 5–4 fiasco. As the latest Yankees shortstop, Murcer might understandably have been distracted, wondering what calamity was about to strike him. (Answer: a speedy demotion to Toledo.)

Afterward, the manager tongue-lashed his dispirited team in the visitors' locker room, reserving special abuse for the bungling rookie and the day's losing pitcher, Pedro Ramos. Keane was mortified to pick up the *New York Post* the next day and read details of the private meeting, which had been supplied to Maury Allen, it turns out, by a furious Elston Howard.

"Elston was angry that Johnny Keane couldn't handle the star players, and that he picked on Ramos, who was Hispanic, and Murcer, who was just a baby, for their mistakes," the writer recalls. Howard also didn't like it when in spring training Vern Benson ridiculed Murcer's fielding, telling the youngster, "You've got the worst hands of any player I've ever seen." The normally serene catcher, whom Al Downing calls "the nicest man I've ever met," confronted the coach.

"If I hear you say something like that to him again," he said heatedly, "I will personally kick your ass."

Perhaps because Howard had to bide his time for five seasons before finally becoming a starting catcher at age thirty-one, the Yankees' disintegration left him particularly disillusioned, and, above all, feeling betrayed by his fellow players.

Allen, a close friend until Howard's death in 1980, reflects, "It was very difficult for a proud man like Elston to see teammates who had carried this team to such glory not only losing their skills, which was bad enough, but not seeming to care about it. He refused to accept that some of these big-name stars weren't playing as hard as they could, so he blamed management—Johnny Keane, and, to some degree, Ralph Houk. It really ate him up."

The day the *Post* story broke, Keane convened his players in the Cleveland clubhouse for yet another meeting. Today's topic: spilling secrets to the papers. When the manager asked point-blank for the source to identify himself, Elston Howard leapt up and launched into a tirade against the "traitor." Arms flapping, he declared, "We ought to find the guy who said these things and fine him a thousand dollars!" Everyone in the locker room, with the exception of Keane, realized this was Howard's roundabout confession.

"It got to be a joke with the other players," says Allen, who was briefed on *that* meeting as well. The clubhouse now crawled with more informants than KGB headquarters. "When you work a ball club where there is antagonism toward the manager," he explains, "there are always players ready to tell you what happened. I had as many as eight real good contacts."

Allen, who like most of the New York press sympathized with and genuinely admired Keane, winced at the toll the rising tension was taking on him. Even the players who were at the root of much of Keane's misery couldn't help but feel sorry for their embattled skipper.

"Every day he looked a little shorter and a little older," says Jim Bouton. "The team had always won under somebody else, and now it wasn't winning under him, and John took it personally. I think his puritan ethic made it even worse for him, because he didn't have an outlet. At least we could go out and party."

Not entirely in jest, the pitcher adds, "Maybe John should have stayed out late a few nights like us."

Though generous with their compassion, the players continued to withhold their support. "Everybody was hoping a change would be made," says Hector Lopez. Ralph Houk's declaration to the press, "Keane's job is not in jeopardy," sounded a little more hollow with each loss—they dropped eight in a row through April 25. Another Houk comment that was meant to prop up the manager, "We can't go on like this," assumed a decidedly different meaning as the floundering Yankees ended a disastrous homestand 4–15 on the year.

The team fled west to Anaheim, new home of the Angels, accompanied by rumors that Houk was about to resume command. "When everybody heard that," Ray Barker recalls, "they all got smiles on their faces." The players, the press, and no doubt Johnny Keane himself knew what awaited him in California, as far away as possible from the glare of the Big Apple.

Friday night the Angels caned winless Whitey Ford 7–4, imprisoning the Yankees in last place. The next afternoon, May 7, Dan Topping and CBS officially canceled The Johnny Keane Show. Houk summoned him to his hotel room and tearfully discharged the man he'd brought to New York, recalling the task as "the toughest thing I ever had to do."

Keane accepted the news almost gratefully. "It was clear that he certainly was not unhappy it had finally happened," observes Maury Allen. "He came downstairs to the lobby after he'd been told, and he didn't seem shocked, he seemed relaxed."

Next Houk called in Vern Benson. "Ralph still had tears in his eyes," the coach remembers. "He said, 'We had to let John go, and we're going to make a move with you too, Vern.' To be honest, I was relieved to be relieved." Once reassured that he'd be paid in full for the season, Benson said, "Ralph, thank you very much. Now, I just ordered a steak down in the restaurant, and if you don't mind, I'll go ahead and finish it." Benson wasn't out of work long, hooking on as Cincinnati's third-base coach by the All-Star break and continuing in baseball as a coach and scout until his retirement in 1992 at age sixty-eight.

That evening Keane, in a blue suit, addressed his squad for the last time. "I've been replaced," he began, then went on to thank the players for their efforts and wish them luck. "I'm just sorry things didn't turn out better," he added wistfully.

"He cast no blame on anybody; he took the blame himself," Bobby Richardson remembers admiringly. "He was certainly a pro about it."

"Classy," agrees Hector Lopez. Ironically, on that day the players demonstrated more respect for Keane than at any other time during his reign. One by one they shuffled into his office to bid him farewell, heartfelt and otherwise. For some it was the most personal contact they'd ever had with the man. Rookie reliever Dooley Womack, one of the few pleasant surprises of 1966 (7–2, 4 SV, 2.64 ERA), brought up the line's rear together with Mickey Mantle.

"Mick," he asked, "what do I say?"

"Hell, Dooley, I don't know," Mantle replied, perplexed. "This has never happened since I've been here." The Yankees hadn't let a manager go midstream in over fifty years.

To their credit, the players publicly showed remorse. Mantle, still seeking his first home run of the season, graciously told reporters, "I want to say that I feel I let this man down, and I'm sorry about it."

In fairness to Keane, although his rigid manner did not serve him well in New York, few outsiders could have pried their way into Yankees hearts still beating loyally for Ralph Houk. Even the ever-popular Yogi Berra, himself an insider, discovered that. Perhaps it was a portent of Keane's brief, unhappy tenure, that his first day at Yankee Stadium he got lost in the building's maze of tunnels and couldn't find the clubhouse.

Over a quarter-century later, Houk's voice betrays sadness as he tries to analyze what went wrong. "I still think Johnny was a good manager," he says. "The personalities just didn't click with our club. I don't know. It just didn't seem like New York was his place, and . . . things just didn't work out.

"I hated being the man to replace Johnny," Houk adds.

The Yankees couldn't have been more ecstatic. "Everybody on the team said, 'All right, Ralph's back!' " recalls Steve Hamilton. " 'Everything's okay, and now we're going to win.' "

Houk possessed that ability to build morale in the face of all reason, whether on the ballfield or the battlefield. As an army second lieutenant in World War II he'd earned a chestful of medals for bravery. Once, when the men in his patrol found themselves hemmed in by a German tank unit, Houk slipped off through the woods, commandeered an empty armored vehicle, and single-handedly wiped out the enemy. At war's end, he was promoted to the rank of major.

"The Major." That's the image Houk's players fondly held of him— poised on a ridge, or at the dugout steps, spitting a stream of tobacco juice and exhorting his men on to victory. His first day back in uniform, the blunt-featured forty-six-year-old told his moribund team, "We're gonna play baseball, and we're gonna have fun."

III

FOR A WHILE, they did. Pumped up with enthusiasm, the Yankees charged onto the field like the Rough Riders up San Juan Hill and outstripped California 3–1 behind Fritz Peterson. The next day, an 0–3 Al Downing finally got into the win column, 5–2, scattering nine hits. Then, in Minnesota, Mel Stottlemyre held off the Twins 3–2, buoyed by home runs from Pepitone, Maris, and, at long last, Mantle.

To shake the Bombers out of their doldrums, Houk initiated several changes, such as installing rookie outfielder Roy White, off to a .300 start, at the top of the lineup and showing faith in Pepitone by batting him cleanup behind Mantle. He also stayed with the defensive move he'd dictated to Keane in late April, which bumped Clete Boyer to short and brought in Tom Tresh to third. While Boyer, originally a shortstop, applauded the experiment, it did not sit so well with Tresh.

"I win Rookie of the Year as a shortstop and they move me to the outfield. Then I win a Gold Glove Award there in 1965 and they move me to third." He laughs. "I couldn't figure out what position I was supposed to prove I could play."

In its first month under Houk, New York went 18–9, reviving visions of pennant contention. But while The Major may have been able to re-create his first term's winning atmosphere, once his euphoric welcome wore off he discovered he no longer enjoyed steadfast allegiance from all his troops.

"Those first three years Ralph managed, we thought he walked on water," says Clete Boyer. But in 1966? "It was a different feeling altogether." For one thing, players who revered Houk the field general felt he had been out of his depth as general manager, with the result that his reputation as a baseball wunderkind was marred.

"Ralph ran into the Peter Principle," Jim Bouton contends. "He rose to his level of incompetence, which was picking other people and managing at a higher level." A $25,000 raise notwithstanding, Houk's homecoming from the front office was in essence a demotion. "He was no longer the general, he was a colonel again," suggests Al Downing. A chastened colonel too, painfully aware that certain Yankees would not easily forget tangling with him over contracts.

After three years spent building up his players, Houk, as general manager, had to argue why they *weren't* worth the money they sought. "The guys now saw two sides of Ralph," says Boyer. A cunning, at times Machiavellian, persona seemed to emerge the moment Houk tied his first Windsor knot.

"Here we are after the '63 World Series, and he's been my manager, and we get along pretty well," recalls Steve Hamilton. "And Ralph's going to negotiate my contract for next year. Well, the first letter he sends me says, 'We can't give you a raise because we played only four games in the Series last year.' " Hamilton chuckles at the flimsy logic, musing, "I wonder what an agent would do today if somebody used that argument?

"But I didn't dislike Ralph for it!" he adds quickly. "We talked and laughed, and he ended up signing me cheap. And when he returned as manager I still felt good about him."

Not all Yankees were so forgiving. Jim Bouton butted heads with the new general manager in a salary dispute that provoked irreparable ill will. In today's era of astronomical paychecks, a 21–7 record with a 2.53 ERA would fetch an easy seven figures. In 1964 Jim Bouton asked for $20,000, up from $10,500. The Yankees wanted to split the difference.

On the eve of spring training, $1,500 still separated the two sides. Number 56 boldly held out. After two weeks passed with no sign of the pitcher, The Major reared back and plunked Bouton in the wallet: for each continued day of absence, he threatened, the Yankees would deduct $100 from their final offer, an ethically questionable tactic. Can management, in effect, fine an employee for not accepting the terms of a contract? The twenty-five-year-old Bouton, representing himself, as was the norm in the days before sports agents, caved.

"We all learned," says Bouton, "that once he became GM, Ralph the 'players' manager' was just another snake. So when he came back, that 'Pardner' shit of his didn't go down too well." Certainly not with Roger Maris, who never forgave Houk for doubting the severity of his hand injury the year before—and then voicing his skepticism to the newspapers.

"Ralph spread the word among the press that Roger didn't want to play," says the *New York Post*'s Maury Allen. "Many of the writers just went along with the club party line that the guy was a malingerer, which really poisoned the air."

Houk can't be totally faulted for doubting Maris. The bone fragments lodged in his throwing hand had eluded not only the team's own Dr. Sidney Gaynor, but two other orthopedic surgeons as well. Finally, in September, the frustrated right fielder consulted, on his own, a prominent New York specialist, who by X-raying the hand from several different angles discovered the cause of Maris's distress.

That Maris had to arrange and bankroll his own surgery "terribly embarrassed the Yankees and Ralph Houk, to such a degree that they tried to disassociate themselves from him," Allen continues. "And that was really the end of Roger's relationship with the ball club."

Maris's career in the Bronx had been prickly almost from the start. Upon learning of his trade to New York in December 1959, the blunt North Dakotan complained that he didn't want to play there. Over the next seven years little would occur to change his mind.

Maris's only truly happy season as a Yankee was his first, 1960, when he won Most Valuable Player honors and impressed New Yorkers with his impeccable defense and aggressive base running. Sleek in pinstripes, the club's newest Number 9 resembled a Bronx Bomber out of central casting: six feet, 195 pounds, with sinewy forearms that rocketed balls over the right-field fence. A splendid future in the nation's largest city seemed assured.

Then came 1961, equal parts dream season and nightmare. As Maris, age twenty-six, and Mickey Mantle, twenty-nine, pursued Babe Ruth's magic 60 home runs neck and neck, the media and the public began to turn on the younger, less-established, of the two. Baseball fans are by nature traditionalists who take great comfort in the orderly, neatly structured quality of the game, the history of which is expressed in tidy columns of gray statistics. Most reacted with outrage that a relative upstart then carrying a .258 career average was challenging the legendary Babe, a .342 hitter. Better that Mantle should break the thirty-four-year-old record, was the general consensus.

"Roger and Mickey got into that race," recalls Clete Boyer, "and the media turned Mickey into the good guy and Roger into the bad guy, because that sold papers." Ironically, Maris's presence took the heat off his teammate, a longtime target for fan hostility. "He made a star out of Mickey," says outfielder Lou Clinton, the Yankees' top pinch hitter in 1966 and the Boston right fielder the day Maris clubbed number 61.

Mantle, struck down by injuries late in the year, eventually stalled at 54, leaving Maris to chase Ruth's record alone and to absorb the onslaught of media attention. During September, every day he would find dozens of reporters clustered around his locker, most of them barnacles from out of town, freshly assigned to the Yankees as Maris inched closer and closer. These unfamiliar faces would then assault him with questions that could range from the merely obnoxious to the downright insulting.

"Why didn't you hit one tonight?"

An older, more sophisticated personality might have appreciated the absurdity of the query and responded with a good-natured wisecrack. "But Roger wasn't a smooth person," says Steve Hamilton sympathetically. "He was a very honest person." One who replied with undisguised impatience, "What do you mean, 'Why didn't I hit one out tonight?' I swung the bat, it didn't go out of the park. What else can I say?"

Hal Reniff, then in his first season, and a good friend of Maris, recalls, "A sportswriter once asked him, 'What would you rather do, hit sixty home runs or bat .300?' " As if he had a choice.

Maris fired back, "What would *you* rather do?"

"Well, *I* think it'd be better to hit .300."

"To each his own," Maris grunted and walked away.

"What idiot would say hitting .300 is better than hitting sixty home runs?" asks Reniff. "He calls himself a sportswriter? But then this was yet another writer who would decide that Roger was a pain in the ass."

Maris was typically portrayed as the quintessential Angry Young Man with a personality as bristly as his blond crew cut. Not accurate, say teammates close to him, who describe a friendly, considerate, but deeply private family man.

"Roger just wanted to do his job and be left alone," says Bill Stafford, the winning pitcher on October 1, 1961, the Sunday that Maris hit his historic home run in the 162nd, and final, game of the season. "I don't think that's too much for a person to ask."

Maris's fourth-inning wallop provided Stafford the only run he needed to blank the Red Sox 1–0. Boston's Lou Clinton, watching the ball soar over his head, hoped it would strike the upper deck and bound back down to him. A Sacramento restaurateur was offering $5,000 for home-run ball number 61. "And I was making about nine thousand dollars then," explains Clinton, now a Kansas oilman. The money went instead to a young truck driver from Coney Island, Sal Durante, who was fortunate enough to be sitting in section 33, box 163D.

After having watched his hair fall out in clumps from tension, Maris felt mostly relief over his achievement, which was already tainted. To the delight of old-timers everywhere, ossified baseball commissioner Ford Frick had decreed over the summer that he would append an asterisk to a new home-run record if accomplished in more than 154 games, the number played during Ruth's era. The commissioner, however, never proposed a second asterisk, to denote that Maris actually hit his 60th in four fewer plate appearances than the Bambino.

During his life, which ended from cancer at age fifty-one in 1985, Maris was never able to exorcise the asterisk from his record, nor the subsequent, and perhaps understandable, chip from his shoulder. From then on, whatever he did was inevitably compared to 1961. "There was a lot more pressure on him," says Bill Stafford. "The next year he hit thirty-three home runs—that's not too bad!—and everyone wondered what was 'wrong' with him."

Maris, hypersensitive to slights both real and imagined, was deeply wounded by the Yankees' fighting him at contract time that winter. "He got disillusioned," says Boyer, his road roommate of five years. "Not with baseball, but with the front office." The ever-widening rift split for good in 1965 over management's contesting his broken hand.

He played out his final season in pinstripes like an inmate checking off the days of his sentence, sulking and talking of quitting to run a beer distributorship. "The guy went nuts on me," Ralph Houk confided to *Newsday*'s George Vecsey.

For the third year out of the last four, injuries kept Maris to under 400 at-bats. Trying to score against the Tigers in mid-May, he took a shin guard to the left knee courtesy of catcher Bill Freehan. One week later, Maris robbed Angel Jimmy Piersall of an extra base hit with a spectacular over-the-shoulder grab before crashing full-force into the Stadium's newly padded right-field fence. Typical of his recent luck, he managed to find an exposed, one-inch metal hinge with his knee.

He probably should have rested through the All-Star break, if not longer, as was borne out by his meager 1966 statistics (.233 BA, 13 HR, 43 RBI). But the front office, concerned over declining attendance, again pressured its $70,000 star to play hurt. "It was like they had to have either Maris or Mantle in the lineup," says Hal Reniff. "So if Mickey couldn't make it for some reason, Roger had to play.

"I'll tell you: when this guy went out on the field, he wanted to do his best and help the team. But he knew he couldn't do the job if he was hurt. He'd say, 'Hey, wait a minute; you don't have to have one of us out there. If it was somebody else, you'd let them heal. Just let me get this thing right; then I'd be happy to play every day.' 'Well, we'd rather have you out there.' That went on for quite a while."

The notion that Maris was begging out of the lineup finally filtered down to the fans, who were already unenamored of him. In an August game against Baltimore, when Number 9 seemed to loaf to first base on a routine grounder, the home crowd showered him with boos. Maris, known to give hecklers the finger, responded sarcastically by tipping his cap.

Two innings later he broke open a 2–1 pitcher's duel with a two-run cannon shot over the auxiliary scoreboard in right-center. The crowd erupted in cheers, but Maris toured the bases stone-faced. Why not acknowledge the applause with a nod of the cap? he was asked afterward.

"I'd never do it then," he replied stubbornly. "Not after I had to take all that crap." Maris's hard feelings toward the Big Apple well outlasted his baseball career, which ended happily in St. Louis. He repeatedly turned down invitations to appear at Yankee Stadium for Old Timers' Day, convinced that New Yorkers would turn the air blue with invective. When he finally relented, for the championship flag-raising ceremony in 1978, much to his surprise the fans embraced him warmly, chanting his name.

"I don't think Roger ever adjusted to the fact that he was a star," observes Lou Clinton, adding somewhat sadly, "I felt sorry for him that he couldn't enjoy what he had accomplished." Clinton, like Ralph Terry and a number of Maris's peers, believes that baseball (which sheepishly rescinded the asterisk in 1991) has again mistreated him by failing to elect Maris to the Hall of Fame. "He was a two-time MVP and broke the season home-run record," argues Terry. "I don't know what game these writers on the committee are watching, but if that ain't enough to get you into the museum, why even have one?"

IV

AFTER FOUR INTOXICATING weeks, reality came back into focus, and the Yankees began to level off.

Ralph Houk proved no more fortunate than Johnny Keane in avoiding player casualties. Whitey Ford, again victimized by blocked circulation, spent most of the season on the sidelines, winning but two games. His left arm worsened to the point where he couldn't even shave without pain.

That August, he required a second operation, in which a six-inch vein from his leg was transplanted to his shoulder. The thirty-seven-year-old fully intended to come back in 1967, leading Hal Reniff to quip, "Yeah, you'll have a great arm, but now when you follow through your leg will collapse."

On June 10, having just added Ford to the disabled list, the Yankees radioed Kansas City for pitching help. The A's sent over twenty-four-year-old right-hander Fred Talbot and batterymate Billy Bryan in return for Roger Repoz, Bill Stafford, and prospect Gil Blanco.

Talbot went 7–7, which just about placed him at the top of the staff. Al Downing drifted through his second straight mediocre season (10–11), while Jim Bouton's limp right hose produced a 3–8 record. And in the surest sign of the apocalypse in the Bronx, Mel Stottlemyre inexplicably went from 20-game winner to 20-game loser.

The only starter to finish above .500 was rookie Fritz Peterson (12–11, 3.31 ERA), who on the Fourth of July came within five outs of a perfect game against Chicago. With one out in the eighth, Jerry Adair slapped a grounder toward the mound. "I was so nervous," Peterson remembers, "I threw it into right-field for an error." John Romano then followed with a seeing-eye base hit that just scooted past recently acquired shortstop Ducky Schofield to end the no-hit bid.

Mickey Mantle aided the 5–2 effort with a single during an offensive barrage that temporarily hushed whispers he was through. Disgusted with his .253 batting average and 7 home runs, on June 28 The Mick jolted two Jose Santiago curveballs out of Fenway Park, igniting a streak of 11 home runs in eleven days. The exhibition recalled the Mantle of old who can still inspire catcher Doc Edwards to rhapsodize, "Whenever Mickey came up to bat, it was like somebody plugged home plate into an electric socket."

No pitcher could stop Mantle; it took a leg injury to do that. During a July 8th twi-night doubleheader at Yankee Stadium, Number 7 touched Washington's Dick Bosman for a home run in the opener, then in game two parked a Jim Hannan pitch 450 feet away in right-center. It was his eighteenth circuit clout of the season, putting him just three behind league leader Boog Powell.

His next at-bat he blooped one down the left-field line that got past lumbering Frank Howard. Mantle decided to go for two. As he turned first base he felt the hamstring muscle in his left thigh snap; the injury bought him two weeks on the bench. Ten years earlier Mantle might have smashed a watercooler in frustration, but the thirty-four-year-old was so used to his legs betraying him that he joked with teammates as he hobbled around the clubhouse. Although he was never the same that year, he finished at .288 with 23 home runs and 56 RBIs, excellent numbers for just 333 at-bats.

The injury might have upset Mantle more were the season not already out of reach. By the All-Star break, the Yankees had faded to ninth place, twenty and a half games out of first. "Everyone knew we weren't going to regroup," says Clete Boyer. "It wasn't there no more. It was over, and you couldn't hide it."

During the second half of the season, the Yankees' descent went into freefall, and the team landed in the basement on September 7. Under Keane, players could always delude themselves into believing the club was better than its record indicated. That they were now the caboose of a ten-car train—with The Major at the controls—brought the magnitude of their decay crashing home, making for one dejected clubhouse.

"The Yankees not the happy family I see in '64," Pedro Ramos understates. "It seem like somebody *die* in the family."

On September 22, a Thursday afternoon, only 413 pallbearers came out to support the Bronx Bombers as they headed toward their final resting place. Distributed among Yankee Stadium's 67,000 seats, that's a whole lot of emptiness. "I don't even know if there were *that* many people," says Steve Whitaker, the Yankees' rookie center fielder that dreary, drizzly day.

"We were joking before the game, 'How are they gonna pay us today?' During the game, you didn't want to chatter—'Hey babe, c'mon babe!'—because everything echoed, and you could hear every little thing." So much so that Dooley Womack, who pitched in relief as New York bowed to the White Sox 4–1, was able to carry on a conversation with third baseman Clete Boyer from the right-field bullpen.

Yankees management was not as appreciative of the black humor inherent in such a sorry spectacle. Announcer Red Barber asked for a camera shot of the sparse crowd, but director Jack Murphy refused. Barber then phoned the front office and repeated his request. Again denied. Days later the witty, urbane Old Redhead, a New York institution, was dismissed from his mythical Catbird Seat. More dreadful public relations, which made the club look not only pathetic but paranoid.

The curtain mercifully fell in Chicago on October 2, which marked Bobby Richardson's final appearance. It was not an enjoyable end to a fine career. "Probably the most frustrating time I've ever experienced," he says of 1966. "My thinking was, *Why did you come back? You should have retired.*"

Richardson played in his first Old Timers' Day game the following summer, on his thirty-second birthday. He spurned Ralph Houk's generous offers to coach, manage in the minors, or become a Yankees broadcaster, opting instead for a publicist's job with an insurance company. Then in 1970 Richardson returned to the sport as baseball coach at the University of South Carolina, a post he resigned in 1976 to run for Congress on the Republican ticket at President Gerald Ford's request. "Out of 128,000 votes, I lost by three thousand," he says. "Jimmy Carter campaigned against me twice." Richardson later coached college baseball again through 1990.

"Busier than ever" in retirement, he now operates the Baseball Chapel, which arranges locker-room devotionals for every team in the major and minor leagues. The Bible-quoting second baseman, whose two sons became pastors, used to hold Sunday-morning services for the Yankees. That he sometimes had to hector them into attending and preferred Ping-Pong to booze and skirt chasing never affected his immense popularity with teammates.

"It was sort of a joke," he says. "They might use some profanity, look over at me, and go, 'Oh, Rich—sorry!' "

Even in his final game, Number 1 displayed the intelligence that made him so valuable for twelve seasons. With the Yankees holding a 2–0 lead and speedy Don Buford on second, Ralph Houk signaled for Dooley Womack to relieve starter Al Downing. Richardson met the rookie in center field as he rambled in from the bullpen.

"Dooley, do you know the situation?"

"Yeah. It's two outs in the eighth, Buford's on second base, Skowron's hitting, and he's the tying run."

"No, no. Didn't you read the paper this morning? Buford is trying to win the stolen-base title." The White Sox third baseman entered the game tied with Kansas City's Campy Campaneris. "If you watch me, we may be able to pick him off."

"We did," says Womack, "on an 0-and-1 pitch, to end the inning."

After winning their 70th game against 89 losses, the Yankees dressed a little more slowly and somberly than usual, aware that many faces would be gone next season "You could see, it wasn't as smiling," says Hector Lopez. " 'We'll get 'em next year.' It was tough. The whole year was tough." He chuckles softly. "I don't even want to remember it."

But 1966 was to be well remembered as the year the Bronx Bombers finished in back of the American League for the first time since 1912. Catcher Billy Bryan, who as a Kansas City Athletic the past two seasons knew what it felt like, may have been the most dumbfounded person on the club. "When I left the A's for the Yankees, I thought the only place I could go was up," he says, still marveling at his bad luck. For an added dollop of humiliation, even the Mets escaped last that year, climbing to the heady environs of ninth place.

V

How DID IT all come apart so quickly? It didn't. The roots of New York's disintegration first took hold back when the club still breezed to the pennant year after year. To appreciate the depths to which the Yankees sank, it helps to first understand the true grandeur of the former dynasty, the likes of which baseball has ensured will never flourish again.

The Yankees initially climbed to the top on the backs of the Red Sox. Not long after winning the World Series in 1918, Boston's financially strapped owner, Harry Frazee, started unloading players to the Bronx in exchange for warm bodies and, more importantly, infusions of cash from the deep pockets of Yankees co-owner Colonel Jake Ruppert, a brewery baron. Over the next few years, New York happily appropriated more than a dozen Bosox at bargain-bin prices, just so that Frazee wouldn't have to go belly up.

On January 3, 1920, Frazee waved goodbye to Babe Ruth in exchange for $125,000 and a $300,000 loan, instantly turning himself into the most hated figure in Boston since King George III. The twenty-four-year-old Bambino, coming off his second consecutive home-run title, was about to blossom into the most awesome slugger the game had ever known.

Three years later the Red Sox watched glumly from the bottom of the American League as New York reveled in its third pennant and first World Championship. Four fifths of the 1923 Yankees' starting rotation had arrived by way of Beantown, for beans.

With Croesus for an owner, the Yankees were virtually guaranteed success during an era when minor-league ball clubs operated independently and auctioned off their prospects to the highest bidder. The free-spending Colonel Ruppert entrusted his checkbook to business manager Ed Barrow, another Boston refugee, and his New York scouts merrily combed the country, picking up such talents as Lou Gehrig, Tony Lazzeri, Bill Dickey, and Lefty Gomez.

By the time the Yankees purchased twenty-year-old Joe DiMaggio in 1934, for $25,000 and five players to be named later, they had embarked on a more economical course. Emulating the revolutionary system devised by St. Louis's visionary Branch Rickey, Barrow and farm director George Weiss started procuring and operating minor-league franchises, weaving a network of more than a dozen across the United States. Other teams followed suit, but none was able to cultivate future stars in such abundance as the Yankees, who won ten more pennants in the 1930s and 1940s.

But the years following World War II saw sweeping changes in the American way of life that would eventually bring down the sun on the sprawling Yankees empire. The single most influential factor: television. Once fans were able to watch big-league stars in action from the comfort of their living rooms, they no longer flocked to the local minor-league ballpark, thus putting many farm teams out of business. The Yankees' chain shrank almost in half, to seven franchises, by 1964.

Even had the minors continued to thrive, they couldn't have filled their rosters as before. Boys who would have entered baseball just to earn the approximately $75 a month paid to bushers during the

Depression could now earn better wages in other fields. Or they had joined the swelling ranks of college graduates.

Another factor in the shrinking of the talent pool was the competition from professional football and basketball in the 1960s. Tom Tresh, who signed with New York in the mid-1950s, recalls, "When guys my age were growing up and trying to decide what we wanted to do as athletes, baseball was really the only sport paying any money. I was a good football player and basketball player too, but there was never any thought at that time to go into anything other than baseball."

For years baseball's downtrodden clubs had been plotting to share player talent more equitably, and at the annual winter meetings in December 1964, they succeeded. Over strenuous objections from the affluent Yankees, Dodgers, and Mets, the czars of baseball brought socialism to the national pastime.

Under its new two-phase free-agent draft, on June 8, 1965, teams would claim the rights to prospects in inverse order to their place in the standings. In other words, no more open market. "Communistic!" huffed New York's farm director, Johnny Johnson. In each round, the first-place Bombers picked next to last—nineteenth, thirty-eighth, and so on—by which time the most promising recruits had gone to their competitors.

These developments aside, the Yankees had to accept much of the blame for their current predicament. Eight American League titles in the 1950s had made the club complacent.

For instance, New York lagged far behind other teams in signing minorities. In response to charges of racism and NAACP pickets outside Yankee Stadium, George Weiss, general manager since 1947, issued the statement "When a Negro comes along good enough to make the Yankees, we'll be glad to have him." Was it that simple, or did blacks perhaps not fit the indelible Yankees image of the tall, taciturn white warrior epitomized by Gary Cooper as Lou Gehrig in the film *Pride of the Yankees?*

New York did sign a few minority players but then either let them languish in the minors or traded them. Team photos included no black faces until Elston Howard was brought up, belatedly, in 1955, *eight years* after Brooklyn's Jackie Robinson broke baseball's unspoken color barrier.

Al Downing agreed to a Yankees pact shortly after George Weiss retired in November 1960. The sophomore at Muhlenberg College also counted Washington, Pittsburgh, and Philadelphia among his suitors. "Had Weiss still been with the Yankees, there's no way I would have signed with them," he says. "Because I hated the Yankees and the things that Weiss represented as far as a willingness to bring black ballplayers into New York went. He just refused to do so.

"And I think that this ultimately caught up to the Yankees," says Downing, "because they had no black ballplayers in their farm system and everyone else did." One only has to consult the record books to see the immediate impact minority athletes had on the national pastime.

The Yankees suffered for their arrogance in other ways. At a time when teams began opening up their purses to so-called bonus babies, paying as much as $200,000 just for the right to sign a young player, the notoriously frugal Weiss snapped his shut. He'd been used to enticing prospects to New York for less money than they might pocket elsewhere by dangling the promise of a World Series check in front of them. During the late 1950s and early 1960s other clubs outbid the Yankees on such future stars as Carl Yastrzemski, Rico Petrocelli, and Sam McDowell.

Expenditures slowed to a trickle when in 1962 Dan Topping convinced partner Del Webb that the time had come to peddle their valuable asset in the Bronx. A rival team's general manager reflects, "They'd been selling off everything—the Kansas City farm team and the stadium there, the Newark farm team and the stadium there. They'd even sold the land under Yankee Stadium. Finally they got down to selling the club itself."

Topping's health prompted the decision. The well-heeled, well-tanned businessman, though just forty-nine, was suffering from emphysema and a heart condition and wanted out. To lure prospective buyers, he and Webb started scaling back in all areas. "They made the books look real good," says Ralph Terry. "Meanwhile, guys who were having really good years in the minor leagues couldn't get a fifty-dollar-a-month raise."

The scouting department, for decades the organization's golden goose, was allowed to atrophy. Some of the team's best talent hunters retired without adequate replacements. And, most significantly, the Yankees were slow to stake their claim in the California gold rush of young ballplayers, an outgrowth of America's shifting demographics after World War II.

Rookie crop failure was the result. Steve Hamilton observes, "The farther along we got—1966, '67, '68—the less talent we had. It really came home to me in 1971, when I was traded to the San Francisco Giants, and I saw the minor-league talent they had: George Foster, Dave Kingman, Garry Maddox, Gary Matthews. I remember thinking to myself, 'Good gosh, we didn't have *anybody* in the Yankees organization that was even close to these guys.' "

Bleak minor-league reports would have prompted prudent owners to swap a star or two for several promising youngsters. Topping and Webb, looking ahead no further than the next couple of years, were more concerned with the cachet of owning name players, and did nothing.

Imagine the talent a Kubek, a Richardson, a Ford, or a Mantle at his peak would have brought. Instead, all four retired. No return. Contrast this with the foresight shown by St. Louis's brain trust when the World Champion Cardinals slumped to seventh in 1965. That winter the club stunned the Show-Me State by trading three quarters of its veteran all-star infield: Ken Boyer to the Mets, and Dick Groat and Bill White to the Phillies. While neither deal could be called a blockbuster, the Redbirds did receive a few valuable additions that aided their recovery by 1967, the first of two consecutive World Series appearances.

Ultimately, Topping and Webb pitched their FOR SALE sign in a gleaming, empty shell. On June 8, 1962, the pair struck a tentative deal with the moneyed New York investment firm Lehman Brothers, contingent upon a complex tax ruling. But after a two-year dalliance, on July 17, 1964, the buyer backed out.

Topping rang up William S. Paley, whom he'd run into a year before at the exclusive 21 Club. The CBS board chairman had mentioned in passing that he might want to land the Yankees should the pending sale fall through. Within a month of that phone call, the transfer of the Yankees to CBS was complete.

VI

DAN TOPPING RELINQUISHED the team presidency and his remaining stock on September 19, 1966, placing the Yankees fully under CBS domain. The corporate giant installed Mike Burke as new president and chairman—perhaps his penance for having encouraged Bill Paley to purchase the club as vice president in charge of investments.

Burke gave the Yankees hierarchy its second war hero. As a member of the Office of Strategic Services (OSS), he went undercover behind enemy lines in German-occupied Italy to smuggle out an important pro-Allies weapons inventor. Hollywood later turned the daring mission into a motion picture titled *Cloak and Dagger*, with Gary Cooper in the role of Burke.

For a more accurate portrayal Warner Bros. might have picked Cary Grant. Burke, tall, slender, and distinguished-looking, displayed a similar style and refinement. A prep-school grad and English major, he was, most likely, the only baseball-team president who displayed a copy of James Joyce's *Ulysses* in his office bookcase. At his introductory press conference, the modishly attired Burke spoke eloquently about reviving the club and its attendance. His first priority, he said: a new general manager.

A few weeks later, Burke presented Lee MacPhail to the press. The forty-eight-year-old picked to lead New York into an uncertain future also represented a link to its Olympian past. From 1949 to 1958 he'd worked in the Yankees' front office, the last few seasons as assistant general manager.

His father, Larry MacPhail, once co-owned the Yankees. In 1945, the fiery redhead convinced millionaire's son Topping and construction mogul Webb to purchase the club for $2.85 million from the estate of the late Colonel Jake Ruppert, who had died six years before. Mac-Phail's rapport with his partners can best be described as tempestuous. "His rapport with *everyone* was tempestuous," his son says good-naturedly.

The triumvirate fell apart following the Yankees' narrow victory over the Dodgers in the 1947 World Series. To celebrate the win, the club repaired to the Biltmore Hotel. "There was a 'misunderstanding,' " the younger MacPhail says. "My father had a little bit too much to drink and ended up in a battle with George Weiss. They called it The Battle of the Biltmore." Twenty-four hours later, Topping and Webb were putting up $1 million apiece to be rid of him.

Larry MacPhail wasn't in favor of his son's returning to the Yankees, but then, he hadn't wanted him to make baseball a career to begin with. When Lee graduated from Swarthmore College in 1939, he approached his father, then the president of the Brooklyn Dodgers, about a job.

"I had assumed I was going to work for him, but he told me he didn't really want me to go into baseball," says MacPhail. "Finally he said, 'Look, give something else a try for a couple of years. And if you're not happy in it, I'll see if I can find a spot for you.' " The "something else" turned out to be the Florida livestock business of a family friend. "For a city boy," says MacPhail, who grew up in Columbus and Cincinnati, "that was quite a change."

World War II further delayed his entry into the game until 1946, when MacPhail finally got his opportunity in the Yankees' chain. He rose swiftly to the office of general manager of their Kansas City farm club, where he befriended a catcher: Ralph Houk. It was Lee MacPhail, in fact, who started The Major up the managerial ladder, offering him the job at Denver in the American Association. A decade later Houk returned the favor by recommending MacPhail as his own successor.

MacPhail was experienced at rebuilding teams from the ground up, having spent seven seasons in Baltimore as GM and then president. Upon his arrival, in 1959, the former St. Louis Browns hadn't fielded a winning club since moving to Baltimore five years earlier. The next season, a radically redesigned, youthful Orioles team kept pace with the Yankees until late September.

From then on, Baltimore regularly muscled its way into the pennant race but could never quite come out on top. MacPhail left the Orioles after 1965 to take a post as administrative assistant to the new commissioner of baseball, retired Air Force general William "Spike" Eckert. His last act for the Orioles was to pilfer Frank Robinson from Cincinnati. "A lot of us felt that deal was the finale that would put us over the top," he recalls. It was. The Orioles had their way with the AL in 1966, then swept the Dodgers four straight in the World Series, while Robinson captured the Triple Crown and became the first player ever to win an MVP award in both leagues.

On his return to the Yankees, MacPhail was surprised to find the system he'd supervised as farm director in the 1950s utterly in ruins. "We had a big rebuilding job to do, no question about it," he says. His conservative prediction at the time: five years, just to be competitive. "We knew it was going to be a long process."

With a laugh, MacPhail adds, "And it was."

That winter he set down to work. In the kind of trade the Yankees should have been making to sustain the dynasty, he dealt Clete Boyer, still in his prime at twenty-nine, to Atlanta for Bill Robinson, a much-heralded rookie outfielder. Next, Roger Maris was finally sprung from the Bronx. His destination: St. Louis. Indicative of how low Number 9's stock had fallen, the most the Yankees could get in return was an itinerant third baseman named Charley Smith.

Boyer, who'd hoped one day to set the club record for games played at third base, calls the trade "a big disappointment." After winding up his career in Japan, he went into coaching. In 1988, and again in 1992, he returned to the Yankees to flash signs from the third-base coaching box.

Maris, on the other hand, grinned broadly when informed of the swap. Although his hand injury reduced his power to just 14 home runs in 1967 and 1968, he played a key role in bringing pennants to St. Louis both years. Maris, as if he had undergone a personality transplant, neither sulked nor baited the St. Louis press or fans, and the city took him to heart.

Hal Reniff, himself traded to the National League in mid-1967, recalls chatting with his ex-teammate before a Mets-Cards game. "Roger said, 'Man, this is a hell of a lot greater. I finally got my leg taken care of, they treat me super, and nobody's playing up this Babe Ruth crap to me.' He was *much* happier." Following the 1968 World Series against Detroit—Maris's seventh in nine seasons—Cardinals owner Gussie Busch handed him the beer distributorship he'd promised the thirty-four-year-old outfielder in return for a twelfth and final season.

The motive behind MacPhail's initial flurry of moves was to remold the Yankees into a more youthful team. "That was really based on Ralph's thinking more than mine," he says. "We decided to open up holes for young players." And also, he concedes, to clean house of disgruntled veterans. "Ralph felt the morale on the team had really gone downhill, and we needed to do something to change it. To start fresh."

VII

BOBBY AND BETSY Richardson, in Houston that winter for a Billy Graham rally at the Astrodome, visited Johnny Keane at home. Despite new employment as a special scout for the California Angels, "he was down," says Richardson. "He didn't show it, but you could tell he felt that he had failed." Apparently even the Yankees' last-place finish under Houk afforded Keane little solace.

Perhaps had he lived to see the club struggle another ten years he wouldn't have been so hard on himself. But on January 6, 1967, one of the saddest sagas in baseball history came to an end when Keane collapsed and died. He was fifty-five—an old fifty-five.

A massive heart attack was given as the cause of death, but Bobby Richardson is not alone when he says, "I really think Johnny just died of a broken heart."

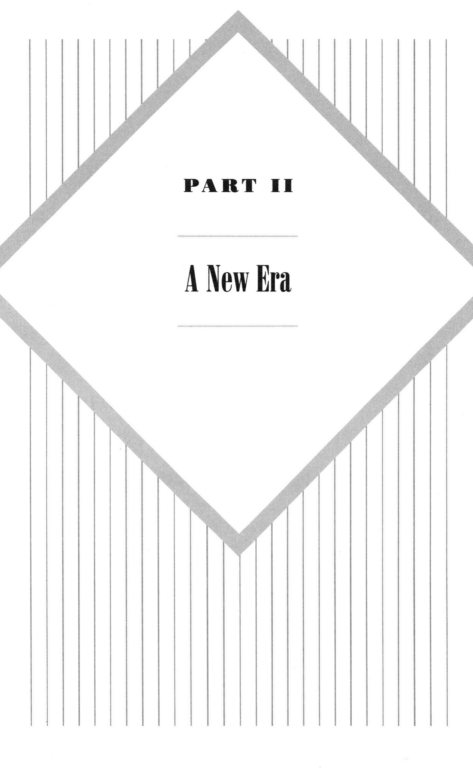

PART II

A New Era

1967

Mel Stottlemyre
Fritz Peterson
Al Downing
Fred Talbot
Bill Monbouquette
Steve Barber

Mickey Mantle (1B)
Horace Clarke (2B)
Ruben Amaro (SS)
Charlie Smith (3B)
Tom Tresh (LF)
Joe Pepitone (CF)
Bill Robinson/Steve
    Whitaker (RF)
Elston Howard/Jake
    Gibbs (C)

Dooley Womack
Steve Hamilton
Thad Tillotson

I

"A NEW ERA."

So proclaimed Mike Burke, and Opening Day 1967 did allow for such cautious optimism as the reconstructed Yankees shellacked the Senators 8–0. President Lyndon Johnson stayed long enough to see rookie Bill Robinson's first major-league home run highlight the Yankees' seven-run third inning. Mel Stottlemyre, still under the cloud of last season's 12–20 record, twirled a two-hitter.

With no other American League teams scheduled, New York could bask in first place, if only for a day. Rookie outfielder Steve Whitaker, 1-for-1 with a double, recalls the club as upbeat despite a 13–17 spring report card.

"We went in with some expectations, because we figured some of the players were going to come back from injuries." The prevailing attitude, he says, was one of "Man, we're gonna turn '66 around and get back on top again."

But the Yankees would fare little better in 1967. Not only was this one of the franchise's worst lineups, except for its frequently crimson faces it was also colorless.

The infield had undergone a complete transformation from the year before: at third base, Charley Smith; at shortstop, John Kennedy; at second base, Horace Clarke; and at first base, Mickey Mantle, anchored there ostensibly to protect his ailing legs. Joe Pepitone, tops among American League first sackers in fielding percentage the past two years, bid the infield goodbye to take over Mantle's pedestal in center.

"That move probably wasn't the greatest for Mickey," says Mike Hegan, a graceful reserve first baseman who frequently spelled Number 7 in the late innings. "The motions at first base are quick and lateral," he explains, "which, when somebody has knee problems, obviously aren't the best kinds to be making." Three innings into the new season, Mantle pulled up lame from a strained leg muscle.

Game two provided a more accurate barometer of the Yankees' caliber of play. John Kennedy booted an easy ground ball to open the second inning, setting the table for a nine-run Washington feast. It was the shortstop's second error in two games; number three if you count the ceremonial toss from LBJ prior to the Presidential Opener.

Instead of having the chief executive pitch to a single target, both teams were lined up in front of him, to minimize the risk of embarrassment. Kennedy, in the middle of the pack, scrambled for the throw and dropped it. He hobbled away with a spiked foot and a bumped nose for his effort.

Ironically, New York had recently obtained him specifically for his glove (with a .213 lifetime average, what else?). "So I went from the first-place Dodgers to the last-place Yankees," says Kennedy, a redheaded six-footer who got to see quite a bit of America in the course of a twelve-year career. "I was upset at first.

"When I joined them, Ralph Houk told me, 'All we're concerned about is you playing defense.' I said, 'I can't guarantee you anything about hitting, but I can definitely catch the ball!' And then as fate would have it, I started off terribly in the field, but I was batting .429."

Fritz Peterson, on the receiving end of Kennedy's miscue, wound up the 10–4 loser. "That started me off on a defeatist attitude," says the left-hander, winless until the day before the All-Star break. Poor control contributed to his sophomore woes, but this had more to do with a twenty-five-year-old's immaturity than with pitch placement.

"I'd had my best spring training ever and was really mentally and physically ready," Peterson reflects. "It hurt me that I didn't get to pitch the opener, because I did have the best year in '66.

"I didn't know how the hierarchy in baseball worked: that the person who was the ultimate good pitcher—which was Mel, certainly—automatically got the first game. Nobody ever bothered to tell me this, and I began the season in the wrong frame of mind."

A twenty-one-year-old Red Sox rookie named Bill Rohr spoiled the Yankees' April 14th home opener, no-hitting them through eight and two thirds innings. Tom Tresh, leading off the ninth, drove Carl Yastrzemski back to the auxiliary scoreboard, but Boston's left fielder made a heroic leap to snare the ball in his outstretched glove.

After Joe Pepitone flied out, Elston Howard stepped up, momentarily startled by the sound of hometown fans rooting against him. Rohr appeared to fan Number 32 on a 1-and-2 pitch. He pumped his left hand in the air, but umpire Cal Drummond ruled it a ball. Then as little John-John Kennedy, sitting in the stands with his mother, waved his Red Sox pennant, Howard laced a full-count curveball into right field. A tidal wave of boos submerged the relieved cheers of William S. Paley and a small contingent of Yankees executives behind the New York dugout. Rohr disposed of Charley Smith on the next pitch, to come away with a 3–0 one-hitter.

A week later, at Fenway Park, the two teams staged a sequel starring the same hero and villain. This time Howard broke up Rohr's bid for a shutout with a two-out, top-of-the-ninth single to left-center.

The catcher's clutch hitting brought him sacks of hate mail. "It was not a very nice thing you did to Bill Rohr," read one unsigned letter. "I despise you for it." According to John Kennedy, many contained racial epithets. "It's an unfortunate thing to have happen to anybody," he says, "but especially to a nice guy like Ellie. Besides, what was he supposed to do? Go up there and strike out?"

The Yankees rebounded from Rohr's one-hitter to take three straight at home, two of them shutouts by Stottlemyre and Whitey Ford. Both artful exhibitions played to near-empty galleries, however. Ford's 3–0 gem against Chicago drew a mere 3,040.

Mike Burke, having entrusted all baseball decisions to Lee MacPhail and Ralph Houk, aimed to reverse the team's shrinking attendance. Although the championship-caliber Bombers used to fill the ballpark regularly, it was often with an equal ratio of out-of-towners to hometown supporters. Phil Linz recalls, "Sometimes you'd hear as many cheers for the opposing team as for us." But when the Yankees ceased to be one of the sports world's seven wonders, tourists began x-ing The House That Ruth Built off their list of Fun City must-sees.

Nineteen sixty-six's paid attendance, 1,124,648, was the team's lowest in over twenty years. Though Burke once managed the Ringling Bros. Circus, it would take some doing to convince New Yorkers that Yankee Stadium still hosted the Greatest Show in the Bronx, much less on Earth. The home opener's meager turnout of 14,375 made that gloomily apparent.

After fielding a competitive team, the first order of business was to overhaul the charmless Yankees image. To that end, Burke created the position of special-projects director for Howard Berk, a CBS draftee and onetime Yankees office boy.

"We faced an enormous task," Berk recalls, "because whether justified or unjustified, the Yankees had a terrible image at that time: cold, uncaring, not involved in city life, more interested in General Motors executives coming to the games than the fans."

The rush to rehumanize the club in time for the upcoming season began with sprucing up the dreary ballpark, which Burke described as "not a Mary Tyler Moore, but a grand old girl." Aunt Bee from *The Andy Griffith Show* was more like it. Over the winter the once magnificent stadium received a $1.3 million face-lift. The drab-green grandstand seats were coated a rich royal blue. Modern fiberglass bleachers replaced the splintering wooden pews. And additional lighting was installed inside and out to soothe fears about encroaching crime in the surrounding slums.

"A lot of the changes were cosmetic," Berk admits, "because we were dealing with an old ballpark and a lousy team."

But 3.7 million square feet of brightly painted walls and seats alone wasn't enough to enliven stagnant Yankee Stadium, which in the absence of a winning club had none of Shea Stadium's Mardi Gras ambience. Outfielder Ron Swoboda played for both New York teams during losing eras. Now a TV sportscaster in New Orleans, he compares the atmosphere in each venue in the light of his new home: "Yankee Stadium was like a funeral; Shea Stadium was like a *jazz* funeral."

How could two failed ball clubs elicit such different responses in the same city? In plotting their future course, the Yankees analyzed the remarkable success of the Mets, whose attendance jumped each year of their existence—to just under 2 million after five seasons.

The Amazin's did possess an unfair advantage, in that New York traditionally pledged allegiance to the National League, no matter how many flags the Yankees brought home. Even during the four years that they had the city all to themselves, the Bombers' bite of the Big Apple rose only marginally. Strangely, in 1958, the season following the Giants' and Dodgers' defections, 60,000 *fewer* fans journeyed to the Bronx to see Whitey Ford, Mickey Mantle, and Co. roll to a fourth straight title.

The Mets lured NL devotees as planned. Besides taking up residence in the Giants' old home, the expansion club filled its roster with recognizable senior-circuit veterans such as Richie Ashburn and Frank Thomas, and ex-Brooklynites Charley Neal and the beloved Gil Hodges. "Even the design and colors of the Mets' uniforms were an amalgam of the Giants' and Dodgers'," points out Swoboda, who wore the white, blue, and orange from 1965 to 1971.

Certainly, the Mets' birth couldn't have been more fortuitously timed, coming at the dawn of the New Frontier. The nation, its spirit reawakened by a young, vigorous president, eagerly anticipated a luminous future that pledged a man on the moon by the end of the 1960s. A culture that had long clung to the comfort of tradition grew obsessed with *newness*. Contemporary styles. Modern appliances. Space-age technology.

Enter the Mets, an entity with no past and no expectations. So what if they played like one big hapless family, finding countless entertaining ways to blow ball games? They were fresh and exciting. "And they had nowhere to go but up," notes Howard Berk. New York's junior club soon moved to a smart new ballpark resembling a pop-art mosaic. That Shea Stadium bordered the grounds of the 1964 World's Fair only reinforced the Mets' image as the team of tomorrow.

The New Frontier's promise outlived John F. Kennedy's assassination, at least for a time. By 1964, with the Cold War beginning to thaw, the specter of mushroom clouds no longer blackened the horizon. America appeared more secure than at any time since the end of World War I. Greater prosperity created more leisure, which opened up room for reflection, which in turn fostered a climate of changing values, as Americans began to question the mores of society.

In a tumultuous year that witnessed the escalation of both the Civil Rights movement and the smoldering conflict in Vietnam—and, with the arrival of the Beatles on these shores, a burgeoning and influential counterculture—the Bronx Bombers' win-win-win ethos now seemed outdated. To many, the coldly imposing Yankees, baseball's aristocrats, symbolized the establishment, which young people in particular were viewing with an increasingly jaundiced eye. This damaging perception was to follow the organization well into its decline, dragging down attendance even further.

The misfit Mets, on the other hand, became the center of a veritable populist movement. Though the club appealed to nonconformists of all stripes, it counted an especially large constituency of teenagers and college students who treated the players more like pop stars in spikes than all-American heroes.

"In the summer we saw tons of kids," recalls Swoboda, a Shea

Stadium favorite. "I used to say that the Mets were the biggest baby-sitting service in the city. Parents weren't afraid to send their kids on the subway to Shea. It was safe.

"And we related to those kids up in the stands. Tug McGraw, Ed Kranepool, and I would come in early for batting practice, and we'd just rap with them. It was wonderful."

That the 1967 Mets' starting lineup had a younger average age than the Beatles explains some of the fan identification. The Yankees, averaging closer to thirty—the chronological Mason-Dixon Line of the emerging generation gap—seemed like graybeards by comparison. But in addition, this age group, soon to unify through its opposition to the Vietnam War, as well as through rock-and-roll and the drug culture, was drawn to the unique sense of community existing among Mets fans.

In a society that traditionally exalted winners, rooting for Flushing's lovable losers took on an almost subversive appeal. Imagine: a team that actually played by the credo "It's not whether you win or lose . . ." At Yankee Stadium such a notion would have been almost communistic.

Mike Burke, taking his cue from the Mets, tried to promote a similar youthful, family feeling. His predecessors had watched games from a private box like Kremlinites dispassionately reviewing a military procession. The Yankees' accessible new president and ambassador of good will could be found roaming the stands, patiently answering questions and, in later years, flashing the peace sign to hippies. Burke, a progressive thinker, let his silver-gray mane grow until he resembled a corporate Timothy Leary.

Befitting his showman's background, Burke sought to convert Yankee Stadium from a museum into a house of fun. "He used to say going to the ballpark should be a nice 'outing' for the family," recalls Howard Berk. "A day of entertainment." The Yankees began shamelessly imitating some of Shea Stadium's sideshow antics.

Dan Topping and Del Webb would have turned up their noses at the measures instituted in 1967. Comely hostesses in striped miniskirts and fedoras now greeted visitors. Vendors, too, were outfitted in brightly colored smocks. The most startling novelty of all, however: courteous ushers.

Under the old regime the stadium's notoriously cranky staff patrolled the aisles checking ticket stubs. It could be the ninth inning, the ballpark two-thirds deserted, and Yankees brownshirts still shooed children out of otherwise empty season boxes, brandishing their dust-cloths like nightsticks. "The public image was that these guys were mean and ruthless, and some of them were," concedes Berk, who was charged with operating the stadium. "We had to overcome that.

"Strangely enough," he adds, "it was the same group that worked at Shea—the same union!—so a lot of it was a state of mind. At the beginning of the season Mike wrote a pamphlet called 'Going First Class,' which stressed that these were guests in our ballpark and were to be treated as such."

Burke also moved to restore the First Amendment within the walls of Yankee Stadium. No longer were banners confiscated, not even those bearing derogatory slogans on the order of WE MUST BE DOING SOMETHING RONG. Only the season before, security guards scuffled for fifteen minutes with a bleachers felon caught unfurling a sheet singing the praises of Mickey Mantle. The Mets, meanwhile, hosted annual Banner Days at which fans competed for prizes by marching around painted bedsheets that mostly poked fun at the team's ineptitude.

To curry favor with a no-longer fawning press, Burke wisely installed a policy of *glasnost* and encouraged players to cooperate with reporters. "The old Yankees may have been winning on the field," says Vic Ziegel, then of the *New York Post*, "but they were bereft of winning personalities." One exception was the impish Whitey Ford. "You had to wait every fifth day until Whitey pitched before you could have any fun after the game.

"It's funny," Ziegel muses, "but when players lose, they're often much better in the locker room. They open their hearts more. They're more willing to answer questions because they're confused, and they need to try to understand what the hell is happening to them. Now, the *bad* Yankees teams had delightful people, like Bouton, Peterson, Hamilton, and Tresh."

Ralph Houk, previously contemptuous toward writers, underwent a particularly dramatic transformation, presumably on orders from the top. "He no longer spat on your shoes and tried to intimidate you by yelling at you and calling you a cocksucker," George Vecsey recalls. "He was actually pleasant. He'd sit in the dugout and talk baseball. I remember Ralph sitting between Vic Ziegel and me at Fenway Park with his arms around us, and me and Vic making eye contact and both thinking, *Whoa, this is kinda weird.*"

For all of Burke's efforts to improve the Yankees' image, ultimately a team's personality is shaped as much by its fans as by its personnel. And that, more than anything, explained the pall that gripped Yankee Stadium until the rebuilding movement could attract a new breed of loyalist.

Even during the dynasty years, when they had something to cheer about, Yankees partisans rooted with an almost British decorum. Of course, with the final score rarely in doubt, what was there to get excited about? The Mets fan experienced baseball with an aesthetic sense foreign to his Yankees counterpart. The former was likely to gaze contentedly at the lush green carpet, sometimes oblivious of the action, while the latter kept meticulous score, blind to the game's beauty.

The *joie de vivre* radiating from Shea Stadium and its great unwashed irritated Yankees elitists no end. Rob Gardner, who pitched for both New York clubs, recalls, "I got a letter from a Yankees fan in 1966," his second season as a Met. "He was a mechanic for American Airlines. The gist of the letter was that he was sick and tired of seeing Mom's bedsheet paraded in front of the stands at Shea Stadium. He wrote that he was much happier to be sipping champagne at Yankee Stadium than guzzling beer with the denizens of Shea.

"I felt it only appropriate to answer that letter," says Gardner. "I wrote back that with the way the Yankees were going, he'd be lucky if he could even *get* beer there in a couple of years. I never did hear from him again."

II

THE ATTENDANCE DRIVE in the Bronx hit a Bruckner Expressway–size pothole when another drawing card fell from the Yankees' deck. On May 30, Whitey Ford announced his retirement, due to arm trouble. Ironically, his circulatory problem wasn't the culprit but a recurring bone spur in his left elbow.

The shame of it was that Ford had been pitching as if reborn, reflected in a 1.58 ERA through his first five starts. Then on May 12 he was trailing Baltimore's Jim Palmer 1–0 in the third when the elbow acted up, forcing him to the trainer's room. The Orioles promptly rocked relievers Jim Bouton and Hal Reniff for thirteen runs. Toward the end of the 14–0 trashing, disgusted fans struck up a chant of "Let's Go Mets!"

Nine days later, the thirty-eight-year-old veteran took the ball in Detroit. This time he lasted only one inning. "You could tell the elbow was hurting him," says catcher Jake Gibbs. "He threw the last pitch and walked off the mound in pain. I think he knew that was it." Ford was halfway back to New York before the Tigers had finished mauling the bullpen to win 9–4.

Number 16's final appearance was briefer still. Prior to an afternoon doubleheader against Minnesota, he jogged onto the field in a dark blue suit. As the cheers of 41,000 New Yorkers washed over him, the normally lighthearted pitcher waved back woodenly, his face pinched in a tight smile. A minute later he seemed to vanish.

"Whitey ran for that dugout," recalls Dooley Womack. "Not only did he have tears in his eyes, most of the players did too. It was a very sad day." Ford, voted into the Hall of Fame in 1974, departed baseball with the highest winning percentage in modern annals, .690 (236–106).

While The Chairman of the Board took his curtain call, Mickey Mantle sat on the dugout steps, watching wistfully. Had he invested his salary as wisely as his buddy, Number 7 might have quit right then himself. Seeing the winds of change scatter his friends like leaves took the fun out of the game, as did playing alongside replacements he would later describe as "extras."

Steve Whitaker, then in his first full year, observes, "I think Mickey was let down by what had happened to the great New York Yankees." He adds frankly, "I felt responsible." Yet Mantle kept his disenchantment to himself. Unlike some waning superstars, who play out their careers as ghostly, detached presences, he was always genial and approachable.

"Mickey and I were the only players who lived in Manhattan, and everywhere he went, he'd take me along," Whitaker says appreciatively. Rumor had it that when Mantle was a rookie, he'd felt snubbed by the great Joe DiMaggio and vowed never to be so removed from his teammates.

Mantle entered his seventeenth season needing four home runs to reach the magic 500 mark. With two days left in April that figure remained unchanged. An average of .200 for 30 at-bats prompted sports editors to ready his professional obituary. The Mick himself began to wonder if the doomsayers weren't correct at last.

On Saturday, April 29, he crashed his first round-tripper of 1967, a tape-measure job that came to rest in the right-field bleachers. The next afternoon, in game one of a Cap Day doubleheader, Mantle broke up a 1–1 tie in the tenth by embedding a ball in the upper deck with two men on. The weekend raised his average to .282 and sent the circling buzzards off to find new quarry.

Mantle paddled 14 more homers before the All-Star break, hurtling him past two milestones: number 500, off Baltimore's Stu Miller on May 14, and numbers 511 and 512 on July 4. The latter two, coming in a losing cause at Minnesota's Metropolitan Stadium, consigned the late Mel Ott to fifth on the all-time home-run list behind Mantle, Jimmie Foxx, Willie Mays, and Babe Ruth.

Sad to say, at this time Mantle was the only Yankee to stand up to opposing hurlers: the team's .225 combined 1967 average was the lowest in the history of a club once renowned for its combustible offense. At one point his 11 home runs equaled the total output of New York's other nonpitchers, which explains why staffs around the league made the Yankees' cleanup hitter use his bat as a walking stick almost every fifth trip to the plate.

The season's two biggest fizzles bracketed him in the batting order. Joe Pepitone and Tom Tresh, both expected to one day wear Mantle's crown, connected for just 13 and 14 home runs, respectively, down from 31 and 27 the year before.

Tresh had reported to Fort Lauderdale exuding confidence, eager to lead the Yankees through their reconstruction. "I was thinking, *Yeah, new era,*" he recalls. "*We need me and Joe to become the backbone of this club.* Supposedly your prime physical condition is between twenty-eight and thirty-three. I was twenty-nine years old. I was ready to roll."

In the second exhibition game of the spring, the Yankees' Gold Glove left fielder cut off a ball in the corner. His momentum carrying him toward the line, he gunned a throw across his body. Just as it left his hand, Tresh heard a popping sound and felt his right knee give way. The next thing he knew he was rolling on the ground in agony.

Two weeks later Tresh sat next to Mantle in the trainer's room, wrapping elastic foam over the steel-hinged brace that adorned his leg. What the team's Dr. Gaynor diagnosed as a strain would prove far more serious: loose cartilage. Tresh says he was told to play on it "and see what happens." Although he claims to harbor no bitterness, in retrospect he feels the club pressured him back to work prematurely and in doing so irreparably damaged his career.

"It was a bad decision, but it wasn't mine to make. No choice was given. It would have been much wiser had they taken me in for surgery right away, before I had a chance to really destroy the knee. Because over the course of the season my knee gave out five times."

Perhaps had the Yankees been further removed from past glories, the front office wouldn't have delayed the operation. "They didn't want to lose, see?" says Tresh. "We were close enough to the last win that they still thought we could get there. But I was taught to play baseball according to what management said. They owned me. So I played the best I could."

Number 15 gamely returned to left field, but not to his old form. In mid-June he was batting .170, nearly 100 points below his lifetime average. Tresh's statistics stood at .219 BA, with 14 HRs and 53 RBIs, the day in September he ran down a triple at Fenway Park and the knee buckled again.

"I walked into the dugout and said, 'That's it. I'm done for the year.' At that point I'd played in more ball games than any Yankee, and I was probably the most severely injured." Tresh spent his thirtieth birthday in New York's Lenox Hill Hospital recuperating from knee surgery. When his physicians seemed less than encouraging about his future as an athlete, he hastened his preparations for a life without baseball. That off-season, Tresh returned to Central Michigan University, where he'd been pursuing a degree in physical education since the late 1950s. "It took me four terms to graduate," he jokes. "Eisenhower, Kennedy, Johnson, and Nixon."

Tresh's knee injury came less than a year after the trauma of losing his father, to whom he was exceptionally close. Mike Tresh, a White Sox and Indians catcher in the 1930s and '40s, longed to see his only child follow in his footsteps. He trained young Tom, a natural right-hander, to switch hit by pitching him Ping-Pong balls. Diagnosed with cancer in early 1966, Mike was in failing health when the Yankees flew into Detroit, the Tresh family's home, for their final appearance there of the season.

Tom wanted badly to hit a home run that series, knowing it was the last time his father would see him play. He clubbed three, one in each game. In his final at-bat he blistered an Earl Wilson pitch off the upper deck in right. As he trotted around the bases, the son searched the stands for his father but couldn't find him. A late-night chill had driven the elder Tresh into the Yankees clubhouse, where he heard the play-by-play on radio.

Afterward the two bid each other goodbye. "I remember my dad standing by the bus, and us shaking hands and saying, 'See you in October,'" Tresh recalls emotionally. "And getting back to my seat, and the tears streaming down my face. It was very hard for me to get my head into baseball when I knew, there's the father that I love, and I may never see him alive again. And I can't go see him because of the job I have."

With two games left to play, Mike Tresh's doctor contacted Tom in Chicago. "He said, 'Your dad could go at any time.' They had sent him home from the hospital and were giving him a lot of drugs for pain. So I went into Ralph Houk's office and told him. He immediately called Bruce Henry, the traveling secretary. 'Bruce, I want you to get Tom here on an airplane as quickly as you can and get him home. Tom, you're finished for the season. You need to be with your father.'"

In a choked voice, Tresh says, "You don't know how important that was to me." Mike Tresh passed away three days later at age fifty-two.

Several Yankees privately wondered if Number 15's subsequent decline wasn't due in part to lingering grief. Tresh denies that. It was the knee, he says. "I was unable to perform the way I had earlier. You run at three-quarters speed, can't cut like before, and hurt every time you swing." It had taken him several seasons to learn to leave his frustrations at the ballpark. Now they resurfaced in a major way.

"I can't say that I handled it all that well when I had my knee problems and my statistics went down. That was very hard on me, to know that at one time I was probably as good as most of the guys in the game." Tresh was considered such a rising star that in 1966 the Red Sox contemplated trading Carl Yastrzemski for him, even up. Over their first five seasons, New York's left fielder both outhomered and outscored his Boston rival, now in the Hall of Fame.

"But after playing three more years with my knee basically destroyed," Tresh continues, "my numbers fell to where they dragged down my overall statistics to those of an average player." In 1968 he batted a subterranean .195. When the scoreboard flashed his average, Tresh would avert his eyes and try tuning out the boos. "It hurts you inside," he says.

In 1969 Tresh's infirmities reached new proportions. "I was a physical wreck," he says, laughing. "I'd gotten hurt. I'd gotten phlebitis. And I had a strep throat." Realizing he no longer fit into the Yankees' plans, he requested a trade to the Tigers, to be near his family. On June 14, Lee MacPhail was able to accommodate him.

Although Tresh slugged 13 home runs for Detroit, in spring training 1970 management insisted the eight-year veteran report to the minors to work on rehabilitating the knee. "I said, 'Give me my release; I'm finished.' " He'd always planned on retiring after ten seasons, a concession to his wife. "She didn't like the game of baseball, basically," says Tresh, who has since divorced and remarried. "So it didn't make any sense to continue.

"To leave baseball at thirty-two was not easy. But I had to get out. I was not happy."

After owning and operating a Kentucky Fried Chicken franchise for a short while, Tresh went to work for his alma mater in the areas of fund-raising and career placement. Since 1984, he's helped Central Michigan University's baseball team to five Mid-American Conference championships as a part-time assistant coach.

Reflecting on the dashed promise of his career, Tresh says, "I'm kind of embarrassed when I look at my statistics. Everybody asks,

'What was your career average?' Well, my career average [.245] is not an indication at all of what I was when I could swing the bat well and play."

The same could be said of Joe Pepitone, whose lifetime marks in no way reflect his talent. Unlike Tresh, however, Number 25's problems were psychological rather than physical. Easily distracted by personal demons, this deeply sensitive man forever resisted the notion that he was expected to report to work on a daily basis.

"If Joe played today," Al Downing observes, "nobody would pay much attention to him." But in a still repressive era, when ballplayers resembled boot-camp recruits, the rebellious, impulsive Pepitone, with his artfully styled hairpieces and long sideburns, stood out like a corked bat.

From the time he was a teenager growing up in Brooklyn, turmoil seemed to follow Pepitone as predictably as boos after an intentional walk. At seventeen, a classmate at Manual Training High School accidentally shot him with a .38 revolver. The bullet pierced Pepitone's upper abdomen and exited his back, shattering the blackboard behind him. Miraculously the teenager survived without any serious complications.

That same year he suffered an even greater misfortune when his construction-foreman father died of a stroke at age thirty-nine. Willie Pepitone, a harsh disciplinarian with a volcanic temper, was alternately loving and abusive. Pepitone himself has attributed his problems as an adult to his problems with his father. Whatever the reason, writer George Vecsey describes him as "a man out of control."

Pepitone's baseball ability came so naturally that at fourteen he began attracting the attention of major-league scouts. Befitting a hot dog, he played center field for Nathan's Famous of Coney Island in addition to his high-school team. The Yankees signed him not long after the shooting incident and eventually converted him to a first baseman. For the 1963 season they committed themselves to Pepitone's enormous potential by trading Bill Skowron, a fixture at first since 1954. His successor's .271 batting average, with 27 home runs and 89 RBIs, silenced critics.

Pepitone inherited his father's ability to brighten a room with a keen, self-deprecating sense of humor. From the day he joined the Yankees he played clubhouse jester as a way of ingratiating himself with teammates, especially the older players. Maury Allen recalls, "Mantle, Maris, Boyer, and Ford all loved to egg Joe on and see him in confrontations with the club and newspaper people."

For all his clowning, Pepitone was prone to insecurity and depression. The complex young man revered Mantle, took many of his cues from him, and consequently wound up entangled in many of the same predicaments.

Tall and darkly handsome, Pepitone's sullen eyes and prominent Roman nose added to his sex appeal as a baseball Jean-Paul Belmondo. He womanized prolifically, regaling teammates with tales about his many conquests. As for money, he couldn't hold on to a dollar bill even if it were stapled to his hand. By 1965, Pepitone was $50,000 in the hole and paying alimony and child support to his first wife. The Yankees had to appoint him a personal financial adviser, who doled out a $100-a-week allowance. No sooner had the debt been whittled down than Pepitone resumed his reckless spending.

"I remember a trip in 1968, going from Boston to Cleveland," says George Vecsey. "Bruce Henry, the traveling secretary, was groaning because Joe had ordered clothing through room service and put it on the Yankees' bill."

Debt and divorce drove Pepitone to a nervous breakdown in 1965. His numbers dropped precipitously (from 28 HR, 100 RBI, to 18 HR, 62 RBI). Miserable under the authoritarian Johnny Keane, he angrily threatened to quit more than once. At times like those, Tom Tresh, Pepitone's best friend on the club, intervened.

"Joe would listen to me," he says, "because I was the one person who didn't constantly berate him, telling him, 'You can't do this, Joe, you can't do that.' " Tresh, mature and sensible, gently counseled Pepitone. "When he was struggling, I fed him my philosophy: 'You've got to play around that, Joe.' "

With Ralph Houk back in charge the next year, Pepitone smoked a club-leading 31 home runs, his only 30-plus season. But in 1967, when the Yankees desperately needed him to catalyze the offense, "He folded like a tent," says Steve Hamilton. The erratic left-handed hitter began the year at cleanup and slipped down to seventh at one point. His final batting average was a sorry .251, with 13 homers and 64 RBIs.

Al Downing tries to offer insight into Pepitone's reputation for shirking responsibility. "I don't think Joe knew how good he really was," he says sympathetically. "He was great when he came up and had all those great players to take the limelight off him. But he was not comfortable being the star of the ballclub.

"All of a sudden the pressure was on him—'If we don't win, it's Joe's fault'—which was unfair, because the Yankees had always been built around eight strong players, not just one." Furthermore, with fewer good hitters grouped around him, Pepitone no longer saw as tempting a selection of pitches. Why risk a fastball on him when you had Ruben Amaro (.223 BA, 1 HR, 17 RBI) up next?

Ralph Houk, who as a rule never criticized players publicly, named Pepitone the season's biggest disappointment. For The Major, usually able to bridle the most obstinate horses, Pepitone presented his most frustrating challenge.

Ray Barker recalls, "Ralph had Joe in his office one day and was just chewing his ass out, loud enough so that even though the door was closed we could still hear him: 'You dumb son of a bitch! If you want to make thirty-five thousand the rest of your damn career, I'll leave it up to you to do just that. You've got the ability to make a hundred thousand and you're pissing it away!' "

While popular in the clubhouse, Pepitone had few close friends. "Everybody tolerated Joe," says Steve Hamilton, adding, "The majority of players felt that he wasted more talent than anybody that's ever played."

The fans too lost their patience with Pepitone, whose 1975 autobiography, *Joe, You Coulda Made Us Proud*, said it all. They jeered or cheered him with each at-bat. Either way, Pepitone thrived on the attention. Andy Kosco, a Yankees outfielder in 1968, recalls, "I once asked him, 'Joe, doesn't it bother you when the fans get on you?' He said, 'I love it!' " Pepitone then gestured grandly at the stadium and added, "It's like a big stage to me."

III

PEPITONE AND TRESH's failures at the plate left the Yankees so starved for runs, they nearly dealt Mel Stottlemyre to Baltimore for promising Mike Epstein. The twenty-four-year-old left-handed slugger, unable to budge Boog Powell off first, forced a trade by flatly refusing a return to the minors. Epstein happened to be Jewish and from the Bronx, which made him all the more appealing to New York. Rumors swirled throughout April and May that a swap was imminent.

Fortunately for New York, Stottlemyre's right shoulder developed tendinitis, scotching the swap. Epstein, who never achieved the greatness predicted for him, went to Washington, while Stottlemyre was to spend the rest of his distinguished career in pinstripes.

In 1967 the quiet right-hander compiled over 250 innings for the third season in a row, a feat repeated until 1974, the year his troublesome shoulder finally broke down. When he first exhibited the stiffness, a concerned Whitey Ford took Stottlemyre aside and advised, "Listen, kid, this club's not going anywhere. There's no sense in you risking a career-threatening injury."

"But Mel wouldn't listen," John Kennedy says admiringly. "He just kept going out there."

Stottlemyre deserved far better than a 15–15 mark, as attested by a 2.96 ERA. Of New York's starters, none received feebler support than Number 30. On May 23, at the height of the trade talk, he permitted Baltimore's big guns a single run on five hits, striking out seven in seven innings, but lost 1–0. Coming out on the short end of low-scoring games became a recurrent theme over the years. But Stottlemyre, the epitome of class, never complained. Nor did he bemoan his misfortune of having boarded the Yankees' express train just before it derailed.

Whitey Ford's departure left the rotation with only three reliable arms: Stottlemyre, Al Downing, and Fred Talbot. Fritz Peterson was in the grips of the sophomore jinx, and Jim Bouton was in Syracuse, the new site of the Yankees' triple-A farm club. In keeping with its "go young" policy, the front office tried filling the void with untested youngsters.

Thaddeus Asa Tillotson, a spitballing refugee from the Dodgers' chain, briefly summoned memories of early Stottlemyre by racking up his first three decisions. The twenty-six-year-old right-hander never won another, finishing the season 3–9, with a 4.03 ERA. Joe Verbanic, a converted reliever acquired from Philadelphia for Pedro Ramos, shut out Washington 6–0 in his second start. As a spot starter and set-up man, he produced a 4–3 record, with 2 saves and a slim 2.80 ERA, but two years later ran into shoulder trouble that curtailed what might have been a dandy career.

It took two longtime nemeses to fill out the staff. Bill Monbouquette, a Red Sox ace who won 20 games in 1963, was for all intents out of baseball just prior to donning pinstripes. Released by Detroit on May 10, he'd contacted eighteen of the twenty major-league clubs—including the Yankees—about his availability. Only the Mets answered his telegram, and their interest flagged after watching him pitch an exhibition game.

"I said to my wife, 'Gee, maybe this is the end of the trail,' " recalls Monbouquette, today the minor-league pitching coach for the Toronto Blue Jays. He contemplated, without enthusiasm, a future running his rug and drapery business in suburban Boston. A few days later, Whitey Ford threw what would be his last pitch.

"I saw that in the paper and called Lee MacPhail right away." Ford's bleak prognosis forced the Yankees to reconsider their earlier estimation of Monbouquette, then thirty. On June 2, they signed him as a free agent. The three-time All-Star thanked them by allowing only 2.33 runs per nine innings, tops on a staff that was fourth best in the league.

The other reclamation project of 1967 was Steve Barber, acquired from Baltimore on July 5. That New York only had to send Ray Barker, two obscure rookies, and $50,000 in return would have been unthinkable at the same time a year ago, when that Yankees-tamer was 10–3. Midway through his seventh season, Barber owned a lifetime .587 winning percentage (91–64), among the game's best.

He'd always had a delicate elbow from throwing a dancing fastball, but in mid-1966 the pain suddenly grew unbearable. "The doctor kept saying, 'It's nothing serious,' " Barber remembers, "and that it just needed time to heal." More time than anyone anticipated. The injury shelved him for the rest of the year, so that Baltimore's top pitcher had to watch his team's World Series sweep from the stands. He calls it both the greatest thrill and the biggest disappointment of his fifteen-year career.

The following spring Barber's arm felt fine. Too fine. "The tenderness I'd always had in my elbow acted as a sort of regulator that prevented me from overthrowing," he explains. Once he'd fully recovered, his control disappeared as mysteriously as socks in a dryer. On April 30 Barber no-hit the Tigers for eight and two thirds innings, but walked ten batters and lost 2–1. "I walked everybody who could hit me," he later quipped.

The left-hander soon fell out of favor with manager Hank Bauer. "Hank always had a whipping boy, if you will," says Barber, "and I'd been it for years. That was fine; I could handle it. But when I started struggling in '67, I finally said to him, 'Look, I've got enough problems of my own; I don't need your shit on top of it.' Which caused a blowup."

On June 4, an unhappy Barber jumped the club for a day and in the process punched his own ticket out of Baltimore. After Washington dispatched him to an early shower, the twenty-eight-year-old opened a can of beer and sat down to feel sorry for himself. "I'm not much of a drinker," says Barber, "but I ended up having what amounted to a beer an inning. And the game went nineteen innings."

The Orioles were about to embark on a lengthy road trip west. On the ride to the airport, Barber decided he needed to see his wife in Wisconsin. "As luck would have it," he recalls, "they pulled the bus up right next to the plane, and as I looked out the window I noticed they were unloading our luggage. So I just got off, grabbed my suitcase, walked inside the airport, and bought myself a plane ticket." He arrived in Anaheim the next day only minutes behind his teammates, but drew a $500 fine and a snarl from ex-Marine Bauer, who exiled him to the bullpen.

Barber came to New York 4–9 and went 6–9 the rest of the way. In between conducting walking tours of the diamond (he averaged nearly seven bases on balls per nine innings), the southpaw displayed flashes of his old form, as on August 18, when he blanked the first-place Twins 1–0.

In camp the next spring, Barber couldn't have located the strike zone with radar. "It was so bad, I was missing the cage in batting practice," he remembers. At his own request Barber went down to Syracuse to try to correct his faulty mechanics, but without success. "My delivery was totally screwed up. Nobody could put their finger on the problem."

Upon his return in June, Barber pitched dependably enough (6–5, 3.23 ERA) that the Yankees stowed him in the bullpen the last month of the season, hoping to raise suspicions about his arm and discourage either of the two new expansion teams from drafting him. The ruse didn't work: in October he went to the Seattle Pilots. Wildness and tendinitis continued to plague him, yet Barber, written off more times than Richard Nixon, hung on through 1974 with five different clubs.

Still, opposing batters never dug in too deeply at the plate. "Our first child, a daughter, was born in '68," Barber recalls. "When they flashed on the scoreboard, 'Congratulations Pat and Steve Barber on the birth of your baby girl,' Dick Young of the *Daily News* got up in the press box and said, 'Thank God Barber had a girl. If it'd been a boy, he would have been born with four balls!'"

IV

NEW YORK WANDERED forlornly into the All-Star break in eighth place, two and a half games from the bottom. Its won-loss ratio of 36–45 (.444) wouldn't have been so disturbing had the team showed signs of improvement. But in its first year, Lee MacPhail's rebuilding effort appeared stalled.

His club riddled with holes at key positions, Ralph Houk was constantly reshuffling the lineup. "Except for a couple of guys, nobody was worthy enough to stay in there day-in and day-out," admits John Kennedy. "We didn't have too much." Kennedy (.196 BA, 1 HR, 17 RBI), who averaged an error every 4.5 games, fumbled away the shortstop assignment to Ruben Amaro in May, but later materialized at the hot corner when Charley Smith flopped (.224, 9, 38) and versatile Dick Howser (.260, 0, 10) broke his wrist. Outfielder Roy White (.224, 2, 18) tried his hand there as well.

The lack of continuity contributed to a league-high 154 errors. At times the club's bumbling play inspired pity. Reserve catcher Billy Bryan, now a recruiter for the Alabama National Guard, divided 1967 between New York and Syracuse. "When I went back home in the off-season," he recalls, "people said to me, 'You know, I'd always been a Yankees-hater, but this year I found myself pulling for them for the first time in my life.' " How the nearly extinct Bronx Bombers of the glory years longed to be despised again.

The Yankees' predicament was unique in that they had to compete not only against their American League rivals and the populist Mets but also against their lofty past. On days when the team looked utterly atrocious, you could almost hear the greats who'd once triumphed there exhorting, "C'mon, kid, bear down." Yankee Stadium was certainly quiet enough.

Newcomers, especially rookies, felt the presence of those ghosts. There probably isn't a Yankee of that era who didn't spend his first day at the hallowed ballpark communing silently in front of the center-field monuments to Babe Ruth, Lou Gehrig, and their manager, Miller Huggins. One awe-inspiring glance around was enough to summon visions of Ruth taking those short, mincing steps around the bases on his spindly legs, or of Joe DiMaggio gliding under fly balls.

"The minute you walked into Yankee Stadium you felt pressure," says outfielder Tom Shopay, who was up for trials in 1967 and 1969. "The tradition. The World Championships. It wasn't a great environment to play in. I saw guys just fall by the wayside, myself included."

It didn't help that the senior Big Apple sportswriters, hacks who'd spent decades filing glowing reports on the best team in baseball, seized every opportunity to savage these pinstriped "imposters." Many considered it a personal affront that New York's ship had sunk and pulled down their own prestige.

"That destroyed the older writers," says Vic Ziegel, "because the Yankees beat had always been *the* beat." He mimics the haughty attitude prevalent among his hoarier colleagues: " '*We're* covering the team that's probably going to be in the World Series.' "

In its desperation to rekindle the old excitement, the press tended to herald certain youngsters prematurely as second comings of former Yankees stars. The next Tony Kubek. The next Clete Boyer. Once the comparison was made, it hung around the neck like an albatross until it proved fitting or ridiculous.

An empathetic Tom Tresh comments, "It was a lot easier coming in when I did than it was for those newer guys. I didn't feel I had the load on my shoulders every day, because someone else was always getting the job done. And," he adds, "we were winning." Tresh had the luxury of blending inconspicuously into a lineup of stars. In 1967, says Lee MacPhail, "We were looking for some of the young players to *be* the stars."

At the top of his list: outfielders Bill Robinson and Steve Whitaker, both twenty-three. The left-handed-hitting Whitaker had impressed the previous August by swatting three home runs his first week in the majors, including a grand slam off Detroit southpaw Mickey Lolich.

"I thought I'd really showed people I could play in the big leagues," says Whitaker, the son of a Tacoma welder who also ran a tavern to support his family of seven. He envisioned himself the starting right fielder on Opening Day. Then the Yankees traded for Robinson, a right-handed batter. Whitaker was crushed to learn they'd be platooned.

"I went to spring training deflated," he remembers. "I'd just gotten there, for Godsakes, and when they did that I took it to mean, 'Well, you came, we saw, and we're really not sure.'" Looking back, he believes his reputation as a hothead and troublemaker soured management on him.

"I was a bad guy," admits Whitaker, now a Florida real-estate developer. "If I didn't hit a home run, I'd go crazy. If I struck out, I'd go *absolutely* crazy. When Mantle came up he was the same way, but he adjusted. I didn't, which is the one thing I regret to this day."

Whitaker raised hell off the field as well as on. While playing for the Yankees' minor-league affiliate in Shelby, North Carolina, the baby-faced outfielder got caught in a compromising position with the mayor's daughter. A local policeman happened upon the two as they were coupling aboard a training aircraft parked in the center of town. "Next thing I know," says Whitaker, "they're sending me back to Idaho Falls," one rung down the ladder.

"In baseball at the time, if you didn't conform to the hierarchy and weren't a straight arrow, you put the monkey on your back right away," he says. Whitaker entered his first full major-league season shouldering a cageful. He's certain he could have improved his '67 figures (.243 BA, 11 HR, 50 RBI) had management assured him 500 at-bats. Then those 0-for-4 days wouldn't have made him press so much at the plate and fret in the field.

Succeeding Roger Maris, whom Whitaker calls "my guru," added an additional burden. "We were hurting, and you could see what they were expecting of you: to take his place. In trying to step right in and fill Roger's shoes, instead of looking to hit the ball into the bleachers,

I was looking to hit it into the upper deck. I would have been much better off not trying to be somebody I wasn't."

Whitaker had mixed emotions the following spring when clubhouse manager Pete Sheehy handed him Maris's old uniform. "It made me feel good one way," he says, "but I also felt like I didn't deserve it. Nine was Roger's number. I would have just as soon stuck with twenty-eight."

The ID change worked no magic. In 1968, Whitaker emulated his idol, all right, but it was the Maris of '66, not '61. He was a forgotten man before Opening Day. "I could see it coming in spring training," he says. "I kept getting the runaround. I thought they were going to cut me." They did, in June, while Whitaker was upstate, putting in time with his Army Reserve unit.

"That was another stake in the heart," says Whitaker. Though recalled in September, "When I cleaned out my locker at the end of the year, I knew I wasn't coming back." Indeed, the Yankees let the incipient Kansas City Royals claim him in the expansion draft.

Bill Robinson's experience in pinstripes was even more nightmarish. To begin with, the even-up exchange that brought him to New York in 1967 had its share of detractors. "The newspaper headlines said that the Yankees traded Clete Boyer for 'Bill Who?' " Robinson recalls matter-of-factly. "That's what they always used to write: 'Bill Who?' "

Virtually every baseball scout in the country could have told them that in 1966 the powerfully built outfielder hit .312 with 20 home runs for Atlanta's triple-A Richmond affiliate and was rated above two phenoms named Reggie: Jackson and Smith. All winter the Yankees' P.R. department vigorously built up Robinson, so that by the time he flew into the Big Apple to start the season, readers of the New York sports pages might have assumed he did so under his own power. "I was billed as the black Mickey Mantle," he says today with a groan.

What the club didn't publicize was the fact that its much-lauded acquisition had recently undergone surgery to repair a damaged elbow. "The Yankees totally mishandled the Bill Robinson situation from the moment they got him," says Al Downing, his roommate. "He came to spring training with his arm in a sling. This guy had a gun, but he couldn't throw the ball fifty feet!

"Rather than them saying, 'Bill, we're going to give you time to heal,' they acted as if the injury didn't exist. Because they were already ballyhooing, 'Bill Robinson! Next spring! Great outfielder for the Yankees!' But the guy wasn't physically ready to play."

Nevertheless Robinson impressed enough in Florida to win the annual James P. Dawson Award for outstanding rookie, voted on by the Yankees' beat writers. Then, he says, he made his biggest mistake as a Yankee: "I hit a home run in my second at-bat of the Presidential Opener.

"And after the game, there were about fifty reporters around me, going, 'This guy can do no wrong! He's going to be the greatest.' " From then on, "I tried to hit home runs. And naturally the harder you try, the worse it becomes."

Going into May, Robinson's home-run total hadn't budged, and his .143 batting average ranked near the bottom of the American League. Give him time to learn the pitchers, the Yankees insisted. As his average slipped farther south—down to .101 on June 3—one by one the theories explaining his failure to hit collapsed. No one was more mystified than Robinson, a sensitive, highly articulate man. "It was really tough for me to accept," he says quietly. "I knew I was a good ballplayer, but I just wasn't putting it together."

Robinson grew up in Elizabeth, Pennsylvania, which proudly calls itself "The Friendliest Little Town in the U.S.A." Fun City, however, never made any such claim. Besides targeting Number 11 with the usual profanities, high-spirited New Yorkers stoned Robinson's car as he exited the players' parking lot.

He remembers, "It got to the point where, when I had another bad day, after the last out I would be back at my locker, showered, dressed, out the door, and heading home before the people from the top deck made it down to the parking lot."

Two and a half months into the season, Robinson at last began to vent steam, batting .353 over a ten-game span. On June 26, his twenty-fourth birthday, he not only banged out three hits against Kansas City but extinguished a base runner with his now healthy arm. Days later in Anaheim, though, Robinson pulled a hamstring while motoring from first to third. The youngster the Yankees had pinned their highest hopes on never regained his momentum, closing out 1967 at .196 with 7 home runs and 29 RBIs.

While Robinson and Whitaker were fizzling on the launch pad, second baseman Horace Clarke's smooth liftoff was all but overlooked. In a season full of puzzles, the twenty-six-year-old Virgin Islander gave New York that rare commodity, a reliable full-time player.

Compact yet speedy, Clarke led the team in five offensive categories and topped the American League in fielding percentage and assists. He also switch-hit, a skill developed by necessity as a boy in Frederiksted, St. Croix.

"We didn't have Little League baseball like we have today," he explains with a melodic Caribbean lilt. "So as kids we formed teams and played wherever we could, usually on Saturdays. If the older players were using the ballpark, we were relegated to a small area right by the ocean.

"Almost all of us were right-handed. And since we were strong enough to hit the ball into the water, we switched sides at the plate, and everybody batted left-handed, so we wouldn't lose the ball."

These days, major-league scouts visit the islands as regularly as tourists. But in the 1950s there were few opportunities for talented players throughout the Caribbean, says Clarke, now a baseball instructor for the Virgin Islands government. "The door opened up after Valmy Thomas, Elmo Plaskett, and Joe Christopher signed, and then me, Alvin McBean, and Elrod Hendricks."

Clarke, originally a shortstop, spent seven years buried in the minors despite three seasons of .300 or better. Along the way, New York shifted him to the keystone in preparation for Bobby Richardson's eventual retirement. While Clarke was batting .301 at triple-A Richmond in 1964, word filtered down that the veteran Yankee was about to hang up his glove, thus clearing Clarke's path to the majors at long last.

Then Richardson changed his mind, not once but twice. With the varsity in 1965 and 1966, Clarke bided his time backstage like an understudy waiting for the principal ballerina to twist an ankle. Finally, in 1967, Number 20's patience was rewarded, and he seized the opportunity, batting .272 with 160 hits and 21 stolen bases.

V

IN THE OPENING contest of a July 23rd doubleheader in Detroit, Clarke's single touched off a game-winning rally that snapped a six-game skid and moved the last-place Yankees past Kansas City. New York was anxious to escape the Motor City, and not just because of its 1-and-3 weekend there.

What began in the early-morning hours as a racial disturbance on the West Side was by Sunday evening billowing into a full-scale riot. Nobody realized the extent of the crisis until they gaped out the bus window en route to the airport.

Detroit was a city under siege, its skyline partially obscured by curling smoke. "You could see fires everywhere," Steve Whitaker recalls. "They were all around us."

For John Kennedy the sight stirred memories of the rampant violence that had racked Los Angeles's Watts district two years before when he played for the World Champion Dodgers. "I was very concerned about getting out of Detroit," he remembers, "and hoping nothing happened to us."

The Yankees landed at La Guardia Airport around the time that National Guardsmen, army paratroopers, and tank units began rumbling into Motown to halt the orgy of arson, looting, and sniping that cut a swath of destruction through the heart of the city. Forty deaths, over 1,000 injuries, and $200 million in property damage made it the worst riot in U.S. history.

No utopia from racial strife awaited the club at home, where only two weeks before, the black ghetto of Newark, New Jersey, had burned. The team bus pulled up in front of Yankee Stadium. As the players walked to their cars, remarking on the hot, muggy night, across the river in East Harlem Hispanic mobs smashed store windows and clashed with police. Similar scenes were being played out nationwide, while in still other cities lids rattled but kept tensions from boiling over. If some of the white players seemed bewildered by the recent eruptions in minority communities, their black teammates understood that this was the inevitable outcome of resentment and hopelessness left smoldering for decades.

A major-league uniform and salary offered no protection from racism. Al Downing, born and raised in Trenton, New Jersey, remembers that during one spring training, "The team was staying at the Yankee Clipper Hotel, and the black players were allowed to eat in only one of its dining rooms.

"For a joke, after dinner Hector Lopez, Elston Howard, and I used to stand in front, because we knew that sooner or later somebody would come up to us and say, 'Hey, mind parking my car?' "

Fort Lauderdale was a bastion of progressive thinking compared to St. Petersburg, New York's former winter home. In 1961 the Soreno Hotel refused entrance to Howard, Lopez, and two other black Yankees, angering their white teammates. The following spring the club pulled up stakes and moved to Florida's East Coast.

Lopez, the first native Panamanian to play in the major leagues, looks back with surprisingly little bitterness on the indignities he and other minorities of his era suffered. "Elston and I knew what to do," he says. "If we weren't supposed to go somewhere, we didn't go. We weren't trying to be pioneers."

Three years after the Yankees released him, the easygoing Lopez did just that. He became the first minority manager in pro ball when he took the reins of Washington's triple-A Buffalo farm club in 1969. Frank Robinson, later to make history as baseball's first black major-league pilot, preceded Lopez by a few months, but in the Puerto Rican Winter League.

Elston Howard, the first black man to wear pinstripes, skirted controversy as deftly as he threw out would-be base stealers. When the Yankees converted him from an outfielder to a catcher in the minors, a black sportswriter sneered that the club was exploiting the young man from St. Louis. Howard insisted that wasn't so and loyally defended the club, a position he took on most matters.

"I wouldn't call Ellie an Uncle Tom, but he was aware of what the front office wanted from him," Steve Hamilton explains. "His wife, Arlene, was very much of an activist. Ellie wasn't that way. He would take management's line on most things and never wanted to upset the applecart."

Beneath his public silence, however, Howard seethed over slights incurred due to the color of his skin. "He'd talk about how much he resented it," says Al Downing. "But Elston was from a different generation." Downing was born in 1941, Howard in 1929. "Being a black man in the Yankees' organization at that time, you didn't say a lot." Perhaps Howard felt he could best further the cause of civil rights by conducting himself with quiet dignity and by commanding respect.

Downing adds, "It was left up to the subsequent generations to speak up."

The racial turbulence of the mid-1960s had a particularly profound effect on Downing, who cites August 28, 1963, as his political awakening. On that day civil-rights leader Dr. Martin Luther King, Jr., led a peaceful march on the nation's capital, climaxed by his stirring "I Have a Dream" sermon.

"It was a tremendous event in this country," Downing reflects. "Over two hundred thousand people at the Washington Monument. And we were playing baseball! I had friends who went on that march. They asked me, 'Why aren't you coming down?'

"I thought, *Well, because I'm a ballplayer.* Then I started thinking, *Wait! Why isn't baseball shutting down for the march?* It was like baseball was outside everything that was going on around it."

Subsequent events further forced Downing to rethink his priorities, which until then had included little else besides the sport. "I had a girlfriend at the time who worked for a military airlift and flew troops to Vietnam," he says. "I asked her, 'Who do you fly back?' She said, 'Bodies.' When my brother went over there, it kind of hit home that this was serious.

"It gave me a totally different approach to baseball," says Downing, one of eight children. "All of a sudden the game didn't seem so important. It was still important in that it was my livelihood. But it wasn't on my mind as much when I left the ballpark, because you couldn't shut out the rest of the world. I became very mad about a lot of things."

Not the least of which included his status as a Yankee. Toward the end of spring training 1967, Ralph Houk stunned Downing by deciding to use him in relief. "I looked around and said, 'Hmm. Lefty Grove's not here. Herb Pennock's not here. He's telling me I can't pitch better than *these* guys?' It was an insult," says Downing.

New York was running out of patience with the inconsistent left-hander, whose lack of concentration on the rubber exasperated his manager and pitching coaches. "I had a lot of problems," Downing freely admits. "I was making a lot of mistakes. I'd get behind a batter and then have to come in with a pitch down the middle. I had a lot of ability, but from '63 through '66 I was still making adjustments and learning how to pitch in the major leagues."

The Al Downing of today is outgoing and opinionated, hosting a sports talk show on Los Angeles radio and announcing Dodger cablecasts. In his early twenties, however, his quiet, inscrutable manner conveyed indifference. Dropping the twenty-five-year-old from the rotation may have been Houk's way of motivating him. If so, says Downing, the tactic worked. "I pitched mad that season."

And more effectively than at any time since his rookie year: 14-10, 2.63 ERA. From the batter's box No. 24 hardly looked imposing as he went into his windup. Then that fastball whistled past, instantly adding height and weight to Downing's five-foot-eleven, 175-pound frame. In 1967 he led the squad in strikeouts for the fourth straight year and painted several masterpieces. Twice the left-hander blanked Baltimore, fanning 13 on May 24 and 12 more on July 7. The next time he walked to the mound it was in Anaheim, representing the Yankees at the 38th All-Star Game, along with Mickey Mantle.

Downing's resentment toward management flared up again on August 3 when New York sent Elston Howard to Boston. On paper it was hard to find fault with the deal, which fetched two minor-leaguers and the $20,000 waiver price in exchange for a thirty-eight-year-old hitting just .196. Downing's objections involved principle.

"Elston came to me and said, 'You know, last week they told me I was going to be a Yankee forever.' Then they turned around and traded him." Howard had worn number 32 for twelve and a half seasons.

"He was unhappy, of course," says his widow, Arlene. "And he felt the team had not lived up to its promise." But ever the organization man, Howard told the *Daily News*, "I can't fault the club. I understand they have to make some moves. This was a good chance for them to get a couple of young players."

Arlene Howard, a strong-willed, outspoken woman who perhaps envisioned greater things for her husband than he ever imagined, didn't temper her anger one bit. "Ellie was a little hurt at first, but I was immediately delighted," she said to reporters before taking a slap at their ex-employer. "The Yankees are not the Yankees we knew and loved. It's a completely different organization. I could never get used to mediocrity, and that's what we have now.

"It'll be different in Boston."

VI

AND IT WAS, as different as first place and ninth place, Boston's and New York's respective finishes. While Howard would thrill to a pennant race again and his tenth World Series, the Yankees were to creak home with a 72–90, .444 record, 20 games back.

August brought forth some homely, *homely* baseball. Playing Baltimore on the fifteenth, the Bronx Bumblers teamed for six errors, to which Dooley Womack added a pair of wild pitches. But through a dozen innings the two clubs played to a 10–10 stalemate. Then Fritz Peterson came on to pitch the thirteenth and balked home the winning run. Two days later, the Orioles hung him with yet another loss, his thirteenth in sixteen decisions.

"My record was so bad and my attitude was so down, I packed my bags and was ready to leave the big leagues," Peterson remembers. "That way, when they told me I was going to the minors, I could beat them to it and say, 'I'm already packed.'

"That's when Ralph Houk pulled me into his office for the first of many talks we would have. He said, 'Look, forget what's happened this year. Let's just start off all over as of the next start.' He did that with me many times, and it really worked." Peterson went 5–1 the rest of the way to complete his sophomore season 8–14, 3.47 ERA.

When it came to fortifying player morale, The Major had no equal. Oddly enough, the true demonstration of Houk's managerial skill wasn't the three pennants won during his first tenure, but the succession of distant finishes that followed his return.

Winning builds confidence. But character, more often than not, is shaped by adversity. Though it went underappreciated at the time, Houk's squads of the rebuilding era displayed their mettle year after year, consistently overachieving. Even the ragged 1967 club.

"We placed ninth in a ten-team league," Steve Barber says drily. "With our talent, we should have been eleventh." The pitcher, like the overwhelming majority of Yankees, calls Houk the best manager he ever played for.

"Ralph got the maximum out of all his ballplayers," explains Barber, now a school-bus driver in Las Vegas. "I can't say any of us felt like we were going to be a contender, but we enjoyed playing, which is what it's all about—having fun. Ralph got us into a frame of mind where we could loosen up and play our best ball." Even before the bell sounded, jockey Houk knew he'd be riding a nag and that too heavy a crop would only make it quit down the stretch, something Johnny Keane discovered too late.

Not that The Major was willing to concede defeat. The Yankees had to chuckle when Houk worked the locker room after each loss, perpetually upbeat, exhorting them to "Hang with 'em!" until it turned into a postgame mantra.

According to Houk, his eternal optimism was no act. "When you manage," he says, "you always feel like you can win. At least I did. I always had that confidence that if we could just make a move here, a move there, we'd be right back in it."

He infused his players with that same confidence. A quick session with the manager, and a puny .175 hitter emerged from Houk's sanctum sanctorum convinced that he could take Cy Young himself downtown. In baseball parlance, that's called "blowing smoke." "Ralph was a great smoke blower, man," Steve Hamilton says. "He made you feel good all the time."

The Yankees manager could pick up a player with some well-timed humor. After the Orioles mistreated Dooley Womack one night, Houk sat him down in the locker room. "He told me, 'Man, you're not throwing like yourself,' " the reliever recalls. " 'You're like a coiled spring. If I cut the rope, you'd spring your ass right out of the stadium.'

"I laughed and said, 'Okay, skipper, what do you want me to do?'

" 'I want you to go home tonight, drink a couple of Bloody Marys, eat a steak, take a good shit, and come out ready to play ball tomorrow night.' The next night I went out, threw one pitch, got the last out, and came into the clubhouse. We were drinking beer together, and Ralph said, 'Isn't this game easy?' "

A favorite Houk tactic for firing up the troops was to unite them against a common foe, such as the press. If a reporter wrote critically of a player, The Major might confront him in his office and loudly threaten bodily harm—leaving the door ajar so that the team overheard. Later he'd apologize privately to the shaken scribe, often an out-of-towner of little consequence.

But usually Houk tangled with the men in blue. During these lean years one of the most entertaining sights at Yankee Stadium was Number 35 railing theatrically at some umpire. This wasn't your routine manager's act of swirling dust around the arbiter's shoes.

"Ralph put on some shows," says Ray Barker. "One time in Washington there was a bad call, and he just flat out raised hell. He covered up home plate with dirt, he threw down his cap, he went up in the umpire's face. We thought, *Oh, boy, don't say anything when Ralph comes in. He's liable to deck your ass.*"

Houk, one cheek bulging with tobacco, jogged back to the dugout and took up his folded-arms stance on the steps.

"Then he turned around," says Barker. " 'How was *that* performance, guys?' Everyone broke out laughing."

VII

NEW YORK FOUND itself a wallflower in that fall's marathon pennant race. Boston, Minnesota, Chicago, Detroit—none would drop. Heading into the season's final week, only one and a half games separated the four teams. The Yankees had hoped to attend in a spoiler's role, but each contender gleefully pushed them aside.

The tightest pennant race in American League history came down to the final day of the season, Sunday, October 1. The Red Sox and Twins, tied for first, faced off, while the Tigers, only a half-game back, could draw even with the winner of that contest by sweeping two from California. Boston dramatically wiped out a 2–0 deficit to defeat Minnesota 5–3, while Detroit won the opener but lost the nightcap.

New York closed out its dismal campaign at home, downing Kansas City 4–3 behind Mel Stottlemyre. Dooley Womack notched the last two outs in what was his sixty-fifth game, tying the club mark for appearances. Womack emerged as Houk's number-one man in the bullpen, going 5–6 with a 2.41 ERA and 18 saves, fourth best in the league.

On August 25, he had preserved both ends of a doubleheader against the Senators. It was his twenty-eighth birthday yet only his second year in the majors. Womack had bounced around the minors like a ball in a roulette wheel for eight seasons, leaving little impression wherever he landed. Despite a decent curve and sinker, managers seemed to notice only his wiry six-foot frame.

Pitching for the Yankees had been Womack's dream since his boyhood in Columbia, South Carolina. "My high-school catcher was on the same page of the yearbook as me," he remembers. "I was in the upper-left-hand corner and he was in the lower-right. He drew a line and wrote, 'Future Yankees!' "

When Womack's struggle reached seven years, the same Cleveland scout who'd signed his older brother took it upon himself to spare the deluded young man further heartbreak. "This guy thought the world of my mom and dad," Womack remembers. "He called them up and said, 'You'd better tell Dooley to come home. He's never going to make it.' "

The skinny right-hander later had the opportunity to confront the skeptic. One winter, Bobby Richardson asked him to attend a coaches' clinic not far from Columbia, where Womack now runs an interior-design firm.

"That scout was there, and I proceeded to cut him apart—in a nice way." He lectured the coaches on discouraging youngsters on the basis of size. "I told them, 'Gentlemen, if I ever hear you tell someone he's too small, so help me, I'll never let you forget it.

" 'Because there's a scout sitting here right now that said I was too small. I proved him wrong. You can't cut a young man open to see how big his heart is. He can be one hundred sixty-five pounds of heart.' And that was my playing weight, one hundred sixty-five pounds."

Dooley Womack (born Horace Guy Womack) was one of the few Yankees who could reflect happily on his 1967 performance. Not among that group was Mickey Mantle, who after a brilliant first half faded. In August and September, Number 7 managed only three home runs, to finish at .245, with 22 home runs and 55 RBIs. Despite frustration over his and the club's showing, Mantle still retained his sense of humor. That fall he called up his golfing buddy and former teammate Lou Clinton, who had been released by the Yankees back in May.

"Lou, I want you to know the team took a vote," Mantle deadpanned. "They've decided to award you a full share."

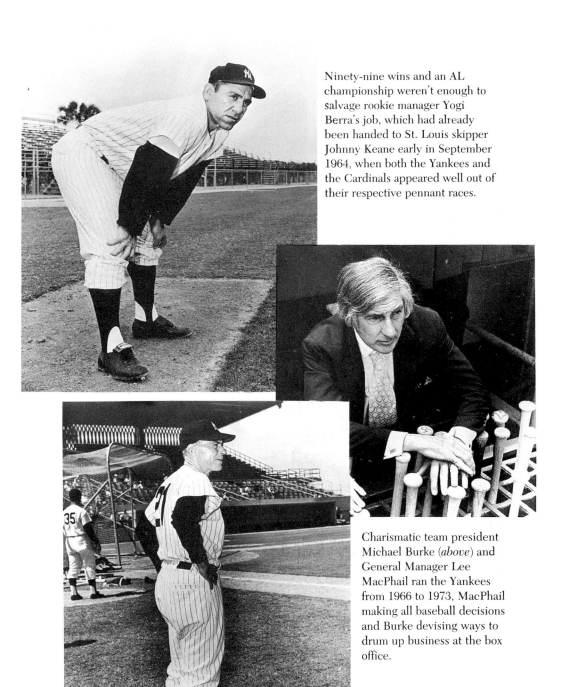

Ninety-nine wins and an AL championship weren't enough to salvage rookie manager Yogi Berra's job, which had already been handed to St. Louis skipper Johnny Keane early in September 1964, when both the Yankees and the Cardinals appeared well out of their respective pennant races.

Charismatic team president Michael Burke (*above*) and General Manager Lee MacPhail ran the Yankees from 1966 to 1973, MacPhail making all baseball decisions and Burke devising ways to drum up business at the box office.

"The Midget." "Squeaky." Those were just some of the nicknames Yankees players coined for newcomer Johnny Keane, who was never able to win their loyalty or respect in his season-plus at the helm.

Keane's clash with the beloved Mickey Mantle helped seal his fate with the other players. Number 7, batting a subpar .255 in an injury-ridden 1965, was so unhappy under the new manager that he contemplated quitting.

With Mantle, Roger Maris, and Elston Howard all hurt, Tom Tresh (.279 BA) carried the offense in 1965. Two years later, a knee injury struck him down in his prime; by age thirty-one he was out of baseball.

In one of the biggest mysteries of 1965, eighteen-game winner Jim Bouton plummeted to a 4–15 record and never won more than four games in a season again.

On May 8, 1966, much to the Yankees' delight, Ralph Houk returned to the dugout from the front office. "Everybody on the team said, 'All right, Ralph's back!' " recalls reliever Steve Hamilton. " 'Everything's okay, and now we're going to win.' " The once-mighty New Yorkers finished in last place for the first time since 1912.

By 1966, star outfielder Roger Maris longed to leave New York, embittered by what he felt was unfair treatment from management, the press, and the fans. That winter he was traded to St. Louis, where he helped the Cardinals to two consecutive pennants before retiring.

On May 30, 1967, the Yankees lost another box-office attraction when Whitey Ford announced his retirement at age thirty-eight. The future Hall of Famer departed baseball with a lifetime .690 winning percentage and a 2.75 ERA.

After two straight losing seasons, the Yankees had run out of patience with inconsistent Al Downing and demoted him to the bullpen. He eventually rejoined the starting rotation and finished a fine 14–10, 2.63 ERA in 1967. "I pitched mad that season," he says.

Joe Pepitone, installed in the cleanup spot, hit just 13 home runs in 1967, and his cavalier attitude toward the game frustrated his manager and teammates. "The majority of players felt that he wasted more talent than anybody that's ever played," says Steve Hamilton.

His name still elicits snickers, but for two seasons Horace "Dooley" Womack was the Yankees' top reliever. The skinny right-hander's 18 saves ranked fourth in the American League in 1967.

After the previous season's numerous freshman failures, the Yankees were grateful to have Stan Bahnsen on their 1968 roster. He won Rookie of the Year honors with a 17–12 record and a stingy 2.05 ERA.

For nearly ten seasons, imperturbable sinkerballer Mel Stottlemyre anchored the Yankees' staff. Despite scant support, he won 20 or more games in 1965, 1968, and 1969.

Catcher Jake Gibbs is probably the only .233 lifetime hitter ever to be given a day in his honor upon retirement. Elston Howard's departure in 1967 opened the door at last for Gibbs, but by 1970 the starting job belonged to a rookie named Thurman Munson. "I don't blame the Yankees," says Gibbs, "I blame myself. I had the opportunity."

In 1968, an overachieving Yankees squad finished above .500 for the first time since
'64. "That ball club was not very good," says third baseman Bobby Cox, a lifetime .225
hitter. "If *I* was on it, it couldn't have been."

Outfielder Roy White was the
only Yankee to suffer through all
eleven meager seasons. He was
rewarded with three pennants in
his final four years. A quiet,
steady player, White came up to
stay in 1968, when he posted a
.267 BA, 17 HR, 62 RBI.

Bobby Murcer arrived in the Bronx in 1965 as a nineteen-year-old shortstop. Converted to an outfielder in 1969, the native Oklahoman blossomed into one of the team's few offensive threats. In his first six full seasons he averaged 23 home runs and 89 RBIs.

With the Mets monopolizing New York's attention, the Yankees had to do something to draw customers. Steve Hamilton developed the Folly Floater, a stop-action lob that bedeviled hitters and delighted spectators. "He found a pitch that could get as many outs as laughs," observes fellow reliever Jack Aker.

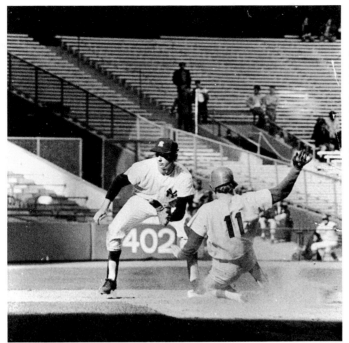

After years of trying everyone from John Kennedy and Ruben Amaro to Tom Tresh and Horace Clarke at shortstop, in 1969 the Yankees found a steady player in Gene Michael. Though known for his glove, "Stick" hit a career-high .272 that season and remained a starter through 1973.

Hamilton, Aker, and Lindy McDaniel comprised a first-rate bullpen in 1970, the year New York finished a surprising second to Baltimore. McDaniel, age thirty-four, went 9–5, 2.01 ERA, and rang up 29 saves.

Yankees fans suspected that second baseman Horace Clarke wore a glove only to keep his hand warm. Somewhat unfairly, he came to symbolize the futility in the Bronx. Though a defensive liability, Number 20 could get on base, and he led the team in stolen bases four times.

In 1972, Rich McKinney temporarily replaced Clarke as a lightning rod for fans' frustration. After batting .215 in thirty-seven games, he was demoted to Syracuse in May. General Manager Lee MacPhail calls the swap of McKinney for pitcher Stan Bahnsen, "the worst I ever made."

For reasons that still defy explanation, McKinney's replacement, Celerino Sanchez, became the most popular New Yorker since Fiorello La Guardia. An eight-year veteran of the Mexican League, he hit just .248 BA, 0 HR, 22 RBI, but knocked in several key runs as the Yankees made a late-season bid for the 1972 AL East flag.

"We plan absentee owner-ship." So declared George Steinbrenner upon purchasing the Yankees on January 3, 1973. By year's end, his meddling had provoked Ralph Houk to quit the organization after thirty-five years.

Fritz Peterson (*above*) averaged 17 wins from 1969 through 1972 but may be best remembered for trading families with fellow left-hander Mike Kekich (*right*). Peterson and Susanne Kekich are still happily married; Kekich's relationship with Marilyn Peterson fell apart shortly after news of the "life swap" was made public during spring training of 1973.

Despite a .307 average through his first four full seasons, the Yankees platooned popular Ron Blomberg against left-handers. Even in the minors, Boomer rarely got a chance to face righties.

New manager Bill Virdon encountered the same kind of resentment as had Johnny Keane. Unlike Keane, however, he didn't let it faze him. Virdon kept the Yankees in the pennant race until the next-to-last day of the 1974 season.

Despite serious injuries that left him hobbling much of the season, Bobby Bonds slugged 32 home runs and pilfered 30 bases in 1975. But Billy Martin wanted him off the team. That winter, Gabe Paul complied, obtaining fleet-footed Mickey Rivers and starter Ed Figueroa. The Yankees could have put World Series tickets on sale right then.

A missed deferred-salary payment by Oakland owner Charlie Finley enabled the Yankees to lure 1974 AL Cy Young winner Catfish Hunter to the Bronx (for $3.75 million over five years). In 1975, Hunter posted his fifth consecutive 20-game season: 23–14, 2.58 ERA.

In 1975, his third campaign in pinstripes, Graig Nettles finally lived up to New Yorkers' expectations, batting .267 BA, 21 HR, 91 RBI. The following year, he led the league in home runs with 32.

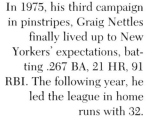

On August 2, 1975, Billy Martin began the first of five tumultuous terms as Yankees pilot. As early as 1976—an oasis of calm compared to later seasons—Number 1 was clashing with George Steinbrenner and drinking heavily.

Thurman Munson, named team captain in spring training of 1976, responded by batting .302 and winning the American League's MVP honors.

Fearless Sparky Lyle
topped the league in saves
in 1976 with 23. His mere
entrance, to the majestic
organ accompaniment of
"Pomp and Circumstance,"
sent ripples of excitement
through Yankee Stadium.

October 14, 1976, AL
Championship Series,
game five: first baseman
Chris Chambliss launches
a Mark Littell fastball
over the right-field wall
to crack a 6–6 tie in the
bottom of the ninth. The
Yankees' twelve-year
odyssey was over.

1968

STARTERS		RELIEVERS
Mel Stottlemyre	Mickey Mantle (1B)	Lindy McDaniel
Stan Bahnsen	Horace Clarke (2B)	Dooley Womack
Fritz Peterson	Tom Tresh (SS)	Steve Hamilton
Fred Talbot	Bobby Cox (3B)	
Steve Barber	Roy White (LF)	
Joe Verbanic	Joe Pepitone (CF)	
Bill Monbouquette	Bill Robinson/Andy Kosco (RF)	
	Jake Gibbs (C)	

I

INSTEAD OF HAVING some general or oily politician throw out the ceremonial first ball, as per custom, the cultivated Mike Burke invited Miss Marianne Moore, the poet, still spry at eighty-one and an avid fan, to do the honors on Opening Day. The Yankees edged out the Angels 1–0 that day behind Mel Stottlemyre, but the first half of the 1968 season would prove anything but poetic.

Once again circumstances forced Ralph Houk to improvise. The projected outfield of Tom Tresh, Joe Pepitone, and the platoon of Bill Robinson and Steve Whitaker disintegrated before the 1–3 opening homestand ended. Pepitone fractured his left elbow, and the two right fielders combined for but one hit.

In Anaheim, on the first road trip of the year, the manager gave Whitaker the hook and penciled in Roy White, who after three seasons of relative inactivity appeared to have run out of opportunities with the Yankees. He'd come up through the system as a second baseman, idolizing Bobby Richardson.

"I liked the way Bobby played the game," says White. "He was a team player. And so I really tried to pattern myself after him." By any measure, he succeeded. White, the product of an interracial marriage that ended in divorce when he was nine, grew up in Los Angeles's Watts district. As a teenager he fell in with a gang and participated in a few crime sprees, for which he received a year's probation. It is difficult to imagine White, the soft-spoken, dependable Yankee, a former juvenile delinquent. During his fifteen-year career, all of it spent in pinstripes, this quiet leader epitomized grace and class.

In 1966, White's first full season, the bottleneck at second shunted him to the outfield. Alternating between left and center, he brightened an otherwise somber April with his speed and power. "I was leading the club in home runs," he remembers. "Then I got home-run hungry and started swinging for it. I ended up with seven—and on the bench."

A .225 batting average made him expendable. The following April, New York loaned him to the Dodgers' triple-A Spokane affiliate as part of the deal for John Kennedy. If he didn't enjoy the Big Apple's finer restaurants and Broadway shows so much, White might have wished the arrangement with the Dodgers was permanent. Especially when the Yankees installed him at third upon his recall in mid-July. "I wasn't really comfortable there," he says, and it showed. After seventeen games, the experiment was pronounced a mistake.

Based on his 1967 stats (.224 BA, 2 HR, 18 RBI), the twenty-four-year-old switch-hitter didn't anticipate much playing time in '68. "I started out as the fifth outfielder," says White. "I was just happy to be there and figured I'd be traded and get a chance to be a regular somewhere else."

He was surprised, then, to find his name in the lineup against the Angels. "I didn't know I was going to be starting," White recalls. "I went 3-for-4 off Jim McGlothlin that night with a home run. The next game, Ralph kept me in the lineup, and I got a pair of hits. And the day after that, two more. From that point on, I played regularly and hit the ball consistently."

When a recovered Joe Pepitone reclaimed center field in mid-May, Houk shifted White to left, where his mortally weak arm would do the least damage. Few left fielders were better at snatching away home runs with acrobatic leaps or sliding across the grass to glove sinking line drives. Nevertheless, New York pitchers occasionally grumbled that opponents ran on him with abandon, costing them runs. "Because of poor Roy's arm, even a base hit to left got the guy over from first to third," says one. To White's lingering irritation, sportswriters rarely passed up a chance to raise his one defensive shortcoming.

"It was annoying," he says, "because I always felt I did enough positive things to compensate. I got rid of the ball quickly and got it to the cutoff man." Besides, White argues, "In Yankee Stadium you weren't going to throw out too many runners, because you had such an enormous amount of ground to cover. You couldn't play a shallow left field.

"I played the percentages. If there was a man on second, and a guy got a base hit to left, I threw the ball into second so the double play would still be in order, knowing that I wouldn't have much of a shot throwing the man out at home anyway.

"I always felt that was an overrated part of the game," he adds, "because there were a lot of guys with terrific arms that would miss the cutoff man, or try throwing runners out at the plate when they really didn't have a chance and let the batter get into scoring position. Nobody ever really looked at that aspect except the manager. But that's what counted."

As of late May, White ranked among the league's leading hitters along with right fielder Andy Kosco, another Yankee who hadn't figured prominently in New York's original plans—nor anyone else's. Over the winter, Minnesota didn't bother to place the twenty-six-year-old outfielder and first baseman on its forty-man roster. And, strangely, after claiming him in the unrestricted draft, neither did Kansas City, which is how he ended up in pinstripes. Not exactly an ego enhancer.

Like White, Kosco had modest expectations of 1968. "I thought I was going to be just a part-timer," he says. Indeed that was the role intended for him, until Robinson and Whitaker both ran aground just out of port. When handed the right-field assignment the first week in May, Kosco knew not to take it as an unequivocal vote of confidence. He was simply the last candidate left. "We're going to see what you can do," manager Houk told him.

Number 18 wasted no time in showing him, homering off Baltimore's Tom Phoebus. A bespectacled, six-foot-three pillar of granite, Kosco carried the club all month and generated excitement with barrages of home runs and clutch hits. Clark Kent, teammates called him. In the ninth inning of a 1–1 duel between Mel Stottlemyre and Washington's Joe Coleman, Kosco planted a pitch 400 feet away to win the game and hoist New York out of the cellar. His May totals came to: .288 BA, 5 HR, 23 RBI.

Other than Kosco and White, the Yankees offense spent most of the year in first gear. The club's .214 mark remains the feeblest in baseball history. Granted, bats were in eclipse throughout the majors that year, part of a continuing pattern that began in 1963 with the enlargement of the strike zone. Averages had shrunk steadily ever since: in the junior circuit 25 points, to an all-time low of .230. The American League saw only one player reach .300 in 1968, batting titlist Carl

Yastrzemski. The ensuing outcry over the game's vanishing offense sparked predictions that baseball was doomed to extinction if it didn't reverse this worrisome trend.

But the national pastime is ruled by ebb and flow. What was the cruelest season ever for batters was the kindest to pitchers since the end of the deadball era in 1920. Pitching records toppled like banana-republic regimes. Detroit's Denny McLain became the first 30-game winner in thirty-four years; Don Drysdale of the Dodgers ran a historic streak of fifty-eight and two thirds scoreless innings; and St. Louis ace Bob Gibson posted the National League's slimmest ERA ever, 1.12.

Even under these circumstances, the Yankees' anemic attack staggered the imagination. "It seemed like every damn time we turned around, we were getting beat 3–2 or 2–1," recalls catcher Jake Gibbs, a .213 hitter that year. "We lost all our power, we didn't have the speed for a running game. Hell, we just struggled." In a June 28th contest against the Oakland Athletics (recently transplanted from Kansas City), New York put seventeen men on base but brought home only two. Twenty-three-year-old Stan Bahnsen incurred the 3–2 loss despite a splendid performance, one of many in 1968. The right-hander from Council Bluffs, Iowa, captured the Rookie of the Year award with a 17–12 ledger and a miserly 2.05 ERA.

Ironically, Bahnsen came to New York via the 1965 inaugural free-agent draft. The lords of baseball had intended the game's paupers to benefit from the selection process, never dreaming that the Yankees would place last and ninth and thus get to draft first in 1967 and third in 1968. Their first-round picks those years, outfielder Ron Blomberg and catcher Thurman Munson, were soon to follow Bahnsen to the Bronx and return respectability to Yankee Stadium.

The fastballing rookie gave the Yankees a solid starting three. Ace Mel Stottlemyre was cruising to an outstanding 21–12, 2.45 ERA season. Of his nineteen complete games, six were shutouts. Fritz Peterson, 12–11, 2.63 ERA, rediscovered his freshman form. He led the majors in control, averaging a mere 1.23 walks per nine innings.

Once again, though, Houk struggled to round out the rotation. Al Downing, expected to be the number-two man, barely pitched after developing a stiff arm in spring training. Fred Talbot, 6–8 a year ago, defied statistical logic by improving his ERA from 4.22 to 3.38 while going 1–9. From July on, he all but disappeared. Bill Monbouquette split eight decisions as a starter before a trade shipped him to San Francisco, while Steve Barber (6–5) seesawed between awesome and awful.

The search for a solution compelled The Major to take even Jim Bouton down off the shelf. On May 20, the forgotten right-hander beat

Washington 6–1 for his first complete game in two years. After ringing up the final out, an exultant Number 56 winged his hat toward the first-base stands. Miraculously, given his rickety arm, it made it over the railing.

Nevertheless, on June 15, New York sold him to the triple-A Seattle Angels, recently tapped to join the American League in 1969 as the Pilots. Whoops of joy could be heard from inside the Yankees clubhouse practically out to Puget Sound. Bouton's outspokenness and at times abrasive personality had made him something of a pariah with teammates.

It wasn't always that way. Not that Bouton was reluctant to express his opinions before. According to Phil Linz, a close friend, "When Jim first came up to the Yankees, he was one of the most popular guys on the team. On the bus he always used to do this impression of Crazy Guggenheim from *The Jackie Gleason Show*. Everybody liked him.

"But he'd get into discussions about religion with guys like Tony Kubek. And ballplayers are not that open-minded. If you had a different point of view, you were *a rebel*." Linz laughs. "Jim would perpetuate these arguments. And he had a lot of good stuff to say. But I'd tell him, 'You're not going to get anywhere with these guys. They're not going to appreciate it.' "

When not on the mound, Bouton took to the soapbox, holding forth on current events to an unreceptive, and frequently hostile, bullpen audience. "Bouton used to piss everybody off," Steve Hamilton says with a hint of the affection a debater reserves for his opponent. "He either wanted to talk about, number one, religion—he claimed he was an agnostic, or whatever—or, number two, gun control. I liked to hunt and did a lot of target shooting. We kept the gun-control debate going for about two years."

"Steve was one of the more broad-minded guys," Bouton acknowledges. "Although his positions were all very conservative, the difference between him and the other players was that at least he was willing to discuss the issues. The other guys didn't want to hear about it. As a matter of fact," he adds, laughing, "they didn't want to *over*hear it.

"So when Steve and I would talk about gun control, or civil rights, or one of those subjects you weren't supposed to talk about, for more than five or ten minutes, somebody was bound to snap, 'Knock it off. Get your heads in the ballgame!' Of course, we could have been talking about women or sports for hours, and it wouldn't have mattered."

If Bouton wondered about his teammates' feelings toward him, it was revealed graphically when he challenged Hamilton for the job of players' representative in 1966. "Nobody wanted to do it," recalls Lou Clinton, not one of Bouton's biggest admirers. "It was a time-consuming pain in the neck. But Bouton actually handed out information and openly campaigned for it." Hamilton won in a landslide, twenty-two to two—three, if you count Fritz Peterson's absentee ballot, which Bouton didn't bother to cast.

Peterson, a rookie that year, was assigned Bouton as a roommate, just as Roger Repoz had been during his freshman season. "Nobody else would room with him," Repoz explains, though he adds, "We got along fine." Bouton took Peterson under his wing, much to the grave concern of "Colonel" Jim Turner, the sexagenarian pitching coach.

"He said Jim was a Communist," Peterson recalls, laughing. But then, the rigid-minded Turner, from Antioch, Tennessee, had a tendency to brand anyone or anything he didn't quite understand "Communust." To reduce the risk of Bouton corrupting any future rookies, management awarded him a single room the following spring, explaining that as a veteran he deserved privacy.

Life as an outsider was nothing new for Bouton. Though handsome enough to work as a TV sportscaster once his playing days ended, he was a homely teenager who suffered the twin curses of acne and braces. Despite his athletic prowess, he nursed a deep inferiority complex throughout his adolescence, something most Yankees would probably find difficult to imagine.

As the issues of the day heated up, so did Bouton's views on matters such as racism, hippies, and Vietnam. By 1968, America's continued military presence there had driven a wedge through the nation.

"Initially, I thought that maybe the war was necessary somehow," Bouton reflects. "But the more I saw deceit going on in terms of the progress we were making there, and the number of men it would take to win, and the predictions not coming true, I realized our government was lying to us. And so I became very much against the war."

As for his peers, Bouton says, "The ballclub was like a microcosm of society, with the younger players thinking that maybe there was something wrong with the war, and the older guys convinced it was the right thing. That was pretty much the breakdown, although it probably was more conservative than in general society. The older players felt about the country the way they felt about baseball: that this was the way things were and the way they were supposed to be, and so you just went along and kept your mouth shut."

Silence was not Bouton's way. He actively supported dark-horse candidate Senator Eugene McCarthy's calls for reassessing the country's Southeast Asian policy. With the Vietnam War emerging as the central issue of the 1968 presidential campaign, the Minnesota liberal sent shockwaves through the Democratic Party when he placed high in the early primaries. While on the road, Bouton snuck away from the hotel to appear at McCarthy campaign-strategy meetings and rallies. (In 1972 he attended the Democratic National Convention as a New Jersey delegate for Senator George McGovern.)

The pitcher also traveled to the October 1968 Summer Olympic Games in Mexico City, where he and other members of the South African Non-Racial Olympic Committee (SANROC) lobbied for South Africa's ouster from future competition. "While we weren't able to get the Olympic Committee to make a decision down there, they eventually did ban South Africa," says Bouton. "And part of it had to do with the efforts of SANROC."

The baseball establishment looked upon his political involvement as "strange," Bouton says, shaking his head. "In 1969, I was having a meeting with Marvin Milkes, the general manager of the Seattle Pilots. He said, 'Well, I know you were down in Mexico City. But *we're going to overlook that.*' Like I had to be forgiven for any of my social activities or interests outside baseball!

"Of course, no one objected when I was winning," Bouton adds pointedly. "On a baseball team, or any sports team, you're as smart and as popular as your earned run average or batting average. As long as you're doing well, people will tolerate you, and even listen to you. But if you're not doing well, forget it; you're a pain in the ass."

II

ALTHOUGH COMPARED TO many of his peers Bouton was certainly an extremist, he typified the modern athlete: more inclined to express himself, less apt to worship the veterans. In the past, being a rookie often meant tiptoeing nervously about the clubhouse and speaking only when spoken to.

"It was like joining a fraternity," says Rollie Sheldon. "They played all kinds of games with me. Whitey Ford would say, 'Hey, rook, go get me a Coke!' And I'd go get him a Coke. I really wasn't accepted until I started winning a few ball games."

"I don't think I said anything to Yogi or Mickey or Whitey for about two or three years," Clete Boyer reflects. "That was the type of respect you had." The freewheeling Joe Pepitone, however, could be found joshing with Mantle and even Joe DiMaggio on one of The Yankee Clipper's locker-room visits. It used to be that when Joe D. passed through, players and sportswriters alike all but averted their eyes; they wouldn't dare try to make small talk with the retired, and retiring, legend.

That all changed in the 1960s, says Ralph Terry. "DiMaggio would come in the clubhouse, and some of the guys would say, 'Hey, Clipper, how's it goin'?' " Terry, himself a bit of a maverick, approved of the younger players' attitudes. "I think that was a good thing," he contends. "The guys that came along were a looser breed. At least the crop that we had—Pepitone, Linz, Bouton—they were more psychologically prepared for winning and losing and all the perceived pressures."

Bobby Richardson, on the other hand, didn't care for what he saw. "For years we had veteran ballplayers with the Yankees tradition," he says. "And then all of a sudden these younger guys came in who weren't as team-oriented. I think the evidence of this was when we divvied up our World Series shares. You had guys on the club for a half-season. The veteran ballplayers would say, 'Well, let's give him a full share.' 'Let's give the batboy a full share.' These new players were more selfish. 'That guy's only been here a half-year? Let's just give him five hundred dollars.' We lost that team spirit. And I think that was part of the team's downfall."

Richardson and others of his generation frowned on the new breed's willingness to engage the media, a taboo during the winning years. But loquacious types such as Bouton, Pepitone, and Linz were extremely at ease in front of notepads and microphones. Their quotes, however, didn't sit well with many teammates.

"At the time, I had no idea that a lot of those guys disliked me, Jim, and Joe because we talked to the sportswriters," says Linz. "But we didn't give a shit what they said; we were going to talk to whomever we felt like talking to."

That tended to be journalists their own age, up-and-comers such as George Vecsey, Steve Jacobson, and Phil Pepe, among others, whose provocative, literary styles were redefining sports reporting. For decades the Yankees' press corps had functioned as a virtual publicity arm for the club, which, incidentally, paid their travel expenses. In return for what was the cushiest job on the baseball beat, these press-box partisans churned out puffery that cast team members in the most favorable light.

The new school covered the New York clubhouse as if it were Town Hall. They didn't shrink from controversy, provided thoughtful analysis, and, best of all, brought the ballplayers to life for readers by asking probing questions and printing the unvarnished replies.

The old guard felt properly threatened. One day Jimmy Cannon, of the *New York Post* and later the *Journal-American*, glanced over at Pepe, Jacobson, and one or two others and sneered, "Look at them, chattering like *chipmunks.*" The tag stuck, as did the writers, while the veteran hacks faded into retirement.

"The young sportswriters were all very progressive and had greater vision," says Al Downing, adding, "I found them to be very enlightening. They were good because they had different ideas about baseball."

Traditionally, the sports pages held up the national pastime as a sanctuary untouched by the world beyond the ballpark, immune from nearly every outside force save the weather. Modern journalists, on the other hand, saw in baseball a reflection of the American condition. They began to chronicle the game in a broader context, evaluating its place in a society that appeared on the verge of a nervous breakdown.

Between the start of spring training and the deciding game of the World Series alone, 1968 bore witness to a chain of national tragedies: in March, a defeated-looking President Lyndon Johnson announcing wearily he would not seek reelection. In April, an assassin's bullet striking down Dr. Martin Luther King, Jr., touching off rioting coast-to-coast. In June, presidential contender Bobby Kennedy shot dead after eking out victory in the California Democratic primary. In August the week of the Democratic Convention, Chicago police brutally clubbing antiwar protestors and innocent bystanders as TV cameras beamed this spectacle of violence into millions of homes.

It occurred to some sportswriters that athletes—at least a select few—might actually have opinions on these and other issues. Al Downing remembers: "The Sunday after Martin Luther King was shot, I was in Miami International Airport getting ready to join the ball club in New York." His injured arm had kept him in Florida for X-ray treatments.

"People were rioting like crazy. A guy stopped me for an interview; I don't know how he knew I'd be there. He asked, 'What do you think about these riots?' I said, 'Martin Luther King was a man of peace. Somebody shot him. So if these people want to riot, it's because they don't feel there's any hope in being peaceful.'

"Some people wanted to hear what you had to say," Downing reflects. "Then there were those that didn't want to listen to you. They'd say, 'You're a ballplayer; what do *you* know?' Well, I know as much as you know. I read."

Any Yankee who made himself available to one of the chipmunks could expect to come under the distrustful glare of Frank ("The Crow") Crosetti, the elderly third-base coach. A Bronx Bomber since 1932, he epitomized the bunker mentality of the old days.

"He was suspicious and hostile," says *Newsday*'s Stan Isaacs. "He would also warn players about those writers who weren't house men, who weren't awed by the Yankees." The Crow's career in pinstripes came to an end in October, when he resigned to join the Seattle Pilots. Since taking up position outside third base in 1949, he'd waved home 15,188 New York runners. The last link to the teams of Babe Ruth and Lou Gehrig, Crosetti seemed a curio on the 1968 club.

If the new generation of ballplayers came across as brash, it was perhaps because more of them were college educated. Having other skills and future plans beyond the game made them less submissive to management's demands. They didn't strive any less to excel. But they were realistic enough to recognize that one day baseball would deposit them back into civilian life.

Jim Lyttle, New York's top draft pick in 1966, skipped his first spring training to complete his spring semester at Florida State University. "The Yankees weren't too happy about that," he recalls with a laugh. "But I felt very strongly that I needed to get my education. I wanted to have something to fall back on."

Lyttle, a math and physical education major, seemed to regard his baseball career as something of a summer job. In 1969 the Yankees promoted him to the big show. After batting .181 in a few dozen games, the twenty-three-year-old outfielder was returned to Syracuse in midseason.

"I'd already made plans to go back to school in the fall, to student-teach," says Lyttle, who now owns a landscape nursery in Florida. "When they sent me back down I asked, 'Are you going to call me up again in September?' They didn't know, so I said, 'Then I'm going back to school.'" Asked if his dedication to academics forestalled his progress in pinstripes, Lyttle replies, "I don't think so. The thing that held me back was, I didn't hit home runs!" Lyttle did spend eight years in the bigs, three of them as a Yankee.

While other Yankees whiled away plane trips playing cards and ogling stewardesses, young Ross Moschitto, an architecture major at Merced College, pored over his homework. "The guys used to call me 'Einstein,'" says the father of four, now a security consultant and a part-time musician who performs as part of an Elvis Presley tribute act. "They'd come over to see what I was working on. Especially Joe Garagiola." Yogi Berra's boyhood buddy broadcast Yankees games from 1965 through 1967 before joining the *Today* show.

"Joe used to crack me up," Moschitto recalls. "He'd pick up my physics book or look at the calculus problems I was doing, and he'd act like he couldn't understand any of it. It just put him in awe that I was a ballplayer and doing this kind of stuff." Athletes' reading lists

rarely contained anything weightier than comic books and skin maga-
zines. But the teasing never turned to ridicule, says Moschitto.

"Not at all. In fact, it was just the opposite." The veteran players,
most of whom signed pro contracts right out of high school, respected
the college men for planning ahead. At the same time, seeing ambitious younger teammates working toward degrees was an unsettling
reminder of their own uncertain futures. Unlike today's athletes, none
would walk away a millionaire. Through 1967, the average annual
paycheck came to $19,000—less than that of the airline pilots who
flew the players from city to city.

III

AT THE ALL-STAR break, the Yankees were parked in eighth place,
36–43 (.456). Stan Bahnsen, making a rare relief appearance, earned
the last of those losses when Baltimore's Fred Valentine took him over
the wall in the ninth inning of a 2–2 tie.

Except for Steve Hamilton (2–2, 11 SV, 2.13 ERA), the bullpen
regulars had been sabotaging games all season. Dooley Womack, so
reliable in 1966 and 1967, tore a rotator cuff while swinging a bat in
Florida. He estimates the shoulder injury took six-plus inches off his
sinking fastball and Lord knows how many years off his career, which
ended not long after. In 1968, Womack tacked only two saves onto a
3–7 record.

On July 13, Lee MacPhail traded Bill Monbouquette to San Francisco for forkball artist Lindy McDaniel. In thirteen seasons, the six-
foot-three Oklahoman had led the National League in saves three
times. As recently as 1966 he'd gone 10–5 (6 SV, 2.66 ERA). A year
later, for reasons he prefers not to discuss, McDaniel landed in manager Herman Franks's doghouse and fell into disuse.

He was still wasting away when informed he'd be taking his virginal
0–0 mark (and zero saves) to New York. McDaniel, who speaks with
a quiet intensity, recalls, "I was ready to go anywhere, because I
wasn't getting any consistent work with the Giants. In fact, I was
pitching so infrequently, I volunteered to throw batting practice. On
two occasions I threw forty-five minutes of B.P., and who do you think
got into the game that night? I did." The surly Franks seemed bent
on ruining him and was close to succeeding. McDaniel admits that at
age thirty-two, "For the first time in my career I was beginning to
doubt myself."

His Yankees debut, against Baltimore, did little to boost his confidence. "The first batter singled off me, then one out later Boog Powell hit a home run over the center-field wall. Not a very good beginning in the American League. So I reared back and struck out four of the next five batters, although we still lost the game by two runs."

Houk, expert at handling firemen, believed in putting riders right back in the saddle after a spill. Later that week he summoned McDaniel to face down a Washington threat: bases loaded, one out, and New York holding a 4–1 ninth-inning lead. The new acquisition fanned ex-Yankee Billy Bryan, then made the final putout himself on a bouncer up the first-base line for the first of ten saves. "From then on," he says, "my pitching went back to normal, and my confidence was restored pretty rapidly."

It helped that American Leaguers had seen a forkball about as often as they held team discussions on Proust. In all of baseball, only McDaniel and Pittsburgh relief ace Elroy Face, his inspiration in learning the pitch, threw one. The forkball, so-named because it is gripped forklike between the thumb, index, and middle fingers, drops sharply just as the batter is certain he's about to make contact.

During August and September, the slender right-hander added four wins in five decisions. Number one came in Anaheim, the first stop on an eleven-game road trip. With McDaniel the pitcher of record, New York rallied for three runs in the ninth to beat the Angels 5–2. In addition to halting a five-game losing streak, the August 12 victory set off a glorious five-week run that temporarily alleviated the pain of being a Yankees fan.

Houk's squad bulldozed California and Oakland seven games to one before Minnesota's Dean Chance tripped Stan Bahnsen 1–0 on an unearned run. Twenty-four hours later, Mel Stottlemyre avenged his teammate with a 5–0 whitewashing, as Andy Kosco belted his third home run in four days. Nine RBIs since flying west gave the broad-shouldered outfielder 48 on the year, to regain the team leadership.

Based on his torrid May, Kosco had seemed sure to reach that number by Independence Day. But his offensive blitzkrieg came to a halt just as suddenly as it began. From mid-July to mid-August Kosco generated only one run. Then once again he spurted to life. Number 18 wound up 1968 at .240, with 15 homers and 59 RBIs, sound statistics considering the spell weaved by pitchers that year.

The night after Kosco's and Stottlemyre's performances, outfielder Rocky Colavito and Al Downing double-teamed the Twins 2–1. Colavito, who signed with New York on July 15, after the Dodgers released him, singled home one run and passed Gil Hodges on the all-time home-run list by lofting his 371st career circuit clout.

New York had procured the thirty-five-year-old Bronx native as much for fan appeal as for right-handed hitting insurance. One of the game's most fearsome sluggers, from 1956 to 1966 Colavito averaged over 30 dingers while wearing the uniforms of the Cleveland Indians, the Detroit Tigers, and the Kansas City A's.

Were it not for a haughty Yankees scout (was there any other kind back then?), Rocco Domenico Colavito might very well instead have starred at Yankee Stadium, only a mile or so from the corner of 173rd Street and Third Avenue where he'd played stickball and punchball as a boy.

He still remembers the Police Athletic League outings to the ballpark and the bus rides across 170th Street, then down Jerome Avenue. "I was a *big* Yankees fan," says Colavito. "I liked Bill Dickey and Charlie Keller. But Joe DiMaggio was my favorite. As a kid I always wanted to be a Yankee."

In 1950 the darkly handsome seventeen-year-old made the pilgrimage to the stadium, this time to attend a New York tryout camp. Soon after, a Yankees scout visited the youngster's home. "He made a bad impression, to be perfectly honest," Colavito remembers. "He acted like there was nobody to sign with but the Yankees, all the while puffing on this great big cigar.

"I made like I had to go to the bathroom and left the room. My older brother came to see where I'd gone. I said, '*You* talk to him.' The attitude just turned me off." New York's $3,000 offer to sign turned him off as well.

"Now, the Indians were very nice," he says. "They took me to Yankee Stadium for the last game of the World Series, the one that Whitey Ford pitched"—and won, 5–2, giving the 1950 Bronx Bombers a four-game sweep over the Philadelphia Phillies. Colavito never made it to the Fall Classic during fourteen major-league seasons but insists he has no regrets about accepting Cleveland's $4,500 bonus contract. "Never. I felt my chances were better with the Indians than the Yankees. At that time they had DiMaggio, Bauer, and Woodling in the outfield."

Now semiretired in Pennsylvania, Colavito still has family in the Bronx. When he finally became a Yankee, "It was like coming home," he says. "The sad part was, they were not the team they once were."

But you sure couldn't have told it from their 8–3 road trip in July, New York's best since 1964. Awaiting the sixth-place Yankees at home: a four-game weekend series versus the league-leading Detroit Tigers. Tom Tresh predicted that if enough team members got hot, a leap to third place was still possible. "Don't laugh," he admonished a skeptic.

In the opening game of a Friday-night twin bill, the .195-hitting shortstop took charge. Tresh's two-run homer provided Stan Bahnsen with all the support he needed to fend off Al Kaline, Norm Cash, Willie Horton, *et al.* for a 2–1 win. The nightcap came within six outs of the reverse outcome when Bill Robinson walked to open the eighth and Roy White followed with a game-tying home run.

Eleven innings and two and a half hours later, the two teams remained deadlocked, 3–3, each at the mercy of the other's bullpen. John Hiller, who entered in the eighth to suppress the Yankees' uprising, stymied them through nine innings on four hits. Lindy McDaniel was even less generous: in seven frames, not a single Tiger reached base. The right-hander worked with the efficiency of an Iron Mike, requiring just fifty-nine pitches to dispose of twenty-one men.

Seven minutes past the league's 1:00 A.M. curfew, Andy Kosco popped to short, and both clubs filed wearily into their respective clubhouses. The game would be replayed Sunday as part of a double-header.

Players' heads had barely hit their pillows before they were back at the ballpark preparing for one of the premier pitching matchups of the summer: 17–10 Mel Stottlemyre opposite 25–4 Denny McLain. A more striking contrast, both on and off the mound, would be hard to come by. One outsmarted batters with sinkerballs, the other simply overpowered them. Stottlemyre was as introverted and unassuming as McLain was gregarious and cocky.

Since he began zeroing in on 30 victories, baseball's twenty-four-year-old bad boy had captivated the public with his swaggering personality and colorful antics. McLain flew his own plane, played nightclubs as an organ soloist, and promoted rock-and-roll shows. In 1970 it came to light that he was also an investor in an illegal bookmaking operation. McLain's admission of guilt led to a three-month suspension and a rapid downfall that culminated in his being sentenced to prison for crimes ranging from cocaine possession to racketeering.

On this day the more prosaic of the two prevailed, although both hurlers performed up to expectations. Stottlemyre recorded no strikeouts while scattering four hits, among them a bases-empty home run by Willie Horton. McLain was equally impressive, fanning six in seven innings. But Roy White's two-run blast in the first stood as the deciding blow.

The Yankees left fielder was beginning to slug like a cleanup hitter, even if he didn't fit the mold. White, five-foot-ten and a taut 160 pounds, choked up so high on the bat that he appeared unsure which end to hit with. Yet his 17 round-trippers on the year were just one shy of team leader Mickey Mantle. White topped New York in every other major offensive category: .267 BA, 154 H, 89 R, 62 RBI.

"I'd never really envisioned myself as a cleanup hitter," he admits in a resonant baritone that seems like it should belong to a much larger man. "But Mickey had been hitting there, and they were pitching around him a lot." As in 1967, Mantle again drew over a hundred free trips to first.

"One day in August, Ralph called me in and said, 'Roy, I'm going to try you at cleanup and let Mickey hit third. You're the only guy on the club hitting well enough where he might get something to hit.'" Batting fourth for the Yankees put White in some rather exclusive company; not too shabby for a ballplayer who'd only begun feeling reasonably secure in his job.

Ask White what's in a number, and he'll tell you: plenty. "When they switched me from forty-eight to twenty-one at the All-Star break, that's when I knew I belonged. And in the off-season, Lee MacPhail called me and said, 'We'd like you to have number six,'" which for years had been the property of Clete Boyer.

White's back-to-back heroics against Detroit earned him a rare day's rest. He sat out the first game of the August 25 Sunday doubleheader, which was played under ugly conditions. The muggy weather that turned Yankee Stadium into a steam bath also lured gangs of gnats and mosquitoes from all five boroughs.

With two days of doubleheaders ahead of him, Ralph Houk crossed his fingers that Steve Barber would be able to give New York's abused bullpen a much-needed respite. But the flu-ridden left-hander got cuffed from the first frame on. When the game appeared out of reach, 5–0 in the fourth, the manager summoned Number 29 to the mound.

Fans checking their scorecards did a doubletake. Rocky Colavito?

Cognoscenti among the crowd might have been aware that he'd hurled three innings for the Indians ten years earlier, also against the Tigers. "As a matter of fact," he notes, "I signed as a pitcher-outfielder with Cleveland."

Upon joining New York, the veteran volunteered his rifle arm for relief duty should the need ever arise. Following Friday's nineteen-inning standoff, Houk called him into his office. "Did you mean what you once said about possibly pitching?" he asked.

"Sure. If you need a mop-up guy, I'll be glad to do it."

"Good. Because I might use you tomorrow."

Colavito recalls, "When I came in the next morning, Ralph was right behind me. He said, 'You're my number one man today.' So I got elevated from mop-up to top reliever." In the second inning, with roommate Barber on the ropes, Colavito hustled down to the bullpen to loosen up.

The veteran was so eager to get into the game he started walking in from right field, until Steve Hamilton pointed to the golf cart that was waiting to chauffeur him. "He was really fired up," says Andy Kosco. "I remember him pounding his glove, and the smile on his face."

During doubleheaders Kosco had the unenviable assignment of replacing Colavito in right, then spelling Mantle at first. "In the first game the fans would be going, 'Kosco? We want Rocky! We want Rocky!' " he says. "I couldn't wait till it was over so I could go to first base. Then in the nightcap all I'd hear was, 'Kosco? We want Mickey! We want Mickey!' Talk about being between a rock and a hard place."

Colavito took the ball, took a breath, and confronted his baptism of fire: Tigers on first and second with one out and dangerous Al Kaline at the plate. Throwing mostly overhand fastballs, he got his ex-teammate to ground out to short, then coaxed a fly ball to left to end the inning.

He returned for the fifth and sixth. Colavito yielded just one hit, a Kaline double, and picked up a strikeout, all the while ignoring his catcher. "He must have shook me off ten times," Jake Gibbs says, laughing. "It was the damndest thing I ever went through. I'd put down a one, he'd want to throw a three. I'd put down a three, he'd want to throw a one." In addition to his fastball Colavito possessed a change-up and a slider that he admits "didn't slide too much."

Says Gibbs, "I thought to myself, *What the hell is going on here?* Finally I told him, 'Rocky, just go ahead and throw what you want to.' "

In the bottom of the sixth, the Yankees having trimmed Detroit's lead to four, New York exploded for five runs. It was only fitting that Colavito score the winning run on Gibbs's single to right. When he failed to materialize for the top of the seventh, 30,000 boos rattled the stands. "They wanted to hang me," Houk giggled afterward. Lindy McDaniel shoveled dirt on the Tigers for the last two innings to preserve Colavito's 6–5 victory.

The afternoon contained still more drama. Stationed back in right field for the nightcap, Number 29 punched a game-tying home run that sent the emotionally drained crowd into a dance of delirium. New York went on to complete its four-game sweep 5–4, pulling the club up to .500. A mark of mediocrity, to be sure, but in the Bronx these days, a landmark.

Monday's twin bill against California made a reliever pro tem out of Gene Michael, whose only mound experience was a few dozen innings in the Arizona Instructional League. Houk put him to work in game two with New York trailing 5–1 in the seventh.

"I was nervous when I came in," recalls Michael, nicknamed Stick for his physique. "Then I struck out the first guy up—the pitcher." In three innings he fanned three all told, including ex-Yankee Roger Repoz with the bags loaded. "Back on the bench, I was telling Stottlemyre and Peterson how easy it was," he says.

"Stick missed his calling," cracks Steve Hamilton. "The guy couldn't hit a lick." Michael's 1968 stats: .198 BA, 1 HR, 8 RBI. The Yankees didn't bless Michael with a stirring comeback as they had Colavito, and a Ruben Amaro miscue helped the Angels to five unearned runs. "But to this day," Michael says proudly, "my earned run average is zero-point-zero-zero."

IV

"MAYBE WE DIDN'T have the greatest players at that time," Lee Mac-Phail says in retrospect, "but we probably had the most intelligent bunch you could put on the field." The infield alone included four future major-league managers: Michael, Mike Ferraro, Dick Howser, and Bobby Cox.

Cox, a twenty-six-year-old third baseman acquired from the Atlanta farm system, began the year with about as much chance of making the squad as a little-known Maryland governor named Spiro Agnew had of becoming vice president. He was entering his ninth season of a career that had taken him to such remote minor-league outposts as Panama City, Florida, and Great Falls, Montana. "Just a normal baseball life," Cox shrugs. "Packing up and traveling all over the world."

He took it in stride when he and his family of five drove to spring training from Selma, California, only to find themselves without a place to stay. "We got to Fort Lauderdale a day early," he recalls, "and there weren't any vacancies anywhere, not even at the team hotel. So we slept on the beach."

With incumbent Charley Smith still recovering from knee surgery, Cox and another rookie, Mike Ferraro, vied for third base. Of the two, the strapping, chiseled Ferraro, twenty-three, was certainly the more impressive physical specimen. Cox's blunt features and plain build raised suspicions that he was actually older than twenty-six, a doubt supported by his grapefruit-league play. He batted just .186, while Ferraro's .351 won him the James P. Dawson Award for outstanding prospect.

Among the players, however, Cox was the sentimental favorite.

They liked the way he cheered on Ferraro even as his job at the hot corner slipped away. "Bobby was what we called a 'gamer,' " says Andy Kosco. "He wasn't a great player, but he knew baseball and worked hard at it. He got to the ballpark early and would do anything to win, like putting himself in front of a ground ball.

"The guys all respected him for that, and deep down everybody was pulling for Bobby."

The day Ralph Houk informed him he'd survived the final cut, he was "thrilled to death," Cox recalls. "I just couldn't believe I'd finally made it." That he'd be riding the bench barely mattered. "I was kind of team-oriented all throughout my life. No point in sulking."

Then the season opened. Ferraro, who'd sizzled in Florida, froze up north. A week before Opening Day a doctor had misdiagnosed him with glaucoma. "He told me I was going to be blind in two or three years," Ferraro recalls. "I had to take this drug that burns your eyes and gives you headaches." Fear of not picking up the ball and getting beaned hampered his play both in the field and at the plate. Less than a month into 1968, the front office optioned him to Syracuse and made Cox the everyday third baseman.

Cox didn't make anyone forget Clete Boyer, but hidden among his undistinguished numbers (.229 BA, 7 HR, 41 RBI) were several timely hits. In Rocky Colavito's pitching spectacle against Detroit, it was Number 14's solo homer that evened the score at five. On September 1, his pair of singles and three RBIs paced the offense for a 5–1 victory over Cleveland.

All in all, a passing grade, but not nearly enough for the front office to view Cox as a cornerstone of its rebuilding program. The next spring, the farm system at last coughed up some worthy young talent. Cox, reduced to utility infielder, encouraged them nonetheless. By 1970 he was back in the minors.

"That was it for me. I wasn't going to play anymore," says Cox. But then what? He'd known no other career since signing with Los Angeles at eighteen. "Going back to school and becoming a coach somewhere was the only thing I could think of." His selflessness and smarts hadn't gone unnoticed during his two seasons in the Bronx, however, and Cox went home that winter the new manager of the Yankees' class-A Fort Lauderdale affiliate.

Characteristically the Tulsa native "worked my tail off" to become one of baseball's most prized pilots, a "player's manager" in the mold of Ralph Houk. "I learned an awful lot from Ralph," says Cox, whose Atlanta Braves reached the World Series in 1991 and 1992, and won their division in 1993. "I really liked the way he treated his players and talked to them as if they were human beings. During my career I'd had managers you couldn't even get a hello out of all season."

V

RIDING ITS WAVE of success, New York charged into the season's final month within striking distance of third. But the euphoria of the last few weeks didn't fool many Yankees into believing they were truly a third-place team.

"That ball club was not very good," Bobby Cox says bluntly. "If *I* was on it, it couldn't have been." But the second week in September, the Bronx Bombers went racing off on a ten-game winning streak that each day thrust a different hero into the spotlight.

September 7: *New York 16, Washington 2; New York 10, Washington 0.* Jake Gibbs, Joe Pepitone, and Roy White crack home runs in game one; Rocky Colavito and Frank Fernandez follow suit in the nightcap to back Fritz Peterson's two-hitter.

September 8: *New York 7, Washington 2.* Bill Robinson goes 2-for-4 as Stan Bahnsen raises his record to 15–10.

September 10: *New York 2, Chicago 1; New York 5, Chicago 0.* Indicative of the serendipity suddenly permeating Yankee Stadium, Cox leaves the opener with a strained rib cage; sub Charley Smith, so inactive in 1968 that he practically needs a map to home plate, comes up with two gone in the bottom of the ninth, the score tied 1–1, and belts his only home run of the year. Joe Verbanic then silences the Sox in game two, aided by Andy Kosco's three RBIs.

September 11: *New York 7, Chicago 2.* In the sixth, New York erupts for seven runs, its biggest rally of the season. White, Pepitone, and Horace Clarke each bangs out two hits.

September 13: *New York 4, Washington 2; New York 2, Washington 1.* Mel Stottlemyre rings up win number 20; Fernandez and Mickey Mantle account for all four RBIs. Robinson, 2-for-4 in the opener, drives in game two's deciding run to make a winner of Stan Bahnsen.

At the beginning of the year, Robinson half-joked that his miserable 1967 season had at least immunized him against a sophomore jinx. But at the All-Star break, a batting average of .179 and 2 home runs put him on a pace to undershoot his rookie totals. Seeing Robinson manage a rare homer in a game against Baltimore rattled Hank Bauer, the Orioles' manager. Bauer, a reformed nicotine addict, "said I started him back to smoking again," Robinson recounts with a laugh. From mid-July on, however, Number 11 suddenly blossomed into the player the Yankees had thought they were getting when they traded for him, batting a clutch .282 to finish at .240, with 6 home runs and 40 RBIs.

September 14: *New York 4, Washington 1.* Al Downing throws the Bombers' fifth straight complete game, while Mike Ferraro's 11 assists tie the American League record. The third baseman claims he set another mark that week: "the fastest recall in the history of professional baseball."

While the Yankees were sweeping Chicago at home on September 10, "I was in my backyard in Kingston, New York, having a barbecue," remembers Ferraro, whose minor-league season had already ended. Then Bobby Cox pulled some muscles in his rib cage. "In the second inning of the first game I got a call to hurry down and join the team. I made it in time for the second game. When I walked into the clubhouse, Mickey Mantle asked, 'What row were you sitting in?' "

September 15: *New York 3, Washington 2.* Peterson's third K.O. of the streak gives New York its twenty-ninth win in thirty-nine games. The fairy-tale dream of a month ago comes to pass as the .533 Bombers (80–70) take title to third place.

Twenty-four hours later, the Yankees' enchanted carriage reverted back to a pumpkin. Detroit chased Joe Verbanic before he'd retired a single batter, then manhandled Steve Barber in a 9–1 rout that whittled that club's magic number down to one. The following night, more than 46,000 of the faithful jammed Tiger Stadium hoping to witness Motown's first pennant clinching since 1945.

Stan Bahnsen and Joe Sparma treated them to a 1–1 nail-biter through eight and a half innings. In the bottom of the ninth, the air thick with tension, Don Wert's two-out single off Lindy McDaniel scored the winning run and sent thousands of exultant fans pouring onto the field. The celebration spilled peacefully into city streets still charred by the racial strife of only a year ago. Drivers got out of their cars to shake the hands of perfect strangers.

From his twelfth-floor window at the Sheraton-Cadillac Hotel, Mickey Mantle watched the revelry below with fascination. In eighteen seasons as a Yankee, he'd never seen such appreciative fans. Mantle, at a point in his career where just tumbling out of bed in the morning inevitably broke some baseball record, needed one more home run to climb past Jimmie Foxx into third place on the all-time ladder.

It was beginning to look as if he might have to wait until 1969. Since hitting his sixteenth of the year in Minnesota, the thirty-six-year-old slugger had gone four weeks without another. On September 19, he stepped in against Denny McLain, still looking for that elusive number 535.

The 30-game winner, leading 6–1 after seven, called catcher Jim Price out to the mound for a word. Talking loud enough for Mantle to hear, he said, "I'm gonna let him hit one." In wafted a medium-speed inside fastball for a strike, then another that Number 7 fouled off. "Switcher," batting left-handed, stepped out of the box with a puzzled look on his face.

"Mickey couldn't believe it," says Andy Kosco, seventh in the order that cool, gray afternoon. "But Denny acknowledged he was going to lay it in there."

Mantle placed an order for a letters-high fastball over the plate, and McLain obliged. *Crack!* Number 7 ripped a clothesline into the upper deck. As he rounded third, Mantle nodded toward the mound and called out, "Thanks!" McLain just grinned. Dooley Womack remembers, "Mickey jumped in the dugout, spun around, and sat down. 'Boy,' he said, 'I've got a new respect for that guy out there.'"

Joe Pepitone, up next, held up a hand to indicate where he'd like *his* fastball served. McLain sent him ducking out of the way instead. After his 6–2 victory, the pitcher, nicknamed "Mighty Mouth," smilingly denied reporters' insinuations that he'd grooved one to his boyhood idol. But according to teammate Pat Dobson, McLain had made his intentions clear prior to the game. "We were all aware of what was going on," he says.

The small Tiger Stadium crowd accorded Mantle a warm ovation, not only for his latest milestone but to bid one of the game's all-time greats farewell. It was widely speculated that The Mick would not suit up next year, and so his final appearances around the league met with similar tributes.

Whether it was Detroit or Chicago, admirers besieged Mantle in public. "It was to the point where he couldn't walk around town," says Andy Kosco, a ten-year veteran. "He couldn't even get on the bus after games." Whitey Ford, back in pinstripes as first-base coach, had to rescue Mantle in a rental car well after the swarms of fans had finally given up and gone home.

"He was like a god," continues Kosco, now in the insurance business. "People just wanted to touch the man." Women of diverse ages and marital status yearned for more personal contact, dropping blatant propositions. "Mickey would say, 'But you're married!' 'As long as it's Mickey Mantle, it's okay.' It was unbelievable, the things you'd hear people say to him."

Mantle, at heart shy and self-deprecating, squirmed at times from the adulation. "Once," says former batboy Thad Mumford, "this guy comes over and is telling Mickey how great he is, when he begins to cry. And Mickey starts crying with him!"

Mantle's teammates were unabashed fans themselves. In the waning days of the season they all lined up to have pictures taken with him as mementos. Most felt certain he would not be back.

"I think it was obvious," says Rocky Colavito, then in his own swan-song season and a confidant of Mantle's. "The thing was the speed. I remember him saying to me, 'You know, now I respect someone like you even more. Because when I used to bounce the ball twice in the infield, I could beat it out.' I said, 'Tell me about it.' Because I didn't run real well."

Rumors swirled that the American League was about to implement a designated-hitter rule. Tailor-made for Mantle and other aging sluggers, it would permit managers to replace pitchers in the batting order with a permanent pinch hitter. Andy Kosco, estimating that the new rule could preserve Number 7's career another three to five years, hoped the talk was true. "Boy, Mickey," he remarked excitedly on the bus, "that would really give you a chance to keep on playing." Mantle smiled politely but knew better.

It was no longer just the wear and tear on his legs that handicapped him at bat. In fact, in 1967 and 1968 he stayed relatively healthy, playing in 144 games both years. His reflexes were going. He couldn't get around on the ball anymore.

"People were throwing fastballs by him," observes Stan Bahnsen. "Occasionally he would comment, 'I can't believe I didn't hit that ball.' He'd lost only a fraction of a second of his timing, but that's all it takes."

On May 30, the rookie pitcher profited from one of Mantle's finest days as a professional: 5-for-5, including a double, 2 homers, and 5 RBIs in a 13–4 censure of the Senators. Afterward the media clamored outside the Yankees clubhouse for Mantle to say a few words.

Only after Lee MacPhail intervened did he come out, a surly expression on his face. "Mickey had a great deal of pride," reporter Maury Allen explains. "He knew what he could do, and when people fussed over things he did late in his career, he found that difficult to deal with. Because to him those things had always been routine."

Mantle eventually warmed up, clearly pleased by his performance. A complicated man, through 1968 he swung back and forth between bemoaning his fading abilities and savoring the good moments. "His last year, he was a pussycat," says Vic Ziegel, one of many sportswriters to have received Mantle's savage glare in the past.

"He used to be just awful," remembers Stan Isaacs of *Newsday*.

"He would look right through you." The Yankees center fielder was famous for responding to reporters' queries with a gruff "Go fuck yourself," or walking away without a word. "Mickey's terrific now," says Isaacs. "When I talk to him I'm amazed how gregarious and funny he is. He's often expressed regret that he didn't handle the press better."

Almost as if to erase the taint from his 535th home run, Mantle unloaded the very next day at Yankee Stadium against Red Sox right-hander Jim Lonborg. In Boston on Saturday, September 28, the season's next-to-last day, he faced Lonborg again for one at-bat. Number 7, his legs aching all over, popped up to left and limped into the dugout.

As the Yankees went to take the field, he told Andy Kosco, "Good luck. Take care."

"I didn't think too much about it," recalls Kosco, Mantle's replacement at first. He and the others were surprised to tramp into the clubhouse following the 4–3 victory and find Mantle gone. He was back home in Dallas when the Yankees won Sunday's game by the same score to give them an 83–79, .512 record on the year. Their fifth-place finish put an extra $300 in each man's pocket.

At Ralph Houk and Lee MacPhail's joint request, Mantle held off until spring training to make a decision on his future. The night he reported to Fort Lauderdale, he phoned his manager and said simply, "Ralph, I don't want to play ball anymore."

"I knew it was coming," Houk reflects. "It was hard for him to tell me, and it was hard for me to hear. He was the best player I ever managed."

The next day, March 1, 1969, Mantle faced the press at a hastily arranged news conference. "I just can't hit anymore, and there's no use trying," the three-time MVP said in a voice that betrayed no emotion. His lone regret, he said, was seeing his lifetime average slip to .298 after batting a career-low .237 in 1968.

When the Yankees reported to Fort Lauderdale Stadium later that afternoon, Mantle's uniforms still hung in his locker. In 1991 one of them sold for over $70,000. "We didn't know there'd be a market like that one day," Andy Kosco says with a laugh, "or we'd have gotten a lot of things of his."

1969

STARTERS
Mel Stottlemyre
Fritz Peterson
Stan Bahnsen
Bill Burbach
Al Downing
Mike Kekich

Joe Pepitone (1B)
Horace Clarke (2B)
Gene Michael (SS)
Jerry Kenney (3B)
Roy White (LF)
Bill Robinson/Ron
Woods/Jimmie Hall (CF)
Bobby Murcer (RF)
Jake Gibbs/Frank
Fernandez (C)

RELIEVERS
Lindy McDaniel
Jack Aker
Steve Hamilton

I

THE YANKEES ENTERED the 1969 season assured of at least a sixth-place finish. With baseball's expansion from twenty to twenty-four teams, each league was restructured into eastern and western divisions of half a dozen clubs each.

In another major development, baseball's owners dishonorably discharged Commissioner Spike Eckert midway through his seven-year term. That these were the same gentlemen who'd elected the retired general pointed up the inherent impotency of the post, not to mention the absurdity of entrusting the commissioner's fate to the very individuals he was ostensibly to govern.

At one point during the search for a successor, Yankees president Mike Burke's name rose to the top of the list. But on February 4, the owners decided on Bowie Kuhn, a Wall Street attorney who in the past had served as counsel to the National League.

His first day on the job, it appeared the new commissioner would find himself with little to do that summer. For with spring training only two weeks away, players on all twenty-four teams were preparing to strike.

This drastic action arose out of their frustration with the owners' seeming refusal to renegotiate the players' pension fund. In December, after months of fruitless negotiations, the Major League Baseball Players Association urged its approximately 600 members not to sign their 1969 contracts. Only the day before Kuhn's election, 125 ballplayers convened at Manhattan's Biltmore Hotel, where they voted unanimously to boycott. They hinted there might be no baseball at all that season if the dispute wasn't settled equitably.

Individuals had held out before. In one of the most famous instances, Hall of Fame outfielder Eddie Roush sat out the 1930 season rather than accept the contract offered him by the New York Giants. The joint action proposed by the players' union, however, was the first since 1890, when over a hundred ballplayers rebelled over poor salaries and other grievances and formed their own league, which went bankrupt a year later.

The lords of baseball refused to budge on the pension issue, forcing a showdown. This came as little surprise. Team owners had long ruled the game as if it were their private fiefdom. In addition, the Players Association, headed by former labor economist Marvin Miller, was only three years old and untested.

In their arrogance, the owners believed the players' solidarity would disintegrate. But the walkout basically held firm. When camps opened to pitchers and catchers around mid-February, only rookies turned out. Players' representative Steve Hamilton managed to keep every Yankee who'd been on the 1968 roster away from Fort Lauderdale Stadium. In a public-relations coup, he also convinced Mickey Mantle to delay announcing his retirement so that his name could be added to the impressive list of players publicly refusing to sign new contracts. Mantle had already made up his mind to quit and would not personally benefit from any boycott, but he gladly lent his support.

Only about 10 percent of the association broke ranks, most of them obscure journeymen, not stars. On February 25, an agreement was reached on the pension issue, with the Players Association winning considerable concessions. The owners, despite their public threats to break the union's back, caved in—and prematurely. Had they waited until after March 1—the date by which players were contractually obligated to report to work—it is highly likely that the boycott would have begun springing leaks. In years to come, the two sides would spar many more rounds, but by anybody's scorecard, this first one went to the players.

II

MIKE BURKE, IN keeping with his Appeal to Youth, arranged for pop star and avid Yankees rooter Paul Simon to throw out the first ball at the 1969 home opener. Singing partner Art Garfunkel merely looked on, he being a Phillies fan. Small wonder the popular folk-rock duo split up a year later.

Simon and Garfunkel's number-one hit "Mrs. Robinson" contained the plaintive line "Where have you gone, Joe DiMaggio? A nation turns its lonely eyes to you." Now not only was Joltin' Joe absent from the national pastime, but also Mickey Mantle, leaving behind a faceless Yankees club devoid of a single superstar.

Knocks against Ralph Houk are as scarce as right-handed first basemen. But if there is a shortcoming to be found, it's that The Major tended to favor experience over youth. Perhaps this was because the great Yankees clubs he'd played on and managed consisted primarily of old hands, to which rookies were added sparingly like seasoning on a fine steak.

Houk's approach created a logjam at a time when the farm system was finally producing talent. The triple-A Syracuse Chiefs, managed by Frank Verdi, placed fifth in 1968, third the following year, and in 1970 won the pennant and the International League Championship.

"We had a lot of good ballplayers," says Verdi, a New York farmhand in the 1940s and 1950s. "But these kids were not appreciated by the Yankees. For one reason or another Ralph Houk preferred to have guys like Gene Michael and Horace Clarke, and kind of surrounded himself with older players.

"I used to push them to use these kids, because I believe youth is the way to go if you want to improve. I think that might have been part of my downfall," he claims. "People say they don't want yes men, but when you disagree with them, they don't particularly care for that kind of talk." The organization let him go in 1973. Verdi, today the baseball coach at Florida's St. Leo College, went on to manage the Mets' Tidewater triple-A club, where he helped develop future stars Jeff Reardon, Mike Scott, and Mookie Wilson.

Tom Shopay, along with Steve Whitaker and Ross Moschitto, believes he was victimized by the organization's impatience. A spray hitter with some speed, Shopay remains highly critical of his former skipper.

"People said that Ralph Houk was a great manager. But I'll tell you this: he hurt my career. And I saw him hurt some other young ballplayers' careers. You had rookies down in triple-A who'd had two, three good years. But there was no way they were going to make the ball club unless they literally shamed management into keeping them." Shopay, vying for a reserve outfielder spot, lost out to thirty-year-old Billy Cowan and Dick Simpson, a seven-year veteran. Neither lasted beyond July.

"The only reason you'd get called up was because somebody got hurt," Shopay goes on. "Then, when you got up there, Houk still stuck with those veteran ballplayers, no matter how poorly they were doing or whatever place the team was in. When I was called up in '69, he told me, 'I'm going to play you against all right-handed pitching.' I started two games against right-handers and hardly saw any action again." Puny numbers (.083 BA, 0 HR, 0 RBI in 48 AB) may have had something to do with that. But, as hitters will remind anyone within earshot, it's tough finding consistency at the plate when you're in and out of the lineup.

Shopay was relieved to escape to Baltimore, where he played sporadically from 1971 through 1977 despite a .201 career average. His sickly stick inspired Orioles teammates to coin the verb "to Sho-*pay*"— to tap weakly back to the pitcher.

Houk defends himself against charges of snubbing rookies. "I always wanted younger players," he insists, "but at the time we just didn't have anybody in the farm system to bring up."

In 1969 that began to change. Bobby Murcer's return from a two-year army hitch stirred up welcome excitement. In spring training he batted .380, and barely a news story failed to trumpet the striking similarities between him and Mickey Mantle: both hailed from Oklahoma, both began their careers as shortstops, both caught the eye of the same scout, Tom Greenwade. The Yankees, not about to discourage comparisons, made it a point to award Murcer Mantle's old locker. In addition, he inherited Bobby Richardson's number 1, at the retired second baseman's request.

Bill Robinson had wobbled under similar pressure, but Murcer bore up well. A handsome, clean-cut twenty-two-year-old whose harshest expletive was "Dadgummit!" he shrugged off the New Mantle label. "It was the similarities they were talking about, not the ability that each of us had," he says in retrospect. "I didn't really worry too much about being compared to Mickey Mantle. I mostly worried what Mickey thought about being compared to me!"

Murcer was slated to share the infield with Number 7 in 1967 when Uncle Sam suddenly beckoned. With the draft in effect then, eligible ballplayers between eighteen and twenty-six years of age were expected to meet their military obligations like anyone else. Most were able to do so without infringing on their careers, by serving in the reserves part-time. But the Yankees shortstop of the future got trapped in a political rundown that resulted in his having to put in two full years.

"At the time I really couldn't talk about it, but I suppose I can now," he says. "Basically, what happened was: when I graduated from high school, just like everybody else I went down to be classified with my service board. And I was classified 1Y, which was a deferment of some kind. Why they gave me that, I have no idea. And I didn't question it." At that time, a 1Y classification by the Selective Service System disqualified a person on the basis of physical, mental, or moral reasons but, unlike a 4F ("registrant not qualified for military service"), was subject to review.

The following year, Murcer's status changed with the suddenness of a pickoff play at first base. "Out of the clear blue sky I got a 1A classification ["available for military service"] in the mail along with my draft notice," he recalls. "That was a little bit strange. Obviously we were wondering what the deal was."

According to Murcer, the deal was this: he was being made an example of. In an atmosphere of increasing public discontent with the Vietnam War, accusations were flying that the troops overseas were inequitably drawn from minorities and the underprivileged.

"Me being a nineteen-year-old kid, I was getting a lot of publicity in New York," says Murcer. He goes on to claim, "The Kennedys got involved with my draft board in Oklahoma, wondering why in the heck I wasn't serving my time. It became a political issue." Robert Kennedy, then junior senator from New York, was a staunch supporter of a lottery-type draft.

As a college undergrad in the off-season, Murcer should have qualified for a student deferment. But because he'd already been drafted—five times in the course of a year—his request was turned down. When he inquired at his local draft board ("the same one as Mickey Mantle's, by the way"), "I was told that the heat was just too much, and there wasn't anything they could do about it."

Murcer appealed his case all the way to Washington. Once again his classification came back 1A. "I took off the very next morning to be processed into a reserve unit," he says, "but within fifteen hours they'd drafted me yet again." On March 6, 1967, he was inducted into the army.

"I certainly didn't have any qualms about serving my country," he stresses. "It was just the way it came about that I questioned." Though he would be just twenty-two when discharged, as far as Murcer was concerned, his career was all but over. "Being a baseball player back in those days, if you lost two years it was almost like the end of the road." He laughs. "When you got into your twenties, you were already getting a little too old."

His twenty months as a radio operator turned out much differently than Murcer had expected. "What I thought was going to be a horrible experience was really a positive thing for me in the long run," he says. "I learned responsibility and, obviously, a little bit of discipline. When I got out I was ready to proceed with my baseball career on a much more mature level."

Murcer arrived in camp infinitely more confident than the nervous rookie who'd literally trembled inside his uniform and prayed the ball wouldn't be hit to him. "I was just nineteen," he reflects on his original appearance in the bigs. "I really wasn't prepared to play a major-league shortstop. I think if I'd had the seasoning and the time behind me, maybe I would have turned into a fairly decent shortstop, though not a great one." The Yankees evidently agreed, shifting him to third base upon his return.

At five-foot-eleven, 160 pounds, Murcer hardly fit the prototype of a power hitter, nor did he consider himself one. Yet over his first five seasons he was to average 26 home runs and 90 RBIs. He provided a glimpse on Opening Day 1969 by homering in front of the nation's new chief executive, Richard Nixon, and didn't slow down until jamming his ankle over the Memorial Day weekend. At the time, his numbers read: .321 BA, 11 HR, 43 RBI (the latter stat being tops in baseball).

Yankees sufferers rejoiced. After years of false prophets sent to lead the team out of the desert, they had their first legitimate star of the new era. (Roy White quietly put up comparable figures but didn't quite possess Murcer's flair or fan appeal.) One lingering area of concern remained, however.

In thirty-two games, the Yankees third baseman committed a horrendous fourteen errors, several of them overthrows that sent spectators behind first base scrambling. During a May series in Oakland, he let fly a pair of javelin tosses to second that landed in the outfield.

Murcer remembers, "Later on, somebody hit me a two-hopper, and as I grabbed it a voice in the stands yelled, 'Watch out, he's got it again!'

"After we got the out, I walked into the dugout. Ralph Houk said to me, 'Young man, tomorrow you come to the ballpark and take some fly balls in the outfield.'

" 'How come?'

" 'Because I want to get you as far out there as I can. I hope they *never* hit you a ball.' "

A few nights later, Murcer was pawing the grass in right field at

Seattle's Sicks Stadium. "I made an error on the first ground ball hit to me," he recalls, laughing. "But I felt relaxed the moment I was out there."

Murcer's banishment to right field restored Jerry Kenney to his old turf. The black infielder-outfielder from Beloit, Wisconsin, had debuted as a shortstop in the closing weeks of 1967 and hit .310. He was all set to fill the vacancy left by Murcer when he too got called up for military service.

Upon his return to civilian life, Kenney figured to challenge Tom Tresh and Gene Michael for the starting shortstop job. He soon learned that the team had other plans for him—namely, center field—not that anyone in management thought to inform him of this. "A friend pointed it out to me in *The Sporting News*," remembers Kenney. "That's how I found out. I didn't think too much of it at first, but my father always told me, 'If you're a ballplayer, you play anywhere.' "

Just as he was beginning to feel comfortable there, Houk took him aside in Seattle and asked if he would mind moving to third, a position Kenney hadn't played since high school. When do you want me to start? he asked. Tomorrow night, Houk replied apologetically.

The rookie acquitted himself well, finishing one point behind league leader Brooks Robinson in fielding percentage and batting .257 from the number-two spot in the order. Coyote-lean and quick, Kenney injected speed into New York's previously one-dimensional offense. His 25 thefts were second to leadoff man Horace Clarke's 33. All told, the 1969 team stole 119 bases, tops in its division and the most by a Yankees crew since 1931.

Kenney shared spring camp's outstanding-rookie award with pitcher Bill Burbach, New York's number-one pick in the very first amateur draft. The seventeen-year-old high-school senior grew up in the tiny town of Dickeyville, Wisconsin. On June 8, 1965, he and a friend drove three hours to Chicago to cheer on the Milwaukee Braves against the Cubs. In the middle of the game the Wrigley Field scoreboard flashed his name and the news that he'd been selected by the American League Champion Yankees.

"I kinda choked when I saw it," is his recollection of that moment. "I called home and found out it was true. We went back and partied for about two days." The Yankees assigned the burly six-foot-four right-hander to its rookie-league club in Johnson City, Tennessee.

From there, Burbach inched his way up through the organization: class-A ball at Greensboro in 1966, double-A ball at Binghamton the next year, then a promotion to triple-A. Just as the 1968 season was getting underway, the pitcher's father died suddenly of a heart attack at the age of sixty-three.

The tragedy left him badly shaken. "I went to Syracuse and was 0–9," he remembers. "I just kind of gave up. But then I had a little talk with myself and a gentleman I'll always remember, Harry Craft." Whatever the Yankees scout said apparently had an effect, for the twenty-year-old won his next nine decisions.

Still, he was a long shot to make the Yankees staff in 1969 and probably wouldn't have if the veterans had reported to camp on time. "During those two weeks they were on strike a lot of us kids got a chance to impress people," says Burbach, whose meteoric fastball had Ralph Houk turning cartwheels on the sidelines.

His control was another matter. "I should have stuck with the fastball more," he says in retrospect. "When I went to another pitch, I got in trouble." In the last exhibition game of the spring, against the San Francisco Giants at Yankee Stadium, "The first batter up was Willie Mays, and I proceeded to hit him. I thought I was going to get booed out of New York City." The Say Hey Kid may have left the Big Apple over ten years before, but he remained an icon there. The traumatized rookie peered nervously at Mays. "As he walked to first, he looked at me and said, 'Relax, kid!' " Burbach recalls. "After that, everything was fun."

Burbach never enjoyed himself more than in his second major-league start, when he whitewashed the Tigers 2–0 on four hits. But from there Number 50's career rumbled downhill like a soapbox-derby racer. A 6–2 loss to Boston on July 16 put his record at 6–8, which is where it stayed through the end of the year.

"I really didn't pitch much after the All-Star break," he says. "I still wonder about that. I felt like I was on the proverbial shit list. Probably my biggest mistake was not going in and asking why." Burbach hung on by his fingertips to make the staff in 1970 and thought he might be able to redeem himself, but he didn't get enough work to find his control. New York optioned him to Syracuse in May and a year later traded him to first-place Baltimore.

"I was really excited," he says, "until I realized they had four twenty-game winners." Burbach was assigned to the Birds' triple-A Rochester affiliate with the promise that he'd be recalled once he notched a few wins there. When he ran his record to 7–0 and no telegram arrived from Baltimore, he began running his mouth.

Somewhat remorsefully, he recalls, "I went into the manager's office and said I wanted to know what the hell was going on. Well, I didn't pitch after that. I just sat." And grew disenchanted with the game. Burbach reels off his final destinations dispassionately.

"I got traded to Detroit over the winter. Went to spring training. Quit. Came back home. They suspended me. Then signed with Minnesota in June of '72 and spent two months in Tacoma. Went to spring training with them in '73 and quit. The next year, went with St. Louis. And I quit again."

Baseball breeds hundreds of Bill Burbachs every year, athletes who earn a fling in the majors only to wind up interred in the catacombs of the minor leagues. One day they decide they've had enough and quietly exit the game, often in sharp contrast to how they entered.

Burbach, now a salesman in Johnson City, Tennessee, where his career began back in 1965, expresses only one regret. "I just wish I'd been born fifteen years later," he says. "As mediocre as I was, I hate to think what I'd be worth at today's salaries."

III

BURBACH'S THIRD WIN came against the White Sox on June 8, 1969, the day the Yankees gave Mickey Mantle a proper send-off. Between games of a Sunday doubleheader, Mantle's number 7 joined Babe Ruth's number 3, Lou Gehrig's number 4, and Joe DiMaggio's number 5 as sacred symbols never to be worn again by mere mortals.

From the moment Mantle poked his head out of the dugout and ambled onto the field, cheers swept through the Stadium. *"We Want Mickey! We Want Mickey!"* For eight minutes the volume never ebbed.

Yankees broadcaster Frank Messer, master of ceremonies for the between-games ceremony, recalls, "I didn't know what to do. This wasn't in the script!" He attempted to introduce Mike Burke, who'd planned on delivering a few words, but it was like shouting into a jet engine. "Finally Mike called Mickey over and urged him to go to the microphone and try quieting down the crowd."

Mantle wasn't any more successful than Messer. He stood there with his hands in the air and a look of embarrassment on his face while the outpouring of affection continued. *"We Want Mickey! We Want Mickey!"*

"Mantle does not show emotion very much," observes Messer. "But I really believe he was upset by the length of the applause." At last the roar subsided. Joe DiMaggio presented Mantle with a plaque that was to hang by the center-field monuments commemorating Babe Ruth, Lou Gehrig, and Miller Huggins, and Whitey Ford handed Mantle his famous uniform. Then Number 7 stepped up to the microphone.

"I was amazed by the speech Mickey gave and his demeanor," says Messer. At one point Mantle evoked Lou Gehrig's famous address from thirty years before, when the dying Yankees great also stood surrounded by a stadium full of worshipping fans. "I never knew how a man who was going to die could say he was the luckiest man in the world," Mantle said. "But now I understand." Though visibly moved, few among the 61,157 probably realized just how deeply he identified with Gehrig, who lost his life to a paralyzing disease at thirty-seven, the same age as today's honoree. Mantle had worried that he'd break down in tears, but he maintained his composure throughout.

"The most emotion I saw Mickey show," says Messer, "was when he in turn presented a plaque to DiMaggio, which was a complete surprise to Joe. Mickey said, 'I'm proud my plaque will be hanging up there, but this one has to hang maybe a little higher than mine,' which I thought was a great tribute."

The ceremony concluded with a chauffeured drive in a bullpen cart around the field where Number 7 made so much baseball history. Then, as the crowd called out to him, a waving Mantle strolled off into the pages of Yankees history and back to his new life as owner of a restaurant franchise and a clothing-store chain. Both failed, repeating an unfortunate pattern from the earliest days of his business ventures.

Ten years after retiring, the Yankees legend found himself reduced to a sideshow attraction, appearing at suburban shopping malls to judge Mickey Mantle look-alike contests and whatnot. Suddenly in the 1980s, collecting baseball cards metamorphosed from a kid's hobby into a big kid's investment opportunity. And, with it, a vigorous market emerged for promoters of baseball-card shows and the old-timers who earn handsome fees signing autographs at these events. Mantle, who as a player never cleared more than $100,000 annually, can now score $30,000 in a single weekend.

The sight of Number 7 and former greats such as DiMaggio, Ford, and Berra gathered together in a festive, bunting-lined stadium brimming to capacity must have nourished the souls of the twenty-five current Yankees. They played like champions for the occasion, torpedoing Chicago 3–1 and 11–2.

The sweep evened New York's record at 28–28 and moved it into a fourth-place tie with Washington. But already the season's aspirations had to be drastically scaled down. The runaway Orioles, in their first full season under manager Earl Weaver, were to win 109 games and sneer at the notion of an American League East race. When the Birds strutted into town on July 1, the Yankees were floundering twenty games back.

Meanwhile, who should have the entire country humming with excitement but those insufferable neighbors from Flushing. Buoyed by a host of young arms and bats, the Mets—*the Mets!*—were wedged right behind first-place Chicago in the National League East. Yankees rooters tugged uncomfortably at their collars. It promised to be a terribly bleak summer. A dog-day summer.

"It really was the dog days," says Tom Shopay, today the owner of a security-guard firm in Florida. "When you know you're out of it, you still want to win and all, but to be perfectly honest, ballplayers are thinking about raise time and trying to put up good numbers. Statistics are important." Reminded of today's long-term, guaranteed contracts, Shopay corrects himself. "*Were* important. Nowadays a guy can hit .250 and still make eight hundred thousand a year."

Several Yankees performed well enough to merit salary increases. Second baseman Horace Clarke flirted with .300 in early September, then tapered off to .285. Though never known for his skill with the glove, he also led the league in twin killings. Despite a .230 average the year before, Clarke had always demonstrated he could handle major-league pitching. The same could not be said for double-play partner Gene Michael, a .196 hitter through 1968. Number 17's .272 stood out as the most unexpected improvement of 1969.

The thirty-year-old shortstop entered his eleventh pro campaign praying New York wouldn't jettison him back to the minors, where he'd idled for eight years in the Pittsburgh chain. A lanky six-foot-two basketball guard at Kent State University, Stick had spurned a contract from the Detroit Pistons when he was twenty-three. Six years later, he was offered a second chance at dribbling for a living. Again Michael said no, even though as a Dodgers utility man his dreams of achievement on the diamond were rapidly fading.

When he did crack the lineup he played stiffly, worried that a muffed grounder or a strikeout could earn him a pink slip. Going into 1969, he made a conscious effort to relax. "I was scared with the Pirates, I was scared with the Dodgers, and I was scared when I came to the Yankees," says Michael, who even as a young man possessed distinguished good looks and a noble bearing.

"In '69 I said, 'The heck with it. I'm going to play the game as I did when I was a kid.' And I had success. It really was a pivotal year for me." Michael replaced injured Tom Tresh at short on May 27 and locked up the position through 1973.

At the All-Star break, the Yankees were napping in fifth place, 46–52 (.469). Mel Stottlemyre, however, who was on the road to winning 20 games for the third time, got the tap to start for the American League. Roy White, his .313 halftime average proving 1968 no fluke, joined him at Washington's recently renamed Robert F. Kennedy Stadium. Unfortunately the National League continued its recent domination of the midseason competition, winning for the seventh time in a row. Whereas one run had decided each of the previous four affairs, this year's 9–3 laugher featured five home runs, including two off the bat of San Francisco's Willie McCovey.

It was the kind of explosive baseball that pleased baseball's owners. To counter 1968's dearth of offense, the game's rules committee not only trimmed the height of the mound from fifteen inches to ten inches but also shrunk the strike zone. Pitchers now had to aim for between the armpit and the top of the knee instead of between the shoulder and the lower knee.

The effort to restore the game's equilibrium had the desired effect: American League batting averages jumped 16 points in 1969; New York's, 21 points, although its .235 still placed last among its Eastern Division rivals.

If you were a pitcher who threw with a sidearm or a three-quarters motion, chances are you adapted without much difficulty. But for an overhand fastballer like Stan Bahnsen, it took months not to feel as though he were pitching uphill. The 1968 Rookie of the Year lost his first six decisions, and although he recovered in the second half, his overall figures (9–16, 3.83 ERA) suggested the sophomore jinx.

"Lowering the mound took maybe a yard off my fastball," he says. "I just couldn't get on top of it. But I really think it hurt my curveball more than anything." In a familiar story, the "Bahnsen burner" of a year before had to substitute savvy for speed, learning to throw more sinking pitches.

He also learned to avoid the off-season rubber-chicken circuit. Bahnsen's selection as top AL freshman made him the toast of Council Bluffs, Iowa, which he then called home. "They had a day for me," he remembers. "The lieutenant governor came." A park there even bears Bahnsen's name.

"I went on the banquet circuit that winter, speaking at Little League dinners and those kinds of things. I guess I didn't work as hard as I did the year before," he admits, "because I know I wasn't in as good a shape in spring training."

IV

BASEBALL, CELEBRATING ITS one hundredth birthday in 1969 amid much fanfare, appeared to be undergoing a centurial crisis. Besides tinkering with the mound height and strike zone, other changes intended to rejuvenate the game were under consideration.

David Merrick, the famed Broadway producer, attended the centennial dinner in Washington the night before the All-Star Game and later handed down his thoughts on baseball's shortcomings: "Not enough show business." His suggestions to spice up the action included adopting an offensive-defensive platoon system similar to football's, and limitless substitutions. As if fans flocked to the ballpark hoping to see both teams' third-string catchers get their at-bats.

In an increasingly fast-paced, disposable culture that craved convenience and efficiency, often at the expense of simple pleasures, baseball came under suspicion as having fallen out of step with the rhythm of modern life. The most often-heard complaint concerned the game's length. Too long, too slow, said critics.

Too slow? Part of baseball's appeal is the prospect of spending a lazy day at the ballpark or in front of the TV without once checking your watch. The longer the game, the longer you've dodged some frightful responsibility.

At one point it was even proposed to pare down whiffs to two strikes, and walks to three balls. Strike two, you're out? Heresy! But in the Age of Aquarius, it was practically one's duty to seek alternatives to convention, especially if you were under thirty.

In mid-August over 400,000 young hearts congregated at a Bethel, New York, farm for the Woodstock Music and Art Fair. Conceived as the largest rock-and-roll concert to date, and a gathering of like-minded people mostly from the fringes of society, it flourished into something far greater, a human experiment that took on the name Woodstock Nation.

Early media coverage of the event adopted a hysterical, mocking tone. Bethel and nearby towns were warned to brace for three days of hippies flouting every law and morality code imaginable. While open nudity and drug use were widespread, the peaceful throng confounded skeptics by behaving civilly in the face of driving rains and shortages of food, water, and toilet facilities. Woodstock forced mainstream America to swallow its antipathy and reexamine some of the counterculture's utopian ideals. Maybe, just maybe, these kids were on to something.

Interestingly, in the process of lauding the festival-goers' conduct, commentators drew frequent comparisons to spectators at sporting events, noting that if you assembled an equal number of beery bleacherites under similar conditions, they'd probably dismantle the stage and cart off every square inch of turf as souvenirs—once the brawls subsided, that is.

Though many professional ballplayers belonged to the same generation as the Woodstock crowd, the majority of major-leaguers no more identified with this group and its concerns than did your average middle-age Republican from Peoria. Anytime the Yankees team bus pulled up at a red light in some American League city and someone spied a longhair on the street corner, insults inevitably came hurling out the window.

"If they weren't standing there in a business suit, the players would have something derogatory to say," recalls Jim Bouton, who spent 1969 pitching in Seattle and Houston. He reflects: "Many of the players were feeling the social earthquakes going on in the country. But like a lot of our leaders and politicians, they tended to blame things on these longhaired people with bare feet who didn't bathe and smoked pot.

"They said, 'That's what's wrong with this country. If it weren't for those hippies, Communists, and agitators, the war would be going okay and we wouldn't have civil-rights problems.' They saw those people as the problem."

Mike Kekich was one of the exceptions who found a good deal of value in the underground movement. But then, a pitcher known to read poetry in the bullpen was hardly typical of his peers. "He was from another world," observes sportswriter George Vecsey. The Yankees discovered this the moment they acquired the cerebral Kekich from Los Angeles for Andy Kosco at the 1968 winter meetings.

Vecsey, who by then had left *Newsday* for the *New York Times*, recalls sitting in the hotel suite as Lee MacPhail announced the transaction. "Lee was talking about this promising young left-hander and how 'We know his best years are ahead of him.' One of the Los Angeles writers piped up, 'Oh, you mean Crazy Mike?' And there was this pause. *Crazy Mike?*"

The L.A. scribe explained himself. "Well, you know about the black leather jackets and the long hair and the motorcycle and the peace and love . . ." Judging from MacPhail's surprised expression, apparently not.

Kekich hated having to leave Los Angeles, his home since he was fourteen. "In the early sixties, it was a great place: good baseball, sunshine, surf, the whole bit," he says fondly. The six-foot-one pitcher, an avid biker and sky diver, blended quite happily into southern California's pleasure-seeking lifestyle.

"My whole perception of everything was a baseball diamond and pretty skirts," he says in retrospect. "I wasn't really consumed by anything else back then. When I was twenty and with the Dodgers, I felt like I was hot stuff. I had a World Series ring, I drove a Corvette, I had a pretty wife.

"But as time went on, toward the late sixties, early seventies, a lot of things started not making sense to me. I became more introspective in a variety of areas: from how I felt about my immediate environment to the extent of my religious pursuits. I became involved, maybe not actively, but at least conscientiously, in a number of other things. Like rock music and what it was saying. And what was happening on college campuses around the world, and what they were saying about our political system."

The more Kekich's priorities changed, the more impatient he grew with the often myopic world of baseball. For a dose of perspective he used to chat for hours with the young fans who waited outside the players' parking lot after games.

"There'd be anywhere from five to twenty-five youngsters on the other side of the fence," he remembers. "I'd sit on the hood of my car, and we'd start off talking about the game. Before the evening was over we were talking about all types of social and political issues. Some nights I wouldn't get home until one, two in the morning."

As evidenced by Kekich's nickname, "Nutsy Mike," teammates didn't always appreciate his voracious curiosity. Other open-minded players who operated around the majors were similarly distanced from the mainstreams of their clubs—such notorious "flakes" as Boston's Bill Lee and Seattle's Steve Hovley, were dubbed "Spaceman" and "Orbit," respectively.

"We tended to take a real hard look at what was going on. There was a spirit among us," says Kekich, who adds Ron Swoboda's name to this short list. The rugged Mets right fielder came over to the Bronx midway through the 1971 season. An early and outspoken supporter of the youth movement, he too looks back on the times with affection. "I have a lot of respect for the intellectual things that period represented," he says. "There was a goodness at the heart of it, and a sincere attempt at trying to understand."

Swoboda refers to William Least Heat Moon's *Blue Highways*, a chronicle of the author's travels through America via its back roads. "There's a wonderful quote in there from a Hopi Indian. He basically said that you could distill the Hopi philosophy down to two tenets. One, don't go around hurting people. Two, try to understand things. To me, that's what the whole hippie era was all about. And on a very oversimplified basis, that's as good as anything we have, isn't it?"

Aside from Swoboda, Kekich, and a few others, most major-leaguers felt the effects of the counterculture only peripherally, through the changes it wrought in music and fashion. In the summer of 1969, songs like the Beatles' "Get Back" and the Rolling Stones' "Honky Tonk

Women" rang out from the Yankees clubhouse, traditionally a haven for little else besides country-and-western.

"Wow, man, you'd hear everything," says Jerry Kenney, a promotion man for Brunswick Records after his baseball career ended. "Everybody had their portable radios."

A tour of the locker room provided a musical sampler. You had Kenney listening to rhythm-and-blues, Horace Clarke digging jazz, Steve Hamilton meditating to classical, Jake Gibbs humming along to country, Joe Pepitone boogying to the Top 40. Fiftyish bullpen coach Jim Hegan liked the old barbershop quartets and would try to enlist volunteers for four-part harmonies. "He'd always get mad at me because I could never blend with anyone," admits Hamilton. "I'd start going off in the opposite direction."

Lockers brimmed with fashions that even Elvis might have rejected as too outlandish—crushed-velvet bell-bottoms, ruffled shirts, Nehru jackets, suede boots—a welcome relief from the drab slacks and sweaters right out of *Golf Digest* that were formerly ballplayers' usual off-field wardrobe.

Kekich, Pepitone, and Al Downing led New York in sartorial self-expression. The nonconformist Kekich naturally chafed at club orders that everyone wear matching blue blazers and gray slacks on the road. "So he wore the jacket, but no shirt underneath," recalls pitcher Gary Waslewski, a Yankee in 1970 and 1971.

Hairstyles were a little slower to achieve hipness. One of Bowie Kuhn's earliest decrees as commissioner was to ban beards, mustaches, and sideburns below the ear. But gradually hair could be seen tickling collars (for certain black players, moderate Afros sprouted out the sides of their caps), even if in Pepitone's case it wasn't his own.

New York's first baseman suffered from prematurely thinning locks—in baseball speak: "bad grass." After games he would fuss over his thatch like an obsessive gardener, though he finally gave up in favor of a hairpiece that he styled to mod length with a blow-dryer. Crusty Pete Sheehy, who'd been keeping Yankees in clean towels since 1927, was appalled.

"Boy, I'll tell ya," he'd lament, "those old Yankees would turn over in their graves if they ever saw a hair dryer and a wig in this locker room." The clubhouse manager seemed convinced that ballplayers in panty girdles would be the next step in baseball's de-evolution.

Although Pepitone casually left hairpieces lying about his cubicle, he was highly self-conscious about the fans learning his secret. "Joe was one of the vainest people I've ever met," recalls batboy Thad Mumford, who went on to Hollywood as a writer and producer of such

TV shows as *M*A*S*H* and *Roc*. "It was so funny watching him during the National Anthem. He'd take his cap off real carefully, so the whole wig wouldn't come off with it."

V

THE YANKEES FINALLY ran out of patience with Pepitone after he went AWOL twice. On August 12, he was a no-show for a home game against Minnesota. The next morning Pepitone meekly informed Ralph Houk by phone he wouldn't be making that night's contest either. As for why, "Personal matters" was all he'd say.

Management knew of Pepitone's ongoing legal entanglements: an alimony suit with his first wife and a custody battle with missus number two, from whom he was separated. It's what they didn't know that concerned them most. His propensity for running up debts plus his alleged associations with Mafia wiseguys made for a potentially dangerous equation.

"At the time he jumped the club," sportswriter Maury Allen recalls, "there were rumors he was involved in drugs. There were *always* rumors about drugs."

Pepitone rejoined the team in time for a weekend series in Chicago. Houk listened to Pepitone's woes and decided the most prudent action was to take none at all against the highly sensitive first baseman. "Joe was like a little boy," he says paternally. "He wanted to do well. He just got misled a couple of times."

Two weeks later it happened again. On August 26, a Tuesday, Pepitone begged out of the lineup with a stiff neck for the second straight day. But before game time, he quietly slipped from the bench and, without permission, left Yankee Stadium.

This time The Major was enraged. Wednesday he summoned Pepitone to his office and ordered him to suit up and remain in the dugout all game. A few innings into New York's 6–3 victory over the White Sox, however, Houk glanced down the bench: no Joe. He had all day Thursday, an off-day, to decide upon an appropriate punishment.

When Pepitone arrived at the ballpark Friday afternoon for a night game against Kansas City, Houk socked him with a $500 fine. The twenty-eight-year-old listened impassively, then bolted from the ballpark, at which point Houk imposed an indefinite suspension on top of the fine.

Through the Labor Day weekend Pepitone's exact whereabouts

remained a mystery, even to his worried mother, whom he'd gotten to make his excuses. "She called in for him, like you call in for a kid going to school, to say, 'Joe can't make it in today,' " Tom Shopay remembers. "It was sad."

The Yankees players shrugged off Pepitone's truancy as just his latest exploit. "After a while," says pitcher Jack Aker, "it became something of a joke with us that if we didn't see him at his locker by batting practice, we'd try to guess what he was doing this time: on a sailing excursion? Maybe he'd gone off to California. We never knew where he was going to be.

"I guess if we'd been in a pennant drive, we'd have really gotten upset with him, because he was a key player for the club." That fact often got overlooked amid all the attention paid to Number 25's antics. He stroked a team-high 27 home runs in 1969 and for the third time led the league's first sackers in fielding percentage. In his absence, Houk had to start Jimmie Hall (.236 BA) and Len Boehmer (.176).

"But there wasn't any real animosity," continues Aker, acquired in a May trade with the Seattle Pilots. "Pepi had such a great personality, that even if we did get upset with him—maybe we were counting on him to play and he didn't show—the next day he'd walk in as if nothing had happened, crack a couple of jokes, we'd laugh, and we'd all be buddies again. I think even Ralph had to laugh sometimes, when he'd get on Pepi about something and Joe came up with some off-the-wall excuse. Only first he'd go back into his office and close the door."

An uncharacteristically contrite Pepitone emerged from seclusion on Monday to publicly apologize to his manager in front of a barrage of press. At $250 per, the five games missed bled an additional $1,250 from a $40,000 salary that in all likelihood already belonged to someone else. Bleary-eyed from lack of sleep, Pepitone did surprise many at the press conference with his admission that he was exhausting his employer's tolerance.

"If I continue like this, what do I have?" he said. "Maybe not a year."

Prophetic words. On December 4, the Yankees found their problem child a foster family. Pepitone tried putting a positive spin on the deal that sent him to the Houston Astros in exchange for outfielder Curt Blefary, saying he welcomed the change of scenery. But there was sadness, on both sides, that the native New Yorker's tenure in pinstripes had come to an end.

To no one's great surprise, Pepitone's promise that "things are going to be different in Houston" turned out to be as empty as Texas skies. From the start he clashed with the strict Harry Walker, whom no one ever accused of being a player's manager. After incurring his second fine in late July Pepitone staged a sit-down strike and a week later found himself in a Chicago Cubs uniform.

The Windy City took to him warmly, and he responded for a while, batting a career-high .307 in 1971. But the following season he abruptly retired in May, only to reconsider a month later. Pepitone's teammates, fighting for a pennant, did not appreciate his routine one bit.

"It was completely different than on the Yankees," says Aker, who joined him there in 1972. "There was a lot of animosity toward him." Steve Hamilton, also a Cub that season, was curious to see if the passage of time had matured Pepitone any. Nope. "Joe was still Joe," he says. "Had a new woman and a motorcycle. That was the big difference."

Sent to Atlanta in 1973, he played three games for the Braves before quitting once again. From there, Boltin' Joe took off to Japan, where an American ballplayer could prolong his career at several times his former salary. Ex-Yankees Clete Boyer, Roger Repoz, and Jim Lyttle all played there after leaving the majors.

It's not nearly as idyllic as it sounds. Resentful teammates frequently ostracize foreigners, or *gaijin*. And U.S. pros can be driven batty by the Japanese's anal-retentive approach to the game.

"They played what I called 'Pearl Harbor Baseball,' " says Lyttle. "It's all a surprise. Anything that shouldn't happen will happen." He offers an example. "I played six years for the Hiroshima team. One time against Nagoya we had a two-run lead early in the game. Their shortstop was up with men at second and third. He was a good fielder, but he couldn't get the ball out of the infield. So we played the infield in, and he hit a little hopper up the middle that just made it to the outfield grass. Both runners scored, and we lost, 3–2.

"I went to our head coach, who spoke pretty good English, and suggested that if we'd played at regular depth, only one run would have scored. I said, 'Early in the game, give them the tying run, but don't give them the go-ahead run.' He said, 'You're right, we shouldn't have done that.'

"Lo and behold, the very next day, the exact same situation: same score, same everything. And again we play the infield in, and this time their shortstop hits a one-hundred-ten hopper that just makes it into the outfield, both runs score, and we lose, 3–2.

"I went back to the coach. He just held up his palms and said, *'Japanese style.'* The coaches over there won't change anything, because if they do and the team loses, they get fired. It's a land of tradition."

Repoz, a survivor of six seasons in Japan in the 1970s, says, "Of the

Americans who have gone over there, I'd say maybe seventy percent don't last a year. I've seen guys fall flat on their faces because they can't take the system."

Needless to say, in a society as conservative as Japan's, Joe Pepitone's behavior practically stirred up an international incident. "Joe played for a team called the Yakult Atoms, and he really pissed them off," Repoz recalls. "He got advanced money, then jumped on the plane and came home, went back, then made it real obvious he didn't want to play over there, which really upset them." Pepitone's inglorious Japanese career lasted all of two weeks, but the fallout lingered long after he'd split back to the States on the pretense of trying to patch up his marriage.

"The next year I played for Yakult," says Repoz. "Normally there were twenty-four foreigners allowed, two per team. But Joe had pissed off the Atoms so much, they wanted only one import player for a while. So I played my first two years there as the only American on the team."

Pepitone seemed to believe that playing baseball for a living exempted him from responsibility and, at times, the law. Stripped of that status, his life took a sad turn when in 1988 he spent four months in Riker's Island Penitentiary for criminal possession of drugs and weapons.

New Yorkers seem willing to forgive lovable Number 25 almost anything, however. At Old Timers' Day he still elicits ovations that light up his face. Pepitone hams it up for the affectionate crowd, comically feigning a heart attack as he chugs from first to third on a base hit. His act may not play on Broadway anymore, but, ah, listen to those cheers.

Veteran Al Downing also bid the Bronx adieu under a cloud in 1969, although by that time many Yankees followers had probably forgotten he still belonged on the roster. The left-hander started only twelve games in 1968 (3–3, 3.52 ERA) and fifteen in 1969 (7–5, 3.38 ERA).

His problems began in spring training of 1968 with a mysterious sore arm that limited him to a dozen innings through July. In exasperation the Yankees sent their pitcher to the Mayo Clinic, where doctors came up with a startling diagnosis.

"They were examining me for my arm, and I fell asleep on the examining table," Downing recalls. "The doctor asked me, 'What's wrong with you?' I told him I'd been doing this since the fourth grade." Number 24's talent for napping anytime, anywhere had long been a source of amazement on the club. He'd been known to snooze in the trainer's room before crucial starts; even in the bullpen during the 1963 World Series. Tests revealed Downing suffered from narcolepsy.

Unfortunately, he says, "Their cure was worse than the disease: drugs. This was another thing that totally kept me out of the picture. I was taking Ritalin, which made me irritable and wired. So then I'd take Valium to go to sleep, but I'd end up getting maybe two hours of sleep a night. I lost sixteen pounds in two months.

"My girlfriend told me, 'Throw that stuff away; it's making you an evil person.' And it was. It changed my personality. So I stopped using the drugs."

The narcolepsy was never cured, though it doesn't appear to interfere with Downing's busy schedule. In addition to his radio talk show and Dodgers cablecasts, he runs a California baseball school. "I still doze off," he explains nonchalantly.

When Downing went in to discuss money for 1969, he was outraged to discover the Yankees expected him to take a pay cut. Though his contract contained a clause stipulating he could not be penalized due to injury, the club persisted anyway, claiming the pitcher hadn't been hurt, just sleepy. Downing refused to sign.

Because he didn't report to camp until mid-March, still a holdout, Number 24 stayed behind in Florida to work himself into shape. A few weeks into the season he called to say he was throwing the ball well and ready to come north, figuring the club would be pleased. Instead, club official Johnny Johnson told him, "You can't come yet."

"I said, 'I'm coming,' and I went," says Downing. "If they hadn't reached a settlement yet, that was their problem." The pitcher was having an accountant-agent negotiate on his behalf. "I got to New York, and they said, 'You can't suit up, because you haven't signed a contract,' " he recalls.

It was Downing's contention that he already *had* a contract, since under the traditional reserve clause then in effect a ball club could automatically invoke an expired contract for another year whether the player agreed with its terms or not. Had New York continued to bar Downing from playing, it is likely he could have become baseball's first free agent.

"In the end they conceded I'd been hurt and gave me the same salary as the year before," he says. "This was all over seventy-five hundred dollars, by the way, which in those days was a lot of money. But it was so unnecessary. After that, I felt like I couldn't trust them anymore."

Twenty-four hours after New York bounced Joe Pepitone to Houston, it sent Downing and catcher Frank Fernandez to Oakland for Danny Cater and Ossie Chavarria. "I was ready to go," says Downing, a 20-game winner with Los Angeles in 1971. "Actually, I was ready when Elston Howard left. It was like, 'Get me out of here.' "

VI

FEWER THAN 6,000 FANS were on hand for what would be Downing's last victory in pinstripes, an 8–2 thrashing of Cleveland on September 30. Compared with some other Yankee Stadium attendance figures during the final weeks of the season, that constituted a decent day at the box office.

While the Bronx Bombers chased the .500 mark, the "Miracle" Mets were shaking the Big Apple to its core with excitement. Nine and a half games behind Chicago on August 15, manager Gil Hodges's team of destiny kept gnawing away at the panicking Cubbies' lead until, on September 10, only a half-game separated the two. The Yankees, by now used to their precocious younger sibling grabbing New York's attention, drifted through September feeling utterly abandoned.

Night after night, The House That Ruth Built sat as deserted as a church on Super Bowl Sunday. "Mike Burke used to joke, 'We're playing private matches,' " vice president Howard Berk recalls. "Once I happened to be standing by the switchboard operator. She asked me, 'There's someone on the phone who wants to know what time the game starts.'

"I told her, 'Whatever time he can get here.' It was very depressing."

Many regulars only half-watched the action on the field, more absorbed in the Mets' play-by-play that blared from the radios they pressed to their ears. Batboy Thad Mumford describes the atmosphere in the old ballpark this way: "It felt like flies on a dead body."

The night the Amazin's swept past Chicago into first, that other New York baseball team was coming within five outs of being no-hit by Washington's Dick Bosman, 6–1. The only excitement was watching Steve Hamilton (3–4, 2 SV, 3.32 ERA) show off his new Folly Floater, a stop-action lob that arced high in the air, then wafted down as if by parachute. He'd been putting the crowd-pleasing pitch to use whenever a lopsided ballgame desperately needed enlivening.

Hamilton, then in his seventh Yankees season, unveiled the Folly Floater in April to a stunned Don Wert. The Tigers third baseman stood with his bat welded to his shoulder as the ball dropped tantalizingly through the strike zone and Hamilton flashed a sheepish grin. Next, Number 39 tried it out on Andy Etchebarren and caught the Baltimore catcher on the big toe. "But the umpire didn't let him go to first," he remembers, "because he didn't try to get out of the way."

Most batters fell into the appropriate spirit, laughing as they hacked away madly—but not all of them. In a July game at Yankee Stadium, the silver-haired left-hander tossed it up to serious-minded Frank Howard of Washington. Hondo was signaling for a time-out even before the Folly Floater touched down gently in Jake Gibbs's mitt for a strike.

"Frank asked, 'Mr. Ump, is that legal?' " Gibbs recalls. Ron Luciano assured him it most certainly was. Says Hamilton, "The first thing I learned about the Folly Floater was to pick the right umpire. Anytime Luciano was back there, you could throw it. He was a little off-center himself, so he loved something like that.

"Whenever I did throw it, I was really nervous," Hamilton confides, "because it's out of the ordinary. And in baseball, when you do something out of the ordinary, man, it's like you're spitting on the flag or something! I had a great fear of somebody hitting it out of the stadium and everyone thinking I was making fun of the game." The veteran's worries were groundless: in 1969 not one batter hit the blooper pitch safely.

Jack Aker, New York's top reliever in 1969 (8–4, 11 SV, 2.06 ERA, including a streak of 33 scoreless innings), points out, "The fans would laugh and all, but Steve was serious about trying to get hitters out with it. At that point in his career he was beginning to struggle a little bit, and he found a pitch that could get as many outs as laughs."

VII

FOR THE FIRST time since the downfall, the Yankees could look back at the end of a season and, with a bit of squinting, perhaps, discern genuine progress. There were the fine showings of Mel Stottlemyre (20–14, 2.82 ERA), Fritz Peterson (17–16, 2.55 ERA), and Roy White (.290 BA, 7 HR, 74 RBI), but especially Bobby Murcer.

After a sluggish June and July, the inconsistent rookie roared across the finish line at .259 BA, 26 HR, 82 RBI. Mickey Mantle, in his first full season, produced three fewer home runs and only five more ribbies. The Yankees felt confident enough in Murcer's ability and, just as important, his character, to install him in center field for the last five weeks of the season.

It was a deliberate symbolic gesture, designed to position him as a budding star in the tradition of Mantle and DiMaggio. "I was too young and naïve at the time to really think about what they were trying to do," Murcer says. "But obviously it made for a great story."

Despite these flickers of promise, 1969 severely tested the devotion of the ever-dwindling corps of Yankees supporters. Attendance dipped yet again to 1,067,996, fewer than half the number of New Yorkers who crowded into Shea Stadium that year. It's safe to assume some of them used to do their rooting up in the Bronx.

For those who kept the faith during the Mets' ascendancy, it was a painful, lonely vigil, not unlike hearing laughter echo from a party to which you—and only you—weren't invited. True Yankees fans looked with scorn upon those wayward brothers and sisters who strayed.

"Despicable frauds, worthless front-runners, precursors of yuppies," Bob Costas calls them. The ubiquitous sports broadcaster was then a high-school senior on Long Island and a Yankees rooter since early childhood.

"When you're a kid," he reflects, "if baseball really means something to you, you know that *your team is your team.* You can't change your team like you change your coat. There's something dishonorable about just attaching yourself to a new team, unless you have a damn good reason."

Costas still remembers vividly the first game he attended at Yankee Stadium, on the second-to-last day of the 1959 season. "I was seven years old," he says. "Afterward they used to open up the gates, and you could walk around the warning track.

"When we got to the monuments of Gehrig, Ruth, and Huggins in center field, I was so moved that I began to cry. Because having seen *Pride of the Yankees* and *The Babe Ruth Story*, I thought that they were buried there beneath the Yankee Stadium sod, which seemed entirely appropriate. My father tried to explain that while they *were* dead, they were buried someplace else. But I'd have none of it; I thought he was just trying to console me."

Costas remained true to his team throughout its decline but admits, "September of '69 felt really strange. Without Mickey Mantle, there was no focus. It was the first year I didn't have some connection to their glory years or some personal devotion to a player, although I kind of attached myself to Bobby Murcer. Then the Mets came out of nowhere.

"I remember watching the Mets on TV the night they clinched the pennant and listening to the Yankees game on the radio." The Yankees were in the process of falling to Boston 1–0 in overtime at Fenway Park. The contest was so far removed from most New Yorkers' consciousness, it might as well have been taking place somewhere in the Himalayas.

"Jerry Coleman was calling the play-by-play the moment the flash came across that the Mets had clinched," Costas recalls. "And it just felt pathetic and sad that this once-great franchise had been reduced to the point where their game is on the radio, it's utterly meaningless, and they have to tip their caps to *this team*."

The Amazin's had whipped St. Louis 6–0 at Shea Stadium, setting off a citywide celebration. All across the country, in fact, their miraculous reversal from ninth to first elicited cheers even from folks who'd never consulted the standings in their lives.

Like no other ball club before or since, the 1969 Mets served as a metaphor for all that was good about America: a shining example of baseball's underclass transcending expectations and circumstances to realize a seemingly impossible dream. Their subsequent upsets over the Atlanta Braves in the National League play-offs and the prodigious Baltimore Orioles in the World Series took on near-religious overtones as inspirational evidence that the meek had inherited the earth.

It was downright *sickening*.

Mike Burke graciously wired his Mets counterpart, M. Donald Grant, a message that encapsuled the feelings of Yankees' partisans everywhere: "As a New Yorker I am ecstatic. As a baseball person I am immensely pleased. As a Yankee I consider suicide the easy option."

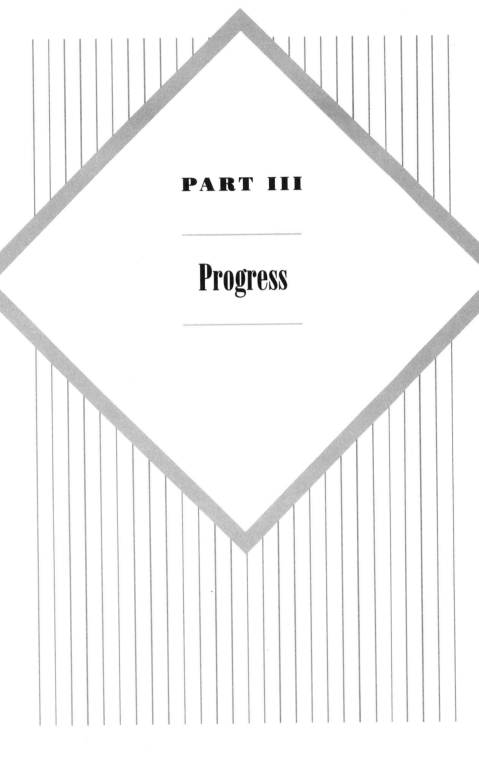

PART III

Progress

1970

STARTERS
Mel Stottlemyre
Fritz Peterson
Stan Bahnsen
Steve Kline
Mike Kekich

Danny Cater (1B)
Horace Clarke (2B)
Gene Michael (SS)
Jerry Kenney (3B)
Roy White (LF)
Bobby Murcer (CF)
Curt Blefary/Jim Lyttle/
Ron Woods (RF)
Thurman Munson (C)

RELIEVERS
Lindy McDaniel
Jack Aker
Ron Klimkowski
Steve Hamilton

I

THE NEW YORK Times's Dave Anderson once said of Ralph Houk's eternal optimism, "If he found a bomb on the *Queen Elizabeth II*, he'd tell the passengers how much they'll enjoy the lifeboats."

Each spring training, Number 35 would repeat his annual prediction: "We're a lot better than people think." No one took him too seriously, least of all Yankees fans. But in 1970, The Major strained credulity with his declaration that he'd been comparing the Yankees' and Mets' rosters, "and to be honest, I think we have the better team."

A chance to find out arrived two weeks into spring training, and the Yankees couldn't wait. The previous fall, when the entire country was consumed with the Mets' charge toward the pennant, not a word about it was uttered in the Yankees' clubhouse. "We completely avoided the subject," says Jack Aker, who finished his career with the Mets in 1974. "We never even acknowledged that the Mets played in the same town."

In fact, the Yankees seethed with resentment. Chief among the Mets-haters was Fritz Peterson. "The Mets had a lot of people who could use their mouths pretty well, like Tom Seaver," he recalls sourly. "They thought they were tremendous.

"I just could never see anybody being a Mets fan. And I still can't to this day! To me the Mets still aren't a real team." Peterson's harangue may defy all the evidence, but then, don't most baseball-related arguments?

His first few seasons, the left-hander could comfort himself by looking around and seeing legends such as Mantle, Ford, and Howard. "I used to say, 'I'd come out to see Mantle anytime before I'd go see the Mets.' But later, I didn't have that to fall back on, because we didn't have a whole lot for the fans to come see.

"I was just jealous," he finally admits.

The Met whom Peterson most wanted to see get hit with a fastball— or a paternity suit—wasn't Seaver, the brash, outspoken pitcher. "I respected him in a lot of ways," he says. Surprisingly it was Bud Harrelson, the comparatively mild-mannered shortstop. Why Harrelson?

Peterson ponders the question, then replies, "You know something? I don't even know! Except that Stottlemyre didn't like him. And anybody that Mel didn't like automatically had to be bad." He chuckles. "Real intelligent, huh?"

On March 18, the Mets swaggered into Fort Lauderdale Stadium for a Wednesday-night contest that was being televised back in New York. Both teams insisted the outcome didn't matter. Of course not. That's why Gil Hodges started his number-three pitcher, Gary Gentry, and not a rookie, and Ralph Houk countered with Stottlemyre and tapped Peterson to relieve. The Yankees trampled the World Champions 8–1 in a game Peterson calls "my most thrilling night in a uniform."

In addition to hurling six strong innings, Number 19 stroked a 375-foot home run off Mets relief ace Tug McGraw. "After I got the final out," he remembers, "Danny Cater and I both walked off the field holding our fingers in the air: 'We're number one.' We knew the game was on TV, and we were tired of seeing that stuff with the Mets the year before."

The win was the sixth in a row for the Yankees, who posted an 18–9 mark on the spring, their best in fifteen years. Most encouraging of all, the farm system had once again delivered an impressive pair of rookies.

Twenty-two-year-old Thurman Lee Munson came to camp assured of the starting catcher's job. At the urging of scout Gene Woodling, a former Yankees outfielder, New York had made him its top draft pick in June 1968, signing Munson out of Kent State University.

Gene Michael, another Kent State alumnus, already knew about him from visits to his alma mater. "The varsity baseball coach there told me how good Thurman was. After his junior year, he said to me, 'This kid will hit .300 in the big leagues right away.' I said, 'Three hundred? You're going to tell me he can hit eighty points higher than Jake Gibbs?' He insisted, 'I'm telling you he can hit .300 right now.' "

A $75,000 signing bonus in hand, Munson reported to the Yankees' double-A Binghamton club midseason and batted .301. He quickly established a reputation for cockiness, as Michael, soon to become a good friend, recalls:

"They'd scheduled a Binghamton game before our game at Yankee Stadium that summer, believe it or not. Thurman was on the bench, and I came out to watch. The first thing he said to me was, 'Hey, Stick, you're in on everything up here. When are you guys bringing me up?' " Michael was speechless. "He'd only played a portion of a year!"

Munson forced the Yankees to speed up their timetable by ravaging International League pitching in 1969. When promoted from Syracuse in August, he brought a .363 average with him. Although Number 15 didn't overwhelm during his two months in New York (.256 BA, 1 HR, 9 RBI in 26 games), the front office felt confident enough to pack off Frank Fernandez to Oakland.

To look at Munson, you'd hardly have figured him for an athlete, much less the Yankees' top prospect. Of course, the same thing was once said about an awkward-looking receiver named Lawrence Peter Berra. The youngster's doughy, nondescript face, distinguished only by a cleft chin, didn't take on character until he grew a droopy mustache years later. And Munson's chunky five-foot-eleven, 190-pound build made him a prime target for insulting nicknames, among them Squatty Body, Turtle, Round Man, and Pudge. "We loved to tease him," Jack Aker recalls.

Gibes about his physique were nothing new to Munson, who had been undersized as a boy. He had no compunction about giving it right back, but mostly he let his bat and glove do the talking, all the while projecting a cool confidence that said, "Just watch me play."

"Thurman came in very brash, from the first day," says Aker, "and we wondered if he could back up his words. But once we saw him catch and throw, we were amazed. None of us had ever seen a catcher release a ball to second base so quickly. It was just unbelievable."

A .368 BA in spring training wasn't enough to win Munson the team's annual James P. Dawson Award. That honor went to John Ellis, Munson's physical opposite. The twenty-one-year-old from New

London, Connecticut, stood a bullish six-foot-two, 225 pounds, all of it muscle. Had he not been a Yankees diehard since boyhood, he might have found fame on the gridiron.

"Football was my first love," says Ellis, a punishing high-school fullback and middle linebacker. "I was offered some college scholarships, but I opted to play baseball, only because I wanted to wear the Yankees pinstripes."

Ellis, also a catcher, was playing two levels below Munson but beat him to the majors. In May 1969 the Yankees ran into a temporary shortage behind the plate and summoned him from their class-A team at Kinston, North Carolina. In 62 at-bats, he hit .290 with 1 home run and 11 RBIs, then went down to triple-A about the same time that Munson received his call.

"I thought I was going to be the number-one catcher in 1970," Ellis recalls. "I'd never heard of a Thurman Munson; didn't know what it was." Their careers finally intersected in the off-season, when the Yankees decided Munson was by far the superior defensive player.

"Lee MacPhail told me they were going to trade Joe Pepitone and give me an opportunity to play first base," recalls Ellis. "I said, 'What the hell for? I'm the greatest catcher that ever lived.' Subsequently he told me about this guy Munson. Being a flexible individual, I went to learn first base in the instructional league, met Thurman in spring training, and we became good friends.

"Overall," Ellis concedes, "Thurman was a much better catcher than I was."

That spring, Number 23 put on a remarkable batting exhibition, driving home 18 runs in 18 games while putting up a batting average of .358. "John had the greatest spring I've ever seen an athlete have," recalls reserve first baseman Pete Ward, a veteran of two decades in the game as a player and minor-league manager. "He absolutely crushed the ball. To me he looked like he was going to be another Mickey Mantle."

On the day that the spring's outstanding rookie was being presented with his James P. Dawson Award watch, in another corner of the clubhouse the 1967 recipient, Bill Robinson, was packing his duffel bag for Syracuse, never to suit up again in a Yankees uniform.

After having raised his average to respectability in the second half of 1968, "I really thought I had it all together," he says. "And then the next year it started again: just trying too hard. It was the same shit, different day." Robinson hit a mere .171. Once the Yankees acquired outfielder Ron Woods for Tom Tresh in mid-June, he mostly warmed the bench.

He arrived for spring training 1970 half-expecting not to make the club. And after batting only .091 in Florida, his option to the minors, a week before Opening Day, came as little surprise. "Ralph Houk called me into his office," he remembers. "Elston Howard was there too." The former Yankees great had returned in 1969 as first-base coach. "The three of us began crying our eyes out. Ralph said, 'Hey, you're killing yourself. We're going to send you down to triple-A, where you can get off to a good start. This is probably the best thing in the world for you.' "

Robinson, praising Houk as "a man I've always loved," didn't argue. "I was hurt beyond belief, but Ralph had tried everything he could with me. I knew I had to go down, for my own sanity."

Robinson sank into obscurity for two and a half seasons, which turned out to be a blessing. "I wasn't in the limelight, highly visible in New York," he points out, "I was back in the minor leagues and trying to reestablish myself." In 1972, last-place Philadelphia recalled him from Eugene, Oregon, just as he was contemplating quitting.

"They brought me up along with Joe Lis, a first baseman–outfielder who was being ballyhooed as the guy the Phillies could really count on," Robinson recalls. "Joe had all the pressure on him, and I had none at all. I kind of snuck in through the back door, finally got a chance to play, and had a real good year in '73."

Batting .288, with 25 homers and 65 RBIs, dramatically resurrected his career at age thirty. Robinson went on to play another ten years in the National League, enjoying back-to-back .300 seasons for Pittsburgh in 1976 and 1977. The former Yankee who used to break bats in frustration became a highly respected batting coach and in 1992 assumed the managerial reins of the San Francisco Giants' minor-league affiliate in Shreveport, Louisiana.

II

THE OPTIMISM OF spring training vanished in a puff of smoke, as both Thurman Munson and John Ellis got off to abysmal starts, recalling all too vividly Bill Robinson's hellish beginnings.

Following a 3–0 blanking by Oakland that dropped New York into last place on April 25, Munson was hitting .155, with no home runs. In his first 30 at-bats the rookie catcher managed just one hit, including an 0-for-24 stretch.

Ellis's figures were even uglier: 3-for-28, .107 BA, 0 HR. "Ralph called me in and said, 'Lookit, I've got to take one of you two nuts out of the lineup,' " he recalls. " 'You're the one to go, because Thurman can catch.' " Only two weeks earlier, the Yankees were lauding Ellis as a star of the future. And now he was to ride the bench? Like a smoking inside fastball, it took him by surprise.

"I was really looking forward to the season," he says. "The night before Opening Day, I was introduced to Mrs. Eleanor Gehrig. I can remember meeting Paul Hornung and Frank Gifford, and being interviewed by them. And having people want to manage the ten dollars in my bank account."

On Opening Day, Lou Gehrig's widow sent him a note. "To John," it said. "For thirty years I've been looking for Lou's successor (if not better), and I'm rooting for you."

With every eye in the ballpark riveted on him, the phenom of spring training went 1-for-3, singling and scoring a run in the Bombers' 4–3 loss to Boston. He was just twenty-one years old and already the cleanup hitter for the New York Yankees.

"I really have to admit, I was awed by my position on the team," Ellis says in retrospect. "I was so distracted by meeting all these wonderful people, I probably lost focus on what I was supposed to do."

At least Ellis and Munson didn't have to feel solely responsible for the Yankees' 6–11 record. There was plenty of blame to go around. The starters had yet to complete a game. Mel Stottlemyre, winner of his first five decisions in 1969, was 0–3 and complaining of arm stiffness. The offense had produced a mere eight home runs, while Horace Clarke, Roy White, and Danny Cater were the only regulars hitting better than .250.

For the thirty-year-old Cater, a six-year veteran, New York was his fourth stop despite a .275 lifetime average, seventh best in the league. "I never did figure out why I kept getting traded," he says, but adds, "As long as I was playing, I didn't care where I was." He carried his bat from city to city like a mercenary toting his gun from war to war.

Cater guesses his subdued demeanor might have rubbed some managers the wrong way. "In the minors, everywhere I went I heard that I'd never make the major leagues because I didn't yell." Not that anyone would have heard him: the Texan speaks in a hoarse, high-pitched voice that reminds you of Andy Devine.

"Kerby Farrell, who managed me at Buffalo, and Frank Lucchesi, who managed me at Little Rock, both told me the same thing, that I needed to be more of a rah-rah guy. I said, 'That's not my way. If I can't make it with my bat, then I just won't make it.' " Ralph Houk didn't care if Cater took a vow of silence, pointing out that Joe DiMaggio was a pretty quiet fellow too.

Under The Major, Cater enjoyed his finest season: .301 BA, 6 HR, 76 RBI. Normally a first baseman, he opened 1970 at third, displacing Jerry Kenney. "I hated third," he says. "I was terrible there. But John Ellis had such a great spring, they had to put him somewhere." When Houk axed the rookie from the lineup, Cater returned to his favorite position and consistently hovered around .300 all year.

The Yankees owed several of their few early wins to Number 10. On April 20, he singled, doubled, and homered in an 11-2 romp over the Senators, then three days later rapped out four hits against Washington in an 11-6 bombardment. The weekend of May 1 he hit safely in all four games against the Milwaukee Brewers (last year's Seattle Pilots relocated and renamed, but with the same wretched roster). New York swept the series to boost its record to 13-12.

Monday, May 4, was a travel day to Oakland. When the Yankees checked into their hotel rooms and turned on the TV, news bulletins broke in with word of a violent disturbance at a previously little-known Ohio university named Kent State.

Some one hundred National Guardsmen had fired without warning upon student antiwar demonstrators, killing four and wounding nine. One of the fatalities, a twenty-year-old coed, wasn't even involved in the protest, but on her way to class, a hundred yards away.

A horrified Gene Michael, born in Kent, Ohio, couldn't believe what he was hearing.

"When I started school there in 1956, it was the most conservative, laid-back community you'd ever want to see," he says. "A pretty little town. It was called the Tree City. The school was laid back too. It was nice and easy.

"I thought, *Jeez, if it can happen there, it can happen anywhere.*"

Tuesday, while the Yankees practiced for their night game against the Athletics, Thurman Munson worried aloud if any of his friends still attending Kent State had been hurt in the incident. Details were still sketchy. National Guard officials initially insisted their troops had shot in response to sniper fire, a claim that was never substantiated. As the facts slowly emerged, it proved even more tragic than first imagined: an avoidable case of jittery, ill-prepared Guardsmen, many no older than the taunting, rock-hurling protestors, panicking and firing thirty rounds into a crowd that had already begun to scatter.

In the days immediately following the Kent State shootings, student unrest whipped higher. Violence flared at the University of California at Berkeley, a hotbed of activism not far from the Oakland Coliseum. There students skirmished with police, broke windows and set fires to buildings and a U.S. Army truck. To ease tensions, many colleges

and universities wisely shut down for the rest of the week. By the time
the Yankees left for Anaheim, on Thursday evening, the atmosphere
on the nation's campuses had cooled considerably.

Then it was the other side's turn to present its point of view. Days
after the club's return home in mid-May, tens of thousands proclaiming
themselves the "Silent Majority"—construction workers, housewives,
businessmen, secretaries—marched through Lower Manhattan in
support of President Richard Nixon's Indochina policies. The chasm
between left and right, young and old, never seemed more unbridge-
able.

Most Yankees, some of them Guardsmen themselves, sided with
the men in uniform. But apart from Michael's and Munson's concerns,
the violence at Kent State created barely a ripple in the New York
clubhouse. "Hardly anybody talked about it," recalls Mike Kekich,
one of the few players at that time who opposed the war.

"You have to understand that ballplayers are totally removed from
things like that," he says. "We have a totally structured life. We don't
even have to think for ourselves. We go through motions, and most
of those motions are not from some thought process, they're physical."

Another possible factor in the seeming indifference is the fact that
very, very few professional athletes faced the prospect of serving on
the front lines, making the distant war even more abstract. Of the
1970 Yankees, only pitcher John Cumberland set foot in Vietnam, and
he volunteered.

The other eligibles were able to enroll in the reserves, a six-year
obligation that required six months of active duty, weekly drills, and
two-week training camps each summer. As Stan Bahnsen can attest,
the frantic commuting from barracks to ballpark and back again sometimes took its toll.

"I'd be up for roll call at five in the morning, be out on the ranges
all day, then have to pitch a ballgame at eight at night," says Bahnsen,
a corporal in the First Battalion of the 389th Training Regiment at
Fort Dix, New Jersey. "I was never very sharp or effective mentally,
because I'd be tired by the time I got to the park." Midway through
his third full season, his record on days when he traded khakis for
pinstripes was 0–7. The right-hander finally won his first on Sunday,
August 16, 1970, against the Royals.

"One time I had to fly to Kansas City and be back the next day in
time for formation. It was a real tough situation. But," Bahnsen adds
gratefully, "I was still able to go after my profession."

Whether accurate or not, there was a growing public perception of
athletes as a privileged class exempt from having to fight—another
reason, perhaps, that few sports figures spoke out against the war.

"Once in a while you'd get a letter saying, 'My son died in Vietnam and you're over here ducking the draft,' " recalls Steve Kline, a twenty-two-year-old rookie right-hander who went 6–6, 3.42 ERA in 1970. Kline, from Chelan, Washington, served in the National Guard.

"I could understand those people's feelings, the resentment and antagonism," he says. "It was like it was being thrown up in their faces. So as far as being critical about the war, no, I wasn't."

III

WHILE STALLED IN his early-season slump, Thurman Munson had warned, "When I break out, it's really going to be something," sounding insanely confident for an .033 hitter. The Yankees secretly would have been thrilled to see Munson reach .250 by year's end. "Nobody expected much," recalls Jack Aker, "because anybody who could catch and throw like he did didn't have to hit a whole lot."

On April 20, the rookie from Canton, Ohio, added three hits to his grand total of one and from that point on scorched the ball at a .322 clip. His college coach probably collected on a few bets that fall, as Munson ended at .302, with 6 home runs and 53 RBIs. He was a near-unanimous choice for Rookie of the Year, becoming the sixth Yankee ever to win the award.

Opponents quickly learned to respect his arm as well as his bat. In 69 steal attempts, 40 would-be thieves trotted back to the dugout shaking their heads. But the young receiver still had much to learn behind the plate.

"At that time Thurman was thinking too much about his bat, and it bothered his catching a little bit," Ralph Houk recalls. "I don't think he really knew how important it was to call the right pitches." More than once Number 15 had upset the normally imperturbable Mel Stottlemyre by signaling for an overabundance of sliders, a poor game plan when your pitcher is bothered by a stiff elbow.

For all Munson's cockiness, he approached baseball with the old-fashioned work ethic of his blue-collar hometown. As a boy he practiced long after the other kids had gone home for supper. As a first-year pro he worked tirelessly with bullpen coach Jim Hegan to improve his game. "You've got to give Thurman a lot of credit," Houk says. "He made himself into a real fine catcher."

In front of family and friends at Cleveland Municipal Stadium, Munson banged out six hits in a manic May 24 doubleheader highlighted by eleven home runs. The Yankees came from behind to take both games, 6–5 and 8–7 in eleven innings, making a dual winner of Lindy McDaniel. Poor Indians reliever Fred Lasher went home a two-time loser.

New York's other offensive star, John Ellis, singled, doubled twice, and clubbed a pair of homers. In the eighth inning of game two, the forgotten rookie put one over the center-field fence with two aboard to shatter a 6–4 Tribe lead. But the next night in Detroit he resumed his seat on the bench because a righty was on the hill. That's the way it went all summer, resulting in a .248 average, 7 home runs, and 29 RBIs in 226 at-bats.

"Thurman went on to become Rookie of the Year," he reflects without bitterness. "I sometimes wonder, had I been allowed to stay in the lineup, maybe my statistics would have been at least as good." Though Ellis was to enjoy a respectable thirteen-year career playing for New York, Cleveland, and Texas, he never did find happiness in the uniform he'd wanted to wear most.

"I began to doubt Ralph Houk's belief in me," he says. "What convinced me was when we had a team meeting in Minnesota in August, and he asked everybody to write down which pitchers they found it difficult to hit against. 'Ellis,' he said, 'you put down "Everybody." ' In front of the whole team." For Houk to embarrass a player like that was extremely out of character.

"We're getting you in the lineup tonight, to see what you can do," the manager told him, to which Ellis replied pointedly, "Skip, I can't do it if I don't play."

"That night I went three-for-four with a home run and a double," he remembers, "and I still didn't get into the lineup the next day. I always requested to be traded. But they always tell you nobody wants you."

Ellis, married and a father of two, is surprisingly soft-spoken for a man remembered by teammates as a "powder keg," to quote Gary Waslewski, a reliever and spot starter picked up from Montreal in May. After a strikeout, the big first baseman would stalk back to the dugout, snap his bat in two like a twig, then bang his head against the wall in frustration. All that pent-up energy from sitting on the bench tended to expend itself as much off the field as on, landing Ellis in frequent trouble.

"John would have a couple of beers and become a wild man," says Waslewski. Ellis's reputation for bar fights and other mischief became so well known to the Fort Lauderdale police that during spring training, Waslewski recalls, "When John was with us, we'd have ten squad cars following us wherever we went, even if nothing was going on."

Ellis chuckles when reminded of his intemperate youth. "I was never invited to go with the guys anywhere," he protests. "I guess they didn't want to go with me. Fritz Peterson once said he took out insurance whenever I hung around."

These exploits did not enhance the youngster's standing with Yankees brass. "Lee MacPhail didn't like that type of publicity at all," Steve Kline remarks. "I think in the long run that kind of hurt John and had a lot to do with why he didn't play, and why he got traded, ultimately."

Waslewski, a fellow Connecticut Yankee, observed at the time that beneath Ellis's rough-and-tumble exterior lurked "a scared kid."

"John was looked upon as the next Messiah who was going to bang out all these home runs," says the pitcher, several years Ellis's senior. "Things were happening so big for him in New York, I don't think he really knew how to handle it at first. I think he felt more accepted by getting into fights and getting drunk and causing all kinds of problems. And guys thought that was great, something to laugh about. 'Oh, John, you're nuts!' He loved to hear that stuff."

Ellis doesn't deny it. "I'm not defending my own stupidity," he says. "This is going to sound really terrible, but I *liked* a good fistfight now and then." He had been thrown off his high-school baseball team for brawling.

After retiring from the game at thirty-three, Ellis faced the toughest fight of his life when he was diagnosed with Hodgkin's disease. "My brother had passed away from it, and my sister also, prior to that. I really didn't expect that I would live . . ."

The cancer extracted a good deal of weight as well as some of his old pugnaciousness. Ellis, his illness in remission since 1986, says the ordeal made him realize that "It's a blessing to live life every day." He now runs his own real-estate business back in New London.

IV

ONCE AGAIN NEW Yorkers were invited to a pennant race, only this year the Bronx, as well as Queens, played host. A 15–11 May delivered the Yankees home from the road in second place, seven and a half games behind Baltimore.

The first half of June the club rolled to an 11–1 record, and for the first time in quite a while, ushers at Yankee Stadium found themselves actually busy during games. Bat Day attracted a gate of 65,880, baseball's largest since 1965. Not everyone came just for the free bat, either.

Besides winning, Ralph Houk's crew was stirring excitement with a style of baseball that was new to the Bronx. Only Bobby Murcer and Roy White reached double figures in home runs on the year; obviously this Yankees club couldn't rely on the old five o'clock lightning. Instead, it finessed its way to victory, seeming to follow a new script each day.

Against Kansas City on June 4, Horace Clarke roped a single to foil Jim Rooker's 1–0 no-hit bid in the ninth, then scored the tying run on a Murcer double. In the bottom of the twelfth, the little second baseman lofted a bases-loaded sacrifice fly for a 2–1 New York win.

"I'd been no-hit once in the minors," Clarke says, "and it didn't leave a good taste in my mouth." Apparently not, because over the next four weeks he broke up two other no-hitters in the ninth, victimizing Sonny Siebert of Boston, then Joe Niekro of Detroit.

No one better exemplified the Yankees' battling spirit than Gene Michael. On June 13, the resourceful shortstop employed the ancient hidden-ball trick to snuff a Kansas City rally in a game New York eventually took in overtime, 9–4. Royals rookie Joe Keough had just tied the score at three apiece in the sixth and hustled into second on the throw home.

Michael casually walked the ball back to the mound and pretended to hand it to pitcher Gary Waslewski. Then he jogged back to his position, making sure to subtly give Emmett Ashford a glimpse of the ball still in his webbing so that the second-base ump wouldn't miss the play.

If there *was* to be a play. Keough, happily replaying his clutch hit in his mind, wouldn't budge off second, while Michael hovered nearby and Waslewski racked his brain thinking of ways to stall without time being called.

"I don't know whether it was thirty seconds, a minute, or what, but boy, it seemed like an eternity," he says. "What the heck do you do? I walked around behind the mound, picked up the resin bag and put it in my glove so they saw something white there, walked around some more, bent over as if to fix a shoelace. Jesus, I was trying everything. Just as I was about to give up, I heard the ump shout, 'Yer out!' "

Waslewski asked Michael how he'd finally gotten Keough to leave the bag. "I asked him to move so I could clean it off," he replied innocently. Later that summer the shortstop embarrassed California's Jarvis Tatum, also in a critical situation.

"It was easy enough to do," Michael says of the hidden-ball trick. "I didn't know it was going to get so much attention, or I would have done it more!"

A throwback to an earlier era, Number 17 would likely have felt right at home among wily John McGraw and Wee Willie Keeler on the legendary Baltimore Orioles teams of the 1890s. What he lacked in physical talent he made up for in cunning. It kept Michael in the majors as a player until he was thirty-eight despite a .229 career average.

"Gene was a scrapper," says Waslewski. "Very crafty and very quick. What he accomplished—he earned every bit of it. If you needed a double play, he was one of the guys you liked to have handling the ball. I don't know how many times I saw him stand there on the pivot, turn the double play, get killed, then get right back up and get into the middle of another one, without flinching.

"He was also great for that low throw to first base. In the minors I'd seen him drill runners between the eyes. I mean, they carried guys off the field. Gene Michael had a reputation, boy: you'd better get down, or this guy's going to put one right through you."

Michael and two other regulars, Jerry Kenney and Curt Blefary, all hit below .215 in 1970. Fortunately, off-season trades had strengthened the bench. Ralph Houk made judicious use of newcomers Pete Ward (.260 BA) and Ron Hansen (.297), along with Jake Gibbs. The trio, all onetime starters now limited to reserve roles late in their careers, could be called on for timely hitting.

Ironically, Gibbs, thirty-one, achieved career-high numbers in average (.301) and home runs (8) the same year he lost the starting catcher's job it had taken him so long to claim. The native Mississippian spent ten years in the major leagues wondering if he'd been right to choose baseball over football back in 1961.

Gibbs, a stocky six-footer, starred at quarterback for the University of Mississippi, leading the undefeated Rebels to the Sugar Bowl in 1960. He was also an infielder, and attended school on both a baseball scholarship and a football scholarship. The summer before his senior year, the Milwaukee Braves offered him a $100,000 signing bonus. But Gibbs, feeling obligated to fulfill his four-year commitment to Ole Miss, turned them down.

Braves scouts watched him from the stands every Saturday during his final college-football season. "I can remember, we was 6-0 and rated the number-one team in the nation," Gibbs recalls in a lazy drawl, "and we went down to play Tulane.

"It was homecoming, and there was about seventy-two thousand people in the stands. On one of the plays, I rolled out to my right, and after I threw the ball, some tackle hit me and drove my right shoulder into the ground. I don't know if he hit a nerve, but it started hurting real bad.

"I knew those Braves people were up in the stands, scouting me.

As I went running off the field, I saw all those dollar bills just flying away. Fortunately it wasn't a serious injury."

After graduation Gibbs had five teams clamoring for him: the Braves, the Yankees, and the expansion Houston Colt .45's, as well as the football Houston Oilers and the Cleveland Browns. Gibbs, then twenty-two and about to be married, returned home to Grenada, Mississippi, where his daddy had been a three-term county supervisor, to mull over his future.

"It was a heavy decision to make," he says. "Of course, down in the South, football is king. I think I upset a lot of people when I went with baseball. But baseball was my first love. When I was a boy I used to listen to the *Game of the Day* on radio. And it seemed like most of them were between Detroit and New York.

"And here's a little old country boy that became a Detroit Tigers fan in 1950. I could name their whole starting lineup: Hoot Evers, Vic Wertz, Johnny Lipon . . . I never had any feelings about the Yankees.

"But as I grew older," he continues, "I started following them, because they had such a great team. They had the history, all those great ballplayers, and they won everything. When I was in high school I did a book report on Lou Gehrig. And I think that's probably one of the main reasons I chose the Yankees over the other ball clubs, because of their winning tradition."

Gibbs accepted New York's $105,000 offer to sign, a huge wad by Yankees standards, and started off in triple-A at Richmond. He batted .270 in 1961 and .284 the next year, playing shortstop. While putting in his six months of basic Army training at Fort Benning, Georgia, the winter of 1962, Gibbs found out that the Yankees weren't viewing him as the eventual successor to Tony Kubek.

"One morning this captain asked me, 'Are you the Gibbs that plays baseball?'

" 'Yep.'

" 'Well, I've got this friend in Augusta, and he tells me you're gonna be a catcher come spring training.'

"Nobody in the Yankees organization had ever mentioned the word *catcher* to me," says Gibbs. "I told him, 'Your friend must be mistaken. I just had a pretty good year at shortstop.' And I kind of let it go."

The first day of spring training Ralph Houk confirmed the rumor, telling Gibbs that because of his football background the front office felt he could quarterback a ball game from behind the plate. "It's the quickest way up to the big leagues," The Major said, which was true. Kubek was just twenty-six at the time; Elston Howard, thirty-three.

In four years of absorbing hits by 250-pound defensemen, Gibbs never suffered an injury. His first year wearing the tools of ignorance he busted two fingers. Plus, his legs, unaccustomed to the squatting, ached all the time. He concentrated so much on catching that he neglected his hitting, slumping to .233. His 1964 average was just .218. "I took a lot of pride in becoming a good defensive catcher, and I got into some bad habits at the plate," Gibbs says. "It took me a long time to get out of them."

The bad breaks, literally and figuratively, continued. New York promoted Gibbs in September 1964 and added him to its World Series roster. As unhappy as he'd been the past two years, it was worth it to finally be a part of the winning legacy that had attracted him to the Yankees. The day after clinching the pennant, Yogi Berra started Gibbs in the season finale, a meaningless affair against Cleveland.

"In the thirteenth inning, I broke my finger," he recalls dryly. "They had to take me off the eligible list for the Series and put on Mike Hegan." Gibbs would have been far more distraught had he known his sole chance to play in the Fall Classic had just passed him by.

When Johnny Keane sent him down to Toledo the following spring, Gibbs could no longer ignore the nagging feeling that he'd made a terrible mistake signing with this club. "That really hit me right in the nuts," he recalls. "Since joining the Yankees, I'd played third, short, second, and first. And here I was a catcher now.

"Never in my life had I raised my voice to a superior, 'cause we weren't raised that way, but I said, 'Johnny, I've done every damn thing in this organization that y'all have asked me to do except pitch. When are y'all gonna make me a pitcher?' "

Gibbs angrily told Keane, "I'm not sure that I'm *going* back to the minors. I'd just as soon pack my damn bags and go home to Mississippi, get me a high-school football coaching job, and say the hell with it." By then he was twenty-six, with one young son and another on the way.

After discussing it with his wife, Gibbs reported to triple-A after all, and received a second call to the majors that June. He averaged a meager .221, but in 1966 batted a respectable .258 while platooning with Elston Howard. On August 3, 1967, his chance to take over behind the plate arrived at long last.

Hearing of Howard's trade to Boston called forth mixed emotions. "I hated to see Ellie go," he says, "because we had become good friends, and he'd helped me a lot as a catcher. But his leaving was my break to step in and take over."

It never happened: Gibbs batted .233 in 1967 and .213 in 1968, his one full season. By mid-1969 the Yankees were fixing their sights on the two youngsters, Munson and Ellis. Gibbs says he understood. "I look back and I don't blame the Yankees, I blame myself. I had the opportunity. If I'd hit .270 in '69, then it would have been a battle the next spring training. But I didn't." He batted only .224, with no home runs.

For Gibbs, 1970 was bittersweet. "Tough but enjoyable," he says. Number 41 could plainly see that his replacement was a burgeoning superstar. "I never felt any animosity toward Thurman. In fact, I worked with him, giving him pointers about the pitching staff. Like all Yankees back then, we helped one another."

Although Gibbs never developed into a catcher of Munson's caliber, he did achieve his goal of becoming a defensive asset. "I'm not trying to demean Elston Howard in any way," says Steve Hamilton, "but Jake was the best catcher I ever threw to. He's a smart baseball man." It's indicative of the respect Gibbs commanded that when he decided to retire at the end of 1971 and return to Ole Miss as head baseball coach, the Yankees fêted him with a farewell *à la* Bobby Richardson and Mickey Mantle.

"I feel very fortunate," he reflects, still tickled at the memory. "Here you have an old country boy with a lifetime average of .233, and they give you a day! They recognize you, I guess, for your dedication and effort. No, you wasn't a star, but you gave your all," says Gibbs, a Yankees coach in 1993. "In my den I still have the big painting they gave me, of me swinging the bat, and Yankee Stadium in the background."

In Boston on June 20, Gibbs went 2-for-4 and drove in two runs in New York's 8–3 win. The next day it was back to warming up pitchers in the bullpen, which is where he remained during both ends of a madcap June 24 doubleheader against the Indians at home. Game one was shaping up as fairly routine when 34-year-old Steve Hamilton came on to pitch the ninth with Cleveland ahead 7–1.

Leading off was Tony Horton, who in May had joined Boston's Rico Petrocelli as the only batters to get a hit off the Folly Floater in a regulation contest. Before the game, Horton collared Number 39 and pleaded for another chance.

"You threw me that pitch and my whole life passed in front of my eyes," he said. "Throw it to me again. I can hit the ball out of the park."

"Nah, Tony, no one can hit the Floater out of the park," drawled the tall left-hander.

"*I* can hit it out," Horton dared. He'd smacked 27 round-trippers in 1969 and at the age of twenty-five was considered one of the league's up-and-coming stars.

"All right, I'll throw it to you."

Hamilton picks up the story: "So I get to face Horton. He's looking at me, and I nod at him. But he's not real sure yet. I throw him one Folly Floater, and he fouls it off. He then walks out in front of the plate and says, 'One more!' holding up a finger. So I in turn make the 'okay' sign."

The crowd of 32,000 roared as Hamilton gingerly arced the ball to the plate. Horton nearly screwed himself into the ground trying to belt it into the upper deck. Instead he popped up weakly behind the plate. While the stadium went bonkers, Horton tossed his bat in the air, threw up his hands, then crawled back to the visitors dugout in mock shame on his hands and knees.

"The pinnacle of the Folly Floater," says Hamilton, who was traded that September to the White Sox. He now serves as athletic director at Kentucky's Morehead State University, his alma mater.

Game two also featured its share of entertainment. The fifth inning alone included Indians outfielder Vada Pinson colliding with Stan Bahnsen in a bang-bang play at home, then blindsiding the pitcher with a left hook to the jaw, and Cleveland catcher Ray Fosse dancing behind home plate after a cherry bomb hurled from the stands exploded at his feet.

Bobby Murcer's bat provided the afternoon's biggest blasts. The center fielder tied a major-league mark by collecting four home runs in four consecutive at-bats: one in the opener, three in the nightcap. His fourth, off Fred Lasher in the eighth, tied the game at 4–4. The Yankees then sent across another run and held on to win.

The next night, Murcer came to bat in the first, looking to break the record shared by Mickey Mantle and Ted Williams, among others.

"They had this young phenom just out of college pitching, Steve Dunning, and Alvin Dark, the Cleveland manager, was calling all the pitches from the dugout," he remembers. "The first time up, they walked me. This kid was throwing me 3-and-0 breaking balls! I guess Dark was determined not to let me hit the fifth home run." In the third inning, Number 1 checked his swing at a slider and popped up.

Dark halted Murcer, but not the Bronx Bombers, whose 3–1 win upped their record to 42–27 (.609). Only two and a half games stood between them and Baltimore. The newly confident Yankees couldn't help peeking at the scoreboard to see how the Birds were faring.

"There was no doubt in my mind that we could win the son of a bitch," says John Cumberland, a chunky left-handed spot starter and long reliever and today the Milwaukee Brewers' minor-league pitching coordinator. "If you went around the league, maybe we didn't have the talent of the other clubs, but we were right in the hunt. It was almost like the '69 Mets. With a ball bounce here, and a ball bounce there . . ."

The 1970 club's starting trio of Mel Stottlemyre (15–13, 3.09 ERA), Fritz Peterson (20–11, 2.91), and Stan Bahnsen (14–11, 3.32) stacked up against any threesome in the league. Only the Orioles' Jim Palmer, Mike Cuellar, and Dave McNally won more games, and they benefited from unparalleled offense and defense.

One department in which New York could claim superiority was the bullpen, outstanding for its depth as well as its effectiveness. Anytime the Yankees took a lead past the sixth inning, the outcome was rarely in doubt. Rookie Ron Klimkowski (6–7, 1 SV, 2.66 ERA) excelled in middle relief, then either Lindy McDaniel (9–5, 29, 2.01), Jack Aker (4–2, 16, 2.06), or Steve Hamilton (4–3, 3, 2.78) would come in to slam the door shut.

McDaniel, a lay preacher who published a monthly newsletter called *Pitching for the Master*, provided especially divine intervention, setting a new team high for saves. Number 40 had been so discouraged with his 1969 performance (5–6, 5 SV, 3.55 ERA) that over the winter he'd considered quitting baseball to tend to his ministry at the Pruett and Lobit Street Church of Christ in Baytown, Texas.

On the mound the forkball was his strength, but off the diamond it was the Bible. "All during my career I'd been engaging in religious work during the off-season," says McDaniel. Aside from one year of formal Bible study in college, he describes himself as "basically self-educated."

When McDaniel took a $50,000 bonus to become a St. Louis Cardinal in 1955, the nineteen-year-old made it clear that Sunday-morning services would have to take precedence over pregame practice. "It was a condition of my signing," he recalls. "And that was passed on to every organization I played for. Since it was a conscientious position, I never had a problem with any manager over it."

Twenty-one years in the major leagues certainly must have convinced McDaniel, a man of delicate sensibilities, of the desperate need for preachers. He saw so many, many souls that needed saving. How did he reconcile teammates' profanity, promiscuity, and other behavior that clashed with his religious convictions?

"I accepted it as just part of what you deal with in life," he says. "As a friend of mine once put it, 'Lindy, if we associated only with angels, we wouldn't do them any good, we'd only corrupt them.' So my philosophy is, you have to work with people and deal with them where they are. If you can have an influence on them, fine. I wasn't trying to reform everyone," he emphasizes, "or buttonholing them concerning my beliefs."

Even so, in the past, McDaniel had sometimes been made to feel like an outsider. But not in New York, he says. "I look back on my time with the Yankees as some of my most enjoyable years in baseball. I was fully accepted by the players from the beginning."

That didn't prevent them from ribbing him mercilessly in the hopes of coaxing a wry smile. Jim Lyttle, whose conversations with McDaniel about the Bible led him to convert from the Baptist Church to the Church of Christ, recalls, "We were on the bus to the ballpark one day when a convertible with a very good-looking girl in it pulled up alongside.

"Some of the guys were knocking on the windows, trying to get her attention." McDaniel wasn't one of them. To Pete Ward, sitting across the aisle, this seemed a shameful waste of a perfectly good window seat. "Pete said, 'Lindy, if you're not going to look at her, I'll give you a dollar for your seat.' Lindy smiled, and then everybody cracked up."

Gary Waslewski adds, "We used to get on Lindy about these young ladies we'd see leaving his hotel room. Supposedly he was talking the Bible to them. Guys would say, 'Lindy, what are you doing, putting the *fear of God* in her? And was that her in there yelling, "Oh God! Oh God!"' We used to really get him going."

McDaniel's post-baseball calling as a full-time preacher has taken him to such places as Merriam, Kansas, Las Vegas, New Mexico, and, most recently, Selma, California.

"It becomes a matter of where you think you can do the most good," explains McDaniel. "We have about one hundred people in our congregation. Lots of Asians and Hispanics, and people from Texas and Oklahoma. For me it's the most challenging thing I could be doing."

V

ON JULY 7, McDANIEL faced the awesome challenge of digging himself out of a bases-loaded, none-out jam in the tenth inning of a tie ball game, the first of three crucial matchups between the Yankees and the Orioles. Crucial to New York, that is, which came into Baltimore five and a half games out. For their part, the nonchalant Birds acted more concerned about an upcoming series against third-place Detroit.

The Yankees had already reeled themselves in from the brink of defeat once tonight. Mike Cuellar was one strike from putting away the ball game, 2–1, when John Ellis drilled a single to send Roy White pedaling home. Ralph Houk then called on his top reliever, 7–2 on the season thus far.

In the tenth, a contested walk, a base hit, and a botched force play at second by Gene Michael put McDaniel in his present predicament, which deepened with each delivery to Brooks Robinson. The Yankees battery was certain that home-plate umpire Jerry Neudecker secretly sported an Orioles T-shirt under his blue jacket.

"I was hitting the corner, pitch after pitch," McDaniel recalls, "and they were all being called balls. Robinson should have been struck out three times." Thurman Munson argued one pitch, bringing Houk rumbling out of the dugout, and beefed about yet another, to no avail. The Orioles third baseman then plowed McDaniel's full-count offering into the left-field stands for a game-ending grand slam.

New York demonstrated its resiliency once again in game two, overcoming deficits of 3–0 and 6–5 to climb on top, 8–6. Going into the bottom of the ninth, Houk depended on Number 40 to preserve the win.

Frank Robinson led off with his second home run of the night, a 450-foot moon shot. Three batters later, McDaniel found himself in the same situation as the night before: Orioles perched on each base and nobody out.

Earl Weaver, following by-the-book strategy, sent up two left-handed pinch hitters. McDaniel, however, required a different reading list than most right-handers. "Evidently, managers didn't figure out that I got lefties out better than righties," he says. Feeling he didn't have full command of his other pitches on this warm evening, McDaniel decided to go exclusively with the forkball, which was dropping as sharply as a jet plane encountering wind shear.

In came three low-and-away forkballs to Terry Crowley. *Whoosh. Whoosh. Whoosh.*

Three more to Elrod Hendricks. *Whoosh. Whoosh. Whoosh.*

Pesky Don Buford, a switch-hitter, stepped in from the left side. Swing: strike one. Swing: strike two. That made eight swinging strikes in a row. "The greatest piece of relief pitching I've ever seen," Pete Ward calls McDaniel's performance.

With the count 0-and-2, Munson didn't even have to put down a sign. "Normally you don't throw nine pitches all the same in a row," McDaniel acknowledges. "That violates all the rules of pitching. But there wasn't any question between Thurman and me that we would go with the forkball, because it was practically unhittable. It didn't matter if they knew it was coming."

Buford, looking like a man about to try catching a bullet in his teeth, lunged at the pitch and sent a feeble roller into the gap between first and second. *Just past* Danny Cater's reach. *Just past* Horace Clarke's outstretched glove. As right fielder Jim Lyttle charged in, one run was already across, and the Birds' third-base coach was frantically windmilling Davy Johnson around.

Lyttle fired home, a bit up the line. Munson gloved it, spun, and dove onto an empty plate, for Johnson had slid past him in a hail of dirt with the winning run. The rookie catcher lay there for several minutes while a deflated Yankees squad shuffled toward the clubhouse.

"Ralph came into the locker room livid," recalls Curt Blefary, whose two-run blow in the top of the eighth had supplied the Yankees their fragile 8–6 lead. "I'm surprised the man didn't have a heart attack. He kicked a large trash container, not realizing it was full of beer and ice, and almost broke his leg."

McDaniel sat in front of his locker, second-guessing his pitch selection. "That was probably one of the biggest disappointments in my whole life," he says. "I felt terrible. Because that was a situation where a pitch was too good. If I had thrown a fastball, it wouldn't have even been swung at. It's one of those things you look back on and say, 'What if?' "

The Yankees salvaged game three, but not without an assist from Mother Nature. For the third night in a row they flipped off an Orioles advantage, pulling ahead 7–5 on three unearned runs in the top of the sixth. Two outs remained in the home half when the soggy skies that had been toying with the action all night opened up.

Ralph Houk paced the dugout and waved frantically at reliever John Cumberland to hurry up and retire Don Buford. Under the existing rule, should the contest be called without completing the inning in its entirety, the final score would revert to 5–4, Baltimore. "Cumberland kept stopping to get the mud out of his spikes," recalls Jerry Kenney, 3-for-3 with three ribbies. "Ralph was pretty upset." Buford struck out to end the inning, making the game official.

The rain stopped, then returned in the eighth. This time Houk beseeched the heavens to keep on pouring. After a forty-minute delay, at 11:35 P M umpire Hank Soar declared the game over. New York, having lost ten of its last twelve, celebrated with champagne, although in keeping with the team's recent ragged luck, "I popped the cork, and it hit Mickey Mantle," a clubhouse visitor, "right in the jaw," Cumberland remembers. The moral of the night seemed to be: when playing the Orioles, try never to let the game go beyond the eighth.

On the ride to Washington, their next stop, memories of those 6–2 and 9–8 heartbreakers were hard to shake. "It was dark and quiet on the bus," says pitcher Steve Kline, who had just been called up from Syracuse, "when all of a sudden a voice went, 'It looks like the only way you're going to beat Baltimore is with knives and guns.'

"Ralph Houk leaped up in front. 'Stop the bus! Stop the bus! Who

said that?' It was Joe Trimble from the *Daily News*." The Major proceeded to revile the reporter at the top of his lungs, then growled,
"The next guy who tells me we can't beat a ball club is going to walk
from here!"

"Ralph would have done it, too," Kline says, laughing. "In my mind
I pictured poor Joe in the red taillights, walking down the freeway
with his bag and typewriter."

Though the players applauded Houk's tirade, most privately agreed
with Trimble. Going into the series, former Oriole Curt Blefary had
attempted to rally his teammates, insisting, "We can beat these guys.
They ain't got no S's on their chests." The three games suggested he
take a closer look.

Baltimore, en route to a 108–54 record and the World Championship, was simply invincible, a dynasty in the mold of the great New
York clubs: great bats, great gloves, great arms, and the psychological
edge you get from believing that the breaks of the game will go your
way and that victory is inevitable. "When you're the number-one
club," says Gary Waslewski, "the little dribblers go through, and the
umpires give you the close calls. It felt like we were playing against
thirteen guys out there."

That series also awakened the Yankees to their very real shortcomings. "It made us realize we didn't have that one special performer on
our team," John Ellis reflects. "We put up our best, and it just wasn't
enough. I think everybody believed right then that the season was
over."

As Blefary puts it, "The fizz went out of the soda pop."

VI

JIM BOUTON RETURNED to haunt the Yankees in 1970, not between
the lines but between the covers of a book. Its premise hardly sounded
promising: the diary of a thirty-year-old marginal pitcher trying to
stay afloat with the last-place Seattle Pilots and the pennant-chasing
Houston Astros.

But *Ball Four: My Life and Hard Times Throwing the Knuckleball
in the Big Leagues* turned out to be a milestone in sports journalism,
an iconoclastic, unexpurgated look at the national pastime and the men
who played it, told with playful humor.

There were revelations of substance abuse, a colorful lexicon of
clubhouse scatology, and such shockingly comic scenes as ballplayers
kissing one another and "beaver shooting," a popular practice that

basically boiled down to high-tech voyeurism. Though relatively tame by today's standards, *Ball Four* sent shock waves through the sports world. The book shot to the top of the best-seller list.

"A landmark," praises sportswriter Vic Ziegel, who adds as one of his personal criteria, "You can tell what a good piece of work you've done by the enemies you've made." Within the game, Bouton could count hundreds.

Curt Blefary, a teammate of Bouton's on the 1969 Astros, recalls, "The Yankees players were really up in arms." Despite a flattering portrayal in the book, he has no kind words for its author in return. "The clubhouse is a sanctuary," says Blefary, where ballplayers observed the rule What you see here, what you do here, what you say here, let it stay here. "And Bouton violated that sanctity for his own personal gain.

"Ballplayers are human," he continues. "All the public needs to know about us is what we do on the field. If we go out and have a drink, that's our business and nobody else's. He infringed on that privacy that we are entitled to as human beings. You just don't do that.

"He got some players divorced, and he desecrated greats like Mickey Mantle and Elston Howard." The New York catcher-turned-coach was depicted in *Ball Four* as a man cowed by management and spineless on the issue of race. "I remember Ellie saying that if he ever saw Bouton on the street, he'd kill him right there," Blefary says.

Pitcher Mike McCormick, acquired for John Cumberland in mid-July, balked at having to wear The Bulldog's old number 56 and was given number 29 instead. But many of those who professed to loathe the book never actually read it. Mike Kekich picked up a copy on the plane one day and couldn't stop laughing. "The guy was saying a lot of truthful things," he says, "and I thought a lot of it was very poignant and very humorous. I remember getting glares from many of my teammates and coaches."

Bouton quit baseball midsummer, probably wisely, to bring his caustic wit to the airwaves as a New York TV sportscaster. When he arrived in Fort Lauderdale in his new jacket-and-tie uniform the next spring, players around the majors conspired to render his microphone all but useless.

"Nobody would talk to him," says Blefary. "He came to spring training camp with about a hundred rolls of tape, and went home with about ninety-nine. The only one who did talk to him was Fritz Peterson." Bouton, unofficially but effectively excommunicated from pinstripes, has never been invited to Old Timers' Day.

Not surprisingly, while the younger, hipper sportswriters showered

Ball Four with praise for bringing realism to baseball writing, the book aroused the eternal ire of the older scribes. They would never forgive Bouton for ripping down baseball's wholesome façade, which they'd spent the better part of their lives polishing.

Nor would those folks who idealized ballplayers as role models for youth and who looked to baseball as one of the last strongholds of such traditional values as sexual morality and sobriety. To them Bouton will forever remain the cad who stole baseball's innocence, even if beneath that prim demeanor the old gal was really a floozy, and always had been.

These days the ex-hurler pitches fantasy: Big League Cards, baseball cards bearing *your likeness*. Bouton has come up with other products too, including Big League Chew, bubblegum "chewing tobacco" for kids, minus the carcinogens. He also does motivational speaking for corporations.

Sitting in his New Jersey offices, he reflects, "What *Ball Four* did was to show that baseball wasn't different from the rest of the country, the way they [conservative writers] wanted it to be. And the same problems that were racking the country were also racking baseball. That meant that these guys weren't immune either. There wasn't a private world that they could write about and keep it away.

"These were basically older guys. The world simply was not working out like they'd wanted it to. I mean, the frustration of these people, to go down to the water and hold up their hands, and the waves were knocking them over. But they couldn't hold it back. They could not stop the changes that were going on."

Sports columnist Dick Young of the *Daily News* thundered against Bouton as if he were a child pornographer, accusing him of poisoning impressionable minds across America. Young would occasionally use his pulpit in the sports pages to sermonize on What's Wrong with This Country, and inevitably fingered sissy longhairs, their rackety music, antiwar protestors, and so on, in reactionary love-it-or-leave-it prose.

The true source of Young's vitriol toward *Ball Four*, according to its author, was guilt. "Here was a guy writing a column called 'Clubhouse Confidential,'" Bouton observes, "and some ballplayer, of all people, writes about what's *really* going on in the clubhouse. It made it look like Dick Young was covering up—which in fact he was."

Ball Four's tales of debauchery may have been new, but the behavior itself was as ancient as the spitball. Babe Ruth, for example, was a prodigious womanizer, once sampling an entire St. Louis brothel in a night. Most times, though, The Sultan of Swat didn't need to pay for play. Stories of female groupies, known as *Baseball Annies* and *Bullpen Shirleys*, date back to the nineteenth century.

Certainly they existed in the 1950s, supposedly a decade of repressed sexuality in America. "Baseball Annies were always around and were always available," says Bouton. "It was almost an accepted part of the baseball lifestyle. More of us were involved in that than were not.

"It started in the minor leagues. The older guys had girls back at the hotel, and then you'd go to another minor-league town, and there'd be girls there." In 1959, twenty-year-old Jim Bouton divided his first summer in the Yankees chain between Auburn, New York, and Kearney, Nebraska.

"To the girls in Kearney we were pretty exciting," he says, "especially compared to the guys in their town. You were a little taller and a little stronger and a little better looking. And you had a lot more money and were more sophisticated. So we were mini-celebrities in the minor leagues. Then we got to the big leagues, and we became major celebrities. We were not only 'special,' but, hey, our pictures were in the newspapers.

"We were also fairly safe for women for a one-night stand. You could do worse than to go to bed with a ballplayer, because what was he going to do with you? He had to get on the bus the next day and go to the ballgame. And he most likely had a wife and family at home and wasn't going to cause any problems. And there was a certain amount of cachet; a girl could tell her girlfriend that she did this guy or that guy. And she'd get tickets to the ball game and sit there and extend it on to the next day. 'See that third baseman over there?' "

The freer sexual mores of the late 1960s and early 1970s made procuring willing bed partners easier still. "Women were becoming much more assertive and aggressive," recalls Bouton, who shelved his television career to make a brief comeback at age thirty-nine with Atlanta in 1978. "Now it wasn't always a situation where the ballplayers had to go find women—women were coming to find them."

Mr. Laffs, on First Avenue between Sixty-fourth and Sixty-fifth streets, was a popular hunting ground for women looking to bag professional athletes. "We were the hottest place in Manhattan," says Phil Linz, a co-owner with former New York Giant Bob Anderson. "Joe Namath was in there every night. Rod Gilbert. Tucker Frederickson. Frank Gifford. Mike Ditka. They were all there."

The former Yankees utility man opened the club in 1965 mainly as a lark. "My partner and I lived in this building on Sixty-fourth and First where there were about three hundred airline stewardesses, all single," he explains. "I'd been having parties in my apartment for years, so we knew a good hundred of them by their first names. We opened, they came. Of course, once the ballplayers found out the stewardesses were there, *they* came. And then *more* stewardesses came once they found out the ballplayers were there.

"Our place was like a fraternity party. Before us," he recalls, "everything was very formal: all Mafia-run places, with captains in dinner jackets, theater ropes, two-drink minimums at the tables, and piano bars. It was pretty boring. I mean, it was really dry. It was still an era in which it was unusual to see a lot of girls at the bar unless they were hookers." Linz, now a corporate-insurance salesman in Connecticut, owned Mr. Laffs for twenty years and at one point ran three other nightspots.

"Anybody and everybody wanted to be seen there," recalls Steve Whitaker. During his rookie season, he lived in Linz's apartment upstairs from the club. "We had an elevator that came down the back side, so I didn't have to stand in line for a block and a half to get in.

"I'd get set up at my favorite little table in back, and Phil would run around, trying to figure out who were the nicest-looking girls in the place. He'd bring 'em over, parade 'em in front of me, and do the introductions. I'd give him the high sign or the low sign. If it was a high sign, and we got along good," says Whitaker, "I was out the back door going up the elevator again."

The public could tolerate ballplayers messing around, explaining it away as boys sowing their wild oats. But *Ball Four*'s revelation that major-leaguers routinely took stimulants to enhance performance came as a blow to national efforts to curb soaring substance abuse among young Americans.

Baseball, anxious to maintain its virtuous image, denied such a problem existed, when in fact teams had silently condoned amphetamine use for years. The prevalent attitude within the game, mirroring that of society's, drew a distinction between illicit drugs such as marijuana and a prescription upper such as Dexamyl, popular with athletes.

"Amphetamines weren't drugs, they were *medicine*," Bouton explains. "If you stayed out late at night and had a hangover, and you came in needing a greenie or a red heart to get your heart beating, the team position was: That's okay." Some clubs kept jars of pills in the clubhouse for players to grab like candy.

"Pep pills were everywhere," contends pitcher Dock Ellis. "Trainers used to carry them around." The star right-hander, a Yankee in 1976 and 1977, broke in with Pittsburgh in 1968. "When they changed the laws so that trainers couldn't carry drugs unless they were prescribed by a doctor, they'd get doctors to prescribe them for guys who had a 'weight problem.'"

According to Ellis, ballplayers abused substances other than amphetamines. "Marijuana and some cocaine was around," he says. "I remember guys slipping coke in my back pocket while I was on the field." Ellis, who first dabbled with drugs as a teenager, admits to using mescaline and LSD "pretty heavily" by 1970. On June 12 of that year, he ingested a tab of acid, mistakenly believing the Pirates had an off-day, then went out and no-hit the purple-melting-demonheaded San Diego Padres 2–0. "You know that if *I* was doing LSD," he says, "there were others doing it."

What's more, Ellis asserts, management knew. "Sure they knew, sure they knew. Recently my son brought me a video of me pitching in the 1971 All-Star Game. I had never seen it before." The American League nailed a stoned Ellis for a pair of two-run homers to finally break the NL's eight-year lock on the Midsummer Classic, 6–4.

"I watched it, and I thought, *How in the hell could they have allowed me to go out there like that?*" The answer is simple: a team-high 19 wins for the World Champion Pirates. "As long as you were producing," he says, "they didn't care."

Baseball wouldn't come to grips with its drug problem until the 1980s and took even longer to recognize the high incidence of alcoholism among athletes. Here too the sport was no different than society, which needed to be educated that booze was potentially no less dangerous and addictive than pot, coke, or speed, despite its being legal.

"Alcohol wasn't a 'drug,' " says Jim Bouton. "It was simply something you used to celebrate a win or to forget about a bad game. The clubhouse was like a bar, really. Most teams had beer there; a couple had beer on draft. The only rule was that the bar wasn't open until the game was over. Unless," he adds, "you got knocked out of the game early—then you could go to the bar."

Tying one on at night was such a long-accepted practice, some managers, Leo Durocher for one, questioned the abilities of athletes who did not imbibe. Curt Blefary, a self-admitted alcoholic, remembers hearing more than once, "You show me a ballplayer that doesn't smoke or drink and I'll show you a horseshit ballplayer." Says Blefary, now sober through Alcoholics Anonymous, "Drinking was part of the realm."

In baseball's macho culture, it was a badge of virility to crawl the bars till dawn, then come out to the ballpark and bang a home run or hurl a shutout. "The play-hard, drink-hard syndrome," pitcher Sam McDowell calls it. One of the preeminent strikeout artists of his day, McDowell wore pinstripes in 1973 and 1974 but is best remembered in a Cleveland uniform. The six-foot-five left-hander, known as Sudden Sam for his flaming fastball, was Sodden Sam virtually his entire career.

"If you could produce, you were held in awe by your peers," says McDowell, who today runs Triumphs Unlimited, an alcohol-abuse counseling program that works with several major-league teams. "The press would even write it up sometimes." Indeed, it wasn't so long ago that baseball journalism habitually romanticized the image of the athlete executing fantastic feats while half-soused: a cockeyed Grover Cleveland Alexander fanning Yankee Tony Lazzeri with the bags loaded in the 1926 World Series, for instance.

In 1970, the year McDowell registered 20 wins and 304 strikeouts, more than any pitcher in the majors, the Indians were shipping him from psychiatrist to psychiatrist in a futile effort to get him off the bottle. Were he not the organization's glittering jewel, it's doubtful he would have received help. Most ball clubs merely turned a blind eye to a ballplayer's excessive drinking so long as it didn't interfere with his performance.

When it did, says Blefary, "Then they just dropped you like a hot potato. There was nobody back then to say, 'Hey, wait a minute. Take a good look at yourself. You might have a little problem here.. Let's see if we can help you.' "

Blefary's own drinking spiraled out of control in 1970, a bitterly disappointing season for the Brooklyn-born outfielder. After four years in Baltimore and one in Houston, he was thrilled to be coming home and even happier to get a second opportunity with the team that had signed him out of college for $18,000 in 1962. He'd turned down far bigger bonuses to join the Yankees organization, not due to any great love of the team. "I hated them," he says. "I was a Dodgers fan. But I wanted to play in the Bronx. Yankee Stadium was made for me."

As they often did, the Yankees let the solidly built left-handed hitter slip away on waivers in order to pick up veteran Harry Bright for the 1963 pennant drive. "I was very upset," says Blefary. "Almost quit. But I talked to my dad, who said, 'Look, stop with this garbage that you want to come home. *Make them pay.*' "

Blefary did, and with interest. He won the American League Rookie of the Year award in 1965 and consistently pummeled Yankees pitching. "If I had intensified my execution against every other major-league team like I did against the Yankees," he says, "I'd have been the next .400 hitter."

On Opening Day 1970, his first game in pinstripes, "I was more nervous than as a rookie," Blefary recalls. Five busloads of friends and family were in the stands. Though the Yankees' new right fielder blooped a two-run double in the 4–3 loss, he let a George Scott line drive get past him for a triple.

The Yankees hadn't coveted Blefary for his glove. He came to them bearing the nickname "Clank," a term of endearment for a man said to have hands of steel. They got the twenty-six-year-old pull hitter for his bat, which had generated 67 home runs his first three seasons. In Yankee Stadium, with that inviting 296-foot right-field wall, big things were expected of Number 13. But Blefary didn't put one in the seats until June.

Blame it on a dearth of inside pitches to pull, that tempting right-field porch, and a stubborn refusal to shoot for a single up the middle instead of trying to knock one out every time up. On top of which, add the pressure of being back home.

"I let it get to me," Blefary reflects, "and that's not like me at all. I thrive on pressure. But I wanted to do *so* well, I wanted to prove to the organization that it made a mistake when it let me go the first time, and one thing just compounded the other."

In Blefary New York fans had found their successor to previous targets such as Roger Maris and Bill Robinson. They savagely mocked the way he craned his neck between swings and heckled, "Curt, you didn't have your Wheaties!" after pop-ups.

"There was one guy," he says. "I can hear his voice today. And he would get on me constantly. Then he would meet me outside after the ball game and shake my hand. He said, 'I hope you don't take this personally. I'm just having some fun.' I said, 'Fine. At my expense, you're having fun. Just keep coming every day and paying your four-fifty.' "

Blefary can laugh while recalling another encounter with his public: "I'm heading toward the players' entrance to the ballpark one day, and there's this little black kid, couldn't have been more than ten, standing outside on the corner, and he has his autograph book out. He says, 'Mr. Blefary, may I have your autograph?'

"I start to sign my name, and the kid asks me, 'You playing tonight?' I knew there was a lefty pitching, so I said no.

" 'Good.'

"The fans never bothered me," he insists. "I could hear them, but I didn't have rabbit ears."

Blefary was deeply upset, though, when Ralph Houk benched him in August, just as it appeared he was getting untracked. In June and July he clubbed eight home runs. But rookie Jim Lyttle took over in right and gave the Yankees a .310 BA in addition to flawless defense. A banner could be spotted hanging from the upper deck: CURT BLEF-ARY FAN CLUB LOVES JIM LYTTLE.

Not playing gnawed at Blefary. "I lived in Fort Lee, New Jersey, just ten minutes across the George Washington Bridge," he says. "And I'd be at the ballpark at two-thirty for an eight o'clock game. If that lineup was up there, and my name wasn't on it, I was just furious. I became unbearable.

"I started drinking too much, that's for sure. Five or six of us would go out to a different tavern every night, to hash things over. It got to the point where you didn't want to go home because you were going to take it out on your family. It got to be extremely intense." Blefary ended the year at a paltry .212 BA, 9 HR, 37 RBI.

Going into 1971, he realized he'd been squeezed out of the starting lineup. Then three days into the season Lyttle suffered an attack of appendicitis during a workout in Washington. "I didn't have as much grief as I probably should've," Blefary admits.

Playing in place of Lyttle, he belted an inside-the-park home run to down Washington 1–0. "The ball and I got to home plate at the same time," remembers Blefary, no speed demon, "and there was no way I was going to run three hundred sixty feet and let Jim French, the catcher, tag me out. I hit him with everything I had. The ball went one way, the chest protector went the other."

A good omen, thought Blefary. "I felt I was really going to be on a roll. But then Houk started playing his games with me again: in and out of the lineup. In May I went to him and said, 'Ralph, I've got a chance to buy a home in New Jersey. Do you or the organization have any intention of trading me?' Because if that was the case, I would have held off.

" 'No, no, no,' he said, 'you're our number-one utility player'— which really pissed me off—'blah blah blah, don't worry about that.'

"So I went ahead with the deal. We're in Detroit two days later. When Houk sent up Ron Woods to pinch hit in a crucial spot instead of me, boy, the light went on real quick. *I'll be a son of a bitch! I bet they traded me!* Sure enough, Elston Howard came up to me after the game and said, 'Ralph wants to talk to you.'

"I went up to Ralph and said, 'All right, where am I going?' " To Oakland for ex-Yankee Rob Gardner. "Ralph had that little squirrelish grin on his face that he always had. He said, 'Curt, we really need pitching. You're the only one they would take.' So here I am with a family in New Jersey, and I'm three thousand miles away, trying to support two households at the same time. I've already taken ninety percent of our life savings and put it into this goddamn house that I could have held off on.

"Little things like that really piss you off."

Now living and working in Florida, Blefary longs to get back into the game as a minor-league instructor. A father of three, he coached high-school ball in Fort Lauderdale and says he loves working with kids. But the letters he sends by certified mail to ex-teammates now in positions to hire go unanswered.

"I would love to have back the postage money that I spent through-

out the years. I could retire by now," Blefary says, more sadly than
bitterly. "I haven't been to a spring-training game in five years, because it just hurts me to go over there.

"I did some crazy things in the game," he admits. "It isn't that I did
anything different than anybody else, I might have just gotten seen
doing it more. But when I was between those white lines, I was one
hundred percent and ready to play ball and win. Obviously I must
have done something wrong or pissed somebody off big time, and I'm
being punished for it for the last twenty years," says Blefary, who was
out of the majors by 1974.

"It's put a tremendous void in my life because of my love of the
game."

VII

BLEFARY WAS BEHIND the plate as the Yankees and Mets faced off in
the Mayor's Trophy Game on August 17. The pennant had been conceded to Baltimore, but the New York City title remained unsettled.

Fifty thousand fans filled Yankee Stadium. "That was probably the
biggest game of the year," says Gary Waslewski. "We had to win. No
matter how badly things might be going, if we beat the Mets, we had
a pretty good season."

The Yankees started Steve Kline; the Mets, twenty-three-year-old
Nolan Ryan. Rookie shortstop Frank Baker watched three Ryan heat-
ers go by and practically sprinted for the dugout. "I was glad to sit
down," he says. "This was back when he didn't have very much control.
He made me nervous."

Pete Ward then stepped up and hammered a 3-and-2 fastball over
the 407-foot sign. "That's the only time I ever faced Nolan Ryan," says
Ward, who was cut the following spring and now owns a travel agency
in Oregon. "For the rest of the year," Waslewski says, "Pete was a
hero in the Bronx."

The Yankees won decisively, 9–4. Ralph Houk's words from spring
training turned out to be prophetic after all. The Bombers placed a
strong second, 93–69 (.574), the Mets, a flat third, 83–79 (.512). On
September 23, the Yankees clinched the runner-up spot by beating
the Senators at Yankee Stadium 6–4. Afterward they celebrated with
the champagne and whooping once reserved for World Championships.

"The Orioles ran away with it, but we were just thrilled to finish
second," says Roy White, whose .296 BA, 22 HR, 94 RBI, 109 R

established him as the club's best all-around player. "After some real dismal seasons, it seemed like we were moving in a positive direction and that we had some young talent." Mike Kekich, on the other hand, was less impressed. "Maybe the rest of the league just sucked," he suggests.

Much of the credit for the Yankees' winningest season since 1964 belonged to The Major. After the disheartening July series in Baltimore, the club cooled off for a while but refused to go under, a hallmark of Houk-managed crews. *Newsday* sportswriter Steve Jacobson observes, "He was very good at getting a mediocre team to keep playing hard, so that after other teams had quit, it could win a lot of games." In October the Associated Press named Houk the American League's Manager of the Year.

New York's ninety-third victory also happened to be number twenty for Fritz Peterson. It couldn't have come under more dramatic circumstances: a 4–3 squeaker on the final day of the season in Fenway Park, some architect's idea of a practical joke. Its short left field makes it a house of horrors for many left-handers, and Peterson dreaded pitching there.

At midseason he'd been halfway to 20 and seemed a shoo-in. Then the native Chicagoan started fantasizing about becoming a 20-game winner for the first time. The more he set his sights on that magic number, the further away it drifted. From June 26 to August 24 he won only three games. "So I tried pushing it out of my mind," says Peterson.

He had all but given up hope when on August 25 he picked up a gift win in relief against Kansas City. "Looking at the schedule, I saw I had about eight shots left. At that point I started to count them off. I thought, *I've got to get every one of these, because I'll never get another chance to do this.*" He won five of his next seven starts to raise his season record to 19–11.

In baseball, success is measured by the absence of failure. To make an out only seven times every ten at-bats is considered exceptional. With the odds of success so overwhelmingly against them, ballplayers tend to be a superstitious lot willing to try anything that might improve their chances, no matter how irrational.

For instance, Pete Ward went through several weeks of the season wearing the same Hawaiian shirt. He credited it with helping him fatten his batting numbers. "I once got on a subway car with him," Gary Waslewski recalls, "and people started leaving. Because he wouldn't wash the damn thing. Even the flies wouldn't land on it."

Ward, however, couldn't hold a black candle to Peterson, whose rituals included eating the same meal during a winning streak, but never stepping on chalk lines; sitting in the same exact spot on the bench if ahead, but never crossing two bats. In checkmating Washington for win number eighteen, he'd kept his small son's tiny sock in his pocket as a good-luck charm.

So naturally he was horrified to check into the hotel in Boston and discover he'd been issued room 1912. So what, you ask? "That would have been my record if I lost," Peterson explains. "I got out of that; I think I went to the twentieth floor."

On a frigid night in Fenway, Peterson helped his own cause by lashing a double and coming around to score. He took his one-run lead into the ninth. With one out, Billy Conigliaro and Joe Lahoud stroked consecutive singles. Out came Houk.

"What do you want to do?" he asked Number 19. "It's your game."

"Ralph, what would you do if it were the World Series?"

"I'd bring in Lindy."

Peterson recalls, "I gave him the ball and went into the dugout. But I didn't want to stay there." This was another of his superstitions: when removed from a game with a lead, proceed directly to clubhouse.

"I went inside, but you could still hear the fans yelling. So I went into Ralph's office, got under his desk and put three towels over my ears. It seemed like I spent two years under there."

With McDaniel on the mound, it didn't take nearly that long. The Yankees closer retired Reggie Smith on a fly out, walked Ducky Scofield to load the bases, then got Mike Andrews to ground into a game-ending force play. As he accepted handshakes for his twenty-ninth save, which tied Luis Arroyo's club mark set in 1961, McDaniel considered playing a practical joke on Peterson. "I should have knocked on the door and told him how sorry I was," he says.

Pete Sheehy went to deliver the good news, but couldn't find the pitcher. Then he noticed the pair of feet sticking out from under the desk, looked closer, and saw him cowering as if awaiting an imminent nuclear attack.

"Pete didn't smile or anything," says Peterson. "I thought, *Oh boy, we lost.* Then he grinned and said, 'Congratulations, you're a twenty-game winner!'

"That night I didn't want to get out of uniform. I think I stayed at the ballpark until two. Everybody else had gone back to the hotel. But I wanted the moment to last forever."

He adds, "I thought that was going to be the answer to all my happiness, and oddly enough it wasn't."

1971

STARTERS
Mel Stottlemyre
Fritz Peterson
Stan Bahnsen
Steve Kline
Mike Kekich

Danny Cater (1B)
Horace Clarke (2B)
Gene Michael (SS)
Jerry Kenney (3B)
Roy White (LF)
Bobby Murcer (CF)
Felipe Alou/Ron
Blomberg (RF)
Thurman Munson (C)

RELIEVERS
Lindy McDaniel
Jack Aker

I

THE MODEST SUCCESS of 1970 lulled New York into a false sense of security. Ralph Houk went into the new season convinced, he says, "that we'd get back on top." The front office appeared dangerously overconfident, standing pat over the winter. To several Yankees' surprise, camp opened with the same cast as the year before.

"We thought there might be an attempt to get us more power hitting," says Jack Aker, "which was what most of us on the team felt we needed. We had to be able to score more runs to keep up with clubs like Baltimore."

Management had to be concerned when not one prospect was deemed worthy of the outstanding-rookie citation, the first time that had happened in the James P. Dawson Award's twenty-five-year history. The organization's only newsworthy addition that spring was in the broadcast booth.

Bill White joined Phil Rizzuto and Frank Messer to become baseball's first black play-by-play announcer. At a time when the sport was beginning to take heat for its exclusionary hiring practices, this constituted a significant development. The opinionated former National League star would develop into a refreshing foil to the unabashedly partisan Rizzuto, but his debut was memorably awkward.

Messer recalls: "Bill had a contract with a TV station in Philadelphia that didn't free him until a few days into the exhibition season. So he came straight from the Miami airport to Miami Stadium and up to the broadcast booth. We were on radio only that day. At the commercial break, I said, 'Phil, I'm going to leave and let you introduce Bill.' I figured Rizzuto and White would finish the ball game," which headed to the bottom of the ninth with the Yankees and Orioles tied at three.

"All of a sudden Rizzuto, as is his wont, left. The engineer later told me that Phil turned around to Bill and said, 'Oh gee, Bill, there's Joe DiMaggio. I've got to go talk to him about something.' " That left guest broadcaster Whitey Ford to do the honors.

And so, through pure happenstance, the first words uttered on the air by a minority sportscaster were "Thank you, Whitey!"

While compiling an 8–23 spring record, the Yankees watched two major experiments fizzle. John Ellis was tested at third as a way to get his bat into the lineup, but he had neither the soft hands nor the reflexes for the hot corner. And then Frank Baker, who was expected to make the grade as starting shortstop after a promising 1970 preview, flunked out. The twenty-four-year-old Mississippian batted a microscopic .044. Though known for his glove work, he also errored nine times in eighteen games.

"I got sick with a low-grade flu and kept trying to play," explains Baker, now in the oil business back in Mississippi. "I should have told the trainer. But when you're young, you want to prove yourself. I really got off to a bad start and never recovered." On Opening Day in Boston, both Jerry Kenney and Gene Michael were occupying their familiar positions.

Almost as if to prove that they were doing something—anything— three days later the front office dealt pitchers Ron Klimkowski and Rob Gardner to Oakland for outfielder–first baseman Felipe Alou.

"On Good Friday," grumbles Klimkowski, who grew up on Long Island and did not want to leave. A stockbroker these days, he recalls learning of the swap as the team headed off to Washington. "They take my luggage off the plane, and I'm walking through the airport with all my baseball gear. Then I'm driving home, and I hear them announce the trade on the radio. It was a funny feeling."

Although Alou provided a productive right-handed bat (.289 BA, 8 HR, 69 RBI), even he questioned the wisdom of a rebuilding team importing a thirty-six-year-old veteran and adding to the growing clutter at first and in right. Upon his arrival in the Bronx, New York's record stood at 3–3. The Yankees would hover around the .500 mark all year, never able to get untracked.

"I can barely remember the season," says Roy White. "We were pretty flat and didn't build on the year before. There were too many guys who had career years in 1970 and just didn't do it again." Jake Gibbs plummeted from .301 to .218, Jim Lyttle from .301 to .198, and Ron Hansen from .297 to .207. Management might have foreseen those three falling shy of their 1970 numbers. But who would have imagined the club's two .300 regulars, Danny Cater and Thurman Munson, sinking to .276 and .251?

Certainly not Cater, a contact hitter unaccustomed to extended slumps. As of June 1 he was mired at .223 and had yet to hit a home run. "I'd never gone through anything like that before," he says, "and it really got to me. If I went 0-for-4, I'd start worrying that I'd never get another hit for the rest of my life." He experienced stomach pains and insomnia.

"I remember we were playing the Royals in New York and I was hitting .219." Cater can be taken at his word. Early in his career he established a reputation for being able to compute his average down to four places before reaching first base. Fittingly, today he works with figures, examining state tax returns in his native Texas.

"Ted Savage slid into third and kicked me in the ankle," he continues, "and I had to be taken out of the game. I went into the clubhouse and I almost cried. But then we left on a two-week road trip. Ralph Houk told me he was going to play me just against certain pitchers." Cater relaxed. "I came back hitting close to .250," he says. A torrid .343 over the last two months of the season enabled Number 10 to finish where he did.

Munson felt similarly frustrated. Despite his outward confidence, "You could see him get depressed at times," Lindy McDaniel observes. At home Munson would stare intently into a mirror and practice his swing over and over, obsessed with figuring out what he was doing wrong.

But the young catcher was mature enough not to let his problems at the plate affect his defense. In just his second full season Munson blossomed into the league's top receiver. He committed a single error in 1971, and only by getting knocked unconscious.

It happened in Baltimore. Though it was just mid-June, already New York's pennant hopes hung in the balance. The division-leading Orioles were riding off to a third straight campaign of 100-plus victories, while the 29–33, .468 Yankees were clinging to fourth place, ten games back.

After coming up short in the opener, 3–1, the following night New

York's offense staked Fritz Peterson to a quick 4–0 advantage. With Birds catcher Andy Etchebarren on first, Paul Blair rode a ball up the left-center alley. Etchebarren, running as if in quicksand, lumbered around third just as relay man Gene Michael whipped a strike home. Munson took the throw, blocked the plate, and braced himself. The next thing he remembered was waking up in a Baltimore hospital.

Etchebarren barreled into him full force, knocking Munson out cold. Adding insult to injury—a mild concussion, it would turn out—the scoreboard flashed "E2." Peterson was furious.

"I wanted John Ellis, who was our thug, to do his thing and kill Andy on the spot," he says with a laugh. Weeks earlier, in Cleveland, Ellis had distinguished himself during a bench-clearing brawl ignited by an altercation at second between Sam McDowell and Gene Michael. "Ellis was running around like a wild man," Gary Waslewski recalls, "punching everyone on the field. He was swinging at *our* guys as well as their guys."

Ellis refrained from retaliating against Etchebarren, who was guilty only of playing the aggressive brand of baseball Frank Robinson had instilled in the Orioles since coming over from the National League. Three tallies each in both the third and the fifth gave Baltimore a 6–4 comeback victory. New York wrested the third contest by the same score in extra innings but got blown out in the Sunday finale, 10–4.

II

THE SERIES ALL but extinguished the Yankees' chances and spotlighted their sievelike fielding, which gave away a total of nine unearned runs. Except for sure-handed Gene Michael, the infielders should have been paying compensation to the pitching staff. Fritz Peterson (15–13, 3.05 ERA) calculates, "You can take about one run off our earned run averages because of lack of defense."

Inconsistency at the corners certainly contributed to a .977 fielding percentage, the worst in the division. An unhappy Cater had to share first base with Alou and Ellis, while he, Jerry Kenney, and Ron Hansen subdivided third. However, several Yankees blamed the deficiencies more on the *consistency* at second.

Horace Clarke's once bright star seemed to go out overnight in the Bronx. Previously a quiet and dependable asset, he became a symbol of Yankees ineptitude. Some New York sportswriters still jokingly refer to this uninspired chapter in the franchise's history as The Horace Clarke Era.

To single out Number 20 for the Yankees' misfortunes is unjust. A proficient leadoff man, he averaged 80 runs scored for the weak-hitting 1969–71 squads and topped the club in stolen bases four times. But the closer New York inched toward contention, the more glaring grew Clarke's shortcomings at the keystone. He came in for scathing criticism in the sports pages. Eventually, he admits, "The way they talked about my defense, it started to make me doubt myself."

Clarke, reserved but proud, withstood the negative comments in silence. After leaving the game in 1975, however, he decided some response was in order. "I got in touch with Jim Ogle, one of the writers during my playing days, and asked him to get my fielding statistics out," he says.

On the surface, Clarke's numbers seem to contradict the putdowns. For six consecutive seasons, 1967 through 1972, he topped AL second basemen in assists, setting a league record, and from 1968 through 1971 in putouts as well. But those figures don't take into account balls that bounded up the middle untouched, nor the fact that playing behind a staff of sinkerballers is naturally going to give you an abundance of chances on the ground. A more telling statistic is Number 20's fielding percentage, which in 1971 ranked last in the division among second sackers.

Clarke prides himself on having played day in and day out for seven seasons. "I was fortunate," he says. "I never had a major injury that kept me out too long." Teammates might suggest that a reluctance to stand in on double plays had something to do with that good luck.

Curt Blefary, expert at breaking up twin killings, recalls, "I used to roll into these guys at second. But when I was with Baltimore I could never get Clarke, and I couldn't understand what the hell was happening. Finally, when I played with him, I realized what he did: he'd take the throw, then jump straight up in the air to avoid being hit and hold the ball. That's why I could never take out the son of a bitch when I was playing against him.

"It was strange," adds Blefary, "because he was so well built, you weren't going to hurt him."

Learning to settle for force plays became a New York pitcher's way of life. Jack Aker says, "This was the only thing any of us ever questioned Ralph Houk on—why Horace Clarke played every day. As a staff of mostly sinkerballers, we lived and died on ground balls. We played so many close ball games, one more double play could have changed the outcome a lot of times. Horace had the knock on him from the players—and I was one of them—that he bailed out."

According to the reliever, "Several pitchers actually went to Ralph and claimed they didn't want to pitch if he was at second." When that failed, they confronted their teammate to his face. "It was a sore subject with him," says Aker, "and he became upset." Clarke could point to having led the league in double plays in 1969, an accomplishment he was to repeat in 1972. "But we would have turned twice that number with *anybody* else," argues Steve Kline (12–13, 2.96 ERA), one of five New York starters to win ten or more games.

Baltimore's rotation produced four 20-game winners that year: Dave McNally, Mike Cuellar, Jim Palmer, and Pat Dobson. Were the Yankees endowed with a comparable offense and defense, says Stan Bahnsen (14–12, 3.25 ERA), "We'd have put up some big numbers too." Fritz Peterson couldn't help imagining what it would be like to take the hill knowing you had the impenetrable infield of Boog Powell, Davy Johnson, Mark Belanger, and Brooks Robinson behind you. A hurler might be tempted to pitch underhanded just for the hell of it.

"It was frustrating to watch pitchers like McNally, who I felt I was better than, having that support and always winning twenty," Peterson says. "Mel was hurt most of all, because he was a total sinkerballer. That guy would have won thirty games with Baltimore."

Stottlemyre (16–12, 2.87 ERA), the only Yankee remaining from the 1964 World Series roster, went all the way 19 times, driven largely by self-preservation. As if the starters didn't feel victimized enough, the bullpen failed them too, time and again in 1971.

Lindy McDaniel, infallible the season before, suffered his worst season (5–10, 4 SV, 5.01 ERA) since becoming a fireman in 1959. In his first appearance of the season, against Washington, Number 40 came on in the bottom of the ninth to wrap up a come-from-behind 4–3 win for long man Gary Waslewski. The Senators scraped together one run to tie, then Tom McCraw led off the tenth by golfing a flat forkball into the stands.

McDaniel dismantled four other potential wins for Waslewski (0–1, 1 SV, 3.25 ERA), who was still looking for his first victory when he tore up his knee midseason and had to miss the rest of the year. "Lindy was very apologetic. I remember him saying to me, 'Gee, I'm sorry, that's the fifth one in a row I blew.'

"He couldn't figure out what was going on," says Waslewski, now an account executive for the Hartford Life Insurance Company in Connecticut. "His mechanics, he thought, were all right. But the forkball just wasn't working, and he was flustered, because it had been so easy the previous year."

McDaniel says his faith in himself fell to where "I even went to Ralph and asked him not to put me in critical situations," he recalls. "I was really hurting the ball club." The Major may have wanted to comply, but the rest of the pen was equally undependable.

On August 15, Jack Aker (4–4, 4 SV, 2.57 ERA) and McDaniel collaborated to torch a 4–2 lead against Oakland's pitching sensation Vida Blue. The twenty-two-year-old prodigy, 21–4 coming in, was attracting huge gates around the American League, so the Yankees, desperate to drum up business, proclaimed the occasion Vida Blue Day. In addition to printing up blue scorecards for the Sunday game, anyone named Blue got in free.

New York starter Stan Bahnsen felt pretty blue as he warmed up. "I couldn't believe the *Yankees* were doing this," he says, "hyping the opposing pitcher. Then I've got to go out and try to beat him." Number 45 delivered a gutsy performance nonetheless, allowing 12 hits but trailing only 2–0 after six and a half. The way Blue was bringing the heat, though, the margin appeared insurmountable.

Suddenly, unexpectedly, the Yankees solved the mighty Vida. John Ellis drove a bases-loaded two-bagger to left-center, scoring Felipe Alou and Danny Cater. Houk, barking orders from the clubhouse— he had been ejected for arguing a close call at second—sent up Ron Hansen to bat for Bahnsen. The .200 hitter plunked a two-run double down the right-field line, and Yankee Stadium reverberated with more noise than had been heard all season.

But Oakland quickly stunned the crowd of 45,343 (which included 126 Blues) into silence. Before Aker could retire anyone in the eighth, the A's countered with two runs on four hits. Blue helped the rally along by dropping his second bunt single of the afternoon, then coming around to score the go-ahead tally on a wild pitch by McDaniel. Another bunt hit brought in an insurance run, and the AL's dual MVP and Cy Young Award winner held on, 6–4.

The next time the Yankees faced Blue, Mel Stottlemyre left nothing to chance. New York nudged across a run in the first, and Number 30 made it stand up, 1–0, three years to the day after he'd bested Denny McLain, the rifle-armed wunderkind of 1968, in a similar showdown of disparate styles.

"Mel would go after batters with such a workmanlike methodology, that when he got done they knew they'd been had," praises Steve Kline, also a right-handed sinkerballer. "He just picked them apart. And if you had a weakness as a hitter, Lord, he'd feed it to you all day long."

Kline, already drawing comparisons to the Yankees elder statesman, carefully studied Stottlemyre from the dugout. "He had such great control—of his pitches, of himself, and of the game. That's what made him a winner. And you wanted to emulate him." Stottlemyre's coolheadedness inspired more confident play from his fielders. "Watching Mel, you learned that as long as you stayed in control, the players felt you had control of the game," Kline adds. "The minute you lost your composure, they sensed it, and they'd get nervous."

With one exception, the staff came together in Stottlemyre's image. "Gene Michael used to joke that Sam McDowell threw his slider harder than anybody on our team threw a fastball," says Gary Waslewski. Kline, Peterson, and Bahnsen all relied on the breaking ball, were always around the plate, and could be counted on for seven or eight innings.

That made Mike Kekich (11–10, 4.08 ERA) the anomaly of the rotation. A seeker on the mound as well as in his personal life, he spent his entire career searching for the strike zone. "I've fought control all my life," the hard-throwing left-hander admits. In 1989, at age forty-four, he came back to pitch for the Gold Coast Suns in the short-lived Senior League, where he found home plate as elusive as ever.

Kekich, who earned an M.D. in Mexico following his retirement and now runs a business that conducts medical exams for insurance companies, has a neurophysiological answer to his chronic wildness. "I am totally right-handed except for pitching," he explains. "I can't even throw a football left-handed." As a result, he needed steady work to "train" his arm, as it were, to throw strikes.

But his first two seasons in pinstripes, Kekich shuttled unhappily between starting and relieving, going 4–6 in 1969 and 6–3 in 1970. "When I got out of that physical routine, look out!" he continues. "Because no matter how much I focused, I could not make the body respond."

Teammates suspect that Number 18's restless nature also prevented him from realizing his potential. There was the time in August 1970 when he decided to conduct an experiment with the menacing Boog Powell at bat and the score 0–0. The Orioles first baseman promptly crushed a two-run homer into the Yankee Stadium bleachers.

"The ball had nothing on it," Jim Lyttle recalls. "It looked like he was tossing batting practice. Ralph Houk jumped up and down screaming and hollering and charged out to the mound. We could see he was very upset, because he circled the mound several times." After conferring with his pitcher on what he'd thrown, The Major stomped back to the dugout.

"*Forkball?*" Houk exploded. "What the hell's he doing throwing a goddamn forkball? He doesn't *have* a forkball!" Merv Rettenmund cut the tirade short by knocking the next pitch out of the park. When Kekich returned to the bench, he explained innocently to a disbelieving Curt Blefary, "I just thought it was a good time to try one."

"He couldn't concentrate on anything," says Lyttle. "He was always go-go-go. On the bench, he'd be walking around spitting sunflower seeds on everybody, talking about this, talking about that. He had to have his mind going all the time."

Anytime Kekich appeared to be coming unglued on the rubber, Stottlemyre took him aside between innings and calmed him down. That kind of encouragement and support was typical among the starting five, who despite their different personalities formed an unusually close-knit fraternity, with the free-thinking Kekich on the left, the conservative Stottlemyre on the right, and the other three in between. "Maybe that was the key to the chemistry," Stan Bahnsen suggests. "It was definitely unique."

Bahnsen, a veteran of five other clubs, observes, "I played through 1982 and saw the game change quite a bit. It became a lot more businesslike, with a lot less camaraderie. Even though the money is astronomical now, I wouldn't trade all my memories to be able to play today, because I don't think today's players will experience the things we did."

The fivesome's penchant for pulling pranks on one another led teammates to nickname them "The Nursery." "We even had T-shirts made up," says Fritz Peterson, the ringleader and undisputed maestro of practical jokes. Compared to Number 19's inventive schemes, such time-honored clubhouse tricks as hotfoots and nailing shoes to the floor seemed downright pedestrian.

One favorite was to sneak into the victim's locker and chain his street clothes together with a bicycle lock. Steve Kline recalls, with a laugh, "He'd run it through the buttonhole on your shirt, through the belt loop on your pants and eyes of your shoes, lock it, and leave a file on your stool, so you could file yourself out—hopefully before the bus left." Another was to chain and padlock a Yankee's car to a motorcycle outside a biker bar, then hide around the corner and wait for the inevitable fireworks.

Peterson's finest moment involved a king-size water bed Mike Kekich purchased in Chicago, the second stop on a three-city road trip in May. "We told him we were going to sabotage it," says Bahnsen. When the waterbed made it all the way to departure day without getting pricked full of holes, a suspicious Kekich carried it with him to Milwaukee County Stadium.

Just before game time he looked up at the flagpole and noticed something strange flapping in the wind. Peterson had paid the clubhouse boy five dollars to hook the waterbed to the halyard and hoist it up along with Old Glory. Kekich hastened up the ladder to retrieve it, but the scoreboard was locked. "So I had to find the guy who had the keys and climb up there again," he recalls. "Just as I get up to it, at the very top of the scoreboard, they start playing the National Anthem."

"We thought we were going to get into a lot of trouble," says Bahnsen. But who could keep a straight face at the sight of a lone figure in pinstripes perched forty feet above the field? Ralph Houk broke out in giggles. "It's like the chairman of the board," says Bahnsen. "When he laughs, everybody laughs."

Houk wasn't laughing the time The Nursery decided to enliven batting practice by turning shagging flies into a contest. Whoever caught the most balls won. "We'd end up diving and running over one another," says Bahnsen. "Ralph was really livid. He had a meeting with us and warned, 'If any of you guys misses a start, it's a thousand dollars.' Well, I was making only ten thousand, so that put a stop to it."

The manager, however, had no problem with the pitchers' batting competition: Stottlemyre and Kekich versus Bahnsen and Peterson. Whichever pair hit for the lowest combined average over the course of the season had to treat the other two to dinner "anywhere they wanted to go," Bahnsen explains, "and the sky was the limit."

One year the restaurant was in Cleveland, "which was picked because we couldn't spend as much money there." Not that Bahnsen and Peterson, that season's "losers," were overly concerned about the tab. "Fritz and I got hold of Stottlemyre's American Express card," he says. "We went to a Polynesian-type place, with all the fancy drinks and ribs and about thirty different kinds of appetizers.

"It was funny: Mike and Mel kept ordering things they weren't going to eat, just to try to gall us. And we just sat there. The two of them couldn't understand why we weren't getting upset. We put the card back in Mel's wallet the next day, and he didn't suspect a thing. Then in the off-season he got the bill."

III

THE ALL-STAR break hadn't even arrived yet, and already the Yankees were looking ahead to 1972. With his listless team stranded in fifth, Lee MacPhail began to shake things up, if only to improve attendance. The June 25 lineup against Washington included two new faces whom management expected would reawaken New Yorkers' interest.

Batting sixth and playing left field was Ron Swoboda, obtained just that morning from Montreal for Ron Woods. To outfit one of the principals of the 1969 Miracle Mets in pinstripes was less an act of blasphemy than it was sweet revenge: a long-overdue payback for the Amazin's having appropriated Yogi Berra. Just as Yogi had personified the Yankees' winning image, Swoboda had embodied the Mets' brash spirit. A popular figure with fans, he was colorful and quotable. It was his outspokenness, in fact, that provoked Mets management to expel him from Queens a week before Opening Day.

"I had run my big mouth," Swoboda says frankly. "I wasn't playing as much as I thought I should be, and rather than just let my performance do the talking, I suggested they trade me. And they complied! I found that I wasn't real hard to replace." News of the swap came as a crushing blow to the twenty-six-year-old outfielder.

"It was the worst thing that could've happened to me," he reflects. "I handled it totally wrong, because in my heart of hearts I didn't want to leave New York. But that immature part of me that was doing the talking thought this was a way to effect some change in my situation."

When Expos skipper Gene Mauch tried to demote him to the minors, once again Swoboda prompted a change of address by objecting vociferously. "That was a surprise," he says of the trade. "I was ecstatic. I was back in New York. I was back in my house. And I got to walk out of the dugout in Yankee Stadium with the pinstripes on. What a wonderful reprieve." Swoboda celebrated his homecoming by banging out an RBI single as the Bombers' romped over the Senators 12–2.

The other midseason debutant, twenty-two-year-old Ron Blomberg, slammed his first major-league home run into the right-field bleachers that day. The Yankees envisioned many more circuit clouts for the strapping left-handed hitter, the nation's number-one draft choice in 1967. Blomberg, a six-foot-two outfielder, possessed both power and speed. And, as an added bonus, he was Jewish.

The franchise had been seeking a Jewish star for decades to appeal to one of the largest ethnic groups in the five boroughs. In 1942 the Yankees brought up a reserve first baseman named Ed Levy. Levy? Like the rye bread? Management didn't mind at all if that's what New Yorkers happened to believe. But as the *New York World Telegram* quickly revealed, Levy's real name was Edward Clarence Whitner. Club president Ed Barrow had insisted the young Irish Catholic adopt his stepfather's Jewish-sounding surname.

Twenty-five years later, the Yankees unsuccessfully pursued Mike Epstein. It was no coincidence that they drafted Blomberg for a $70,000 bonus only weeks after the proposed Stottlemyre-for-Epstein swap fell through.

For all the attention focused on his religion, the rookie's instant popularity derived more from his hitting ability. In 199 at-bats, almost exclusively against right-handers, Blomberg batted .322 (with 7 home runs and 31 RBIs) and generated excitement with a ferocious, whiplike swing. His boyish good looks and enthusiasm further made him a favorite of the press and public.

He appeared at grand openings and in advertisements for everything from delicatessens to banks to hair-replacement centers, which Blomberg himself frequented on account of premature baldness. His likeness hung in Sardi's and Elaine's. For a wide-eyed boy from Atlanta, very much in awe of New York, it was a heady time.

"I used to go to restaurants and never paid for food. Never paid for cars. Never paid for anything," he recalls wistfully. "Wherever you went, people knew who you were. That was a great feeling."

Blomberg also experienced the darker side of celebrity. During his sophomore year, activist Rabbi Meir Kahane, founder of the militant Jewish Defense League, demanded permission to present an award to Number 12 in a pregame ceremony. The Yankees turned him down, at which point Kahane threatened to march onto the field in the middle of the game and make his presentation anyway.

"That was some fascinating day," says vice president Howard Berk. "We had to track him, to make sure he didn't do that." When an unsuspecting Blomberg pulled into the players' parking lot, a dozen security guards descended on his car. "They said, 'We need to talk to you,' " the player recalls, "and took me into Michael Burke's office."

Blomberg had never heard of Meir Kahane. But hearing words like *radical* and *militant* had him convinced he was going to be shot at first base, his new position. "I didn't know what to do," he says. "Everywhere I went, the dugout and the stands were just full of security people. It was a scary thing." Luckily, Kahane committed a critical mistake that precluded him from getting anywhere near his intended target.

"He entered on a clergy pass," Berk explains, "so we knew when he came in. We were able to follow him all day, know exactly where he was and what he was doing. I had walkie-talkies set up in my office."

Though unnerved by the incident, Blomberg appreciated the fact that members of his faith identified with him and took pride in his success. Only a handful of major-leaguers came from Jewish homes, where traditionally education is emphasized over athletics.

Blomberg's father, a jeweler, supported his decision to make sports a career. "I wanted to become a professional athlete from the time I was thirteen or fourteen," he reflects. "When I told my dad and mom, they looked at me like I was crazy, but they said, 'Do what you want to do.' " At her son's signing, held at Yankee Stadium, Mrs. Sol Blomberg remarked pragmatically to reporters, "He wasn't going to be a doctor, lawyer, or accountant, so why not a ballplayer?"

As a boy in Georgia, Blomberg's aptitude for sports shielded him from anti-Semitism. "Atlanta was a big Ku Klux Klan area then," he acknowledges, "and in high school I played ball against schools that you could tell didn't have any Jews there. But I really never had any problems. Being a good athlete, I got left alone, because they always wanted me to be on the team."

Blomberg also excelled at football and basketball, but baseball was his first love. Hitting, especially. "We didn't have a lot of baseball fields near my house," he remembers, "so I used to go in the front yard, pick holly berries, and toss 'em up in the air and hit 'em with a stick."

When not wrapped around a baseball bat, Blomberg's hands usually clutched a fork and knife. A prodigious eater, in high school he once polished off twenty-eight hamburgers in a sitting. "I loved to eat," he says. "Pastrami, corned beef, hamburgers, steaks, whatever. I lived in delis. My favorite in New York was the Stage Deli. But my metabolism was so high that I didn't gain any weight."

Stories of his voracious appetite and garrulous nature often made Blomberg seem something of a quaint Southern folk hero. More than once the papers referred to him as a "Jewish Li'l Abner." Teammates weren't always sure, though, if his ingenuousness was sincere or a put-on.

The week after Blomberg's promotion, the Yankees traveled to Washington. Their next destination was to be Fenway Park, famous for its towering left-field wall, known as the Green Monster. Jim Lyttle recalls, "We were sitting in the dugout before the game, talking about going to Boston. Bloomie was forever asking questions and never hearing the answers, because another question followed and then another question.

"He asked, 'What color is the Green Monster?' A couple of the guys kind of laughed, and somebody chimed in, 'Why do you *think* they call it the Green Monster?' We went on talking a while, and he spoke up again. '*What color is the Green Monster?*' He was dead serious.

"Ronnie was also gullible. He believed anything anybody told him. One day Dick Howser, our third-base coach, was throwing batting practice in Yankee Stadium and Ronnie hit a ball off the façade in right field! I was standing next to the batting cage, and Howser looked at me and shook his head in disbelief.

"I turned to Bloomie and said, 'Ronnie, as big and strong as you are, you should be able to hit that ball out of the ballpark.' " No one has ever cleared Yankee Stadium's roof in fair territory. Mickey Mantle came closest, bruising a home run off the ornate white façade during a game in 1963.

"Ronnie looked at me kind of funny," Lyttle continues. "The next few days, everybody he came up to, he'd ask, 'Do you think I'm losing my power?' "

Blomberg's presence behind Roy White and Bobby Murcer gave New York a potent 3-4-5 attack, particularly against right-handers. Cleanup man White (.292 BA, 19 HR, 84 RBI) played an errorless left field and thrived in the clutch. His 17 run-scoring sacrifice flies set an American League record—overlooked, perhaps, but representative of a quietly productive career. "That was always an important statistic for me," he says proudly. "I hated to leave a guy on third."

Murcer, batting in the number three spot, afforded White plenty of opportunities to collect ribbies. By mastering the strike zone and learning patience at the plate, he came into his own in 1971, hitting .331 with 25 homers and 94 RBIs. He also showed a marked improvement defensively, especially when it came to intercepting missiles in Yankee Stadium's Death Valley. "Bobby caught some balls going away that probably had moths on them by the time they came down," jokes pitcher Rob Gardner.

In chasing Tony Olivia for the batting title, Murcer at last chased away the ghost of Mickey Mantle. He has always insisted the comparisons never troubled him. Yet Murcer concedes his identity as a ballplayer didn't truly come into focus until his junior year.

"I became more comfortable with who I was," he reflects, "knowing that I was a solid player." And consistent. In the 1970s, only nine major-leaguers accumulated more hits and only eight scored more runs. Unfortunately, because Murcer toiled for mediocre Yankees teams, his considerable talents were never fully appreciated beyond the Bronx.

"Bobby was one of the most underrated players you could ever imagine," says John Ellis. "Sometimes I'd bat behind him and just watch him. He was a great hitter, had huge statistics, and played with a lot of pain." In 1971, Murcer's Triple Crown–caliber numbers won him election to the American League's starting lineup in that year's All-Star Game, the second since voting was returned to the fans after thirteen years. (From 1958 to 1970, the players honored their own.)

Murcer clubbed his twenty-fifth home run in the season finale, a bizarre affair against Washington. The nation's capital was losing its Senators to Arlington, Texas, where they would assume a new identity in the Western Division as the Texas Rangers. The franchise had long been hemorrhaging money. Most days RFK Stadium rivaled the floor of Congress during a filibuster for sparse attendance and deadly atmosphere. Yet when owner Bob Short decided to relocate rather than risk bankruptcy, angry Washingtonians were ready to tar and feather him.

A typically small but unruly crowd of 14,460 attended the city's 10,852nd and last baseball game. In the second inning Yankees shortstop Frank Baker spotted a FUCK SHORT banner unfurled to loud cheers and thought to himself, "Uh-oh, we're in trouble." The mood grew progressively uglier.

New York trailed 7–5 and was one out away from defeat when hordes of spectators stormed the field. "All of us took off into the clubhouse," Baker recalls. Security guards didn't bother trying to restore order, looking on as the mob helped themselves to bases, turf, and even lightbulbs from the scoreboard as souvenirs. Ralph Houk's club came away with a 9–0 forfeit, baseball's first in seventeen years, and completed 1971 a disappointing fourth, 82–80 (.506), twenty-one games back.

IV

THE YANKEES WENT home for the winter wondering if they might one day be subjecting New Yorkers to similar heartbreak. Since the beginning of the year, talk had been flying that unless the city agreed to improve conditions in and around Yankee Stadium, the Bronx Bombers and their subtenants, the football Giants, would consider New Jersey's invitation to move into a lavish $200 million sports complex proposed for the Hackensack Meadowlands, then the world's largest garbage dump.

How close did the Yankees come to crossing the Hudson? "*Close,*" says vice president Howard Berk, a participant in every meeting between the club and the city. "But Mike Burke really didn't want to do it. We were going to give it every shot to stay there."

Once a tourist attraction in its own right, Yankee Stadium had become a deterrent to attendance, which barely exceeded one million in 1971. The temporary face-lift conducted at the start of Burke's reign couldn't rectify intrinsic design flaws such as view-obstructing pillars and rafters.

In addition, the aging ballpark stood in a crime-ridden slum no longer equipped to handle either the traffic or the parking. Motorists arriving around game time could anticipate sweltering in gridlock, then parking blocks away, where they might or might not find their cars when they returned. Fans were also increasingly loath to ride the subway to 161st Street, especially at night.

The Yankees complained to their absentee landlord, Houston's Rice University, without success. (Dan Topping and Del Webb had sold the stadium in 1953.) So Burke took up his case with his good friend the mayor, making sure to use the Garden State's proposition as leverage. "We've got to do something for you," John Lindsay quickly agreed.

"There were two plans," Berk recalls. "One was to dome Shea Stadium and have both teams play there. But we didn't want to go to Shea, and the Mets didn't want us there, because it doesn't work. Everybody loses his identity when you do that. So that plan lasted about thirty seconds. The other was to modernize Yankee Stadium."

On March 2, 1971, Lindsay announced the city's intention to purchase and renovate The House That Ruth Built for an estimated $24 million, the same amount sunk into building Shea Stadium. In the event that Rice University did not wish to part with the ballpark, the mayor hinted he would seize it by way of condemnation proceedings. Despite scattered objections that the project was a white elephant the financially troubled city could not afford, in June both the City Council and the State Legislature opened the way for negotiations to proceed.

Then, on August 26, the Giants dealt the plan a critical blow when they signed a thirty-year lease to play in the Meadowlands beginning in 1975. While Mayor Lindsay insisted he would press on with the rebuilding regardless, City Council President Sanford Garelik and Controller Abe Beame challenged the wisdom of investing at all in a property that would now sit vacant six months of the year. As the 1971 season closed, it appeared Yankee Stadium might go the way of Ebbets Field and the Polo Grounds, both long since demolished.

Lindsay resourcefully executed a squeeze play. He persuaded the City Planning Commission to designate the plan an urban renewal project, thus circumventing the Board of Estimate, where it was likely to meet opposition. Ultimately the board endorsed it by a two-to-one margin—over Garelik's dissenting vote and Beame's abstention—and on March 24, 1972, the Yankees agreed to a thirty-year pact.

The city pledged a remodeled stadium, plus improved lighting, traffic flow, and parking in time for Opening Day 1976. During the two-year renovation, slated to begin in 1974, the Yankees and Mets would share Shea Stadium. Already rising construction costs had pumped the original $24 million estimate at least $11 million higher,

but what did Mike Burke care? The agreement he'd masterfully negoti-
ated placed no ceiling on cost.

Howard Berk reflects, "If there's a tribute to Mike Burke, it's that
ballpark and the fact that the Yankees are still there." Now that the
issue of where they would play was settled, one question remained:
Could the Yankees field a team worthy of their new palace?

1972

STARTERS		RELIEVERS
Mel Stottlemyre	**Ron Blomberg (1B)**	Sparky Lyle
Fritz Peterson	**Horace Clarke (2B)**	Lindy McDaniel
Steve Kline	**Gene Michael (SS)**	Fred Beene
Mike Kekich	**Rich McKinney/Celerino**	
Rob Gardner	**Sanchez (3B)**	
	Roy White (LF)	
	Bobby Murcer (CF)	
	Felipe Alou/John Callison	
	(RF)	
	Thurman Munson (C)	

I

OPENING DAY 1972, A delightful, sun-kissed afternoon. Ralph Houk stood on the dugout steps and let the cool breeze tickle his face. Then the scoreboard clock blinked 2:05—game time—and The Major, smoking a cigar and wearing a brown suit, strolled onto the field, which was empty and quiet.

There would be no baseball today, nor tomorrow, and Saturday didn't look very promising. The electric sign outside Yankee Stadium, under the Longines digital clock, advertised: YANKEE–ORIOLE OPENER SATURDAY 2 P.M. WE HOPE. The players were on strike.

As in 1969, the retirement fund was at issue. The players wanted benefits increased by 17 percent, or $1,072,000 total, to keep pace with the rising cost of living. It seemed a modest demand, especially given that four fifths of that sum could come from an existing fund surplus. Yet the lords of baseball shook their heads no. "We won't give another damn cent," St. Louis's Gussie Busch blustered. Jack Aker, the Yankees players' representative, believed the pension dispute was just a smoke screen for their true objective: to break the Players Association. He'd feared as much over the winter.

"None of us was looking forward to that spring, because we knew something heavy was going to have to happen," says Aker, nicknamed "Chief" because of his part–Native American ancestry. "The owners had already showed that they were going to stonewall any proposals we made. And it seemed like they were going to test us."

The players grimly understood the hazards of a strike, not the least of which would be the financial sacrifice. The union had no strike fund, and many major-leaguers earned surprisingly modest livings to begin with. In 1972, the average annual salary was $34,092, ranging from Atlanta Brave Henry Aaron's $200,000 to the minimum of $13,500. Mel Stottlemyre, who at $80,000 was the highest paid Yankee, would forfeit more than $3,000 for each week spent on the picket line.

"I'm sure there were some players who for their own personal sake were really hoping we wouldn't strike," says Aker. But when he sat down with his teammates in mid-March and put it to them bluntly— "We've got to decide on this thing. Yes or no?"—the vote was unanimous in favor. Nineteen other clubs followed suit. The tally from around the majors totaled an overwhelming 663 yeas, 10 nays, and 1 abstention. If no accord was reached by Friday, March 31, one week before Opening Day, the players planned to walk out.

Once again the club owners miscalculated the Association's unity, rebuffing a late offer by the union to accept an independent arbitrator. Their huffing threats to padlock every ballpark all season long, by God, if that's what it took to teach the ingrates a lesson, served only to alienate the public. Gene Autry, the cowboy singer back in the saddle again as owner of the California Angels, actually blurted, "We ought to close baseball down forever!" The players didn't believe him or the others for a moment.

"We knew the owners weren't going to throw away a whole year's income over this," Aker recalls. "We were prepared to sit out for a while; at the most, we thought, a month, although I don't know why we came up with that figure."

The players' own union leader underestimated their determination to take up the owners' gauntlet. On deadline day the forty-eight team representatives and alternates convened in a Dallas airport motel for an eleventh-hour powwow. When gray-haired, mustachioed Marvin Miller cautiously recommended continuing negotiations and postponing the strike until next year, one by one members stood up to declare that their constituents were prepared to walk.

Nonetheless tensions flared. "It was a very heated meeting," Aker recalls. "Two or three clubs were definitely against striking, and there were some very loud exchanges of words. We finally asked Marvin if he thought we should or shouldn't strike.

"Having heard all these arguments, he didn't really believe that we were solid enough, and he advised us not to." Miller worried that if the strike crumbled, it could spell the end of the still-young Association. "At that point," says Aker, "we asked him to leave the room. We talked it over among ourselves and decided that we would strike."

The final vote was 47 to 0. Los Angeles's Wes Parker, a vocal opponent, abstained. But then, the veteran Dodger had already been quoted in the papers complaining about players' "ridiculously high" salaries. Parker's teammates soon stripped him of his office, and he retired after the season.

That night a drawn-looking Marvin Miller stood in front of the assembled reporters and photographers and announced simply, "Strike."

Saturday morning the sport ground to a standstill. All exhibition games had to be cancelled. Clubs shut down their spring-training facilities and stopped paying players' expenses. "The day we left spring training was probably one of the saddest days in my career," reflects Aker. "It was traumatic for a lot of us who really loved our jobs and loved the cities we played in. And even the conditions we'd been playing under didn't bother us that much.

"But," he emphasizes, "we realized that this had to be done, if not for our sake, then at least for the players of the future."

The union's solidarity marked a turnaround from only a few years before when Jim Bouton would raise to teammates the inherent inequity of the reserve clause—which indentured a player to a club for his baseball life—only to be reprimanded, "Don't be a clubhouse lawyer!"

"If I could have gotten three or more players on the team to strike," he says, "I would have organized one. I would have said, 'Let's march in the streets. Let's carry picket signs. This is unfair.' But baseball players were basically scared people. They didn't want to put themselves on the line.

"I remember one spring Clete Boyer took a poll of the clubhouse to find out what guys thought the minimum salary should be. It was six thousand dollars at the time. They went around the room, and each person said nine thousand, ten thousand, eight thousand, eleven thousand. That was the range. Then they got to me.

" 'Okay, Bouton, what do you think?'

"I said, 'Twenty-five thousand.'

" 'Aw, come on!'

" 'Get outta here!'

"The whole clubhouse went, 'Oh, Jesus . . .'—like, 'What a pain in the ass this guy is.'

"I said, 'Twenty-five thousand—why not? You guys are all Ph.D.s in hitting and pitching. We're at the top of our field. It's a monopoly that makes millions of dollars. Twenty-five thousand dollars is *nothing*.'

"But they couldn't understand that," says Bouton. "They had me marked down as a nut for thinking this way."

While bargaining between the owners and the Players Association forged ahead, Yankees players worked out on diamonds throughout the New York area. A janitor at Pascack Valley High in New Jersey chased Steve Kline and Gene Michael off the school ballfield, fearing the shortstop might put one of Kline's pitches through a window. Obviously the man had never seen Michael hit.

Across the street from Yankee Stadium, teenagers playing ball in McCombs Dam Park noticed a group of familiar faces heading their way with bats and balls: Ron Blomberg, Thurman Munson, Roy White, Bobby Murcer, Jerry Kenney, and Horace Clarke. "They couldn't believe their eyes," Blomberg recalls. "We played a pickup game with them, with about five hundred people standing around watching. It was fun. A nice time."

On April 10, four days into the season, the owners capitulated on the pension issue, agreeing to a 14-percent cost-of-living increase and to a $500,000 rise in health-care benefits. Play ball? Not yet. A new stumbling block arose when the owners insisted that all postponements be made up with no pay. Unacceptable, said the players. And so Marvin Miller and John Gaherin, the owners' representative, picked up their sabers and resumed fencing.

Three more days dragged by, needlessly, it would turn out. To avoid compensating the players, the owners decided to forgo the missed dates altogether. This meant that clubs would see their seasons shortened by anywhere from six to nine games, a scheduling imbalance that was to profoundly influence the American League East race.

With that, the first strike in the history of professional sports was over. The immediate financial casualties amounted to something of a draw: $5.2 million in lost revenues for the owners; $600,000 for the strikers. But in the long run the walkout was a decisive victory for the players, irrevocably altering the balance of power within the game.

"I think everybody was satisfied," says Jack Aker of fellow ballplayers' feelings about the settlement. "We knew, 'Hey, we've really got a players' union now.' And baseball did a complete turnaround from that point on."

Over the next four years, the average major-league salary rose by approximately 50 percent, to $51,501. Then, in 1975, a court decision limiting the reserve system ushered in the era of free agency and sent salaries skyrocketing. Aker, who now runs his own baseball school, says, "If the strike hadn't happened, today's players wouldn't be paid anywhere near what they are." In 1993, the average salary was $1,116,946.

Ironically, he believes the owners' attempt to crush the union instigated the uprising that ultimately overthrew their fiefdoms. "There's a great possibility that had they given in just slightly, we might not have gone on strike. And as a result," says Aker, traded to the Cubs in May, "there might not have been free agency and these sorts of things down the line.

"But by egging us on and backing us up against the wall, they created so much animosity—in '72 and later on—that whenever there was a choice between negotiating and striking, the players got their backs up."

II

OPENING DAY IS baseball's annual day of atonement, when the sins of the past are duly absolved. Never did that rite feel more cleansing than on April 16, when New York's 155-game season finally got underway in rainy Baltimore. The gray skies baptized the participants four times before the umpires finally halted play for good in the seventh with the Orioles ahead 3–1.

Six games and four more losses later, the 2–5 Yankees may have wished the strike had lasted indefinitely. The new season was tracing the disturbing pattern of the old one: reliable pitching undermined by a barren offense and an atrocious defense.

In an 11–7 loss at Fenway Park on April 22, new third baseman Rich McKinney tied a major-league mark by muffing four ground balls. Statistics are not kept on general managers' errors in judgment, but already it was becoming clear that Lee MacPhail had committed a colossal blunder when he parted with Stan Bahnsen for the twenty-five-year-old White Sox utility man.

Like spurned lovers comparing themselves to their former flames' new sweethearts, ballplayers secretly keep tabs on whoever made them expendable. Bahnsen, a 21-game winner in 1972, found it funny that McKinney's miscues should end up wounding Fritz Peterson. "Fritz had said he didn't think it was a bad trade, which surprised me," says Bahnsen, now involved in sports promotion and marketing in Florida. "Then Rich made the four errors in one of his games. It was almost as if Fritz's words came back to haunt him."

Peterson's opinion changed appreciably as he watched balls glance off McKinney's glove and roll between his legs while nine unearned runs streamed across the plate. "At that point," says the left-hander, "I think we realized something was wrong."

In fairness to McKinney, a .271 hitter for Chicago in 1971, he'd worked the hot corner fewer than three dozen times in his career, so just why New York management settled upon him as the answer to its problems there remains a mystery. Lee MacPhail accepts full blame for the transaction, which he calls "the worst I ever made."

"We should have gotten more information about McKinney," he says in hindsight. "He'd played second base for the White Sox, and we thought he wouldn't have too much trouble making the shift to third." MacPhail shakes his head and laughs. "But he certainly did."

McKinney, nicknamed Bozo for the way his curly hair poked out the sides of his cap, never got over that embarrassing afternoon in Fenway. The target of vicious taunts from the stands, he developed a virtual phobia about playing third. "Every game you could see him losing more and more confidence, to where he was afraid to do anything," observes utility infielder Bernie Allen, acquired from Texas the same day as McKinney.

Hal Lanier, another veteran pickup, known for his glove, tried working with McKinney on his defense. "But Rich just didn't want the ball hit to him," Lanier says. "He wanted out of there in the late innings, when an error might lose the game for us."

Ironically, McKinney went the next four weeks without an error. It was his deficieny at bat (.216 BA, 1 HR, 5 RBI) that led the club to funnel him to the minors on May 29. Syracuse, though, wasn't far enough from the Bronx to suit McKinney, who rejoiced when the Yankees shipped him to Oakland that winter along with pitcher Rob Gardner. "He was glad to get out of New York and made no bones about it," says Gardner.

In his brief stay, McKinney had temporarily replaced Horace Clarke as the lightning rod for fans' ire. The day of his demotion, the fifth-place Yankees wore an unflattering 14–19, .424 record. Lee MacPhail's five-year rebuilding movement was not only behind schedule, the franchise appeared to be backsliding, both on the field and at the turnstiles.

Frustration was, of course, also felt in the president's office. The normally ebullient Mike Burke described the first third of 1972 to *Newsday*'s Steve Jacobson as "a very keen disappointment. This was the year we should have delivered. We can't cop a plea of not enough time."

Since CBS put him in charge, he'd left all strategy and personnel decisions to Houk and MacPhail. Burke's only direct involvement with the players was to join them sometimes for games of pepper during spring training. Curt Blefary laughingly recalls, "He'd take off his suit jacket, roll up his sleeves, loosen his tie, and put on a glove. Then we'd hit line drives off his shins until he finally quit."

But as the Yankees slogged through an 11–14 June, Burke seriously contemplated terminating his manager, then in the final months of a three-year contract. A long-time Houk advocate, Burke's faith in The Major was beginning to evaporate.

"We've had a hell of a lot of mental lapses, mistakes that shouldn't be happening," Burke further complained, implying the manager was losing his magic. Indeed, for the first time, Houk's annual declaration that the Yankees would surprise their critics failed to convince the troops. "We'd heard it so many times," says Fritz Peterson, "by then we knew better. We just didn't have the players to win."

Burke dreamed of replacing Houk with fiery Billy Martin. The problem was that Martin belonged to the Tigers, who were currently sitting atop the AL East. As might be expected of a former intelligence agent, the Yankees president parachuted behind enemy lines in the hope of engineering an extraordinary scenario.

"Mike thought he'd trade managers with Detroit," Lee MacPhail explains. "It would stir up a lot of publicity, and Billy Martin was the fighting type that might be good for the Yankees. But Mike knew I'd be against it, so he never even broached it to me. He went to the Detroit club and talked to their general manager, Jim Campbell, who happened to be a very close friend of mine. The first thing Jim said was, 'Well, how does Lee feel about this?' And Mike said, 'I haven't told him ' Jim said, 'Forget it.' So that was the end of that."

Returning home from a miserable 1–9 midwestern road trip in mid-June, New York fell to Chicago's Wilbur Wood 2–0. It marked the third time in four games the club failed to put a run on the board. The Major's usually harmonious Yankees were in disarray, anxious about their manager's status and squabbling among themselves. Several pitchers ripped the team's defense in the sports pages, specifically Roy White and Horace Clarke. Curiously, these anonymous sources spared the sputtering offense, which had generated a mere two dozen home runs in the club's first fifty ball games.

On June 15, the day of the trading deadline, Houk held a rare closed-door meeting with his men to assure them he was still in command and

not destined for Boston as rumored. He also issued a stern warning
that any more whining in public would cost the source $1,000. The
Yankees listened quietly and respectfully, then marched out and pummeled the White Sox, 8–1, after which the complexion of the 1972
season immediately brightened.

New York touched .500 on July 21, as Mel Stottlemyre and Fritz
Peterson muzzled California on four hits each in a twin-shutout doubleheader. The Yankees' one-two combination, once 0–3 and 0–6, respectively, raised their records to 10–11 and 9–11. Stottlemyre's seven
shutouts on the year gave him 36 lifetime, more than any active AL
hurler, while for the fifth straight season Peterson dispensed the fewest
walks per nine innings in the league.

"I liked to think of us as the poor man's Sandy Koufax and Don
Drysdale," he says, adding that the two briefly considered following
the example of the Dodgers' awesome lefty-righty duo of the 1950s
and '60s and negotiating their 1973 contracts jointly. "But Mel was
such a nice guy," says Peterson, "he didn't want to make anybody in
the front office mad."

The next afternoon, Old Timers' Day, Steve Kline tacked on seven
more scoreless innings but was removed for a pinch hitter in a game
the bullpen let slip through its fingers 1–0. Two seasons in the Bronx
had steeled Number 38 to the frustration of pitching well enough to
win yet coming away empty-handed.

It happened repeatedly in 1971, when his 2.96 ERA produced an
anomalous 12–13 mark. But Kline accepted the string of low-scoring
draws and defeats as the breaks of the game. "The tough part, though,
was going in at the end of the year and trying to get more money for
that attitude," he says. "Lee MacPhail told me to my face, 'You're not
paid to have a good ERA, you're paid to win.' "

In 1972, the twenty-four-year-old emerged as one of the league's
most promising right-handers. Kline tamed the Red Sox 3–1 on July
28 to push his record to 10–4. When Mike Kekich rang up his tenth
the next day, it gave the Yankees the first starting foursome in all of
baseball to reach double figures in the W column.

New York still needed a fifth starting arm, especially with doubleheaders soon to pile up in late July and early August. Rich Hinton and
Wade Blasingame had already flunked as spot starters, leaving Houk
little choice but to try Rob Gardner, a journeyman twenty-seven-year-
old sent down in spring training because The Major didn't think he
possessed major-league stuff.

Managers had underestimated Gardner before. A left-handed
breaking-ball artist, he won his first three decisions as a Mets starter
in 1966, his second season. But when one of the club's southpaw

relievers injured himself, Manager Wes Westrum assigned Gardner to the bullpen, where the irregular work ruined his control. He went 1–8 the rest of the way. Later the Cubs and Indians also insisted on molding him into a fireman, with equally discouraging results.

"Rob was one of those people whom baseball's conventional wisdom robbed of a career," observes Ron Swoboda, Gardner's teammate on both New York clubs. "Relieving was not what he did best. He wasn't a hard thrower, but he was really a pitcher, with a capital *P*. A good thinker. You'd never be impressed with his stuff, yet he'd get you out."

As a rookie outfielder for the Mets, Swoboda unintentionally helped to make Gardner's 1965 major-league debut versus Houston all too memorable. "I still have nightmares about it regularly," says Gardner, who was born and raised in Binghamton, New York. "Bob Lillis was the first hitter I ever faced, and I got him to pop the ball up to left. I remember thinking as it went off the bat, *Jeez, my first big-league out. That wasn't too tough!*

"I turned around and saw Ron having a bit of trouble out there. The ball fell behind him, and Lillis wound up on second with a double. Joe Morgan was the next hitter, and he got a base hit, and I was behind 1–0. Then the third batter, Jim Wynn, hit another pop fly to left that Ron also had a bit of trouble with. They ended up scoring five runs before I got anybody out."

By 1969, Gardner was toiling for Cleveland's triple-A club in Portland, with little prospect of making it back to the majors. "I was stinking up the place and thought that could be it," he says. "Then I got the news I'd been traded to Syracuse. Frank Verdi, the manager there, took me aside and said, 'I know you haven't been pitching a lot. I'm going to start you in a while, but I want you to relieve for now.' I thought, *Oh yeah, I've heard this song before.*

"But he did start me. I wound up winning eleven games in half a year. And in 1970 I won twenty: sixteen during the season, three in the play-offs, and one with the Yankees. Frank saved my life. I probably would have been out of baseball already if it weren't for him."

Gardner was named the International League's Pitcher of the Year, but Houk, unimpressed, cut him on Opening Day the following spring. Three days later, he accompanied Ron Klimkowski to Oakland in the Felipe Alou deal, only to wind up back at Syracuse in May as compensation for Curt Blefary. When he failed to make the squad again in 1972, despite an excellent grapefruit-league record, Gardner demanded an explanation.

"Ralph told me he felt I was a little shy of being a big-league pitcher," he recalls. "I asked him to be traded if that were possible, then went to Syracuse, figuring I wouldn't pitch for the Yankees at all that year."

In June he received a surprise call to join the club in Chicago. "Ralph called me into his office and said, 'Lookit, nobody's doing the job here. You say you can do it. I'm going to give you the ball when we go to Detroit in three weeks, and we'll see if you can pitch up here.'

"I said, 'That's all I ever wanted, Ralph. Let's find out.'

"From there we went to Texas and had a day off. Steve Kline and I were on the bus with some of the writers, going to the Six Flags amusement park. One of them said to me, 'Did you hear about the trade? The Yankees just acquired Wade Blasingame from Houston.' Another left-hander.

"So the start in Detroit I was going to get went to Blasingame instead. Now, in this day and age maybe this won't sound so bad, since the only loyalty is to money, but back then your loyalty was supposed to be to your ball club. I sat in the bullpen that day hoping we'd lose," he confesses, "because that was supposed to be my start." Gardner's wish came true: Blasingame, a fading nine-year veteran, walked the leadoff man, then watched three consecutive home runs vanish over the fence. Houk never dared give him the ball again.

Gardner's chance to redeem himself in the manager's eyes finally came in the nightcap of a July 2 doubleheader against Cleveland. The twin bill has since gone the way of the flannel jersey, but the Yankees played over three dozen that year. "Game two was kind of the throwaway," he explains. "You'd put your best pitcher in the first one and whoever was left in the second. I was the last one left."

John Ellis, whose playing time diminished by half in 1972, was to catch. "We both knew this would be our only shot," Gardner recalls. "If we screwed up, it was probably going to be the black hole forever." The former Met stifled the Indians 5–2, while Ellis went 2-for-4 and bailed his batterymate out of a two-out, bases-loaded jam, leaning into the backstop to nab a foul pop.

Like a schoolboy counting down the days until the next vacation, Gardner circled forthcoming doubleheaders on New York's schedule and awaited his next start. Three weeks later, with Ellis again his receiver, Number 39 clinched a split in the Old Timers' Day doubleheader by going the distance over the Angels, 7–1. It was his first complete game since 1966.

Gardner rapidly upgraded his position from spot starter to stopper. Taking the mound after a nine-day enforced holiday, on July 31 he nipped the Orioles 2–1. Ellis added three hits, to match Thurman Munson's output in game one, which the Yankees took 5–2.

Munson, enjoying a .280 BA, 7 HR, 46 RBI season, kept a rally alive in the seventh inning of the opener through sheer hustle. He was on third base when Fritz Peterson nubbed a roller to second. As Number 15 broke for the plate, Bobby Grich scooped the ball and whipped it home to Andy Etchebarren, setting up a turnabout encounter between the two catchers. Munson plowed head-first into Etchebarren, sending his helmet flying in one direction and the ball in another, while Felipe Alou loped across with the inning's fifth run.

III

FOR MUNSON, IT was sweet revenge, and for the Yankees, confirmation that neither they nor the Orioles were the same clubs they were last season. Trading away the inspirational Frank Robinson alone dissipated Baltimore's aura of invincibility. Then slumps engulfed all eight regulars, driving down the Birds' team average 32 points to a division-low .229.

New York's only significant improvement came in the relief department, but what a difference. When Peterson and Gardner showed signs of tiring against the O's, Ralph Houk immediately summoned left-hander Sparky Lyle. A pair of shutout innings in each game, and the new lockup man pocketed two more saves en route to a then league record 35.

The bullpen debacle of 1971 had prompted New York to go fishing for a quality closer over the winter, using Danny Cater as bait. Lee MacPhail initially set his sights on Oakland's Darold Knowles. But Houk had coveted Boston's Lyle for some time, and the Red Sox needed a first baseman after having traded George Scott. The result, midway through spring training, was a deal that would win MacPhail a near-pardon for the McKinney disaster. Lyle, twenty-seven, had a hand in more than half of the Yankees' 79 wins in 1972, going 9–5, with a 1.91 ERA.

In addition to anchoring the bullpen, Albert Walter Lyle, nicknamed Sparky by his father for reasons known only to the elder Lyle, gave the Yankees their most colorful, engaging personality in years. His mere entrance, like that of a matador, sent ripples of excitement through Yankee Stadium.

To the majestic organ accompaniment of "Pomp and Circumstance," Number 28 would hop from the pinstriped Datsun bullpen car, toss his warm-up jacket to the batboy, and stride theatrically to the mound. Then he'd come at the hitter with little more than an average fastball but a devastatingly hard slider, which he'd perfected late one night while playing for the Red Sox's Pittsfield, Massachusetts, farm club.

Lyle wasn't pitching at the time but in bed with his wife, gripping a baseball. Suddenly it came to him how to throw the tricky breaking pitch. He hurried outside and started experimenting against the wall of an adjacent bar, under the dim halo of a street lamp. Lyle's slider wasn't much easier to follow in broad daylight, ducking low and in on righties and low and away on lefties at eighty-five miles per hour.

"He'd just tell the hitter, 'Here comes my hard slider,' " says Bernie Allen. " 'You hit it, you got me. And if you don't, I got you. Now let's get it on.' "

Lyle, along with Oakland's Rollie Fingers and Montreal's Mike Marshall, was the quintessence of the modern short reliever, possessing both star quality and the marble nerve of a trapeze artist. Win or lose, his face, distinguished by a cleft chin and a wad of Red Man tucked in his left cheek, and framed by muttonchop sideburns, betrayed no emotion.

"Sparky was absolutely fearless," says Ron Swoboda. "One time we were playing in Milwaukee, where the lights weren't the best. It was the bottom of the ninth, and the tying and winning runs were on base with two outs.

"The batter smokes one to right-center, and the ball practically disappears out there while Bobby Murcer is chasing it. And here comes Sparky strolling off the mound like the game has ended. Jim Turner the pitching coach asked him, 'Where the hell are you going?'

" 'Well,' said Sparky, 'one way or the other, it's all over.' If Murcer caught it, it was over. And if it landed out there, it was over. Either way his job was done."

The gregarious Lyle kept teammates loose with clubhouse pranks such as squashing birthday cakes with his bare ass. Catcher Jerry Moses, a Yankee in 1973, and before that a teammate of Lyle's in Boston and the minors, recalls, "If you left a cake out, Jim Turner would eat the whole thing. So Sparky used to hide around the corner, waiting for Jim to get ready to cut himself a piece. Just then he'd jump out, sit on the cake and run, with all that frosting hanging off him. One time Jim took off after him with a knife, trying to get him."

Lyle, unhappy his last season in Boston due to lack of work, thrived under Ralph Houk, who more than doubled his innings to 108 1/3 but without wearing him out. In Kansas City on August 15 Number 28 wasn't allowed to so much as warm up in the bottom of the ninth even while Rob Gardner was converting a hard-fought 6–4 lead into a bitter 7–6 defeat. Sportswriter Steve Jacobson observes, "Houk had a gift for being willing to take a loss, knowing that if he used his relief pitcher that day he might lose him for the next two weeks."

The previous week Lyle recorded a win and four saves, three of them relatively easy and one the kind of tense combat that could send his adrenaline pumping: gladiator to gladiator, with the outcome hanging in the balance.

In the August 10 finale of a four-game home stand against first-place Detroit, New York carried a 1–0 edge into the ninth. Steve Kline, on twenty-four-hour loan from Army Reserve duty upstate, had been outstanding, yielding just three singles. "My usual game," he calls it. "A bunch of ground balls, a cloud of dust, and I'm out of there." But Houk felt he'd thrown enough pitches and phoned the bullpen for his closer. He got no argument from Kline, then in the midst of a thirty-seven-inning scoreless streak that reduced his ERA to 1.61, the best in the majors. "You knew that when Sparky came in, the door was going to get slammed shut," he says.

Lyle protected the young righty's thirteenth win, but not with his customary dispatch. Gates Brown drilled a leadoff double, followed by a strikeout, an infield hit, a ground out to first, and an intentional pass, which loaded the bases. Up stepped pinch hitter Ike Brown.

The Yankees left-hander missed with his first pitch, and the crowd of 40,000-plus stirred uneasily. Then he got a fastball over for strike one. A slider for a swinging strike two. With the crowd on its feet, Lyle delivered another slider that Brown waved at helplessly to give New York the series, three games to one. An exultant Thurman Munson heaved the ball into the outfield.

"It was a tremendous ball game, and a real uplifting one," says Kline, "because Billy Martin had come into town saying the Tigers were going to put us away and drop us back into fourth place where we belonged."

New York, 27–15 (.643) from July 1 on, and now 55–49 (.529) overall, was very much in contention, even if only because the American League East pennant race resembled the three-legged kind, with Detroit, Boston, and Baltimore all stumbling along as if none wanted to face the West's awesome Oakland A's in the play-offs.

Ambushing the Tigers elevated the Yankees to within two and a half games of first and made an overnight saint of twenty-eight-year-old rookie Celerino Sanchez. In eight seasons in his native Mexico, the right-handed third baseman failed to surpass .300 but once, and in 1966 batted .448.

A Mexican newspaperman had tipped off the Yankees to Sanchez, who'd long dreamed of playing north of the border. When the Mexico

City Tigers refused to let their star go, Sanchez forced a deal by threatening to retire. As a nonroster player, he pounded the ball in spring training. But the Yankees were still committed to using Rich McKinney at third and sent him to Syracuse.

Recalled on June 10, Sanchez hit a modest .248 BA (with zero home runs and 22 RBIs) for New York, but collected a number of key hits. In the Detroit-series opener, Sanchez's eighth-inning sacrifice fly put the Yankees on top, 3–2. Ron Swoboda followed with a run-scoring single, and Sparky Lyle held the Tigers in check for a 4–2 victory.

The next afternoon, undefeated Rob Gardner picked up his fourth win, 2–1, after Sanchez delivered a clutch two-run single late in the game. As an unexpected dividend, Number 10 also provided plucky defense. In the eighth, he blocked a hard grounder with his chest, recovering in time to get the inning's final out. Gardner came over to express his gratitude, but without an English-Spanish dictionary handy had to settle for patting his teammate on the back. "Mostly he'd just smile a lot and say hi," recalls Jerry Kenney.

If anything, the language barrier enhanced Sanchez's near-mythical status among fans as a Mexican Joe Hardy. The following season he played only sparingly, after which he returned to Mexico, where he now owns a sporting-goods store in Guanajuato. But for several weeks in the summer of 1972, Celerino Sanchez was the most popular New Yorker since Fiorello La Guardia.

The Milwaukee Brewers followed the Tigers into town. On August 12, New York held its annual Latin American Day. Sanchez, who was being honored along with Felipe Alou and Horace Clarke, whacked an RBI triple that put the Yankees ahead to stay. But right fielder Johnny Callison, whom the Yankees got the previous winter from the Cubs, outshone everyone in the 10–6 slugfest. The onetime National League star knocked in six runs on three hits, including his fifth career grand slam.

At midseason, Callison, thirty-three years old and batting .216, was contemplating retirement. Then the Yankees demoted disappointing rookie Rusty Torres and installed him in right against right-handed pitching. Over the second half, the former Phillie evoked memories of the '64 all-star who would have been a shoo-in for that year's NL MVP award had Philadelphia not taken its legendary swan dive. He powdered the ball at a .300-plus clip to wind up at .258, with 9 home runs and 34 RBIs.

Without Callison and other indispensable part-timers such as Alou, John Ellis, and Bernie Allen, New York's pennant surge would have been a ripple at best. Of the regulars, only Bobby Murcer was posting outstanding numbers (.292 BA, 33 HR, 96 RBI, and a league-leading

102 R). Ron Blomberg (.268 BA, 14 HR, 49 RBI) continued to impress, but against righties only, while Roy White tailed off to .270 BA, 10 HR, 54 RBI.

The reserves took up the slack. Alou (.278 BA, 6 HR, 37 RBI) batted .345 off the bench and led the league in pinch hits. Ellis made the most of his infrequent appearances, hitting .294. And Allen, an eleven-year veteran, contributed 9 home runs, several in clutch situations.

Credit the manager for the bench's productivity. Houk wove his subs in and out of the lineup masterfully. Just as important, he kept them psychologically primed between starts. Few pilots showed a greater appreciation of the second-stringer's frustrating plight than The Major, himself a former *third*-stringer behind Yogi Berra and Charlie Silvera.

"I think that from all the years I spent in the bullpen, I understood more what the players down there went through," he reflects. "So I always tried to make each person on the club know he was valuable and what his job was. Because I've always felt that pennants aren't really won by the front nine," Houk contends, "but by those guys you don't read about who win the one or two or three games for you."

Infielder Hal Lanier says, "I remember Ralph always telling me that if I ever became a manager, the people to keep happy are the guys sitting on the bench. The nine guys on the field, all you really have to do is pat them on the back." As the rookie skipper of the Houston Astros in 1986, he won a division title.

Lanier, San Francisco's starting shortstop for seven seasons (and the son of Max Lanier, a splendid pitcher for the Cardinals and the Giants), spent most of his time in pinstripes riding the pine. "During really tight situations," he remembers appreciatively, "Ralph would walk down to where me, Callison, and Allen sat and ask us, 'What would you do in this situation?' To keep us in the game."

The day after Callison's offensive barrage, the Bronx Bombers swept a Bat Day doublcheader in front of 56,238 souls, the league's largest attendance of the season. Since the drive toward first shifted into high gear, New Yorkers began descending upon Yankee Stadium like prospectors at Sutter's Mill during the Gold Rush days.

This new generation of fan, for whom evidence of the team's proud tradition existed only in history books, rooted with an enthusiasm that reminded Ron Swoboda of Shea Stadium in the exalted summer of 1969. When the Brewers mounted a late-inning threat against Mel Stottlemyre in the 5–3 opener, the crowd chanted rousingly, "*Dee*-fense! *Dee*-fense! *Dee*-fense!"

Game two's come-from-behind 5–4 victory generated such deafening noise that winning reliever Fred Beene recalls, "Me and Thurman had to yell just to hear each other." In the seventh inning, pinch hitter

Ron Blomberg overturned a 3–2 Milwaukee lead by poking a two-run homer off Jim Colborn. Indicative of his strength, the sophomore first baseman broke his bat on the swing yet put enough distance into the ball that it dropped just over the right-field fence. Two pitches later, Bernie Allen winged one in the exact same spot for an insurance run.

"I never wanted to go to the ballpark so much as when we made that run for the pennant," Rob Gardner reminisces. "You couldn't wait for the next game. And you could feel it from the fans. There was an electricity pervading the whole stadium. From the first pitch to the last, they were in it."

In late August, Ralph Houk announced that he would go to a four-man rotation down the stretch, with Gardner to replace a struggling Mike Kekich. Despite Kekich's sad second half (1–4, 6.21 ERA), his Nursery fraternity brothers felt he'd been wronged by the shift and were decidedly cool to the interloper.

Gardner brushed off the snubs and in his first outing as the number-four man shut out Texas through seven innings in a game the Yankees won for Sparky Lyle in overtime, 2–0. The last two months of the season, Gardner and Fritz Peterson (17–15, 3.24 ERA) provided the slumping staff's only consistency. Steve Kline, 14–5, 1.61 ERA, on August 19, developed tenderness in his elbow and faded out at 16–9, 2.40 ERA, while Mel Stottlemyre deflated after the All-Star break to end up 14–18, 3.22 ERA.

At 8–5, with a 3.06 ERA, Gardner was convinced he had a job for next year. "Then in November I got a telegram from Lee MacPhail saying, 'We regret to inform you . . .' " The Yankees had traded him to Oakland, *again*, and for another Alou, Felipe's younger brother Matty. "Surprised and disappointed," was Gardner's reaction. His disappointment grew as months passed without a welcoming phone call from A's owner Charlie Finley.

"It got around contract time, and I still hadn't heard from him, so I wound up calling him. I asked him, 'Charlie, why did you trade for me? You've got the best pitching staff in baseball!' He said, 'Well, we like to have insurance.' To me that meant they liked to have insurance *at Tucson*," Oakland's triple-A club. "So that was not a pleasant conversation."

Gardner's career resumed a familiar pattern, as Oakland stashed him in the bullpen. He hurt his arm, got dealt to Milwaukee in May, and then returned to the A's in July, never to win another game in the majors. One small consolation: at least he couldn't be traded for the third Alou brother, Jesus, who was by then an Oakland teammate.

In 1976 the pitcher who never wanted to be a fireman left the game to join the Binghamton Fire Department, in upstate New York, as a medic. He also served as a county legislator from 1982 to 1990. "I don't want to sound sanctimonious about this," says Gardner, a Democrat, "but you're so insulated when you play baseball. I had taken a lot of things on this earth for granted, and I was trying to give something back."

IV

ON LABOR DAY, Gardner restrained the Orioles 5–2 after they'd handed the Yankees a disheartening 4–3 defeat in the opener. It marked the third time he'd salvaged a doubleheader split. As the season entered its final four weeks, the knot at the top of the American League East had tightened so that Baltimore and Detroit shared first, while Boston and New York each lurked a half-game back.

To be this close this late in the year would have been unthinkable for the Yankees back in June, when their manager's status was tenuous. A 38–25 (.603) July and August had made Houk's rehiring a foregone conclusion, and over the Labor Day weekend both he and Lee Mac-Phail signed new three-year contracts.

As the Yankees prepared to host Baltimore on September 15, all four contenders sported identical win totals:

	W–L	Pct.	Games Back
Boston	74–62	.544	—
Detroit	74–64	.536	1
Baltimore	74–65	.532	1½
New York	74–65	.532	1½

"Everybody felt we had a good chance to take the pennant," says Hal Lanier. "You could feel it," adds Steve Kline. "The momentum was on our side."

Funny thing, momentum—so fickle. Jim Palmer's outmatching Mel Stottlemyre 3–1 in the Friday-night opener started the Yankees down a slippery 5–11 slope that would ultimately land them in fourth place, six and a half games out.

"We peaked just a tad early, then hit a slump at the worst possible time," says Rob Gardner. No one department deserved more blame than another, although a tired Sparky Lyle did stumble in the final month, despite delicate handling. In Detroit with one week left, he incurred the loss that wrote the Yankees out of the race.

New York was carrying a 5–1 lead into the eighth when singles by Willie Horton, Al Kaline, and Duke Sims chased starter Steve Kline. Enter The Count, who days before had earned his thirty-fifth save. A single and a sacrifice fly shrank the lead to one.

In the ninth, the Tigers won in torturous fashion. First, Ed Brinkman and Horton singled. Next, pinch hitter Tony Taylor dropped a bunt that caught third baseman Hal Lanier flat-footed, loading the bases.

Number 28 had escaped jams like this before, and he appeared to have fooled Kaline with an 0-and-2 fastball. But umpire Don Denkinger ruled it a ball, which sent Thurman Munson into a rage and rattled the normally unperturbable Lyle. He fell behind, 3-and-2, then came in with a pitch that Kaline skied deep enough to tie the game and move the winning run to third.

Houk waved in his outfielders, since in this situation a long fly was as good as a hit. After taking a strike, lefty Duke Sims lined a single into left center for a 6–5 Detroit victory. Murcer caught up with the ball and in frustration hurled it into the upper deck. He'd signed with the Yankees as an eighteen-year-old in 1964 expecting to play for a pennant winner, and eight years later this was the closest he'd come.

"We never had the club," he says in retrospect. "We were always short. We were getting much closer, gaining ground each year, but we were still short."

Back in the Bronx, the Yankees let the clock tick out on 1972 by dropping their last five contests. Sportswriter George Vecsey recalls, "I have a vivid memory of seeing Mike Burke sitting all alone in left field, watching the game with his sleeves rolled up, just melancholy, because the Yankees had crumbled again." New York's 79–76 closing record didn't do justice to a thrilling campaign, one that for Boston and Detroit rumbled down to the next-to-last day. The Tigers (86–70) won by half a game over the Red Sox (85–70), thanks to the uneven strike-shortened schedule.

New York's season ended much as it had begun: losing before an audience of empty seats. Afterward, Ralph Houk leaned back in his office chair and, with cigar and beer in hand, outlined his team's greatest need—"a guy who can hit twenty-five home runs in the middle of the lineup."

On November 27, he got him: Indians third baseman and left-handed power hitter Graig Nettles. In order to obtain him and catcher Jerry Moses, the Yankees surrendered John Ellis, Jerry Kenney, Rusty

Torres, and Charlie Spikes, a muscle-bound Louisianan of unlimited potential. New York was loath to give up the twenty-one-year-old outfielder but Cleveland made it clear that any deal involving Nettles hinged on Spikes being part of the package.

In announcing the six-man trade, Lee MacPhail acknowledged that the Yankees were ransoming the future for immediate results. "We traded tomorrow for today," he said. "Our fans have waited long enough. Now we feel we have as good a club as anybody in baseball."

Several weeks after Nettles's arrival, another prominent Clevelander would make his presence felt in the Big Apple.

PART IV

Enter the Shipbuilder

1973

STARTERS
Mel Stottlemyre
Doc Medich
Fritz Peterson
Pat Dobson
Sam McDowell
Steve Kline

Felipe Alou (1B)
Horace Clarke (2B)
Gene Michael (SS)
Graig Nettles (3B)
Roy White (LF)
Bobby Murcer (CF)
Matty Alou (RF)
Thurman Munson (C)
Ron Blomberg/Jim Ray
Hart (DH)

RELIEVERS
Sparky Lyle
Lindy McDaniel
Fred Beene

I

ON JANUARY 3, 1973, MIKE Burke faced a phalanx of reporters and made the stunning announcement that he and a consortium had purchased the New York Yankees from the Columbia Broadcasting System for $10 million—$3.2 million less than the entertainment giant had paid Dan Topping and Del Webb for the team.

Burke stood surrounded by enlarged photographs of scenes from the club's banner years, which, back in 1964, CBS had naturally assumed would continue under its ownership. Chairman William Paley believed he had acquired a cash cow. Instead, the ball club *lost* $11 million of the parent company's money over the next eight years.

Not only did gate receipts sink—attendance bottomed out at 966,328 in 1972, despite the pennant run—but annual radio and television revenue toppled from more than $1 million at one time to less than $200,000 for the upcoming season. By contrast, sponsor Rheingold Beer paid the Mets $1.25 million for the broadcasting rights to their 1973 games.

Rumors had been circulating for several years that CBS might consider disposing of its dubious asset. But before seriously entertaining any offers, Paley wanted to ensure the Yankees' future in the Bronx. Already deeply embarrassed by public opinion that it was somehow responsible for the franchise's decline, the company did not want history to show the Yankees escaping New York on its watch as well.

Once the ball club signed a thirty-year lease with the city on August 8, 1972, Paley gave Mike Burke the green light to cut it loose. By this time the team presidency was part of Burke's blood. He decided to form his own syndicate and began hunting for investors.

Cleveland Indians president and general manager Gabe Paul suggested a group that had recently sought to buy the Tribe, a consortium headed by an Ohio shipbuilder named George Steinbrenner. Brought together by Paul at Manhattan's 21 Club in November, Burke and Steinbrenner mapped out a strategy for taking the club off CBS's hands. Steinbrenner could scarcely believe it when Burke said the Yankees could probably be theirs for $10 million cash. Two of the game's scrubbiest franchises, the Indians and the Seattle Pilots, had recently gone for $10.8 million each.

Although Burke contributed relatively little money to the partnership, his involvement gave it the inside track over a group assembled by former San Francisco Giants manager Herman Franks that was preparing to bid in the neighborhood of $14 million. Burke and Steinbrenner presented their offer to Paley on December 19. That CBS accepted within three days, during Christmas week, should convey some idea of its eagerness to unload the club.

The Yankees now belonged to general partners Burke and Steinbrenner and twelve limited partners, a disparate group that included theater impresario James Nederlander, Nelson Bunker Hunt (of the Dallas oil dynasty), and General Motors executive John DeLorean.

None attended the press conference at the Yankee Stadium restaurant. When it came Steinbrenner's turn to speak, he demurred, "We plan absentee ownership as far as running the Yankees is concerned. We're not going to pretend to be something we aren't. I'll stick to building ships."

Forty-two-year-old George M. Steinbrenner III, born into a wealthy Ohio family, had done phenomenally well. A shrewd, hard-nosed businessman, in 1963 he'd salvaged his father Henry's foundering cargo-ship company, then bought into the American Ship Building Company, and as president more than tripled its volume.

But Steinbrenner was no newcomer to sports entrepreneurship. In 1960 he bought a semipro basketball team called the Cleveland Pipers and entered it in the short-lived American Basketball League. A portent of things to come, Steinbrenner achieved notoriety as the only owner in pro basketball history to be penalized with a technical foul for berating an official. The venture ended unhappily when the league folded two years later. Since then, Steinbrenner had invested in the basketball Chicago Bulls, a racing stable, and a harness track.

The Yankees, despite their recent difficulties, remained baseball's crown jewel. Steinbrenner had to pinch himself. He now owned 20 percent of the legendary ball club he'd held in awe while growing up in the Cleveland suburb of Bay Village.

Broadcaster Frank Messer remembers his introduction to the new owner in spring training. "We were chatting, and Whitey Ford wandered by. George said, 'Oh, excuse me, there's Whitey Ford! I've got to go talk to Whitey Ford!' Like a little kid seeking an autograph. And with that, I was completely forgotten, maybe forever, as George went to find Whitey."

Another detail of their conversation also stuck with Messer. "The first thing George said to me was, 'Well, Frank, your job is not in jeopardy.' Which, until he said it, hadn't entered my mind!"

Mike Burke didn't yet realize it, but by teaming up with Steinbrenner he'd paved the way for his own departure from the organization he loved. When the Yankees ownership assembled for a press conference at the 21 Club on January 10, yet another limited partner was introduced: Gabe Paul. According to vice president Howard Berk, he and Burke learned of this change only the night before. "That's when I said to myself, *Self, this is not a good relationship,*" he recalls.

Paul, an executive with Cincinnati and Houston prior to Cleveland, took on the ambiguous title "administrative partner in charge of business affairs." Burke tried to play down his presence. "This is a nice way for Gabe Paul to close out his baseball career," he told reporters. "He's sixty-three and intends to retire to Florida in a couple of years." That came as news to Paul.

"When I first heard it," he claims, "I was flabbergasted! I'd joined the group with the understanding that I would be made president. As a matter of fact, when the deal was consummated at Kennedy Airport, Mike, George, and I shook hands on it." Burke, he says, was to move upstairs as chairman of the board and tend primarily to public relations.

Howard Berk contends, however, that when his boss called to inform him of the sale, he'd stressed that his capacity would remain the same as before. "I'll give you his exact words. He said, 'There's been a little change. The Columbia Broadcasting System'—Mike always referred to it that way, never as CBS—'has finally sold the team to a wonderful fellow from Cleveland named George Steinbrenner. I'm going to be the managing partner and continue as president, and George is going to be an absolute absentee owner.' "

Berk's concerns about the Cleveland contingent's motives multiplied one Saturday toward the end of spring training. "I was in the Yankees office in the hotel, and my wife came up and said, 'I have to talk to you right away.' She said she was having breakfast by the pool with the kids, and Steinbrenner was at the next table with some friends. Turned out to be his cronies. They hadn't legally taken over yet, and all he was doing was badmouthing Mike.

"He said, '*When we get this club, we'll make that Irish son of a bitch flap in the breeze!*'

"Just then, Mike came walking down the hall," Howard Berk continues. "I said, 'Mike, Phyllis wants to tell you something.' We went into a little utility closet, with pails and mops. Mike was a very private guy and a great poker player. Expressionless. He listened, 'Mm-mmm, mm-mmm, mm-mmm,' said softly, 'Thank you, Phyllis,' and gave her a peck on the cheek."

Burke privately confronted Steinbrenner the next day during a Yankees grapefruit-league game. Later, in the sixth inning, he appeared next to Howard Berk's seat, tapped him on the shoulder, and gave the thumbs-up sign. "I'll talk to you tomorrow," he said with a smile.

"He called me," Howard Berk remembers, "and said, 'Everything's worked out. It was all a misunderstanding.' George did not deny what he said—to his credit, I guess. But at that point Mike still knew there was something very, very wrong."

II

BORN ON THE Fourth of July, George Steinbrenner ardently championed the traditional American values that to him the Yankees symbolized. So he was mortified when Fritz Peterson and Mike Kekich revealed on March 5 that during the off-season they'd exchanged wives, children—even the family dogs. It wasn't some tawdry wife swap, Kekich emphasized, but "a life swap." Unfortunately for the four parties involved, by and large the public did not see the distinction.

The two left-handers were closer than brothers, and their families socialized regularly. Over time, Peterson and Susanne Kekich found themselves falling in love, as did Kekich and Marilyn Peterson. Susanne was easygoing, like Fritz, while Marilyn shared Mike's intellectual interests.

One Saturday night in July 1972, both couples attended a dinner party at writer Maury Allen's house. Afterward Mike went home with

Marilyn, and Fritz with Susanne, an arrangement that continued on and off through the end of the season. It was decided that come October the husbands would quietly switch households for a two-month experiment.

Peterson moved into the Kekich home in Franklin, New Jersey, and played stepdad to Susanne's two small daughters. Kekich and Marilyn lived in nearby Mahwah with her two young sons. Things proceeded so smoothly that the four discussed having a double divorce and wedding ceremony.

In December Kekich and Peterson returned to their families for a period of reevaluation and possible reconciliation. It took less than two weeks for everyone to conclude that they belonged with the other's spouse. Marilyn and Mike celebrated Christmas together in Montana, Susanne and Fritz in New Jersey.

Yankees management advised both pitchers to go public at the beginning of spring training, in hopes that the matter would run its course and be forgotten by Opening Day. In separate interviews, Peterson and Kekich stressed this was no sordid fling, but simply a case of two couples, married when they were barely out of their teens, finding greater happiness with other partners. Yes, it was unorthodox, they acknowledged, but these were turbulent times in which the very concept of marriage was being challenged. All four adamantly rejected open marriage and other alternatives; they each sought a traditional relationship. Why should anyone find that morally objectionable?

None of them was prepared for the ensuing onslaught of criticism. Even in the sexually liberated 1970s, much of America considered the Peterson-Kekich "trade" scandalous. This type of behavior might have been tolerated from those cocaine-snorting, left-leaning wackos out in the Hollywood hills, but not from ballplayers. Hate mail, including death threats, poured in.

Daily News columnist Dick Young weighed in with a typically windy broadside. Responding to Kekich's contention that neither couple meant to hurt anyone, he railed, "This is the same self-centered rationale used by young dope-takers." (Huh?) And: "One day Mike Kekich will sit down and write a list of those he has hurt. He will be astounded at how long it is."

Steve Jacobson of *Newsday*, who coined the phrase "life swap," finds Young's piety amusing. "Dick was the most promiscuous of men," he claims.

Jim Bouton, then a sportscaster on New York's ABC-TV, observes, "The ironic thing about the whole Peterson-Kekich situation was that nobody ever wrote about the illicit sex that had always gone on in baseball. And now here was an instance where two players gravitated toward each other's spouses simply because their rhythms and their likes and dislikes matched up better.

"As a broadcaster I said, 'This is not a sex story, it's a lifestyle story.' But the media missed the point and wrote about it as a wife-swapping thing."

Most Yankees viewed the affair with mild amusement. Lindy Mc-Daniel, though, couldn't hide his disapproval. "That was very hard for me to swallow," he admits, "because it was something that even people who don't respect God don't normally do."

Team members did their best to sidestep the controversy but found that it wasn't always possible. While in St. Petersburg for an exhibition game, Peterson, Bernie Allen, Mel Stottlemyre, and Hal Lanier took a taxi to a local dog track.

"You guys ballplayers?" the cabbie asked.

"Yeah."

"What team?"

"The Yankees."

Not knowing his passengers' identities, the hack exclaimed, "Hey, how 'bout those two guys who swapped wives and everything!"

Allen recalls: "Mel, Hal, and I just kind of slid down in our seats. We didn't know what to say."

Peterson snapped sarcastically from the back, "Well, which one do you want to know about? Wife number one or wife number two?"

"That cabbie just shut right up," says Allen. "He didn't say another word the rest of the way."

Emblematic of a sexual revolution that failed to take into account guilt, jealousy, insecurity, and other human frailties, Kekich's relationship with Marilyn Peterson collapsed under the weight of public disapproval. The stigma was simply too much for her. "Mike and Marilyn, that should have worked," says Steve Jacobson, a friend of everyone involved. "It didn't because she was afraid."

Shortly after the story broke, she fled to her mother's, outside Chicago, leaving Kekich without his lover, his wife, his children, and without much affection for his ex-roommate. "Sometimes I feel like I'd like to kill him," he admitted at the time. Although Lee MacPhail asserted the Yankees had no intention of trading either player, "You knew one of them had to go," says Allen.

As often happens in a split of any kind, friends took sides. The vast majority lined up behind Peterson, one of the club's most popular personalities. Kekich spent a lonely two months in the bullpen, pitching only fifteen innings before the Yankees dealt him to Cleveland on June 12. "It was a tough time," he says.

Asked if he felt relieved to escape what he calls the "constant bombardment" of media in New York, Kekich replies, "Actually, quite the contrary. I'm one of those people who if he sees an injustice tries to correct it. I wanted the chance to show that no matter what went on in my personal life, I was still *this*. But I was not given the opportunity, which made me pretty bitter."

While pitching against Milwaukee that August, the stress of the past year surfaced in the form of a nervous breakdown. The left-hander's vision suddenly went blurry on the mound and he could barely move. He and Marilyn Peterson continued to see each other sporadically but were never able to rekindle their romance. Kekich remarried in 1978, his last season in U.S. pro ball, and has a daughter with his second wife, Michelle.

The usually carefree Peterson also buckled from the strain. "Fritz was devastated that whole season because of all the hate mail he received and the abuse at the ballpark," pitcher Fred Beene recalls. "I know he drank real bad, which was not like him."

Peterson had always tended to gravitate toward strong personalities like Kekich and Jim Bouton. "He was a follower," says a friend, "always looking for the next thing in somebody else." After his retirement in 1976 he turned to religion and became a born-again Christian. Today the commercial real-estate broker lives in Illinois with his wife, Susanne.

Their half of the infamous love quadrangle survived the public outcry. Although Peterson prefers not to discuss the matter, he surely must appreciate the bittersweet irony that after being charged with undermining the institution of marriage, he and the former Mrs. Kekich should become a model of connubial stability. Wed in 1974, the couple have two daughters together, in addition to children from their previous marriages.

III

GEORGE STEINBRENNER'S PLEDGE of absentee ownership proved as sincere as Adolf Hitler's promise to keep out of Poland. Watching the home opener against Cleveland from his box behind the New York dugout, he frowned when the Yankees removed their caps for the National Anthem.

Several looked a little too shaggy to suit the new owner, who wore his hair neatly trimmed. Not knowing the players' names, Steinbrenner jotted down their uniform numbers. He later handed this list to Ralph Houk, along with the command that the offenders—stars

Murcer, Munson, Lyle, and White among them—get to a barber immediately.

Despite his military background, The Major was unusually tolerant of modern hairstyles and other youthful expressions of individuality. "If a man could hit," he says, laughing, "he could wear his hair clear down to his knees." But orders were orders.

Reserve catcher Jerry Moses remembers, "Ralph held a meeting and said, 'Listen, I have a list here of guys who've got to get their hair cut.' Then he read off the numbers, because that's the way it had been given to him. Ralph was too much of a man to come out and say, 'Steinbrenner told me to do this.' But he read it in a manner that let us know it didn't come from him and that he didn't agree with it." The clubhouse rolled with laughter as Houk announced each number like a caller at a bingo game. "We thought it was funny as hell that George didn't know our names," says Ron Swoboda.

The players weren't sure just what to make of Steinbrenner, having yet to meet him. "For all we knew, it could have been Jimmy Hoffa that bought the Yankees," jokes pitcher George "Doc" Medich, a freshman that year. But the haircut incident did not leave a favorable first impression. "It seemed like the Big Guy in the Sky was always hovering over you," says Fred Beene. "We knew we were being watched."

Already stories were circulating about their new boss's impetuous nature. In the first inning of the home opener, Bobby Murcer popped up with two men aboard. Steinbrenner fumed, "Is that the guy we're paying a hundred thousand dollars?" Murcer, only the third Yankee in history to make six figures, more than earned his 1973 salary, batting .304 with 22 home runs and 95 RBIs.

While the players resented Steinbrenner's intrusion, at the same time they welcomed his presence. "The feeling was, 'At least now we know who the owner is,' " Frank Messer observes. "When CBS owned the ball club, nobody knew. Michael Burke did not put himself in the role of the owner; he was the president. So there was no one person you could look to and say, 'This is the man who's got a tremendous interest in the ball club.' "

Identifying the Yankees' owner became twice as easy on April 28. Prior to an 11–5 romp over the Twins, Burke met with Steinbrenner, Gabe Paul, and Lee MacPhail and tendered his resignation, which the Yankees announced the next day in a terse statement. New third baseman Graig Nettles, as quick with a quip as he was diving to his left, wanted to know, "Was his hair too long?"

The fifty-six-year-old CEO was uncharacteristically tight-lipped about his reasons for bowing out. It came down to a plain incompatibility between the two co-general partners. Vice president Howard Berk recalls, "Mike told me, 'I got tired of going to the mat. Life's too short. It's best for everybody if I resign.' So it had been building for a while." Berk himself had quit the day before, disenchanted with the new regime.

"For six and a half years I'd worked sixteen hours a day, seven days a week, and loved every second of it," he says. "Then I found myself hating to go there. George just had a different attitude toward people. Everything we did, he was violently critical of. It was not an atmosphere I wanted to work in."

The Yankees made Mike Burke a public-relations consultant, knowing full well he had too much pride to serve in that capacity for long. Indeed, he soon went to work in another New York sports landmark, as president of Madison Square Garden. Still, "Nothing Mike did later in life ever equaled the Yankees," says Howard Berk, now a vice president at Viacom International. "He loved it till the day he died." Burke retired to Ireland in 1981 and passed away there six years later, at age seventy.

Tremors from the front-office power play (dubbed "The Cleveland Coup" by one wag) eventually subsided, refocusing attention on the players, who after going 9–10 in April were beginning to justify having been picked as nine-to-five favorites in the AL East.

The additions of Nettles and Matty Alou infused the Yankees offense with such depth that Thurman Munson, a .301 hitter in 1973, could bat eighth. "Our lineup looked super," says Roy White, unaccustomed at the time to so many capable batsmen following him in the order. "We were going to score a lot of runs."

Alou, still speedy at thirty-four, wielded a baseball bat like an archer's bow to zing singles around the diamond. In the 1960s, only Pittsburgh's Roberto Clemente surpassed his .312 average. Nettles, who was awarded Roger Maris's number 9, fell short of fulfilling New Yorkers' exorbitant expectations, even though his .234 BA, 22 HR, 81 RBI constituted standard Nettles production. The twenty-eight-year-old San Diegan also welded the hot corner shut defensively.

In one of the most dramatic modifications of baseball's structure since its inception, the American League had broken with the National League and voted unanimously to adopt the designated-hitter rule on an experimental basis. Initially no club benefited more than the Yankees. Through late May, their lefty-righty DH platoon of Ron Blomberg and Jim Ray Hart boasted identical numbers, 28-for-76 (.368 BA).

Blomberg carries the distinction of being baseball's first designated hitter. On Opening Day in Boston he drew a bases-loaded walk off

Luis Tiant in the first inning. Afterward his bat was sent off to Cooperstown for enshrinement. Despite having DH'd in the minors, it felt odd, he says, not to take the field following the third out.

"I went back into the dugout and sat down—and I didn't know what to do!" Blomberg recalls. "It was miserably cold that day. Bobby Murcer always had a hot-water bottle with him, so I held it the whole time. Then I went in the clubhouse and tried to get loose, but I couldn't. It was terrible.

"I never got adjusted to it because I was too young and energetic. I wanted to play."

Hart, a thirty-one-year-old San Francisco Giants discard, tailed off to .251 while Blomberg sailed into the .400s and docked there through late June. No one since Ted Williams and Stan Musial, twenty-five years before, had crossed that formidable boundary so deep into the season. Yet the Yankees continued platooning him.

In Texas, Rangers manager Whitey Herzog summoned a left-hander to face Number 12 with two gone in the ninth, the tying runs on base, and the count 2-and-0. Houk lifted his .407 hitter, 2-for-2 on the night, for right-handed Felipe Alou, who popped out to end the game. Afterward he offered the explanation, "Boomer doesn't hit lefties."

For that the Yankees had only themselves to blame. Blomberg never got to face southpaws on a consistent basis, not even in triple-A, where youngsters are sent ostensibly to hone their skills. At Syracuse, the top draft pick of 1967 sat against left-handers.

"That hurt my career more than anything," he reflects. "Frank Verdi was a good manager, but to be honest, he knew that most of the players on his team weren't going up to the big leagues, so he wanted to win games. He was shooting for the Little World Series."

Lee MacPhail intervened. "I had a big fight with the Syracuse manager and made him play Ron all the time," he says. Verdi, however, insists he did start Blomberg against lefties; the kid couldn't buy a hit. According to Ron Swoboda, "If a right-hander switched gloves and threw left-handed, he could still get him out."

Statistics suggest otherwise. "My lifetime average against left-handed pitchers was .273," Blomberg claims, "but people didn't realize that. Once you get labeled, it's very difficult to kick it." So he could single, homer and collect four RBIs in a 14–4 drubbing of the Twins and still fidget on the bench the next night because Jim Kaat was on the mound.

"I used to call up Marty Appel, our P.R. guy, and Bill Kane, our traveling secretary, to find out who the opposing pitchers were for the next three or four games. When I was going really strong, they'd throw left-handers at us to get me out of the lineup." Houk let him face southpaws only seventeen times in 1973, and the twenty-four-year-old hit them for a mere .176, including one circuit clout.

"I always wanted to be an everyday ballplayer and get six hundred at-bats," says Blomberg, who finished at .329 BA, 12 HR, 57 RBI in 301 at-bats. Project his first four years' combined totals over 600 at-bats, and you produce a .306 BA, 24 HR, 104 RBI season. The Yankees came under frequent second-guessing for not playing the quick-wristed lefty every day.

"A lot of people wanted me to make a big stink about it," he remembers. "I had calls from all across the country, and the papers always wanted to kill the management. But I didn't want to be a troublemaker. Plus, I thought Ralph Houk was a great manager. I loved the guy."

The Major promised to make him the regular first baseman come 1974, though without a pronounced improvement in his fielding, a job as full-time DH seemed more likely. Blomberg erred eight times in just forty-one games, once obliterating a sure triple play by bobbling the relay to first.

"The only triple play I'd ever seen, and I screwed it up!" he laments, laughing. "Afterward, Fritz Peterson wrote 'U.S. Steel' on my mitt." He returned from the showers to find Sparky Lyle's handiwork hanging in his locker: a large metal pan, bent in half. "Blomberg's glove," read the attached note.

Beneath the joking around bubbled an undercurrent of resentment over his seeming indifference toward developing other areas of his game. "Ron just didn't care about fielding," says Steve Kline. "To him it was something you did while waiting to hit." Ron Swoboda, who tried to work with Blomberg, adds, "I remember hitting him ground balls, and it was hard to keep his attention. He was a completely one-dimensional ballplayer." Several Yankees had a cruel epithet for their teammate: "freak."

"I always had a bat in my hand rather than a glove," Blomberg admits, "even in Little League." One father-manager considered the youngster such a defensive liability that he booted him from the team. Under an assumed name, Blomberg got onto another roster and batted .989.

"Maybe," he muses candidly, "I wasn't made up to be a guy that really worked hard."

IV

ON THE STRENGTH of their potent offense, the second-place Bronx Bombers were breathing down Detroit's neck as June opened. But the starting rotation, New York's saving grace in recent years, had unexpectedly fallen apart. Only Mel Stottlemyre and rookie Doc Medich pitched effectively. Mike Kekich was marking time on the trading block, Fritz Peterson was erratic, and Steve Kline, last year's staff leader, could barely break a pane of glass due to a sore right elbow.

The tenderness that had slowed him down in the final weeks of 1972 wasn't a concern at first. "In your twenties you think you're bulletproof," he says. Warming up before his fourth start of the season, Kline felt a twinge. "I thought, *Jeez, I'll just try to get through this.* And then a few innings into the game I had to come out." The pitcher told trainer Gene Monahan worriedly, "Something isn't right."

"My arm around the elbow joint kept tightening up until I couldn't extend it," he continues. Kline, who'd never missed a turn in his career, began losing starts here and there while waiting for the discomfort to subside.

"We were doing everything you could possibly do. They'd give you enough pills to kill a horse: muscle relaxers and anti-inflammatories, two, three times a day. Putting on hot packs. The whirlpool. But the arm just wasn't responding. I'd pitch on the side and would feel pretty good. Then I'd go into the game and the elbow would tighten back up on me.

"It was frustrating," he says. "Pretty soon you don't know if the problem is real or in your mind. I know that Ralph Houk was scratching his head trying to figure out what the hell was the matter with me."

The Yankees placed the six-foot-three right-hander on the disabled list in late June. Activated a month later, he blanked the Brewers for five and a third innings. But in Kline's next appearance, at Fenway Park on August 2, the Red Sox shelled him for four runs in the first. "I literally couldn't throw the ball over the plate," he remembers. "Orlando Cepeda took me into the net for a three-run homer, I walked Rico Petrocelli, and then Ralph came out and got me."

Kline, 4–7, 4.01 ERA, was declared finished for the year. He went home to San Luis Obispo, California, where he was studying math education at California Polytechnic State University, and worked out with the baseball team there, trying to rehabilitate the elbow.

A year earlier he'd been one of the brightest young pitchers in the game. Now, betrayed by his body at age twenty-five, his future hung in limbo. "Sometimes," he recalls, "I'd look down at my elbow and go, 'C'mon, guy, don't let me down now. You've been doing this for years. I mean, you're finally at the top here! What're you doing?' "

On June 7, the day after Kline's fourth and final win, the Yankees shored up the staff with two major trades. At 9:00 A.M., Lee MacPhail wheedled Atlanta out of right-hander Pat Dobson for four minor-leaguers. Then, at 3:00 P.M., Gabe Paul purchased San Francisco left-hander Sam McDowell for the then hefty sum of $100,000.

Whatever the Yankees' misgivings about George Steinbrenner, his willingness to spend money to build a winner came as a heartening sign. MacPhail insists that CBS never imposed any financial constraints during its reign. In fact, he says, "I remember William Paley asking, 'Can't you just go out and buy good players?' "

Dobson, thirty-one years old, had won 20 games for the Orioles in 1971, and 16 in 1972. "Pat was a big addition for us," says catcher Jerry Moses. "He was really a pitcher, not a thrower. He wasn't going to overpower anyone, but he used his fastball appropriately and had great command of the breaking ball. Plus, he'd been with those great Baltimore teams and brought a winning attitude with him." Hearing they'd nabbed the six-year veteran for a quartet of unknowns prompted several Yankees to wonder aloud if he was suffering arm trouble. "None whatsoever," says Dobson, whose only explanation for the one-sided deal was that the Braves wanted to unload his $58,000 salary.

McDowell, thirty, once the hardest thrower in baseball, arrived in New York with an injured shoulder. "I didn't want anybody to know about it," he says. At first it didn't seem to impair his performance. "Maybe he wasn't the same Sam McDowell he was with Cleveland," Moses observes, "but he knew how to pitch better, and he had great stuff."

The two newcomers each won four of their first five decisions. Dobson, debuting in relief, threw five frames of one-hit ball as the Yankees expunged a 4–0 deficit to win 6–4 and claim first place. Sudden Sam, a perennial league leader in bases on balls as well as strikeouts, beat California 5–1 in his pinstripe premiere. Typically, he fanned six and walked seven in six and two thirds innings. "I must have gone back to control pitching that day," he jokes. Sparky Lyle then disposed of the last seven Angels and walked off with his sixteenth save.

Ralph Houk called the bullpen of Lyle, Lindy McDaniel, and Fred Beene the best he'd ever managed. The trio figured in all but nine of

New York's first 59 victories and overall put up 38 saves and a 21–8 won-loss ledger. Beene, a surprising 6–0, 1 SV, 1.68 ERA, emerged as a fan favorite.

His was the classic underdog story. Five-foot-nine, 155 pounds, he'd weathered eight seasons in the Orioles chain despite a .624 percentage—all because of his size. In 1969, Beene's 15–7 record for the triple-A Rochester Red Wings attracted the attention of a Seattle Pilots scout.

"He told the owner that I was a really great pitcher, but I was too little to pitch in the big leagues," Beene recalls with some exasperation. "I heard that most of my career and carried it as a chip on my shoulder."

Traded to Syracuse before the 1972 season, the Texas native attended spring training expecting not even to touch a baseball, much less make the Yankees squad. He still recalls the words of the letter inviting him to Fort Lauderdale as a nonroster player: "You probably will not get to pitch in any exhibition games."

"Well, I got into the very first game, against the Twins in Orlando, because some guys were ailing," says Beene. "Then I started to get in regularly and had about fourteen innings before I gave up a run." That lone tally happened to decide a 4–3 loss to Baltimore. "I figured they'd cut me," he says. "That's the way I felt: *If you give up anything, you're gone.*"

The next morning Ralph Houk came into work early and spotted Beene sitting alone in front of his locker, head bowed, smoking a cigarette. "Beenie," he called, "c'mere." Beene swallowed hard and shuffled across the deserted locker room like a condemned man going to the gas chamber. "This is it," he thought.

"I know you've had a tough career," Houk said kindly. "I just wanted to tell you, you made my club last night."

"Ralph," Beene replied, "if you want anybody killed, just tell me and I'll do it for you." He says, "I couldn't tell him how grateful I was."

From that day on, Houk was the grateful one. Beene didn't work much his first season in pinstripes (1–3, 3 SV, 2.33 ERA), but in 1973 he developed into a versatile long reliever and emergency starter. When Steve Kline had to be scratched against Cleveland on May 20, the baby-faced right-hander filled in and tossed six innings of goose eggs for his first win, 4–2. Three weeks later, in Oakland, Kline's elbow tightened up in the second inning. Beene came on to set down the first eighteen A's he faced, seven of them on strikes.

On June 19 he tamed Baltimore in middle relief and bagged his second win. Afterward he exclaimed, "I'm as happy as I've ever been in my life." Yet the years of disappointment prevented Beene, then thirty, from fully enjoying his belated success. Despite his perfect record, he still feared being sent down.

"I had a different attitude than a lot of the guys," he reflects. "I was fighting for my life every day in the big leagues, so I never really relaxed until after the '73 season." He confides, "I was scared to go to the park nearly every day."

In the opener of a June 24 Ball Day doubleheader versus Detroit, Beene replaced Kline once again, this time in the fifth, with Billy Martin's team leading 2–1. He allowed the Tigers only one hit over four innings while the Yankees nudged across single runs in the seventh and eighth. Beene then made way for Sparky Lyle, who effortlessly preserved his third victory.

The House That Ruth Built groaned under the weight of 62,107 spectators, so many that thousands of kids went home empty-handed. You couldn't fault management for underestimating the gate; a year ago the same promotion had drawn only 20,482. Attendance swelled to 1.2 million in 1973, the highest total since 1964, as visitors turned out not only to cheer the Yankees on to the pennant but to take a final look around the historic ballpark before it closed down for renovation.

In the ninth inning of the nightcap, the Bombers uncorked some vintage five o'clock lightning. Graig Nettles mauled a Mickey Lolich pitch into the sea of fans in right to end a 1–1 standoff. The blast gave New York a sweep of its seven-game homestand, during which the Yankee Stadium organist fittingly broke into "Seems Like Old Times."

One of baseball's most hallowed, if faulty, tenets holds that the clubs occupying first place on Independence Day will go on to postseason play. This year New York, Oakland, Chicago, and Los Angeles were leading their respective divisions, New York by four games. But these were times that defied tradition. Come the season's final day, only the A's would remain atop the standings.

The Yankees observed America's 197th birthday—and George Steinbrenner's forty-third—by dropping both halves of a holiday twin bill to the Red Sox in front of 41,693 sun-baked fans. The game-one starter, Mel Stottlemyre, carried a 1–0 edge into the ninth. When Reggie Smith poked a leadoff single, the bullpen gates opened, and out rolled the Datsun with its most precious cargo: Number 28.

Carl Yastrzemski pulled a Sparky Lyle pitch past the right side: runners on first and second. The next batter, rickety-kneed Orlando Cepeda, surprised everyone in the ballpark by dropping a bunt, only the second of his sixteen-year career. In his haste to nip the runner at third, Thurman Munson took his eye off the ball and booted it for an error. Bases full, none out. Lyle, his adrenaline pumping, fanned Rico

Petrocelli, then induced what appeared to be a game-ending double-play ball to third.

But pinch runner Tommy Harper plowed into pivoting second baseman Bernie Allen, forcing a bounced relay to first. The ball glanced off Ron Blomberg's glove and rolled behind him. Smith scampered across with the tying run. Yastrzemski, deciding to gamble, came galloping around third.

"Home! Home!" the Yankees hollered. Blomberg stared at the unfolding action as if an observer. He pumped once, twice, before finally heaving a wild throw that skipped past Munson.

"Don't worry about it," Ralph Houk consoled after the unsightly 2–1 defeat, "we have another one." Unfortunately, New York's bats went into eclipse against southpaw Roger Moret, managing just six hits. Doc Medich outpitched him but yielded the game's sole run in the fifth on a walk, a stolen base, and Yastrzemski's bloop single.

"After those two losses, it was real, real tough," recalls Blomberg, who, back in the hushed locker room, patiently answered reporters' questions about his fatal error. "I was always the type of guy that never ran away from problems," he says. "If I did bad, I told the people I stunk."

The July 4 fiasco hobbled the Yankees' momentum. Over the next three weeks they played 11–10 ball to limp into the All-Star break at 57–44 (.564), one and a half games up on Baltimore. Nonetheless, optimism still ran high as the team vacationed at a Catskills resort while Bobby Murcer and Thurman Munson competed in the midsummer classic at Kansas City's Royals Stadium.

"When we went to Grossinger's, my wife and I had already spent our twenty-five thousand dollars," says Jerry Moses. "We knew where our World Series money was going. I just couldn't believe that we weren't going to win it."

The first road trip of the second half took the Yankees to Milwaukee, where they dropped all three games. Then it was on to Boston, the site of eight defeats in their last eight appearances there. The Red Sox snatched Monday's opener 4–3, but New York rebounded the following night. Faced with losing its grasp on first, Ralph Houk's club mounted a three-run uprising in the ninth to pull out a 5–4 victory.

Game three, on August 1, produced another squeaker, tied at two apiece through eight. Once again the offense engineered an eleventh-hour rally. The Yankees had men at the corners, one out, and Gene Michael (.225 BA, 3 HR, 47 RBI) hitting from the left side against southpaw John Curtis. Ralph Houk flashed the squeeze sign.

As Curtis went into his stretch, Thurman Munson charged home from third. Michael squared around to bunt, but the 1-and-0 curve broke low and inside and he missed. Munson, an unstoppable incoming missile, hurtled into catcher Carlton Fisk, bowling him over. The Red Sox receiver angrily removed Munson from his chest by kicking him off. Both men came up swinging, and Munson connected first with a solid right. Fisk, still clutching the baseball, landed a few blows before teammates wrestled Munson to the ground. That's when Michael decided to make this a tag-team match.

Although "Pudge" Fisk outweighed Stick Michael by a good twenty pounds, the Yankees shortstop had a reputation for taking on far bigger opponents, Cleveland's Sam McDowell and Tony Horton among them. "Gene was pretty fearless," says Jerry Moses. "If you looked at him undressed in the clubhouse, you wouldn't think he was real strong. But he handled himself very well."

Michael rained punches down on Fisk, jabbing him in the eye and scratching his face. The two ended up on the ground under a quilt of bodies, as both benches rushed to the rescue. Hal Lanier, who got into a shoving match with Red Sox infielder Mario Guerrero, recalls, "Reggie Smith came flying onto the pile, and Elston Howard just grabbed him in midair and stopped him completely." Even Ralph Houk waded into the fray, to pry Fisk's arm from around Michael's neck. "It was nasty," says Moses. "There were some people who really did not like one another."

Naturally, the bullpen inmates arrived just as the brawl was breaking up. "I remember standing there," says Doc Medich, "when I hear lumbering footsteps and heavy breathing behind me, turn around, and here comes Bob Veale," the hulking Boston reliever. "I thought, *Man, I'm glad this big guy's out of breath.*"

The umpires ejected instigators Fisk and Munson, but not Michael, interestingly. He grounded out to end the threat. In the bottom of the inning, Guerrero, a throw-in in the Sparky Lyle–Danny Cater trade, singled home the winning run off Lyle, now 0–5 versus his erstwhile club.

The donnybrook was the latest episode in an ongoing rivalry between the two teams, and the beginning of a bitter feud between Munson and Fisk, the 1972 AL Rookie of the Year. Munson, who sought recognition as the best catcher in the league, resented the talented newcomer and the attention lavished on him by the media.

Fisk was as handsome as Munson was plain. A noble-featured six-foot-three New Englander, he projected a patrician air. Munson, proud of his ability but sensitive about his appearance, felt underappreciated. It wounded him deeply when Fisk finished first in the 1973 All-Star Game balloting. You couldn't fault the Yankees backstop for feeling slighted. In addition to batting .301, he added power (20 home runs and 74 RBIs) to his résumé and won the first of three consecutive Gold Glove Awards. Fisk's sophomore grades were .246 BA, 26 HR, 71 RBI.

Munson died in a 1979 plane crash; Fisk went on to become a baseball institution, playing into 1993. Surely, Cooperstown awaits him. But during the period when they competed against each other, Munson was unquestionably the superior receiver.

A Yankees pitcher who played alongside both offers anonymously, "As far as I'm concerned, there was no comparison whatsoever. Thurman could beat Carlton in every category except home runs. He was a better catcher—the best I ever threw to. And even though Pudge could steal, Thurman was a better base runner too."

Munson and Fisk's rivalry approached full-scale war. "Thurman hated Fisk," says Steve Kline. "If we didn't get him out, he'd go crazy. 'I want this guy out now! Right now!' " Every morning Munson religiously checked the Boston box score to see how his adversary did.

Jerry Moses, Number 15's understudy, believes the feud ultimately enhanced both men's careers. "I think it drove Thurman and Carlton," he observes. "As you get older you realize there's room in baseball for two extraordinary catchers, but when you're young, as these two kids were, there's only one position: number one. And they both wanted it. It made them better players."

A few of his teammates liked nothing better than to stoke Munson's obsession. "Anytime I could get a picture of Carlton from a magazine, I'd put it in Thurman's locker or slip it under his chair," Gene Michael remembers, laughing. "He didn't know it was me for the longest time. I had him going cuckoo." The week before the brawl in Boston, Fisk graced the cover of *Sports Illustrated*, much to Munson's irritation. Naturally, a half-dozen copies found their way into his cubicle.

Michael qualified as Munson's closest friend, one of his few on the team. Although well liked, the catcher tended to keep others at arm's length. "He was very much a loner, very moody," says Bernie Allen, another confidant. "Some nights he'd want to go do something together. Other nights he'd say, 'No, I don't want you with me.' 'Okay, no problem, big boy.' I gave him his space.

"If Thurman really liked you, he'd do anything for you," Allen continues. "But you had to kind of prove yourself to him." Munson liked to test people by dishing out crude insults. It was his way of expressing affection. Those who didn't know him well sometimes found him intimidating. "He had the lowest tolerance for bullshit of anyone I've ever met," former batboy Thad Mumford says fondly. "If he thought you were full of shit, he'd call you on it."

According to Michael, Munson's outward gruffness was really the protective façade of a private and surprisingly insecure man. "Thurman was a delight in a lot of ways," he reminisces. "It was kind of an act with him, trying to be tough with people. He just didn't want anyone to think he was soft and mushy."

V

THE YANKEES' SIX-WEEK tenure at the top of the division came to an end on August 2 as the Red Sox humiliated them in game four, 10–0. Carlton Fisk, sporting a bruise under one eye, wasted no time in avenging the previous day's boxing exhibition. In his first trip to the plate he took Doc Medich over the Green Monster, then trotted stone-faced past Gene Michael and Munson. Roger Moret again confounded New York hitters, sending eight down on strikes. In dramatic style, he fanned Munson for the final out. A gale of hoots and catcalls nearly swept the fuming catcher back to the dugout.

In hindsight, Pat Dobson calls the series "a turning point for us." The floundering Bombers departed Boston one game behind Baltimore. Third-place Detroit promptly shouldered past them, handing the Yankees their seventh loss in eight games. August would prove as torturous a time in The House That Ruth Built as in the White House, which was nervously monitoring the Senate hearings into its alleged 1972 break-in at Democratic National Committee headquarters.

While the Watergate tragicomedy unfolded daily in the media, New York went into a 9–18 tailspin. Richard Nixon was eventually brought down by his own paranoia and arrogance, Ralph Houk by the pitching staff he thought had been repaired.

With the exception of Doc Medich, the starting rotation stopped winning so abruptly, it was as if someone had flicked off a switch. The rookie captured seven of his last ten decisions to finish a fine 14–9 (2.95 ERA), but everyone else fell on the losing side of .500 after the All-Star break. Mel Stottlemyre (who would close 1973 at 16–16, 3.07 ERA) sank to 4–7, Pat Dobson (9–8, 4.17 ERA) to 3–5. Fritz Peterson (8–15, 3.95 ERA) and Sam McDowell (5–8, 3.95 ERA) never tasted victory again.

A workhorse who'd averaged 238 innings during his seven years in the majors, Peterson developed tendinitis. "I received my first cortisone shot midseason," he remembers, "which allowed me to finish the year." His second-half record was 0–5. "Then my arm fell off."

The left-hander, who was traded to Cleveland in 1974, and to Texas two years later, underwent surgery, but the condition never improved.

"He contracted a lingering staph infection in his shoulder," *Newsday* sportswriter Steve Jacobson says. "The pain was so excruciating, he actually inquired about amputation."

McDowell wasn't sound either, but his 0–7 second half stemmed mainly from a career-long addiction to alcohol that by 1973 had spiraled out of control. Gabe Paul, his general manager in Cleveland, knew he was taking a gamble in acquiring the expensive veteran, about whom a Tribe sportscaster once cracked, "He has a million-dollar arm and a ten-cent head."

"Gabe was the first man in baseball that told me I was a drunk," says McDowell, now recovered. "While I was with the Indians, he sent me to psychiatrists. Then when I came to the Yankees, he sent me to a psychiatrist again. But that doesn't work."

Sudden Sam promised his new teammates a pennant. "The Yankees are going to win it because of Sam McDowell," he boasted. His first month in pinstripes, Number 48 backed up his words, running his record to 5–1. "Nobody was pitching better than Sam," affirms Jerry Moses.

But after games the towering left-hander regularly crawled the pubs. And he doesn't dispute descriptions of him as a mean drunk. "Sam was a blowhard who used to bully people," Steve Jacobson remembers. "He once pissed on somebody's leg in the bar at the Yankee Stadium Motor Lodge. People had a lot of scorn for him."

Following a Friday-night win over the Twins on July 6, McDowell went out to a Minneapolis discotheque, got lubricated, and sprained his ankle. He told Ralph Houk a different story: that he'd gotten the cuff of his pants caught in an escalator at a local shopping mall. For an added touch of realism, McDowell indignantly claimed he was considering a lawsuit.

Nobody believed him, least of all The Major. "They all knew," McDowell acknowledges. He missed two starts and was never the same upon his return, which Moses cites as the biggest factor in New York's August–September slide. "Next to Mel, we were really counting on Sam," he says. "After he got hurt, he didn't throw well anymore."

The following season, McDowell's alcoholism impaired him to the point of uselessness. "The team was trying everything it could to help me," he reflects in a surprisingly soft but intense voice. "They knew that when I was around my family I wouldn't drink; the road was where I did most of my drinking. So for about the last month of '74 they decided that I would join the team in New York, but when we had a road trip I would go home and stay with my family—although

I would fly back and forth to New York once, twice, or three times a week, depending on how often the psychiatrist wanted to see me."

McDowell, 1–6, 4.69 ERA, made only thirteen appearances the entire year. In mid-September he announced his retirement and returned home to Pittsburgh, where he'd grown up the son of a steel-mill inspector. Still only thirty-two, over the winter he contacted Pirates general manager Joe Brown about a possible pitching job.

"The first thing out of his mouth was, 'Sam, we know about your alcoholism. Have you taken care of it?' Of course I said yes." In fact, he was sufficiently "careful" about his drinking to log thirty-five innings on the mound for Pittsburgh in 1975 (2–1, 2.83 ERA). But one night in June, McDowell slipped up for the last time. Relieving Bruce Kison at Shea Stadium, he blanked the Mets for four frames in a game the Pirates came back to win 7–3. "That night I went out and celebrated. The next morning I was still drunk. And that was it for me." Pittsburgh dropped him immediately.

McDowell continued to hit the bottle yet get by, pitching insurance policies instead of fastballs. Finally in 1979 he sought treatment. "It reached a point where I said, 'Enough is enough. I just can't take it anymore.' " McDowell enrolled in a Pennsylvania rehabilitation center. Today a certified addiction counselor and mental-health therapist, he started his own practice, which came to be known as Triumphs Unlimited. Clients include not only local teenagers but athletes from professional football, basketball, hockey, and baseball.

"Our program is proactive," he explains. "We don't wait for the ballplayer to volunteer. We go get him before his family and career are destroyed." Had similar help been available when eighteen-year-old Sam McDowell came up to the Indians in 1961, his plaque might now be hanging in Cooperstown. In fifteen seasons the towering left-hander chalked up a 141–134 record, 3.17 ERA, and 2,453 strike-outs—more than such Hall of Famers as Whitey Ford, Sandy Koufax, and Early Wynn.

VI

MCDOWELL'S SPRAINED ANKLE left New York in dire need of an extra starter. Ralph Houk tapped Lindy McDaniel to face the White Sox at Comiskey Park. It was in Chicago, coincidentally, that he'd become a reliever fourteen years before.

Signed as a starting pitcher out of the University of Oklahoma,

McDaniel won 15 and lost 9 for St. Louis in 1957. But the following season produced a 5–7 mark, and when he showed no improvement in the early part of 1959, his fifth year in the majors, the young right-hander requested a switch to the bullpen. In McDaniel's first relief stint he shut out the Cubs for four and two thirds innings, got credit for a win, and began a second career. He topped the National League in saves that year and the next.

The Yankees hoped for five or six innings from McDaniel against the Chisox. Instead the thirty-seven-year-old went the distance, striking out eleven and yielding just one earned run on three hits. Unfortunately an infield error permitted another tally, which turned out to be the difference in a 2–1 heartbreaker.

McDaniel lobbied to join the rotation full-time. "I needed a lot of work," he explains. "That was the key to my pitching. Otherwise my muscles didn't stretch out properly and my control would suffer." Houk, however, felt he was more valuable in long relief, a judgment that was hard to dispute after McDaniel's August 4th outing in Detroit.

A pulled thigh muscle sent Fritz Peterson limping off the field at the start of the second, trailing 1–0. In trotted the preacher. His forkball was still baffling Tigers batters in the ninth after the Yankees had tied the score at 2–2 on Matty Alou's clutch double. And even after Horace Clarke's home run had put New York ahead 3–2 in the top of the fourteenth, out came Number 40 to nail down his victory. His log on the evening amounted to one run in thirteen innings. "Endurance was never a problem for me," he says modestly.

Despite a terrific season (12–6, 10 SV, 2.86 ERA), management denied McDaniel's request for a two-year contract. The disappointed veteran approved a trade to Kansas City. "I really wasn't too anxious to stay with the Yankees," he says. He came to regret it after discovering, in his words, that "The Royals were more interested in getting rid of Lou Piniella than they were in getting me." Stale from inactivity, McDaniel went 1–4 in 1974 and 5–1 in 1975. At the time of his retirement, only ageless knuckleballer Hoyt Wilhelm owned more lifetime appearances and relief wins.

McDaniel closed out his final season in pinstripes as the bullpen's anchorman. Tendinitis disabled Fred Beene, and although Houk handled Sparky Lyle as delicately as a Fabergé egg, the left-hander inexplicably lost his velocity. By the All-Star break, Number 28 had compiled 26 saves; he added only one more the rest of the way.

At the start of August, Lyle absorbed three defeats in eight games. His frustration flared during a Sunday matinee versus Oakland on August 12. Relieving Sam McDowell with two outs in the top of the seventh, he inherited a pair of base runners and an 11–6 lead. A walk, a double, and back-to-back singles quickly whittled the margin to one. Out hurried Houk, signaling for a right-hander. As Lyle left the mound to scattered boos, he glowered at one heckler behind the New York dugout and thrust both middle fingers in the air.

Before the gruesome spectacle had ended, several other Yankees incurred the crowd's wrath. Rookie Tom Buskey, Lyle's replacement, coaxed an easy bouncer to second that Horace Clarke misplayed. Tie game. In the eighth inning, Graig Nettles botched his second grounder of the day, paving the way for Oakland's winning two-run rally. A charitable official scorer levied only five errors against New York, which was also guilty of numerous mental lapses. On one single, Clarke simply forgot to cover second, allowing the batter to take the extra base unmolested.

Afterward, McDowell blasted the team's performance to reporters. "This game made me sick to my stomach," he fumed, adding, "We don't deserve to have the pinstripes on." The 13–12 embarrassment dropped the Yankees into a third-place tie with Milwaukee, two and a half games off the pace.

"It was in a fit of anger that I made those remarks," McDowell explains. "When you play for the Cleveland Indians, where you know when you leave spring training you're going to come in last, you form this unrealistic perception of who and what the Yankees are—that they're bigger than life and don't make mistakes. So when I got sold over there, I thought, *Wow, here's my chance to finally be in the World Series!* Then when you see them being human, everything gets dashed."

Had McDowell not been battling his own demons at the time, his outburst might have fired up the club, as intended. Instead, says Fred Beene, the general reaction was, "Aw, that's just Sam. Don't pay any attention."

Perhaps the Yankees should have. McDowell's accusations of sloppy play and lack of hustle contained more than a kernel of truth. The defense, leaky for years, had degenerated completely. In one twenty-one-game stretch, New York committed 30 miscues, 23 of them by the infield. Mike Kekich laughingly recounts, "When Pat Dobson came over and saw the fielding, his first comment was, 'Jesus, this is gonna add a point and a half to my ERA!' " And it did.

"We executed very poorly on fundamentals," says Beene, now a scouting supervisor for the Milwaukee Brewers. "I came from the Baltimore organization, where in big-league camp we worked on covering first, pitch-outs, intentional walks. And I don't mean only the little guys, I mean Jim Palmer, Dave McNally, and Mike Cuellar. We did it until it was perfect, and we never beat ourselves.

"The Yankees, we did beat ourselves, like missing the cutoff man.

In that game against Oakland, we threw to the wrong base two, three times, and singles turned into doubles. I guess it's the manager's job to correct that, but we never had any meetings or dressing-downs about it."

Ralph Houk's philosophy on instilling basics mirrored his policy on enforcing discipline: that major-leaguers were professionals and didn't need to be drilled. Ron Swoboda observes, "Ralph's ideas were formed by those great Yankees teams he played on. You didn't have to beat on those players about fundamentals. But we had some guys with marginal mechanics. Maybe," he suggests, "we should have worked a little harder."

And played less hard after hours. Lindy McDaniel, who never needed a curfew, saw a number of teammates who might have benefited from one. "Things began to fall apart on the ball club," he says sadly, "and discipline went out the window, as far as players taking care of themselves."

For the first time, Houk felt the club had gotten away from him. Lee MacPhail, still a close friend, says, "I remember Ralph telling me a couple of times that he didn't think he was doing as good a job as he should be; that he should be getting more out of the team." He adds, "I didn't quite feel that way."

In mid-1972, with his job on the line, The Major had revived a floundering team and guided it into contention. Not this year. Houk seemed oddly distracted. "He wasn't himself," notes Horace Clarke. Although Houk kept personal matters to himself, "Sometimes comments came out that you grasped," says the second baseman. "I sensed he didn't like a few of the things that were happening upstairs."

Specifically, interference from George Steinbrenner. "He was trying to demand who played," Clarke continues, "and calling down to the dugout and calling the manager after games. Like *he* was the manager. That would never happen with a man like Ralph, who was accustomed to having a free hand."

Maury Allen of the *New York Post* adds, "Ralph was very independent and confident, and proud of his achievements. He saw Steinbrenner as just one big pain in the ass; a blowhard who knew nothing about baseball, trying to impose his will."

The owner, a graduate of Indiana's Culver Military Academy, expected Marine-like decorum from his players, which in itself showed an ignorance of the game. "You've got to play baseball loose," explains Jerry Moses, today the owner of a food-service company in Massachusetts. "You can't let everything build up." On the team's first trip to Texas, Steinbrenner just about burst a blood vessel over a practical joke played on Gene Michael.

At Arlington Stadium, Michael set down his mitt on the top step of the dugout and went up to hit. Knowing the shortstop's mortal fear of snakes, insects, and the like, "Hal Lanier cut a hot dog in half and stuffed it up one of the fingers," Moses says. "After the inning was over, Gene picked up his glove, stepped onto the field, stuck in his hand, and screamed.

"The glove went up in the air, and the hot dog rolled over right in front of Steinbrenner," who occupied a box seat alongside the visitors' dugout. "All hell broke loose." Afterward, the outraged owner confronted his manager—holding up the dirt-encrusted wiener and demanding he reprimand the perpetrator. Houk just shook his head in disbelief.

It was also in Texas that Steinbrenner first displayed his Napoleonic side, the off-with-their-heads impulsiveness soon to become legend. On August 17, the opener of a two-week western swing, the last-place Rangers humbled New York, 8–1. When Johnny Callison muffed a fly ball in right, the shipbuilder thundered, "I will not have that man on my team!" and banished him within hours. "Get rid of the son of a bitch" became a familiar Steinbrenner refrain.

Against Houk's wishes, he purged other veterans as well, beginning with Bernie Allen, who was sent to Montreal. Allen, now in sales, recalls, "I went in to pick up my stuff, and Ralph called me into his office. He told me, 'Bernie, I just wanted you to know that Lee and I had nothing to do with this.' "

Next, the Alou brothers were exported out of the league on the same day, Felipe to the Expos, Matty to the Cardinals. The two had looked forward to playing together for the first time since 1963, when all three Alous were San Francisco Giants, but the reunion ended unhappily.

Upon arriving in Montreal, the usually reserved Felipe exclaimed to Allen, "That Mr. Steinbrenner, he's crazy!" Alou retired a year later and joined the Expos organization as a minor-league coach and manager. In 1992, the team named him skipper, making him the first native Dominican to direct a major-league club.

Matty proved a major disappointment in New York. Although he hit for average (.296), "We found out he wasn't an RBI man at all," says Steve Kline. Alou drove in a paltry 28 runs, raising the question why Houk persisted in batting him third the first half of the season.

Interestingly, all three deals were for cash. With the advent of free agency, Steinbrenner demonstrated he would spare no expense to attract talent. But his first season as boss he still had a bit of the old bottom-liner in him. "It's strange when you think back now," Lee MacPhail chuckles, "but he was always after us to get rid of that type of older player. It hurt George to pay their salaries." The Alous earned $150,000 between them, a substantial figure at that time.

MacPhail, who as American League president would have his share of disputes with Steinbrenner, says, "There wasn't too much trouble with George the first half of the season. But then things began to get more and more difficult, and he got more and more involved in the player moves. You could see it definitely wasn't going to be the way it had been, for any of us, under any of the organizations we had worked for."

While Callison, Allen, and the Alous were hardly essential, the flurry of transactions served to unsettle an already troubled ball club. Yankees began wondering who would be next to face either the guillotine or their capricious employer's insults. More than once Steinbrenner had loudly berated his own players from the stands.

"I didn't like the way he treated the players, talking about them in the papers," says Horace Clarke. "I don't think that helps. He probably thought it would stimulate people to do better. But a professional has enough pride to want to go out every day and do his best, without somebody showing him up."

The owner's unbecoming conduct all but destroyed morale. As an anonymous Yankee later told *The New York Times*, "Guys were thinking more of George Steinbrenner than what we should be doing on the field."

It showed. On a grueling four-city road trip, New York dropped eight straight and tumbled out of the race. "I'll never forget it," says first baseman Mike Hegan. After five years with Seattle, Milwaukee, and Oakland, the son of bullpen coach Jim Hegan rejoined the Yankees on August 19. "Within ten days we went from three games out to ten and a half. The Orioles won fourteen in a row, and it was over."

Baltimore's bold management had transformed the team over the winter by trading some of its depreciating stars while they still had value. Earl Weaver's starting nine featured five new faces, among them Don Baylor, Bobby Grich, and 1973 Rookie of the Year Al Bumbry. The Birds nested atop the AL East the last two months of the season, leaving second-place Boston eight lengths behind.

The Yankees? They streaked through the .500 barrier and embedded themselves in fourth place, seventeen games back. "It was a sad time," says Fritz Peterson, "because we were going nowhere—again. And there was just no hope. The day we got Nettles, I'd said to Susanne, 'We just won the pennant.' But it still wasn't enough."

New York drifted through an 11–16 September. Catcher Duke Sims, claimed on waivers from Detroit with a week to go, says, "When

I got over there, it seemed to me the club had quit." No one could ever say that before about a Ralph Houk team.

Number 35's appearances on the field met with jeering choruses of "Goodbye, Ralphie," bellowed to the tune of "Good Night, Ladies." Fans' memories, of course, are notoriously short. In taunting Houk, they were forgetting the three pennants of the early 1960s and the surprising finishes of 1968, '70, and '72. But this year's second-half dive sent long-simmering frustrations boiling over.

Compounding the angst in the Bronx was the sudden ascent of the Mets. On August 31, manager Yogi Berra's mediocrities extricated themselves from the National League East cellar. Fortunate to belong to the weakest division in the majors, they rose to first and on the last day of the season backed into the title with the lowest winning percentage ever, .509. The Cinderella team of 1973 then dismantled Cincinnati's Big Red Machine in the playoffs and came within one game of capturing the World Series. For Yankees zealots, the sight of merry Mets fans jabbing index fingers in the air and flaunting the slogan "You Gotta Believe!" was harder to swallow than a stadium frank.

VII

THE BRONX BOMBERS had hoped to commemorate Yankee Stadium's fiftieth anniversary the same way they'd dedicated the majestic ballpark, with a championship. Instead, the final game played there was a meaningless 8–5 loss to Detroit that attracted only 32,328. When baseball's grandest stadium first opened—on April 18, 1923—nearly that many spectators had to be turned away, as a record 74,200 passed through the turnstiles.

Babe Ruth christened the house with a three-run swat. Duke Sims, whose career in pinstripes lasted all of nine games, crushed the last home run the graying building would see, a Ruthian belt into the bleachers. "My claim to fame in baseball," jokes the Nevada businessman.

In the eighth, the Tigers pounced on Lindy McDaniel, scoring six times. When Ralph Houk came out to change pitchers, boos filled the air. "That hurt," he admits in a quiet voice. "People say you don't hear it, but you do."

Banners hanging from the mezzanine and upper deck demanded HOUK MUST GO! and FIRE HOUK! That wouldn't be necessary. A few days before, in Milwaukee, The Major had decided to quit. "I just thought, I'd been there so long, it was time for me to get away from New York," he says. Lee MacPhail tried talking him out of it, then Gabe Paul and George Steinbrenner, but, says Houk, "I'd made up my mind."

Extra security had been hired in anticipation of the inevitable post-game mob scene. But some ticket holders didn't wait for the final out to assist in demolishing The House That Ruth Built. Fred Beene remembers: "The relievers started the game in the bullpen, but by the third or fourth inning they advised us to go into the dugout, because it was getting dangerous. People just started destroying the place, ripping out pipes and seats."

At 4:41 P.M., Mike Hegan flied out to center and an estimated 20,000 souvenir hunters swarmed onto the field. "Elston Howard got a hold of first base," Beene recalls, "and some guy was trying to take it away from him. Ellie had him around the neck and was choking him. He said afterward he wasn't going to let anyone get that base." The canvas bag had been promised to Mrs. Eleanor Gehrig, while Mrs. Clare Ruth was to receive home plate. An intrepid private cop protected the white-rubber slab by planting himself on it and refusing all bribes. Vandals did, however, make off with second and third.

While the crowd set to work tearing up turf, in the locker room Ralph Houk tearfully informed his players he was stepping down. Asked to recall his emotions on that day, he replies, "Not good. It was tough to do."

Few Yankees kept their composure enough to remember his words. "He just said he couldn't function in the situation there, he wasn't happy, and so it was best to get out," Beene says. "It broke the club up, I'll tell you. Everybody was practically crying, like there'd been a death in the family. I know *I* cried. Ralph was like a father to me."

"I was absolutely stunned," recalls Doc Medich. "I thought Ralph was a Yankee in every cell of his body." Fritz Peterson, however, suspected the manager might not return, "because he could not work with George."

Still wearing his uniform and clutching his trademark cigar, Houk trudged off to the press room. The 35 on his back equaled the number of years he'd belonged to the organization. Eleven seasons at the helm had brought 944 wins, 806 losses, three American League flags, and two World Series rings.

In October, MacPhail followed Houk out the door, relinquishing the general managership to succeed Joe Cronin as league president, a position he held until 1983. Now retired, he visits Yankee Stadium whenever the Minnesota Twins, of which his son Andy is general manager, are in town.

Back in 1969 Mike Burke had prophesied, "I've always thought of Ralph, Lee, and myself as a sort of team; that we'd build a winner or we'd go all together." That is precisely what happened. Less than a year after George Steinbrenner's ascension to power, the Burke-MacPhail-Houk stewardship ended. Although no pennants flapped from the flagpole, their seven years had produced slow but steady progress: more good trades than bad, the revival of the scouting and farm systems, and much-improved public relations.

The smoke and debris from 1973's late-season crash obscured the fact that from next to nothing the triumvirate assembled the nucleus of the 1976–78 championship squads: Thurman Munson, Graig Nettles, Roy White, Sparky Lyle, Fred Stanley. Other players added during their watch, such as Lindy McDaniel, Pat Dobson, and Doc Medich, would be traded to obtain additional key components. As Gene Michael, twice a Yankees general manager, points out, "I know some people say George took over a team with no tools on it, but that wasn't true at all. In spring training we'd been picked to win. We were competitive."

On the negative side, the Yankees brain trust tended to maneuver with excessive caution. Houk especially looked upon drastic action as panicking, preferring to stay the course. As a result, New York often held on to players too long. Clete Boyer offers this opinion: "Even with their baseball backgrounds, they never had the knack of knowing who could play in the big leagues." While his assessment is overly harsh, because the roster remained relatively stable from year to year, eventually both manager and general manager grew too close to some of the players to objectively evaluate their talent.

Similarly, by 1973 Houk's comfortable rapport with his men became more a detriment than an asset, contributing to the decline in discipline and conditioning. Michael, also a two-time Yankees field manager, offers as harsh a criticism of Houk as you're likely to hear: "If anything was wrong with Ralph, he wasn't critical enough."

Even by quitting, The Major hadn't fully exorcised George Steinbrenner from his life. On October 11, he signed on to manage Detroit, which had been trying to get him for years. "I had thought it was time for me to spend more time with my family," says Houk, then a fifty-four-year-old father of three. "But Jim Campbell called me immediately and said he had to make a big change." The Tigers had let combative Billy Martin go at the beginning of September. "He made it sound so good, I decided to do it."

The Yankees, however, refused to release Houk from his contract, which had two years left at $80,000 per. The matter dragged on through mid-December, eventually landing before the league president. "We had a hearing in Boston," Houk explains, "and they called in the lawyers and one thing and another. I'd signed the contract [in 1972] through CBS, before George was there. So Joe Cronin ruled that I could go ahead and manage Detroit." Jim Hegan, a Yankees coach since 1960, accompanied him.

Unfortunately for Houk, the aging Tigers had lost their bite. Once again he was saddled with the thankless task of overseeing a rebuilding movement from the foundation on up. It took five years—until 1978— to get Detroit above the .500 mark, after which The Major declined a new contract and went home to Florida, ostensibly to retire. "Again we thought, 'Hey, we just can't stay in baseball all our lives,' " he says. "When I left Detroit I had no intention of coming back at all."

But two years later, Boston general manager Haywood Sullivan wooed him away from a life of golf, fishing, and hunting with a lucrative deal. "We also had some family up there," Houk explains. "Our daughter. My wife said, 'If you think you want to manage again, I would go to Boston.' " Before finally calling it a career, Houk worked part-time for Andy MacPhail in Minnesota as vice president of baseball and later as a consultant. Asked if he's enjoying retirement after more than fifty years in the game, he purrs, "I sure am."

Houk remains the only Yankees skipper to leave George Steinbrenner's employ voluntarily; the rest have all been fired. From 1974 through 1990, the year Commissioner Fay Vincent suspended him for consorting with a known gambler, The Boss replaced ten different managers a total of seventeen times.

Houk's quitting sent a signal. Says Steve Jacobson of *Newsday*, "Right then, all of us knew that the Steinbrenner era was going to be a bitch.

"And it was!"

1974

STARTERS
Doc Medich
Pat Dobson
Dick Tidrow
Rudy May
Larry Gura
Mel Stottlemyre

Chris Chambliss (1B)
Sandy Alomar (2B)
Jim Mason (SS)
Graig Nettles (3B)
Lou Piniella/Roy White
(LF)
Elliott Maddox (CF)
Bobby Murcer (RF)
Thurman Munson (C)
Ron Blomberg/Roy White
(DH)

RELIEVERS
Sparky Lyle
Cecil Upshaw
Mike Wallace

I

ON DECEMBER 13, 1973, THE Yankees introduced Ralph Houk's replacement at a restaurant high above the grounds of the 1964 New
York World's Fair, in Flushing, their new temporary home. Proving
that the pinstripes still retained their allure, for the second time in a
decade New York snagged the skipper of the reigning world champions.

Dick Williams had shocked the sports world by quitting the Oakland
Athletics moments after their seventh-game win over the Mets in the
1973 World Series. TV cameras recorded his resignation while Reggie
Jackson, Catfish Hunter, and the rest of the bickering, battling A's
celebrated noisily in the background.

The forty-five-year-old Williams was widely considered one of baseball's finest field generals. In six seasons his clubs reached the postseason four times. As a crewcut freshman, he led the 1967 Red Sox from
ninth place to first, a feat that earned him AL Manager of the Year
accolades. But Williams's outspokenness and authoritarian style troubled the Boston front office, which let him go two years later.

In 1971, he assumed command in Oakland. The A's hadn't won a pennant since 1931, when they belonged to Philadelphia. Williams apparently fell under the West Coast's radical influence, growing his hair long and sprouting a mustache. He delivered a division title right away, then back-to-back World Championships. He was that rare commodity, a manager with box-office appeal, and the Yankees wanted him badly—although his hirsute Athletics never would have passed one of Boss Steinbrenner's inspections.

Ironically, Williams had given notice for the same reason as Houk: an intrusive owner undermining his authority. Charlie Finley, who routinely ground up pilots (nine in the decade between 1961 and Williams's arrival), infuriated him during the '73 World Series by humiliating one of his favorite players. Second baseman Mike Andrews errored twice in the twelfth inning of game two's 10–7 marathon, greasing the Mets' winning rally. Finley promptly axed him from the roster on the pretext of a phantom shoulder injury. In a shameful charade, he browbeat Andrews into signing a phony physician's medical report.

Commissioner Bowie Kuhn reinstated the veteran in time for game four, but after three years of Finley's antics, Williams had had enough. He confided to his players that, win or lose, he was gone. True to his word, after Oakland's determining 5–2 victory on October 21, Williams quit in front of a national audience. Finley, standing alongside, graciously expressed his appreciation.

Days later, however, before a league meeting in Chicago, George Steinbrenner and Gabe Paul were dumbfounded when the controversial owner denied them permission to sound out Williams about managing in New York. His contract, Finley claimed, bound him to Oakland for two more years.

Why the abrupt about-face? Vengeance, no doubt, for all those years the A's served as Yankees doormats. Ever since, Finley had been obsessed with subverting the mighty New Yorkers. It was Charlie O., you'll recall, who tried blocking the club's sale to CBS. He also once proposed the Bombers be forced to raise Yankee Stadium's right-field wall, to cut down on cheap home runs. When that measure failed, he brought his own right-field fence in some twenty feet and smirkingly dubbed it the "pennant porch." But the commissioner and the league president ordered Finley to restore Municipal Stadium's original dimensions. That the fortunes of the A's and the Yankees were now reversed in no way deterred him from his divine mission.

Finley held his ex-manager for ransom. First he declared he'd let Williams go only in exchange for either Bobby Murcer or Thurman Munson. New York countered with Horace Clarke and $50,000. Then the demand centered on two prize rookies, pitcher Scott McGregor and first baseman–outfielder Otto Velez. Not even for Williams, Walter Alston, and the ghost of Connie Mack, huffed the Yankees. Steinbrenner, meanwhile, decided to try his own hand at extortion and informed Detroit that he expected compensation for Ralph Houk's services.

The three sides reached an impasse, pending a league ruling. Charlie O. clearly enjoyed watching the Yankees twist in the wind. Steinbrenner finally ran out of patience, of which he did not have an endless supply. On his attorneys' advice, he went ahead and signed Williams to a three-year deal. At the December 13 press conference, Gabe Paul neatly sidestepped questions about probable legal action from Finley, preferring to focus on the season ahead. Williams offered few specifics, though he did announce plans to play Ron Blomberg every day.

He never got the chance. A week later, Joe Cronin dealt the Yankees a double blow, nullifying their pact with Williams while upholding Houk's Tigers contract. According to the outgoing president, New York had acted in bad faith by hiring Williams despite Finley's objections.

Cronin's decision sent the embarrassed Yankees scurrying for a manager like last-minute Christmas shoppers. Elston Howard had been campaigning for the position. Other names bandied about included Whitey Ford, Frank Robinson, Bill White, Hank Bauer, Dave Bristol, Eddie Stanky, and Bill Virdon.

With spring training only a month away, on January 3, 1974, New York selected Virdon, manager of the Pittsburgh Pirates the past two seasons. Said Gabe Paul in a ringing endorsement, "We had to do something . . ."

For Virdon, the new appointment brought his career full circle. In 1950 he was signed out of a Missouri try-out camp by Tom Greenwade, the Yankees superscout who'd discovered Mickey Mantle the year before. But Virdon couldn't crack Casey Stengel's outfield, so New York traded him to the Cardinals. A .281 BA, 17 HR, 68 RBI performance won him National League Rookie of the Year honors in 1955.

When he started slowly his sophomore year, St. Louis inexplicably shipped him to Pittsburgh for a pair of journeymen. The six-foot center fielder put together a .319 average and spent the rest of his twelve-year career there, batting .267 overall.

Yankees rooters remembered Virdon all too well from game seven of the 1960 World Series. It was his ground ball that took a freakish hop and caught Tony Kubek in the Adam's apple, touching off a five-run Bucs eighth. The contest went to the bottom of the ninth tied

9–9, which set the stage for one of the most dramatic moments in sports history: Bill Mazeroski lofting a Ralph Terry pitch over the left-field wall and trotting home accompanied by most of Pittsburgh.

As Danny Murtaugh's successor in 1972, Virdon inherited another championship squad. His maiden season, the Pirates ran off with the NL East but threw away the pennant on a wild pitch in the play-offs finale against Cincinnati. The next year contained more setbacks than some managers encounter in a lifetime. First a New Year's Eve plane crash claimed the life of star right fielder Roberto Clemente. Then nineteen-game winner Steve Blass reported to camp suddenly unable to locate the plate, a mental block that defied psychotherapy, hypnosis, and meditation. The right-hander's ERA swelled from 2.49 to 9.85. Blass never regained his control, and an excellent career ended prematurely the following year. Sore-armed number-two starter Dock Ellis also fell off his 1972 form, although not so precipitously.

Yet Virdon kept the team in contention. Pittsburgh sat three games back of first-place St. Louis when management dismissed him in early September—unfairly, most Bucs felt.

New York's insistence on a one-year contract aroused speculation that Virdon was merely warming the manager's chair for Dick Williams. *New York Times* columnist Dave Anderson claimed that the former Pirate had agreed to step aside once Williams became available, perhaps as early as midseason. "Not true," says Virdon, although his denial is conspicuously mild. "I don't think that was ever talked about, really.

"A lot of people asked me, 'Do you have a problem with the fact that Dick Williams was their first choice?' At the time, Dick was probably the best-known manager in baseball, so I didn't mind being second best, not when you were talking about the best in the business."

The new pilot's first spring in pinstripes paralleled that of the late Johnny Keane, whose number 21 he was given to wear. Virdon too came from the National League and faced the unenviable task of trying to win the allegiance of players still devoted to Ralph Houk.

Unlike his popular predecessor, Virdon kept his distance from the team. Infielder Fred Stanley recalls, "Bill was there to get a job done his way, and that way was not to be particularly friendly with a whole lot of people." Stoic, inscrutable behind wire-rim glasses, he often communicated to players through coaches Dick Howser, Elston Howard, Mel Wright, and Whitey Ford, the new pitching tutor.

"Going from Ralph to Virdon was like going from one extreme to another, with no happy medium," says Pat Dobson. "I don't know that a lot of the players were very happy changing so much in one year"— he being one of them.

Virdon felt that, like the rest of the country, the Yankees had suffered an energy crisis in late 1973. "We died," Gene Michael agrees. "We went on a West Coast trip and became a pretty tired ball club." Accordingly, the new manager ran a grueling spring training that was heavy on fitness and fundamentals.

"It was like boot camp," says Stanley, a refugee from the San Diego Padres. "The toughest one I'd ever been in." Duke Sims, on the other hand, found the three-hour workouts no more rigorous than those he'd experienced in ten seasons with Cleveland, Los Angeles, and Detroit. "I thought Bill was all right!" he exclaims. "But some of the guys thought he was a Little Hitler because he made them work harder than they'd ever had to before. There was a lot of grumbling."

In a reprise of 1965, the Yankees didn't wait long to test the new boss. Whereas Keane was rattled by their defiance like a window in a tempest, his authority forever impaired, Virdon stood firm. "There were a couple of times in spring training when we were going through drills and guys were fooling around," Mike Hegan recalls. "Bill stopped everything, brought us all in, and said in no uncertain terms, 'This is what we're going to do. There's no Sunday school here anymore.' A lot of guys didn't like that." But everyone complied.

"I don't think I asked them to do anything that I wasn't willing to do myself," says Virdon. Still trim and hard-muscled at age forty-two, he liked to flaunt his bulging biceps around the locker room. Asked if maintaining a brawny physique is useful when it comes to enforcing discipline, Virdon, economical with words, replies, "I think it helps, yes."

A superb center fielder, he subjected the outfielders to a drill devised to improve reaction time. Elston Howard would fungo sinking line drives at a trio of Yankees positioned just beyond the infield dirt until they were drenched in sweat. Mickey Mantle, in camp as an instructor, praised, "That's the best outfield drill I ever saw." The three participants didn't necessarily agree.

Sportswriter Joe Donnelly of *Newsday* remembers, "At one point the outfielders were complaining, so Virdon took the bat from Elston and started hitting shots at them himself. Bobby Murcer came in, claiming he had to puke." But that year New York outfielders finished one, two, and three in the league in assists. Murcer topped the majors with 21.

"It was one of the first positive signs of the team coming back," reflects Donnelly, "and it was Virdon instilling it."

Even some Houk loyalists welcomed Number 21's approach. "A lot of guys didn't like Bill as a manager, but I did," Ron Blomberg says, despite his still being platooned against left-handed pitching. "He made us work double hard in spring training, he took no nonsense, and he was a winner. At that time, we needed some different atmosphere on the club.

"We needed to win," Blomberg says intently. "We needed *to win*."

II

IN HIS FIRST team address, Bill Virdon warned that virtually no one was untouchable. The Yankees were to learn quickly this was no idle threat.

On April 26, second-place New York edged Texas 4–3 at home for its eleventh victory in nineteen games. While the players exchanged congratulations in the clubhouse, pitchers Fritz Peterson, Steve Kline, Fred Beene, and Tom Buskey were quietly summoned to the manager's office.

Virdon informed them they'd been traded en masse to the Indians for two right-handers and a first baseman.

Buskey, the spring's top rookie, was happy to go anywhere he might pitch regularly. The other three stood there stunned. Forty percent of the pitching staff—gone. "It didn't seem real," says Beene. He remembers thinking, "This is the major leagues. You don't all get traded to one club. That's not the way it happens."

"We didn't want to trade you, Beenie," Virdon added, but it came as little consolation. "I was getting nauseous by the second, I really was," Beene says. "I'd had such a long, hard fight. I felt like I finally had a home. And then I was just blasted out of it."

Virdon turned to Peterson. "Fritz, I know you're not happy." Demoted to the fifth spot in the rotation, the thirty-two-year-old veteran had recently asked Gabe Paul to trade him anyplace but Cleveland. "He patted me on the shoulder and said, 'Don't worry, young man, we wouldn't do that to you,' " Peterson recalls. "I told Graig Nettles and Sam McDowell, and they said, 'Well, move either to the east side of Cleveland or the west side!' "

Kline took the news in stride. "Anyone want an apartment?" he joked. Most ballplayers accept getting traded as a professional hazard. This was particularly true prior to free agency, when they were mere chattel with no say as to where they worked. Management dealt you to another team, you said your goodbyes, and went.

The transition is often far more stressful and lonely for wives and children whose lives are uprooted without warning. Kline had married his college sweetheart during the off-season. "Linda knew nothing about baseball," he says. "Initially she thought we were always going to play for New York. She figured it was like working for a company: you came back every year and had your job."

Kline reported to Cleveland the next day, leaving his bride of four months to pack up the one-bedroom apartment in Queens, load a trailer with furniture and the couple's new puppy, and make the drive to Ohio alone. "I found us the apartment there," says Kline, "but Linda took care of the rest.

"That was the first time she'd been upended in her life, you know? Get in the car and go. And she was on her own and had to drive quite a number of miles. I think for her it was kind of scary."

As for Kline, 2–2 at the time of the seven-man swap, his first four starts of 1974 allayed fears that he would never throw freely again. He debuted by silencing Ralph Houk's Tigers 3–0. Then he put down Cleveland 9–5. "I thought I had the elbow problem licked," Kline says. But by midseason, "It just became intolerable again. I was at my wit's end."

The tall right-hander faded into the minors, resurfacing with Atlanta briefly in 1977. Over the winter he contemplated his future. "I was thirty years old," he reflects. "Linda and I had gone through a whole season apart. We'd just had our first daughter, and I wasn't even there for the birth.

"I felt like I was going to lose my family if I kept playing, so I decided, 'Well, I'd better do something else.'" That turned out to be lumber brokering in Oregon, where Kline had some relatives. Sounding perfectly content, the father of two says, "We jumped in our van and started a new life."

III

KLINE, PHILOSOPHICAL ABOUT the trade to Cleveland, may have been the calmest man in the locker room that Friday night. "Everybody was angry about it," says Doc Medich, "because those four guys were really well liked." Ballplayers want to win, but ideally they want to win surrounded by their pals. In the heat of the moment it didn't matter that New York was receiving the 1971 AL Rookie of the Year in first baseman Chris Chambliss, a reliable starter in Dick Tidrow, and a proven reliever in Cecil Upshaw.

Thurman Munson squawked, "They can trade those four pitchers back for me!" while Bobby Murcer drawled sarcastically, "At this rate, they [the Indians] are going to have a pretty good ball club soon." A threatened clubhouse meeting to formally denounce the swap, though, never materialized.

The bitter reaction took Gabe Paul by surprise. "But I didn't pay too much attention to that," he says, "because I knew it was a good deal."

Mike Hegan didn't think so, for Chambliss's arrival shattered his dream of playing regularly in New York a second time. He had lost a spot on the team once before, when the Yankees made a first baseman of Joe Pepitone. The night of the mega-deal, reporters swarmed around his locker for an opinion. Hegan, then tied for second on the team in RBIs, was in a state of shock. He suggested that Chambliss, a .282 hitter since coming to the majors, couldn't knock in runs, a remark he later regretted.

"I said some things at the time that may have sounded like sour grapes—and in a way they probably were," he admits. Hegan demanded a trade back to Milwaukee, where he made his home and worked as a TV sportscaster for the local NBC affiliate during the off-season. "I knew the broadcast business was the place I wanted to be when I finished playing," says the photogenic Hegan, today an announcer for the Indians.

On May 13, Gabe Paul accommodated him, in one of *seven* trades consummated that month alone. Lee MacPhail's resignation had freed the Yankees' new president and general manager to place his stamp on the club. At the winter meetings in Houston he went on a shopping spree, buying shortstop Jim Mason and utility man Bill Sudakis from Texas and swapping Lindy McDaniel to Kansas City for outfielder Lou Piniella and pitcher Ken Wright.

In March, a blizzard of activity brought over outfielder Walt "No-Neck" Williams from Cleveland, while the Rangers relinquished outfielder Elliott Maddox for more George Steinbrenner money. Then April saw the blockbuster deal with the Tribe.

"Apparently they don't think we can win," Bobby Murcer sniffed, to which Paul responded publicly, "Never was a truer statement made." Besides looking to upgrade talent, he wanted to break up "the country club," as he put it. Giving the manager a better balance between seasoned hands and newcomers (read: men who hadn't played under Ralph Houk) was another consideration, although some of the resentment toward the front office spattered onto Bill Virdon.

Having played the game himself, he understood the indignation at seeing longtime friends packed off. "But I really thought that was the least of my worries," he says. "Yeah, some players there had been together a number of years. But," he adds, "they hadn't been very successful, either."

The same could have been said of Gabriel Howard Paul, then in his twenty-fourth season as a baseball executive. Prior to becoming the Cincinnati Reds' president in 1951, he'd spent nearly a quarter century in capacities ranging from public-relations director to traveling secretary to scoreboard ad-space salesman. At eighteen, the Rochester, New York, native gave up his sportswriting job to work for the hometown Red Wings, a St. Louis Cardinals farm team.

Although Paul had yet to preside over a pennant winner, he did assemble the 1961 NL Champion Reds. He'd quit Cincy the winter before to oversee the formation of the Houston Colt .45's, but wound up back in Ohio six months later as Cleveland Indians chief.

Paul's track record didn't impress many Yankees. "At that time a lot of people thought that maybe baseball had passed Gabe by," Mike Hegan recalls. They nicknamed the gray-haired, ruddy-complexioned sixty-four-year-old "Dial-a-Deal" and in general felt his furious trading had left the squad a shambles. When Horace Clarke was condemned to the San Diego Padres on May 31, New York resided in last place.

"It was a very sad thing," Clarke says of the deal that cleaved him from the organization after sixteen years. However, Graig Nettles heard the news and quipped, "Some guys have all the luck." The clubhouse resembled a bus depot, with just nine players remaining from the roster of exactly one year ago.

Having to call Shea Stadium home only magnified the vagabond Bombers' identity crisis. "It was like we were guests there, and every game was an away game," says Doc Medich. Yankees fans felt equally uncomfortable. As if setting foot in the Mets' ballpark wasn't sacrilege enough, the 1973 National League pennant taunted them from the flagpole all year.

The Amazin's recent respectability in no way diminished their populist appeal, just as nine threadbare seasons did little to make the Yankees more lovable. Because of Shea Stadium's accessibility, bored Mets fans got into the habit of infiltrating the stands when their darlings were out of town. Bobby Murcer, Thurman Munson, and other Yankees favorites suddenly heard boos at "home."

Although the Mets leased Shea Stadium from the city, for all intents and purposes they were the Yankees' landlord. Mets management not only hoarded all profits from parking and concessions, it forced its subtenant to reduce its groundskeeping crew. "The field during those two years was probably the worst in baseball," says Fred Stanley, an eyewitness to untold bad hops. "When we were on the road the Mets were at home, so it just got beat up. Those poor grounds-crew guys didn't have a chance."

No one missed the Bronx more than Murcer. Balls that would have easily cleared Yankee Stadium's 296-foot sign were merely long outs at Shea, where the foul poles stood 338 feet away. "I hit countless, *countless* balls to the middle of the warning track and up against the wall," he groans. "Even Mickey Mantle felt sorry for me." Murcer didn't muscle his first four-bagger there until the season's next-to-last week.

It wasn't until years later that he discovered why. "At Yankee Stadium I had developed a top-hand swing, not the type you'd want to use in a bigger ballpark," Murcer explains. "When I swung, I was going against my own strength, overpowering the ball. So when I did hit the ball a long ways, it kind of faded at the end, simply because, with the top hand rolling over as much as I had it rolling over, you get a topspin on the ball, and the flight has a downward action to it.

"But nobody was telling me, and I didn't realize what the heck was going on." In 1979 the Yankees hired Charlie Lau, the Albert Einstein of batting instructors. He immediately detected the flaw in Murcer's stroke. "The first time I took batting practice, Charlie called me over to the side and said, 'Why are you smothering the ball so much?' And he showed me exactly what I was doing. All of a sudden my mind just clicked. *I've been doing this for the last five years! Can you imagine how many home runs it has cost me?*"

Murcer's inability to put one over the wall in the new venue kept him up nights. "He felt the pressure all year long," Roy White says sympathetically. "Everywhere we played, the press kept bringing up how Bobby was struggling. It became a mental thing, where he tried to overcompensate by swinging a little harder, and it hurt him." Murcer, who also detested the ballpark for the cold, gusty winds that blew in off of Flushing Bay, saw his numbers droop to .274 BA, 10 HR, 88 RBI.

He was further demoralized when he arrived at Shea Stadium for a game against Chicago on May 28 and found he'd been bumped from center field to right in favor of unproven Elliott Maddox. Bill Virdon had contemplated this shift for some time. Aware that he'd be tampering with tradition—and piquing Murcer's pride—he did not make it lightly. "Before I went ahead," he says, "I checked very thoroughly with the coaches to be sure that everybody thought it was the right thing to do."

"Bobby felt like he'd been slapped in the face," confides a Yankees pitcher. Murcer insists otherwise. "The New York press made a big issue out of this. It didn't make any difference to me where I played. But one day I show up at the ballpark, and he's got me playing right field after I'd been playing center for many years.

"The thing that really set me off was, I went to Virdon and asked him the reason. And he said, 'Because that's the way I want it to be.' " Murcer laughs. "I didn't particularly like that."

At least one fan didn't, either. The next day Virdon answered the phone in his Shea Stadium office. "Is Gabe Paul there?" a man's voice demanded.

No, he wasn't, said Virdon, without identifying himself.

"Tell him if Bobby Murcer doesn't play center field, *Virdon is dead.*"

Murcer may have shot the manager some deadly looks the rest of the year, but Virdon never budged. "Bobby wasn't happy about it," he acknowledges. "I think that's obvious. But he did not refuse to play because of it. He accepted the challenge and did a very good job for us."

His first night back in right, Number 1 expertly played a carom in the corner and held the potential go-ahead run at third with an outstanding throw. An inning later he sliced a leadoff single and came around to score the game-winner in New York's 3–2 victory.

The pitching staff privately applauded Virdon's decision. "A gutsy move," says Doc Medich. Another pitcher, who wishes to remain anonymous, disagrees. "I didn't think it was so gutsy; it was fairly obvious. At the time, I said, 'Boy, this is what we should have been doing for two months!'

"Murcer was more suited to right field. He didn't have the quick reaction time anymore that Maddox did. Elliott got a much faster jump and was more flexible in making catches over his shoulder and diving for balls. Murcer would let balls fall in front of him and get a late jump to boot."

New York would have been satisfied with a .250 average from Maddox, a .239 career hitter through four seasons. But the graceful twenty-six-year-old from East Orange, New Jersey, dwarfed expectations by batting .303. Inserted in the number-two slot ahead of Murcer, he also led the club in runs scored.

"I think Elliott was the best center fielder in the league, both offensively and defensively," declares Medich, who owed his tenth win, a 2–1 cliff-hanger in Kansas City, to Number 27's rifle arm. With the Yankees defending their slim lead in the seventh, Maddox speared George Brett's line drive, then fired a blue dart home to rub out Jim Wolford as he tried to tag up. "Maddox was as accurate a thrower as I ever saw," says Virdon.

Despite the switch's unquestionable success, Murcer never came around. Sportswriter Phil Pepe of the *Daily News* recalls, "He just got into a funk over Shea Stadium and over not playing center field. Bobby always put out one hundred percent, but he became moody and petulant."

Murcer's unhappy year began with his being made the richest Yankee of all time as well as unofficial team captain. George Steinbrenner informed his $120,000 outfielder that he expected him to assume a leadership role, something the quiet Oklahoman had always shied away from.

"I'll tell you why," says Murcer. "Because we felt like our manager was our leader." By the time his star rose, only Mel Stottlemyre remained from the last Yankees championship crew. "We didn't have a whole lot of experience in the leadership category, so what qualified any of us to be a leader? That was my attitude. If the others wanted to look upon me as being a leader, fine, but as far as me telling somebody else what to do, I thought that was the manager's job."

Steinbrenner felt differently and frequently sounded out Murcer's opinions. "George would invite me into the city to have lunch with him," he recalls. "He wanted to know from me how we could make this team a winner.

"It was totally new in the baseball world for an owner to be as involved as George was when he first took control of the Yankees. Until then, the players and the ownership didn't have a one-on-one relationship. If any messages had to be sent, it was always done through the manager."

The Boss delivered his personally and often. "He started calling me just about every day at my house! We'd have a night game, I'd get home at midnight or one, and the next morning at seven-thirty he'd have me on the phone, wanting to know, 'What's going on? What's wrong?'

"At first I didn't know how to react to it, to tell you the truth. But when the owner invites you to lunch, what are you going to tell him— you're not going to go?"

During one conversation, Murcer offered his advice for improving the Yankees: fire the manager and replace him with third-base coach Dick Howser. Getting shunted to right field was merely Murcer's latest grievance against Virdon. "There's nothing to hide," he concedes. "Bill and I did not get along."

Murcer, who was used to Ralph Houk's coddling, chafed at being treated like just another player. "Virdon had no superstars," Fred Beene says approvingly. One of the new manager's first mandates was that Murcer report to the ballpark the same time as everybody else, which set their relationship off on a shaky course.

"Bobby didn't get in tune with Bill right off the bat," says Beene.

"He didn't toe the mark, so to speak." Instead of acting like a role model, Murcer was one of the loudest dissenters throughout spring training. His sneering reaction to Virdon's emphasis on running: "I've never seen so much chicken shit!"

Virdon says he didn't take Murcer's attempted coup too seriously. "A player can complain and be unhappy and so forth, but so long as he does his job and doesn't influence others, then I don't think it's a problem. Some players have a following, and some don't. And I really don't think Bobby Murcer had an influence on any of the players."

Pat Dobson, another of Virdon's most vocal detractors, contends that, to the contrary, there was no shortage of mutineers eager to hang the new captain from the crow's nest. "Murcer was more or less a spokesman for everybody else. I don't think a lot of people were happy with Bill Virdon. Maybe because Bobby had been there for a while and was kind of the fair-haired boy, he felt it was his job to do what he did."

Dobson overstates the level of discontent, although Virdon certainly was not popular among the starting pitchers for his quick hook. Dobson had a couple of confrontations with the manager over not being allowed to finish games. Once in Minnesota he trailed Bert Blyleven 1–0 in the seventh when Virdon came ambling out of the dugout, signaling for Sparky Lyle. Dobson stomped around the mound. "I felt it was a bad decision. He wasn't very happy with what I said to him," he recalls. Lyle yielded a two-run double and New York lost, 3–0. Afterward Dobson grumbled to reporters that the next time the manager intended to lift him in a tight game, he'd need a tow truck.

Virdon held a clubhouse meeting at which he reasserted his authority, all the while flaunting his sculptured arms. "If it takes a tow truck to get you off the mound, I'll get one," he told the six-foot-three right-hander, then struck a Mr. Universe pose. "But I don't think I'll need one. Do *you*, Mr. Dobson?" Dobson held his tongue this time.

The offense also had a complaint: that Virdon played for the big inning and didn't bunt or run enough. "He still thinks he's managing Pittsburgh," more than one Yankee griped. The 1974 club boasted no Willie Stargells or Richie Hebners; only Graig Nettles exceeded twenty home runs. In Texas, the players secretly assembled in Sparky Lyle's hotel room and plotted to advance runners on their own.

Bobby Murcer remembers laughingly, "Lou Piniella, Thurman Munson, myself, we used to give one another signs to bunt, hit-and-run, and all that. And Virdon kept saying, 'You guys can never get the signs right!' But it seemed to work every time." The manager eventually caught on. His reaction? A sly smile.

In June, Virdon's job security was reinforced when Dick Williams signed on to manage the American League's other last-place team, California. Charlie Finley had finally let him out of contractual pillory, with one hitch: Williams could manage anywhere but New York. "I am not a vindictive person," proclaimed the Oakland owner, sounding much like Richard Nixon protesting "I am not a crook."

The sight of Williams sitting behind the Yankees dugout on Opening Day had seemed to underscore Virdon's tenuous status. Now notions of Number 21 as merely an interim manager dissolved. Gradually most of the Yankees warmed up to Virdon. "I grew to like Bill," says Roy White. "He was fair with me, and I could always talk to him."

He didn't feel that way at first. In spring training Virdon announced that White would have to win the left-field job from Lou Piniella. "I wasn't too happy about that, to say the least," White recalls. "I felt I'd proven myself. And I wasn't too happy with Virdon initially, because I thought I'd been prejudged."

White had started in left field every day going back to 1971. In 1974, however, he got into only 136 games, nearly half as designated hitter. When the June 15 trading deadline rolled around, he seemed destined for his second subpar season in a row. White was batting .230 and begging to be sent somewhere, anywhere. But management wisely held on to him. The switch-hitting thirty-year-old came alive and finished at .275. He also excelled in his new role as leadoff man, scoring 68 runs.

Virdon publicly admitted he'd underestimated White. "I really respected him for having the guts to come out and say something like that," says White. "A lot of managers wouldn't have. That was really honest." Unlike Ralph Houk, who could soften the truth to spare tender egos, Virdon was forthright to a fault. Sportswriter Steve Jacobson calls him "the only manager I would swear never lied to me." After the season, the New York Baseball Writers Association named him the recipient of its annual Good Guy Award.

As summer approached, the shock waves from Gabe Paul's spring housecleaning began to ebb and the patchwork Yankees showed signs of pulling together. A less unflappable leader might not have been able to navigate such turbulent waters. Fortunately for Virdon, he didn't have to wrestle George Steinbrenner for the wheel.

On April 5, Opening Day, a special Watergate grand jury charged the Yankees general partner with contributing illegally to Richard Nixon's 1972 presidential campaign fund. There were fourteen counts in all, including conspiracy and obstruction of a criminal investigation.

Subsequent Senate testimony would reveal that a vindictive Nixon administration had strong-armed Steinbrenner into giving generously. Apparently the White House was miffed over his association with its rival party. In 1969 and 1970 Steinbrenner raised nearly $2 million for Democratic senatorial candidates and in doing so became a close friend of Senator Edward Kennedy. The two flew to the 1972 Democratic convention together.

Herbert W. Kalmbach, Nixon's personal attorney, is said to have met with Steinbrenner and to have suggested strongly he come across with a round figure of, oh, $100,000. At the time, the American Ship Building Company was facing an investigation by the Department of Labor into its safety standards and working conditions. Other matters vulnerable to government pressure were pending. The board chairman donated $75,000 of his own money and $25,000 more from American Ship disguised as executive bonuses that were then "voluntarily" contributed to ensure four more years of Richard Nixon.

Although Steinbrenner professed his innocence, he announced he was removing himself from the ball club's daily affairs in order to concentrate on his legal defense. It took a federal indictment, but at last The Boss would uphold his promise of absentee ownership.

IV

GABE PAUL WASN'T through wheeling and dealing. In the space of three weeks he strengthened two critical areas by taking advantage of the turmoil on the Angels, a team racked with dissension and in the process of overhauling itself. First he bought pitcher Rudy May one hour before the trading deadline, and then, on July 8, paid cash for second baseman Sandy Alomar.

Neither transaction sent New Yorkers scurrying to reserve play-off tickets. With Fritz Peterson gone and Sam McDowell incapacitated by alcoholism, the starting rotation consisted entirely of righties Stottlemyre, Dobson, Medich, and Tidrow. Hence their interest in Rudy May, a black southpaw with a hard fastball and a fierce curve. But he lugged with him a record of 0-1 (7.00 ERA), which came on the heels of a 7-17 (4.38 ERA) 1973. The deal took on greater significance just days later, however, when Stottlemyre went on the disabled list for an injury suffered on June 11.

While facing California's Frank Robinson, Number 30 suddenly clutched his shoulder. He flexed it, took a few warmups, and resumed pitching. But he had to come out after the third inning. For Stottlemyre, then 6-7, it was the earliest exit of his career. It would also be his last major-league start. The damage, far more serious than first believed, turned out to be a torn rotator cuff.

May, one month shy of his thirtieth birthday, only had to stroll across the infield to join the Yankees, who came into Anaheim immediately after the trade. He felt more at home in the visitors dugout than he had as a fallen Angel under skipper Bobby Winkles. For reasons he says he still doesn't understand, "The ball club tried to turn me into a sinkerball-slider pitcher, and I couldn't get the hang of it. So they gave up on me. They said I'd lost my stuff."

Not his stuff, just his confidence. A starter all his life, the Oakland native threw only twenty-seven innings for California, mostly in short relief. "I wasn't playing, and I thought, *My career's over*. So when the Yankees took a chance on me, I was really surprised and happy."

On June 23, May four-hit Detroit 4–1 in a downpour that turned the mound into a mudpile. Nine Tigers went down on strikes, six of them swinging and hitting only raindrops. "That game was the greatest thing that ever happened to me," he says. "It turned everything around. Because until that Sunday, I was finished, the guy that couldn't pitch. And I went out in the rain and proved I had a lot of career left in me. Ten years later I was still doing it." May, now a supervisor for a convenience-store chain ("It's a really good job, the first I ever had," he says, laughing), was almost forty when he retired.

During his fourth outing, Number 43 hurt a hip diving for a ball on Kansas City's artificial turf, but three weeks on the disabled list didn't hamper his comeback in the slightest. May returned to action with an 8–0 two-hitter over Boston, the first of three consecutive games in which he didn't allow an earned run. In Mel Stottlemyre's continued absence, he emerged as the club's stopper until tiring in September.

Coming to New York restored May's cheerful disposition, which had inspired Angel Mickey Rivers to call him "Super Dude." The nickname adorned most of the T-shirts he owned. Sandy Alomar, his California teammate since 1969, says, "I saw the change. Rudy was enjoying himself again."

Alomar, a thirty-year-old from Salinas, Puerto Rico, plugged the defense's most gaping hole. Gabe Paul had tried sweet-talking the Angels out of Alomar all winter, but without success. While awaiting a deal of some kind, the Yankees did everything in their power to replace Horace Clarke, as if to let him open the season at the keystone would be the ultimate symbol of their stagnation.

George Steinbrenner appealed to Gene Michael to move to second. Stick didn't think too much of the idea, scoffing to *Newsday*'s Joe Donnelly, "Steinbrenner came off a boat; what does he know about baseball?" At thirty-six, Michael's range wasn't what it used to be. He had to settle for a utility role in his seventh and final season in pinstripes (.260 BA, 0 HR, 13 RBI).

Next, New York tried a journeyman named Fernando Gonzales, obtained from Kansas City during the spring trading frenzy. But he wasn't the answer either (.215 BA) and ended the year in the minors. Finally the Yankees landed their man on what Paul claimed was the 101st try.

Sandy Alomar (born Santos) had wanted out of Anaheim for much the same reason as Rudy May. In spring training the onetime All-Star found himself displaced by ex-Phillie Denny Doyle. California doubted he would ever be the same after breaking his leg the previous September.

"My mobility was okay," Alomar insists in lightly accented English. "I felt like they wanted to make a utility guy out of me right away without giving me a chance. I was still young and didn't have any doubts that I could play. So I asked them to trade me." Bill Virdon knew Alomar's capabilities well, having once managed him in the Mets farm system. He made him his everyday second baseman.

Alomar didn't relish relocating his family of five, which included future big-league stars Sandy Jr. and Roberto, and daughter Sandia ("The smart one," he jokes). However, he quickly came to enjoy the Big Apple, home of a sizable Hispanic population. "I just loved it there," he says. "I'd had some good years with the Angels, but I never got the recognition I did with the Yankees."

The lithe five-foot-nine 140-pounder proved to be the cylinder missing from the Yankees' engine. New York won its first five games with Alomar in the lineup and played .625 ball the rest of the way, leaving last place behind in a cloud of dust. Number 2 switch-hit a career-high .269 and solidified the infield with his absorbent glove and leadership qualities. He immediately took double-play partner Jim Mason under his wing.

Mason, twenty-three, possessed the tools to be a fine shortstop: quick reflexes, zip-gun arm. But an erratic first half raised doubts about his temperament. Bad days in the field tended to follow bad days at the plate. And there were many of those. Through his first forty-five games, the left-handed Mason was hitting .209, three points higher than his career average in three seasons with Texas.

Rudy May observes, "Mase was always a joker, a kid at heart. He could go 4-for-4 one day and do a tremendous job for you, but then he'd go 0-for-21 and not show any emotion about it. That really bothered Sandy, because he took the game very seriously.

"I remember him and Jim having a confrontation about how important Mase was to the team. Sandy really settled him down and got him to concentrate." Mason completed the year at .250 BA, 5 HR, 37 RBI. In a 12–5 thrashing of the Rangers, he lashed four doubles to tie

the major-league record. New York believed it had found its shortstop
of the next decade, for a mere $100,000.

In Anaheim on August 10, Mason and Alomar roved all over the
infield gobbling grounders as Rudy May pinned a 2–1 loss on his
former team in front of his cheering family. The left-hander's fourth
victory in five decisions started the 55–57 Yankees on a 15–5 roll
through the end of the month.

"We just began winning," he recalls. "We got to a point where we
didn't think we could lose, and all of a sudden we were in a pennant
race." In the AL East that summer, a 55–57 record bought fourth
place, six and a half games behind division-leading Boston. All six
teams were hot on the scent; even last-place Milwaukee sat a mere
nine and a half back.

The Yankees headed into the Labor Day weekend trailing by five;
they emerged with only one game separating them and the Bosox.
The offense bulldozed Chicago at Comiskey Park 8–5, 18–6, and 7–5.
Returning home, New York split its Labor Day doubleheader against
Milwaukee. Boston, meanwhile, was getting a jump on its yearly
September slide, succumbing to Minnesota three games in a row.
Then the Orioles' Ross Grimsley and Mike Cuellar gagged them 1–0
in both ends of their holiday twin bill.

On September 4, the Yankees moved into a first-place tie. At the
same time the bewildered Red Sox were enduring a third straight
shutout, Doc Medich was blanking the Brewers for his seventeenth
win. Still a dewy-faced twenty-five, the towering sophomore established himself as the most consistent member of the rotation.

When not operating on hitters with an assortment of fastballs,
curves, and sliders, Medich studied orthopedics at the University of
Pittsburgh Medical School. New York offered him a contract in 1970.
Before he signed, the young man had to consider the practicality of
juggling two demanding careers.

He sought the opinion of someone who had, former Yankees third
baseman Dr. Bobby Brown. "He was practicing cardiology in Fort
Worth at the time," Medich remembers. "He didn't know me from
anybody, but I wrote him a letter explaining that I wanted to go to
medical school and play baseball, and could he help me out with any
advice." Brown, later Lee MacPhail's successor as American League
president, responded with a two-page letter.

"He basically said that things were different back when he played,
and that it was too hard and I shouldn't do it. But I did it anyway."
Medich is now an orthopedic surgeon outside Pittsburgh, not far from
where he grew up. His first two years in med school, "I could play

ball only in the summer because of the basic science curriculum," he explains. "But my last two years, I could do eighteen weeks of clinical rotation when the season was over, then go to spring training. The timing worked out.

"The only thing I had to be real careful about was that I didn't fall behind in my studies." Highly disciplined, Medich pored over textbooks in his hotel rooms and knew all the best libraries around the American League.

Catcher Jerry Moses, dealt to Detroit in spring training, states the obvious when he observes, "Doc was not your typical baseball player. He was a guy of high intellect and commitment. But he didn't use that as a wedge or to make people think he was special. He was well liked." The spring Medich first made the club, on the plane ride north, Sparky Lyle flavored his eggs Benedict with chemically treated road apples purchased in a novelty shop. "My initiation into the big leagues," Medich calls it. "I was the only rookie, so I guess they had to get me."

Against Milwaukee, Lou Piniella gave Number 33 all the support he needed with a first-inning run-scoring double. "It seemed like when Lou hit, we won," says Medich. The fiery, dark-complexioned outfielder batted .305 his first season in pinstripes and, more than anyone that year, embodied the team's indomitable spirit. "Lou was inspirational," Medich continues, "and good for the ball club because he used to make guys bear down by playing hard and taking the game seriously. We used to kid him *not* to take it so seriously."

Managers at every stop along a seven-year minor-league career had warned Piniella to rein in his emotions. "And rightfully so," he reflects. "As I got older, I learned that it's good to display a lot of intensity, but you've got to harness it a little bit. That's probably one of the things that held me back."

Stories of his thermonuclear tantrums are legend. While playing for Cleveland's triple-A Portland Beavers, he once struck out with the bases loaded. Still seething as he took his position, he kicked the right-field fence. A fifteen-foot section came toppling down, knocking Piniella to the ground. Several hysterical teammates had to pull the fence off him.

In his freshman season with the expansion Kansas City club in 1969, Piniella's .282 BA, 11 HR, 68 RBI won him top-rookie honors. A keenly intelligent contact hitter, he improved to .301 in 1970 and .312 in 1972. But the following season he became expendable after he and new manager Jack McKeon clashed and his average plunged to a then career-low .250. "Kansas City intended to put Lou on the bench," recalls Gabe Paul, who had been responsible for signing Piniella to the Tribe in 1962. "The feeling was that he would not take kindly to that.

"Which," Paul adds, "was helpful in making the deal." It stands as one of his most productive heists.

Piniella, thirty, had a reputation as a spotty outfielder whose work habits could stand improvement. He matured considerably under Bill Virdon. The Yankees manager stood over him with fatherly patience and forced him to improve. "Lou was not an openly ambitious player at that point," Virdon says in retrospect. "He wasn't one to chase fly balls unless somebody made him do it. I saw pretty quickly that that's what it was going to take."

Piniella, later a successful manager himself with the Yankees, Cincinnati, and (currently) Seattle, is the first to agree. "Bill helped me become a good outfielder," he says. "I've always been appreciative of that." Not during spring training he wasn't, when Virdon ran him ragged.

"Virdon had this routine he put them through," the *Daily News*'s Phil Pepe remembers. "At the end of practice every player would go from home to first, then first to third, third to home, home to second, second to home, home to third, third to home, and then all around the bases. That's a lot of running for baseball players.

"And Piniella just hated it. He was in agony! One day while circling the bases, he fell down about midway between third and home, and he crawled the rest of the way, cursing and yelling at Virdon, who was standing there laughing."

Virdon still chuckles at the memory. "But as hard as I made Lou work," he points out, "he never refused to do anything I asked him to do. And he became a very good left fielder." In Doc Medich's 3–0 shutout, Number 14 splashed across the rain-soaked turf to rob Brewer Don Money of a triple with a diving, sliding grab.

Such all-out hustle kindled a love affair that has yet to fade between "Sweet Lou" and the city. Non-Yankees fans, unaware of his immense popularity, often appeared puzzled whenever his introduction over the P.A. elicited what sounded like a ghostly chorus of boos, until it was explained to them that the crowd was merely invoking his name—*Loooouuuu!*

Boston extended its losing streak to seven the next day, giving idle New York sole possession of first place. Ironically, just as the Yankees hit the top, their owner was hitting bottom.

On August 9, Richard Milhous Nixon resigned the presidency in disgrace rather than face impeachment proceedings over the Watergate scandal. Two weeks later, George Steinbrenner pled guilty to conspiracy in covering up his illegal contribution to the president's reelection campaign, as well as to another, related charge.

In September, new chief executive Gerald R. Ford reversed his earlier, publicly stated position and pardoned his former boss. Steinbrenner would have to wait far longer for his presidential pardon; three more administrations, to be exact.

His sentence, handed down a week later, amounted to a mere $15,000 personal fine. But the felony conviction prompted Bowie Kuhn to mete out the cruelest punishment possible for an owner as involved in the game as Steinbrenner. On September 6, the commissioner ordered him to sever all contact with his first-place team for at least one month while he mulled over further action.

"George wanted so dearly to be a part of the ball club, I'm sure it bothered him a great deal that he couldn't come into the clubhouse anymore," Doc Medich says sympathetically. Kuhn's edict did not deter The Boss from sending his men tape-recorded pep talks, however. As a onetime high-school and college assistant football coach, he was a big believer in pep talks and fancied himself a galvanizing speaker.

It fell to Bill Virdon to act as envoy. "He specifically said, 'I want this played in the clubhouse.' So I played it in the clubhouse. I told them what it was and why I was playing it." The manager clutched the recorder respectfully as Steinbrenner's stern voice filled the room. *Balls* seemed to comprise his dominant theme.

"Goddamn it, you've got to go balls-out all the time!" he exhorted. "Everything you do. You've got to have balls!"

Says Virdon, "We listened to it, turned it off, and went on from there."

And the team's reaction? "Very casual, if that's the right word."

Maybe not. "A lot of laughter," is Pat Dobson's amused recollection.

Despite their outward irreverence, the Yankees to some extent appreciated their employer's enthusiasm. "I think they kind of liked it when George came into the clubhouse personally," Doc Medich says. "But these were professionals. They knew their jobs inside and out. I don't think many of them got much out of a pep talk."

For a long time, Steinbrenner failed to appreciate that baseball's constant schedule demanded a more even emotional keel than a contact sport such as football, with its gladiatorial contests staged one week apart. "Baseball's not as rah-rah," Fred Stanley explains. "If you get too emotional, a lot of times it will hurt you, because you try to do more than you're capable of. You've got to have yourself under control."

Ron Swoboda remarks, "George always approached baseball with a football mentality: 'We've got to win them all.' " After a while, eyeballs rolled every time The Boss declared this game or that game The Big One. As any ballplayer will tell you, it's impossible to gear up psychologically for The Big One 162 times a year.

V

THE YANKEES VENTURED warily to Fenway Park, site of twenty burials in their last twenty-one appearances, for a two-game set. Boston had regained consciousness over the weekend and pulled even, with a 74–65, .532 record.

In the Monday opener, Doc Medich ignored recent history, repressing the Red Sox 6–3. The following night, September 10, Pat Dobson and Luis Tiant played Russian roulette through eight tense innings. Neither permitted an earned run, but a throwing error by Thurman Munson in the first handed the Red Sox a 1–0 lead. New York had two chances remaining to figure out the Cuban right-hander when Lou Piniella wangled a walk on a 3-and-2 count. Larry Murray, a speedy rookie outfielder, went in to pinch-run.

Chris Chambliss then tore a slider into the right-field corner. By the time Dwight Evans got the ball back to the infield, Murray was across the plate and Chambliss was checking in at third. Suddenly, in rushed Evans, pointing toward the stands. Fan interference, he claimed; ground-rule double. Not so, insisted Whitey Ford, who'd hustled in from the bullpen. According to the Yankees pitching coach, the spectator reached for the ball but never touched it. Second-base umpire Marty Springstead took Boston's side and waved the runners back. The partisan crowd of 33,164 jeered Bill Virdon as he jawed with the man in blue.

"While they were arguing," Chambliss remembers, "I felt something go *thud* into my arm." He glanced over his shoulder. "It turned out to be a steel dart! The fans were throwing darts at me. They were all over the field—about six of them. I had to get a tetanus shot afterward."

The umping crew reached a compromise: Chambliss had to return to second, but the run counted. Now Darrell Johnson hastened out of the home dugout to add a few decibels to the already deafening noise level. He was given the rest of the night off. Tiant stranded Chambliss, and the game went into overtime tied at 1–1.

Dobson, pumped up on his customary half-dozen cups of coffee, took the hill in the tenth and again in the eleventh. "After the first inning, I was cruising and never in much trouble," he says. "As long as I was capable of going out there, I think Virdon was going to let me stay in."

Since the two squabbled over Dobson's early eviction in July, the right-hander transformed what had been a gloomy campaign thus far: 8–13 through the beginning of August. Number 36 fashioned an 11–2 record thereafter, to finish 19–15 with a 3.07 ERA. His 281 innings led the staff, and no one was more commanding down the stretch. He went into the Boston marathon working on a six-game winning streak.

"I just tried to persevere and do my thing," says Dobson. He and Virdon, however, never patched up their differences. "I did my job, but I didn't have to like the guy," he says with a shrug.

A game-saving play by Sandy Alomar helped Dobson escape the bottom of the eleventh. With two out and the potential winning run in scoring position, Cecil Cooper pulled a sharp grounder toward right field. The Yankees second baseman dove to his left, smothered the ball on the outfield grass, and recovered in time to nip Cooper at first.

In the twelfth, the Yankees unwrapped Gabe Paul's latest purchase. Outfielder Alex Johnson, picked up from Texas only the day before, quickly justified the $20,000 waivers fee by parking a Diego Segui pitch in the Red Sox bullpen for a 2–1 lead. Sparky Lyle then came on to set down the Bosox in order, saving Dobson's gem.

Johnson shunned all handshakes upon completing his tour of the bases, but by 1974 most players around the league knew not to take offense at his sullen, often peculiar behavior. The Greta Garbo of baseball, Johnson wanted to be left alone. "Alex just did not speak," says Jerry Moses, a teammate both in California and Cleveland. "And if he did, you really had to try to understand what he was saying, because what he said was not always what he meant."

Despite a .291 average over eleven seasons, Johnson had worn out his welcome in six cities. His problems reached a head in 1971, one year after he won the AL batting title. Johnson exasperated the Angels with lackadaisical play, failing to run out ground balls and loafing in the outfield. A muscular six-footer, he also fostered turmoil off the field. Several teammates claimed to be openly afraid of him.

California tried benching the Arkansas native several times, and fined him twenty-five times—more fines than any player has ever accrued in a *career*. Then, in June, it suspended him without pay. The Players Association sued to win Johnson back his salary, arguing, successfully, that his bizarre conduct clearly indicated the man needed psychological help, not punishment.

"The players wanted a guy with his ability to go out and play," says

Moses. "We resented his actions because we didn't understand that he had a problem. None of us knew anything about it. Alex Johnson was just an enigma to me. I watched him keep a calculus book in his locker for two years, and he would sit and stare at the same page day after day after day.

"That didn't mean he was unintelligent or didn't have any friends," Moses adds. "There were some people on the club that really liked him." Sandy Alomar, one of them, saw another side to Johnson, the older brother of the New York football Giants star running back Ron. "He was a great guy; great with kids," he says. "And whether people want to believe it or not, Alex would do anything for a friend. But he was a loner. The only thing he didn't like was to be bothered when he wanted to be alone. So that's what I did," says Alomar, "just leave him alone." Johnson played without incident in pinstripes, but his New York sojourn lasted about as long as his hitches elsewhere; he was released the following August.

From Boston the Yankees flew on to Baltimore, then Detroit. They took two out of three in each city, capping the 6–2 road trip with a 10–2 pasting of Ralph Houk's last-place Tigers. The win went to Larry Gura, 4–0 since his recall in mid-August. Gura, another of Gabe Paul's springtime bargains, came over from Texas for Duke Sims. When Mel Stottlemyre's damaged shoulder sidelined him a second and final time, Syracuse Chiefs manager Bobby Cox recommended New York fill his spot on the roster with the slender twenty-six-year-old left-hander.

Pitching for the Yankees had been Gura's childhood dream, not the most popular ambition for a boy growing up in Joliet, Illinois, outside Chicago. "I kept it among my friends," he says, laughing gently. He modeled himself after Whitey Ford, relying on precise control and a mastery of several pitches to compensate for a lack of velocity.

His hometown Cubs drafted him out of Arizona State University, where Gura went 19–1 and paced the team to the 1969 national college championship. But manager Leo Durocher didn't think much of Gura's reserved disposition. "Stony," teammates dubbed him. Leo the Lip relegated the Cubs' number-two pick to the bullpen, allotting Gura only ten starts in four undistinguished seasons.

"I finally went to the Cubs and said, 'Either you make me a starter or trade me,'" he recalls. "Well, they traded me." To Texas, with a month left on the 1973 schedule. "I thought, *Okay, maybe now I'll have an opportunity to prove myself as a starter.*"

The following spring he failed to impress new skipper Billy Martin, although he got only one inning in which to do so. "When Billy called me into his office and told me I was going to be sent down to work on my control, I kind of got upset," says Gura, "because control was my asset. And he had guys on that team, like Pete Broberg, David Clyde, and Jim Bibby, who couldn't find the side of a barn if you showed it to them! I just didn't fit into his program."

Virdon, an undemonstrative sort himself, didn't care about Gura's demeanor, only his arm. He put Number 39 to work right away. In his first AL start, on August 25, Gura outpitched California's Nolan Ryan 2–1. His next time out, however, Chicago roughed him up, though the Yankees rallied for an 8–5 win. Afterward, Whitey Ford—Gura's youthful idol and now his pitching coach—sat down next to him on the bus and said reassuringly, "Don't worry about it. You're pitching again Saturday."

"That just made me feel great, knowing the manager had confidence in me," says Gura. "I was walking on air. With the Cubs, I probably wouldn't have pitched again for a month."

In the second game of a home twin bill, Gura gained the Yankees a split by stymieing the Tigers 1–0. Then, four days later, in Baltimore, he pitched his third complete-game victory in four tries—also after New York had dropped the opener. In eight starts he put up a 5–1 mark and a 2.41 ERA.

Gura's 10–2 win in Detroit leavened the Yankees' lead over the second-place Birds to two and a half, with fifteen games to go. The team's unexpectedly lofty standing spelled vindication for Gabe Paul, who had taken harsh criticism months earlier for constantly shuffling personnel. Valuable additions Gura, Piniella, Mason, Maddox, Alomar, May, and Mike Wallace (6–0 as a setup man) cost New York a grand total of one thirty-eight-year-old reliever (Lindy McDaniel), one thirty-three-year-old second-string catcher (Duke Sims), one barely used pitcher (Ken Wright), and approximately $250,000. Says Bill Virdon, "There had to be some changes made, and Gabe made the right ones."

Only the trio acquired in the controversial seven-player swap with the Indians hadn't performed up to expectations, especially its key man, Chris Chambliss. The deal, he says, took him completely by surprise. "I hadn't any idea I was going to be traded. Things were going so well in Cleveland. I'd just hit a bases-loaded double off Nolan Ryan to win a game."

The next morning a limousine whisked him, Dick Tidrow, and Cecil Upshaw from the airport to Shea Stadium, where their new teammates accorded them a frosty reception. Maury Allen of the *New York Post* recalls, "The players were very resentful. Suddenly instead of having Fritz Peterson around, one of the most entertaining guys imaginable, they had Chris Chambliss, this very religious, dignified black gentleman. They thought, *What do we need him for? He's not going to be any fun!*"

Fans didn't take immediately to Number 10, either. As of July 1, he was stranded at a wretched .233 BA, 3 HR, 12 RBI in his new surroundings. Chambliss, the son of a Navy chaplain, dismisses the notion that pressure from having arrived in an unpopular trade contributed to his sluggish start. "I really didn't pay too much attention to that," he says. Rather, he blames it on being platooned.

"Bill Virdon told me I was going to play every day," he recalls. "Then after only a week or two, I wasn't playing against left-handers anymore." Bill Sudakis (.232 BA, 7 HR, 39 RBI) was.

"Chris was not happy," Virdon acknowledges. "But he hadn't proved to me yet that he could hit left-handers. He did very shortly, though, and he ended up playing all the time." In 110 games for New York Chambliss batted .243 BA, 6 HR, 43 RBI. "I did pretty good at the end," he remembers, "but that was my worst season."

Tidrow, 11–9, 3.86 ERA in pinstripes, pitched reasonably well as the number-four starter. But Larry Gura's sudden ascent led Virdon to convert Number 19 to a reliever for the season's final lap. The manager delivered the news in typically blunt fashion.

"He said, 'I've got a problem,'" Tidrow remembers. "'Out of the three guys I'm going to name, which one would you send to the bullpen: Doc Medich, Pat Dobson, or yourself? Dobson's best pitch is his curveball. And Medich takes about twenty minutes to warm up, whereas you can throw ten, fifteen pitches and be ready to go in the game.'" Another reason was that the relief corps's lone right-hander, Cecil Upshaw, hadn't delivered consistently (1–5, 6 SV, 3.00 ERA).

"After all that," says Tidrow, "what could I say?" Virdon bypassed him on September 12, awarding his turn to left-handed reliever Mike Wallace. All he did in his starting debut was shut out Baltimore through seven and two thirds innings. Tidrow then came on to record his first major-league save. Until his retirement in 1985, he pitched almost exclusively out of the bullpen for the Yankees and three other teams.

"I felt bad about it to start with," says Tidrow, nicknamed "Dirt" on account of his perennially unshaven appearance and unkempt uniform. "Because at that time it was ingrained in you to be a starter. But after I got out there with Sparky Lyle and could be in the game every day, I got to liking it."

Two days later, Tidrow picked up a relief win in Detroit. In what had become both a pre- and postgame clubhouse ritual, Bill Sudakis's portable tape player pumped the Yankees' unofficial theme song, Paul

McCartney's recent hit "Band on the Run." Its title expressed this club's image of itself as a pack of bandits plundering the American League.

That so many of them were castoffs from other organizations became a unifying factor. "We all felt rejuvenated," says Rudy May. "Except for Pat Dobson and Sparky Lyle, we didn't have any players that had played on winners before. It was a really loose, close-knit bunch, with Dobber and Sparky the catalysts."

Lyle pitched the entire year without a contract rather than accept management's offer of $70,000, the same amount he made in 1973. He held out in spring training and threatened to sit out the season if necessary and test the reserve clause, which allowed clubs to automatically renew the previous year's salary. A phenomenal 9–3, 15 SV, 1.66 ERA won Number 28 his raise on the last day of the year: $17,500 retroactively, plus an increase to $93,000 for next season. The Count's sixty-six appearances broke the club record shared by Dooley Womack, Pedro Ramos, and Luis Arroyo. And his pranks involving hacksaws and syringes at least equaled the departed Fritz Peterson's inventiveness.

To get back at Ron Blomberg for always hogging the postgame spread, Lyle and Tidrow injected vodka into a whole watermelon. "Bloomie went in and ate it," Tidrow remembers, "and got drunker than a skunk. We knew he would, too."

The hacksaw was used to customize the high-back Early American rocking chair Bobby Murcer kept in front of his locker for relaxation. It had been working overtime this season, as Murcer brooded over Shea Stadium's dimensions. The day after he finally clubbed his first four-bagger at home, Lyle and Sudakis snuck into the locker room early, cut clear through the rocker's legs, then carefully set the seat on top. When Murcer strolled in, the reliever asked him to pose in the chair for a photo.

"Of course everybody was aware of what was going on," says Murcer, "and they were just waiting for me to sit down. So I plunked myself into this rocking chair, and it just kind of exploded! The grounds crew guys took what was left of the chair and glued it to the rocker underneath, and it became the lowest rocking chair in the world."

VI

NEW YORK, VICTORIOUS in twenty of its last twenty-six contests, donned white for a three-night showdown with Baltimore. The series

opener attracted a feverish crowd of 33,781 that hoisted banners proclaiming the Mets-like slogan YES WE CAN!

Earl Weaver's club ruined the homecoming. Jim Palmer and Dave
McNally sandwiched a 10–4 rout with a pair of shutouts, and suddenly
the dazed New Yorkers were a half-game back, in second. But the
club showed its character by snapping right back. A four-game sweep
of Cleveland dumped the Birds out of first. With 154 games on the
books, the 84–70 Yankees held a one-game advantage.

Games 155 and 156, a Tuesday-night doubleheader, were best forgotten, but there was little chance of that.

Boston interrupted its exodus from the race to scuttle New York
twice. Luis Tiant picked up his twenty-first win, 4–0; then, in the
nightcap, pesky Roger Moret handed Larry Gura his first defeat, 4–2.
The Yankees looked lethargic at bat, in the field, and on the basepaths.
One play involving Bobby Murcer set the tone: an apparent triple
became an out when he tripped on some loose dirt after rounding
second and went sprawling to the ground. He lay there damning Shea
Stadium while the tag was applied.

As the miserable evening wore on, the Yankees' second-largest gate
of the season—46,448, including a number of Bostonians who'd driven
down I-95 to see their team in the role of spoiler—grew restless, then
turned on itself. Rioting spread from section to section.

"The place was just rockin' all night," recalls Dick Tidrow. "Every
part of the stadium was going crazy." A wrestling match between two
women set off a brawl in left field. A whiskey bottle struck a young
girl in the head. Tennis balls, trash, and beer fell from the upper deck.
"I hadn't seen anything like it before," says Tidrow, confessing with a
laugh, "I enjoyed watching."

Rudy May, game one's loser, was peering in for Thurman Munson's
signal when he spotted his wife in the stands behind home plate. "She
had a white outfit on, and there was blood all over it." A Yankees
official sitting behind her had tried to prevent the fighting from spilling
over into the section where the players' wives sat, and wound up
bruised and bloodied. "She was telling me, 'Honey, everything's okay,
just keep pitching,'" May recalls.

In an increasingly violent society, such incidents were on the rise
around the major leagues. Earlier that year, Cleveland had to forfeit
a game when hundreds of spectators overran the field. The Indians,
always looking to drum up business, were hosting a Ten-Cent Beer
Night promotion. Passing out complimentary hand grenades would
have been less dangerous. In the bottom of the ninth, with the score
tied 5–5, the drunken rabble converged on Rangers right fielder Jeff
Burroughs. Both dugouts raced to his assistance. Fistfights broke out

between players and fans as bottles and metal chairs came hurtling out of the stands.

Doc Medich, who pitched ten full seasons, observed that between his rookie year and his retirement in 1983, violence at baseball games "seemed to get a little worse each year. The fans became a little more brazen. They started throwing things on the field. If you had a bad night, somebody was liable to toss a rock through your windshield as you drove out of the ballpark."

Boston's twin-bill sweep allowed triumphant Baltimore to dethrone New York once more. Unbowed, the Yankees took off on another winning streak. Medich bested Bill Lee 1–0 in the season's home finale, pitching all ten innings. "I owed them that one," he says. Next they staggered Cleveland 9–3, 9–7, and 10–0. Ron Blomberg (.311 BA, 10 HR, 48 RBI) and Graig Nettles (.246 BA, 22 HR, 75 RBI) paced the attack with three home runs apiece.

Yet the Yankees couldn't chip away at the Birds' half-game lead. Baltimore, in the midst of a 9–0 surge, nosed out the Brewers 4–3. It marked the third time in a row that Brooks Robinson and company had eked out a victory in their final at-bat.

"Baltimore would be losing 4–2 in the ninth," Dick Tidrow remembers, "and we'd go to bed figuring, *They're put away tonight!* Then we'd wake up the next morning, and they'd won it 5–4." New York, 8–2 since the Birds plowed them under at Shea, watched helplessly as their adversaries refused to lose.

"I'll be in a psychiatric ward by the time the play-offs come around," Bobby Murcer joked. Instead, the pressure of the pennant race would put him on the bench with a broken finger.

Following Rudy May's four-hit, thirteen-strikeout performance against the Tribe on Sunday, September 29, the Yankees had to wait at the airport for a commercial flight to Milwaukee, their final destination of the regular season. "Thunderstorms delayed us in Cleveland three, four hours," Murcer remembers. "There were a few too many brews before we got onto the plane." With Monday an off-day, Bill Virdon and his coaches saw no harm in the players unwinding.

Once aboard, however, the banter between two unhappy Yankees turned nasty. Bill Sudakis and Rick Dempsey were both frustrated with their second-string roles. "Suds liked to needle, but when he got it back, he didn't take too kindly to it," says sportswriter Phil Pepe. "He was a strange guy; had a chip on his shoulder." Sudakis once spat on official scorer Joe Trimble for taking away a base hit.

Dempsey, twenty-five, had already requested a trade. New York later accommodated him and he developed into a steady first-string catcher who played twenty-four seasons before retiring in 1992. But as Thurman Munson's backup he saw only thirty-one games behind the plate.

"Dempsey used to go crazy," says Dick Tidrow. "He wanted to play so bad, during games he used to throw himself batting practice in the bullpen at Shea by rifling balls off the brick wall with one hand while holding a bat in the other.

"He and Sudakis were not real fond of each other by that point of the season. They'd tried going at it before, and we'd separated them. We thought something could happen, but we were so preoccupied with the pennant race, nobody stepped to the front."

The exhausted team finally piled into the lobby of the Pfister Hotel at around 10:30 P.M. "Just as we were checking in to get our keys," says Murcer, "it broke loose."

Dempsey and Sudakis, both burly six-footers, had tried to jam through the revolving door at the same time. They emerged with fists flying. A lamp toppled to the floor and a marble-top coffee table lost a leg as the two rolled around exchanging punches.

"Of course everybody jumped in to stop the fight, which was a pretty good one, by the way," says Murcer, "and somebody stepped on my dadgum finger and broke it, and I couldn't play the last two games." As teammates restrained the two, Murcer lay on his back, white-faced. Having drunk a bit too much himself, he didn't realize the extent of his injury until the next morning.

"Just your routine checking into the hotel, routine fight in the lobby, routine number-three hitter breaking his finger and can't play," jokes Doc Medich, who later dubbed the incident "Pfistercuffs."

That night, more grim news: the Orioles widened their lead to one full game by trouncing Detroit 12–6. Heading into October, Baltimore's record stood at 89–71, .556; New York's at 88–72, .550. In the event of a season-ending tie, the two clubs would meet for a one-game play-off at Shea Stadium. (Interestingly, despite the Yankees' aversion to playing there, they posted the division's best home record, 47–34, .580.)

Were it not the end of the season, Tuesday night's game would have been postponed due to inclement weather. As starter Medich drove to Milwaukee's County Stadium with Mel Stottlemyre, snowflakes dusted the windshield. Conditions seemed chillier still when word came down that Baltimore had staged yet another late-inning rally to defeat Detroit 7–6.

With Bobby Murcer rooting from the bench, New York snapped a scoreless tie in the seventh on a walk to Roy White, an Elliott Maddox triple, and a single by Alex Johnson. Medich was five outs away from notching his twentieth win and staving off elimination when pinch hitter Bob Hansen lofted a fly to right. Lou Piniella, there in place of Murcer, drifted back in the quagmire and called Maddox off the ball.

Two weeks before, Earl Weaver had collared Piniella at Shea Stadium and complimented him on his much improved defense. "Why didn't you do that for me at Elmira?" he kidded. Weaver managed Piniella at the Orioles' double-A affiliate in 1965, and the two had been playful antagonists ever since.

"I always had this type of show-you attitude with Earl," says Piniella, "because they traded me away after the season, and I felt he was the one responsible for me leaving the Baltimore organization. I just wanted to prove to him that I could play, so I'd always play as well as I could against the Orioles."

Weaver leveled a finger at Piniella toward the end of their chat at Shea. "You're going to screw up a play in the outfield," he warned ominously, "and it's going to cost you a game and give us the pennant." Piniella laughed him off. "We had these little run-ins during the course of my career. But as far as a hex," he says, "Earl had a lot of false bravado about him. And this was one example."

Or was it?

At the last instant, Number 14 pulled away from the ball, which dropped behind him for a triple. "Either of us could have caught it," Piniella reflects. "I don't know why I backed off." Weaver sent a teasing telegram the next day expressing his gratitude.

Don Money followed with another three-bagger, then scored the tying run on a sacrifice fly. In the bottom of the tenth, the Brewers loaded the bases against Medich. As a warmed-up Sparky Lyle watched from the bullpen, George Scott punched a single to wipe out New York's pennant chances. Medich, 19–15, 3.60 ERA, calmly walked off the mound. He never came that close to winning twenty again.

The Yankees repaired to the locker room, disappointed but proud. From September 1 on, they won 20 of 31 games; the Orioles, an extraordinary 25 of 31. "We didn't choke," Dick Tidrow emphasizes. "They earned it. We would have won it had Baltimore not played like the 1927 Yankees down the stretch."

VII

ON OCTOBER 22, NEW York announced one of the biggest one-for-one swaps in baseball history: Bobby Murcer, once Mickey Mantle's heir apparent, to the San Francisco Giants for outfielder Bobby Bonds, first hailed as the successor to Willie Mays. Murcer's reaction? "Total shock," he says. Only that summer George Steinbrenner had assured him a lifetime in pinstripes.

Murcer, reacquired in 1979, charges Gabe Paul with masterminding the deal. Without going into specifics, he acknowledges that the two did not have a good rapport. "I don't think there was really any reason for the trade other than he saw a window to trade me, and he did."

The timing couldn't have been more painful for Murcer, a beacon of promise during a gloomy era. Now that the Yankees were at long last poised to contend for the flag, here he was being shipped to the fifth-place Giants. Compounding his misery: He'd be playing in that igloo of a stadium, Candlestick Park. Today Murcer divides his time between announcing Yankees telecasts and serving as president and co-owner of the triple-A Oklahoma City 89ers. Asked to describe his feelings when New York did indeed win the pennant two years after his exile, Murcer says sharply, "I should have been a part of that."

Once news of the swap sank in, he thought back to his lunches with Boss Steinbrenner. Among Murcer's recommendations for improving the Yankees: balance the lineup with a right-handed power hitter. And what was Bobby Bonds? A right-handed power hitter.

"George asked me how I thought we could make the club a winner," Murcer reflects ruefully, "and I told him. And eventually it got me traded!"

1975

STARTERS
Catfish Hunter
Doc Medich
Pat Dobson
Rudy May
Larry Gura

Chris Chambliss (1B)
Sandy Alomar (2B)
Jim Mason/Fred Stanley
(SS)
Graig Nettles (3B)
Roy White (LF)
Elliott Maddox (CF)
Bobby Bonds (RF)
Thurman Munson (C)
Ron Blomberg/
Ed Herrmann (DH)

RELIEVERS
Sparky Lyle
Dick Tidrow
Tippy Martinez

I

HAPPY NEW YEAR, Charlie.

New York rang in 1975 by signing American League Cy Young Award winner Jim "Catfish" Hunter as a free agent. Making this historic moment sweeter yet was its coming at the expense of longtime antagonist Finley, whose arrogance had inadvertently set in motion his star right-hander's emancipation.

Hunter's 1974 contract stipulated that the Oakland owner pay $50,000 in deferred salary to an insurance company. When Finley discovered too late that the annuity would not be immediately tax deductible, he either neglected or just plain refused to make the payment, putting the club in breach. On the eve of the postseason, Hunter (25–12, 2.49 ERA in '74) declared himself a free agent, available to any team. The case went before an arbitrator two weeks after the A's rolled over Los Angeles for their third World Series title in a row.

Mediator Peter Seitz's landmark decision to free the pitcher from his $100,000 contract, formally handed down on December 16, sent major-league teams descending upon Hunter's lawyers' offices in tiny Ahoskie, North Carolina, and his 113-acre farm in even tinier Hertford. Only the Orioles and the Tigers declined to participate.

In the mad scramble for Hunter, New York emerged the winner. The elaborately structured five-year, $3.75 million deal included $200,000 in annual salary, plus life insurance policies, deferred income, and attorneys' fees. Other clubs bid more money—the Dodgers, two years at $3 million; the Padres, five years at $4.5 million—but the Yankees were fortunate to have scouting director Clyde Kluttz on their payroll.

Kluttz, a fellow North Carolinian and onetime major-league receiver, had signed eighteen-year-old Jimmy Hunter to the Kansas City Athletics back in 1964. The two remained close ever since, hunting together in the off-season, and Hunter trusted Kluttz implicitly. "Clyde was the main reason I signed with the Yankees," he acknowledges.

Friendship did not transcend financial security, however. Hunter rejected Gabe Paul's initial offer of $1.5 million over five years. But while the Yankees president flew back to New York, Kluttz remained behind. He was about to give up on December 30 but decided to try persuading Hunter one last time the next day.

Hunter remembers, "That morning before I left to go to Ahoskie, I told my wife, 'I'm getting tired of going to all these meetings with these clubs and everything. I'm gonna sign with someone.' So Clyde and I were having breakfast at the Tomahawk Motel there in Ahoskie, and he said, 'Would you sign with the Yankees?'

" 'Yeah, I'd sign with the Yankees.' "

Kluttz named a figure.

"And I said yeah," Hunter recalls. "Just like that."

By early afternoon he, Kluttz, and his attorneys were jetting to New York to finalize the details with Gabe Paul. A few hours before the ball dropped in Times Square, Hunter was modeling a Yankees cap for photographers at a hastily assembled press conference. He returned to Hertford the richest athlete in baseball history.

Such wealth contrasted jarringly with his humble roots. Born on a farm, the twenty-eight-year-old Hunter was one of eight children of Millie and Abbott Hunter, a tenant farmer and logger who never earned more than $10,000 in a single year. Hunter, elected to the Hall of Fame in 1987, still lives in his home town (population 1,941), where the folks call him Jimmy.

"Catfish" was the invention of Charlie Finley. K.C.'s $50,000 bonus baby turned out to be no showboat, so Finley the showman concocted this rustic nickname, along with a fanciful explanation of its origin: that young Jim once ran away and returned home with a pair of catfish that he'd caught. (Another A's pitcher from down South, John "Blue Moon" Odom, came in for similar biographical revisionism.)

Hunter's arrival displaced Mel Stottlemyre as top man in the rotation, although that distinction would have gone to someone else regardless. Due to his torn rotator cuff, Number 30 couldn't even lob batting practice without stiffness. Still, no one expected it when New York abruptly gave the fifth winningest pitcher in club history (164–139, .541, 2.97 ERA) his unconditional release on March 29.

The maneuver recalled the cold-hearted Bronx Bombers of old, with Gabe Paul in George Weiss's penny-squeezing role. Had the Yankees carried Stottlemyre on the roster one more day, they would have been required to pay him one third of his salary. The $30,000 saved wasn't worth the bad publicity earned.

Stottlemyre, unaware of any deadline, was stunned.

"Mel doesn't like to bad-mouth people," says sportswriter Maury Allen, "but he was as hurt as any ballplayer I've ever seen. Because he was cut simply because he was injured, and he didn't have a chance to show whether or not he could pitch. All over a few dollars.

"The whole thing was so ridiculous. He'd been told all winter, 'Take your time, we'll let you get ready at your own pace, we'll take care of you.' And then when he pitched two or three times and was lousy, they cut him. He had been a great Yankee in the old tradition of dedication and pride in the club, and he was terribly angry and bitter. He blamed it all on George Steinbrenner."

The Yankees' owner soon developed a deep respect for the franchise's history, luring Roger Maris out of self-imposed exile in 1978 and finding jobs in the organization for Joe Pepitone, Gene Michael, Graig Nettles, and other New York favorites when their playing days were through. "But George was still new then," Phil Pepe of the *Daily News* points out, "and he really didn't have a great appreciation of what Stottlemyre had meant to the team."

Stottlemyre's teammates, having heard Steinbrenner speak numerous times about mutual loyalty—"If you're loyal to me, I'll be loyal to you"—reacted with disgust.

"I was really angry with the front office for doing that," says Doc Medich. "Mel was such a class guy, I thought he deserved a little more in the way of respect. They could have offered him a coaching position, because he would have been an asset. Instead they just cast him aside."

Roy White, then in his eleventh season as a Yankee, says, "When something like that happens, you start thinking about what's going to happen to you when your time comes."

Stottlemyre tried hooking on with Ralph Houk in Detroit, but the shoulder damage proved irreparable. "Mel came to me one day and said, 'Ralph, I can't pitch anymore. There's no use in me doing this.' Which I really respect him for," says Houk. "He could have hung around and made some money."

The thirty-three-year-old right-hander went home to Grandview, Washington, where he ran a sporting-goods store, then joined the expansion Seattle Mariners as minor-league pitching instructor. In 1984 he returned to New York as pitching coach—wearing a Mets uniform. Stottlemyre, who now works in the same capacity for the Houston Astros, shuns Yankees Old Timers' Day games and barely acknowledges having once starred for the city's other team.

Aside from the uproar over Stottlemyre's mistreatment, Bill Virdon's second spring proceeded peacefully. Secure in a new two-year contract, *The Sporting News*'s Major League Manager of the Year encountered no hostility this time. Contributing to the congenial atmosphere was the fact that of the twenty-five Yankees who traveled north, only eleven had made the trip last season.

A Sparky Lyle prank accounted for Virdon's only headache. The left-hander hobbled into camp on crutches, his left arm and leg encased in fake casts, courtesy of a doctor friend. "Virdon almost had a heart attack," Phil Pepe recalls.

"Sparky! What happened?" he sputtered. Lyle mournfully recounted the details of a tragic car accident until the manager realized he'd been had.

II

VIRDON ASSIGNED DOC Medich the season opener in Cleveland so that Catfish Hunter could make his first appearance at home. Over 26,000, among them Governor Hugh Carey and Mayor Abe Beame, flooded into Shea Stadium to watch Number 29 take on the Tigers. Conspicuously absent was George Steinbrenner. On November 27, 1974, Bowie Kuhn had slapped the Yankees owner with a two-year suspension.

It's just as well that Steinbrenner missed his second home opener in a row. By the time Nate Colbert's three-run homer put Detroit ahead to stay in the fifth, he likely would have been demanding, "Is this the guy we're paying $3.75 million?" Many Yankees faithful were asking that question while Hunter struggled through an abysmal April.

After four starts his statistics showed no wins, three losses, and a 7.66 ERA.

When Hunter couldn't hold on to a 3–0 lead in his second turn, irate fans booed so furiously that you would have thought they were the ones signing his paychecks. More than once he heard "Three million dollars, my ass!"

Hunter didn't act overly concerned. For one thing, he had a history of slow starts. Of his eighty-eight wins the past four seasons, only eight came in the first month. He impressed teammates with his poise, shrugging off the jeers and candidly acknowledging to reporters the pressure of trying to justify his immense salary.

"Catfish handled it great," says Fred Stanley. "He never let anything bother him. And by him not getting rattled, the team didn't get rattled." Despite Hunter's status within the game, he blended right in from the first day of spring training. The Yankees felt free to rib him about his inauspicious debut.

"They'd get on me once in a while," Hunter recalls good-naturedly, "especially Sparky Lyle." Because both pitchers sported bushy mustaches and longish brown hair, autograph hounds frequently confused the two. "He used to walk out of the clubhouse ahead of me, and a lot of the people would shout, 'Hey Catfish!' Sparky would look at them and sneer, '*I ain't signin' that shit for you!*' Then he'd turn around and say to me, 'Ah-ha! Got ya again!' "

New York's other Bay Area acquisition, Bobby Bonds, was also having problems. After a respectable start, the right fielder dipped below .200 in mid-May. "Catfish and I used to talk about how we were going to get *killed* if we didn't produce," says Bonds, a .273 hitter in seven seasons with San Francisco.

"My biggest problem was not knowing the pitchers. I had come from a league where a lot of guys relied on hard stuff. At that time you were challenged a lot more in the NL than in the AL."

As an example, he offers Nolan Ryan. "I'd faced him when he was a kid with the Mets," says Bonds. "On a 3-and-1 count, Ryan would come at you with a fastball. But in the American League he'd throw a straight change-up. So even he adapted to the AL style. And I couldn't believe that these pitchers did this. I kept trying to figure out the league on my own, but it was like trying to learn the alphabet backward."

Bonds commiserated with Oakland outfielder Billy Williams, another expatriate National League superstar. "I was hitting about .190 and Billy was hitting about .175. And he jokingly said, 'Jesus, Bobby, you've got this league all figured out, haven't you!' "

Hunter shook off his slump first, burying Milwaukee 10–1 in front of 41,493 on April 27, his wife's birthday. He held the Brewers hitless into the eighth and ended the game by striking out all-time home-run champ Henry Aaron. As he walked off the mound to cheers, Hunter politely tipped his cap. "That was a big load off my shoulders," he admits.

His next time out, Hunter blanked Baltimore 5–0, one of three shutouts he hurled in May alone. The second, a 3–0 two-hitter, was especially gratifying, coming against his former team. On the eighteenth, he set down the Athletics again, 9–1. The victory was only New York's fourth that month, and all of them belonged to Hunter.

In a pregame meeting, Bill Virdon chewed out the Yankees, who were then stranded in the cellar with a 12–20, .375 record. The puny offense came in for his sharpest criticism. "If you don't start swinging the bat," he warned, "I'm going to tell my pitchers to knock down the opposing hitters, so *you'll* get knocked on your asses and wake up." To jump-start Bobby Bonds, Virdon moved him from third to first in the order. The Giants had used him there almost exclusively even though his average of 27 home runs and 79 RBIs per year more befitted a cleanup hitter.

Number 25 banged the first pitch he saw to the left-field wall for a triple. Over the next two weeks Bonds hoisted his average nearly 40 points. Placement in the lineup "had nothing to do with it," he insists. It was some advice from Thurman Munson that made the difference.

"He was one of my best friends on the team. If it weren't for Thurman, I don't know if I ever would've hit in the American League." After Bonds watched Munson stroke a 3-and-1 curve to the opposite field, "I asked him, 'How can you look for that pitch in this situation? On a 3-and-1 count it's either going to be a hard slider or a fastball, because they don't want to walk you, right?'

"Thurman explained: 'Bobby, in this league they would rather walk you than let you hit the ball out of the park. Never look for anything but a medium slider.' After that," says Bonds, "I began to look slider every pitch, and I began to hit, and we started winning."

New York's season turned the corner faster than a Manhatten cabbie. The Yankees played 10–4 ball the rest of the month, then commenced a 20–9 June by taking seven in a row from Texas, Minnesota, and Chicago. On June 10, little-used Larry Gura pitched them to within one game of first when he tamed Nolan Ryan for the second time in two encounters, 6–4.

Prior to game time, a ceremonial gun battery from Brooklyn's Fort Hamilton honored the U.S. Army's two-hundredth anniversary with a twenty-one-cannon salute. In a scene out of a Mack Sennett comedy, one concussion blew down three panels of green fence in left-center; another tore a hole in right-center. The Yankees had to wait in the dugout while the Shea Stadium grounds crew hastily patched up the holes.

Perhaps the mishap was a sign of things to come, for holes began cropping up in the New York outfield almost daily. During the second week of June, a staggering rash of injuries decimated the starting threesome, beginning with Bobby Bonds.

Though he'd long ranked among baseball's elite, many considered the twenty-nine-year-old Californian a work in progress. The closest he'd come to fully drawing on his awesome power and speed was 1973, when he batted .283, socked 39 homers, drove in 96 runs, scored 131 times, and stole 43 bases. The conventional wisdom held that even those outstanding numbers were merely the prelude to an MVP season worthy of Bonds's idol, Willie Mays. Nineteen seventy-five was starting to look like that year.

Once inserted in the leadoff spot, Bonds feasted on AL pitchers' measly breaking balls. The next three weeks produced a .333 BA, 10 HR, and 21 RBI. At Comiskey Park on June 7, the six-foot-one, 190-pounder clubbed his fourteenth and fifteenth home runs of the season to seize the major-league lead. "There was no question in my mind that I was going to hit over fifty," he says. "I'd never thought that about any season."

In the seventh inning, Bonds put on a defensive display as well. A running, leaping catch on the warning track robbed Jorge Orta of an extra-base hit. Upon landing, however, his right knee buckled, sending him tumbling into the wall.

Trainer Gene Monahan brought out a stretcher, but Number 25 waved it off.

Rudy May, calling him by his nickname, gasped, "Quarter, you can't get up!"

"I'm not being carried off in front of all these people," Bonds snapped. "Ain't no way. Just give me some time to try to get up."

He recalls, "I remember Rudy helping me off the field. I guess it was a macho thing, but there was *no way* they were going to put me on a stretcher. Not that I didn't need it." X rays revealed torn knee cartilage, which would require arthroscopic surgery over the winter.

Bonds missed most of the next three weeks. When he returned to the outfield, it wasn't with the same intensity as before. Not all Yankees followers understood why. "I was hurt a lot worse than people knew," he says. "I probably should have missed the remainder of the season and had the operation then. But the '75 Yankees were one of the best teams I was ever on. I felt we really had a chance to go to the World Series, so I didn't want to come out.

"After the injury my year began to slack off a little bit, because I was playing in a lot of pain," he continues. "In fact, Gene Monahan had to come to my hotel room one night because I got out of bed to use the bathroom, fell on the floor, and couldn't get up. I had to pull myself along the carpet to the phone and tell him I literally couldn't stand."

Four days after Bonds's accident, a strained hamstring interrupted Roy White's best season since 1971 (.290 BA, 12 HR, 59 RBI). Then, most devastating of all, two nights later Shea Stadium's perennially soggy turf claimed Elliott Maddox. "People were pulling muscles all the time there because they couldn't pull their feet out of the mud," says Dick Tidrow. "It was incredible."

Maddox, proving last year's .303 no fluke, had rapped three hits off White Sox pitching to hike his average to .307. In the top of the ninth, while gliding after a Ken Henderson single, Number 27 suddenly slipped and crumpled to the ground. "We shouldn't even have been playing," says Pat Dobson, the 2–1 victor. "There was about a foot of water on the field." Maddox, then completing his bachelor of science in prelaw at Manhattan's Hunter College, filed a $1 million negligence suit against New York City.

Torn ligaments in his right knee cost the twenty-seven-year-old not only the rest of the season but a fine career. By the time he came off the disabled list the following June, a sensational speedster named Mickey Rivers occupied center field. Although Maddox played through 1980, two surgeries couldn't restore his full mobility.

Incredibly, the Yankees' wounded roll kept expanding. Lou Piniella, plagued since April by an elusive inner-ear infection that made him dizzy, joined Maddox on the disabled list the same day in order to undergo minor ear surgery.

"It was a terrible season for me," says Piniella. "I went to quite a few doctors, and nobody could figure out for sure what was wrong. They tried to treat it with vitamins and medication at first, but it just didn't help. Finally I was fortunate enough to go to an ear specialist. He came up with what the hell was wrong with me, and more important, a solution. So I had the operation." The procedure didn't produce immediate results, however. Number 14 returned to the active roster in July just as disoriented as before and unable to hear in his right ear.

"I had the dizziness the whole year," he remembers unhappily. "I couldn't even get on an airplane, so I didn't travel with the team. Even when we were at home, at times I wasn't able to go to the ballpark."

A .291 lifetime hitter over eighteen seasons, Piniella plummeted to career lows of .198 BA, 0 HR, 22 RBI in 199 AB.

"When I went home to Florida that fall, I didn't know if I would ever play again," he says. "It was on my mind all winter." The condition troubled him during spring training, "then it just went away," he says. "I was fortunate, and I bounced back." Piniella played past his fortieth birthday.

Ron Blomberg was not so lucky. A pair of calamities precipitated his retirement at the age of thirty. Ironically, had The Boomer been healthy in 1975, circumstances would have compelled the Yankees to finally start him against both species of pitchers. But during a 10–1 thrashing of Milwaukee in April, Number 12 hacked a ferocious home run. Before he could admire its flight, he felt something pop in his right shoulder.

"I thought I'd been shot," he remembers. "I fell down. Gene Monahan had to come out and walk me around the bases." Team physician Dr. Sidney Gaynor examined Blomberg and determined he'd merely strained a muscle. Blomberg insisted otherwise. "I didn't have any feeling in my right shoulder and right hand!" he says. "But he told me to just rest it. And I rested it and rested it and rested it. They thought it was going to heal by itself. And it did not."

New York's left-handed DH appeared in but thirty-four games all year, batting .255 BA, 4 HR, 17 RBI, and was lost to the club from mid-July on. The following spring, "I couldn't even swing," he says. "I still hit about .300, but it was all singles and doubles. I didn't have the snap. I didn't have the power. So the last game of spring training, I said to myself, 'I'm gonna swing hard.' I swung, and my shoulder went out again."

One week later he was undergoing surgery in Los Angeles. Renowned orthopedic specialists Dr. Frank Jobe and Dr. Robert Kerlan diagnosed him with a torn rotator cuff. "To this day," says Blomberg, "I don't have any idea why they didn't find it in New York That kept me out almost two years."

Blomberg spent all of 1976 lifting weights to strengthen the shoulder, which he calls "the most painful thing I ever had to do." He got into one game that September, all but forgotten in the citywide exhilaration as the Yankees breezed to a division title. Blomberg watched the pennant clincher on TV, his arm in a sling. Not being able to contribute, he says, "killed me. I felt like I wasn't part of the team.

"But I came back." In his first exhibition game of 1977, he powdered a home run that nearly cleared the light tower at Fort Lauderdale Stadium. "All the writers came over to me and said, 'God, that's like you used to do!' " he recalls. "I was having a super spring, my shoulder was super, everything was great. Then, crazy me, at Winter Haven I ran into the left-field wall and ripped up my knee." Lying dazed on the ground, he thought to himself, *It's always me. Why is it always me?*

"And I was out another year."

Blomberg, always something of a clubhouse outsider, didn't elicit much sympathy from teammates, some of whom privately called him "Take-the-Money-and-Run Ron."

Blomberg insists he worked hard to get himself into condition. "My shoulder and knee were real bad. When you're injured, people don't realize that you do everything you possibly can to come back. But also when you're injured, they look upon you as being hexed. Voodooed. You feel like nobody wants to get too close to you because they don't want to get injured either.

"I had to get out of New York," he continues, "because I had so much pressure from all the ballplayers: 'When are you gonna be able to play again?' It was very, very difficult for me to take." Blomberg signed as a free agent with the Chicago White Sox, bypassing the Mets, who'd offered the same four-year, $600,000 deal.

Unfortunately the nearly three-year layoff took the edge off his stroke. Blomberg, .302 for his career in pinstripes, managed only .231 BA, 5 HR, 22 RBI as a part-timer in 1978 before leaving baseball completely. He declined offers to return to New York and work behind a microphone.

"I wanted to get out of sports," says the father of two, since divorced and remarried. "Because I was never a fan, I was a *player*. I don't follow baseball anymore. I've never been out to a ball game."

Blomberg went home to Atlanta and worked for a motivational-speakers agency founded by his friend Fran Tarkenton, the Hall of Fame quarterback. Then he and a partner started their own company, U.S.A. Career Marketing. "We are now the largest corporate-out-placement firm in the Southeast," he says proudly. "We've got a nice, successful little business.

"But if I had my druthers, I'd still be out on the field getting dirty," he adds wistfully. "Like I tell my clients, if you get laid off from IBM after twenty years, you go through a career divorce. Well, I went through a career divorce with baseball."

III

DESPITE THESE CASUALTIES, New York continued to home in on first-place Boston. Manager Virdon resourcefully fashioned lineups from what he had. During an 8–4 span in mid-June, he didn't field the same outfield twice. Neglected veterans Alex Johnson and five-foot-six Walt Williams and rookie reinforcements Terry Whitfield and Kerry Dineen all pitched in, as did two unlikely volunteers.

On June 15, Bat Day, Catfish Hunter handcuffed Chicago 3–0 backed by what the Yankees jokingly dubbed their "three-catcher defense": Thurman Munson and Rick Dempsey flanking the twenty-two-year-old Dineen in center while second-string receiver Ed Herrmann covered the plate.

Even that configuration couldn't stay out of the infirmary. In the opener of a June 17 doubleheader against Milwaukee, Dempsey strained a hamstring while lumbering after a drive off the bat of Sixto Lezcano. Two days later, Dineen (.364 in 22 at-bats) did the same. No sooner had he hobbled off the field than New York purchased outfielder Rich Coggins from Montreal.

Confusion reigned at shortstop too, where Virdon juggled Jim Mason, Fred Stanley, and another new face and old hand, Ed Brinkman. All three managed to keep themselves healthy—though not their bats. Mason, thought to own the territory between second and third into the next decade, flopped miserably. A single play forever tarnished his career in pinstripes, which had shone so brightly the year before. It followed Dempsey's pulling up lame in the eighth inning of a 3–3 tie.

With Lezcano on second, George Scott arced a sure out behind short. Mason drifted back and pounded his glove. The ball landed behind him with a thud as the winning run scored. "He was visibly shaken," says Stanley. From then on, "Things started rolling downhill, and Jim wasn't able to stop the slide." Mason finished the year at .152, a nearly 100-point reduction.

"If we could have figured it out, we would have done something to change it," a still mystified Bill Virdon says. "I had no way of knowing how anybody could change that much in one year, although I'd seen Steve Blass go through the same thing in Pittsburgh. It does happen."

Before the Yankees let him go to Toronto in the 1976 expansion draft, Mason was treated to a healthy dose of public ridicule. When the shortstop held on to an easy pop fly in the 4–2 nightcap, sarcastic cheers rained down from the stands. The Mobile, Alabama, native never adjusted to playing in the Big Apple. "He *hated* the New York fans," says former batboy Joe D'Ambrosio.

On June 24, the night New York evicted the Red Sox from first, Mason took the collar and grounded into two double plays. But Catfish Hunter reeled off his seventh straight complete game, a 3–1 beauty against the Orioles. The next night Ed Brinkman manned short as the franchise completed its first sweep at Memorial Stadium in a dozen years. Thurman Munson's ninth-inning sacrifice fly brought Walt Williams churning home to edge Jim Palmer 2–1.

A four-game dogfight awaited the Yankees in Boston. Their 40–29, .580 record and one-and-a-half-game lead didn't reflect the team's precarious state and growing anxiety. You don't lose three engines like Maddox, Piniella, and Blomberg, all coming off .300 seasons, and stay airborne for long. "You look at the guys on the bench and wonder if they can hold on," admits Larry Gura. "Because most of them are good for two, three weeks, but not the whole year."

Boston's outfield, bulked up by a phenomenal rookie tandem, made the Yankees wince. Center fielder Fred Lynn became the first freshman in baseball history to be named both Rookie of the Year and Most Valuable Player, batting .331 BA, 21 HR, 105 RBI. Left fielder Jim Rice, twenty-two, put up an equally extraordinary .309 BA, 22 HR, 102 RBI.

Lynn's two-run triple in the fourth inning of the opener overturned New York's 1–0 lead. The twenty-three-year-old from USC singled home another run as the Red Sox ended Pat Dobson's personal six-game winning streak, 6–1. Larry Gura and the bullpen managed to muzzle Lynn and Rice Friday night, but the rest of the Bosox lineup maximized its nine hits in a 9–1 runaway.

On Saturday the two teams traded punches like a pair of wobbly boxers waiting for the other to fall. Bill Virdon's squad pulled ahead in the eighth to win 8–6. Thurman Munson, en route to the first hundred-RBI season by a Yankee since Mickey Mantle and Joe Pepitone in 1964, highlighted a five-run fifth with a bases-clearing single.

Slowed down throughout 1974 by tendinitis in his right arm and a bruised right hand, the durable Number 15 improved dramatically from .261 to .318, with 12 homers and 102 RBIs. What's more, baseball fans outside New York finally recognized his talent, electing him overwhelmingly to the All-Star Team. The honor would have been perfect had injuries not limited Carlton Fisk to fewer than eighty games that year.

Munson's archrival and the Yankees were no closer to mending relations than the recently split Cher and Gregg Allman. Over 33,000 spectators wedged into the stadium for game four, swelling series attendance to 136,187, a Fenway Park record. Fisk exchanged angry words with Sandy Alomar over an incident in the third inning. New York's second baseman protested a called third strike by dropping his bat on home plate and leaving it there. Fisk defiantly kicked the lumber away.

When Alomar stepped up to the plate in the fifth, "I told him I never kicked his mask or nothing like that, so he didn't have to be kicking my bat."

"Be a man, not a hot dog!" the catcher barked.

"I am a man!" the tiny Puerto Rican retorted. "And I can drop my bat wherever I want!" Alomar then scorched a double and came around to score the Yankees' second run off troublesome Roger Moret.

Catfish Hunter kept Boston at bay 2–1 through six, but then the siege of injuries came to haunt New York. In the seventh, Cecil Cooper lofted a sacrifice fly to center. Had Elliott Maddox been waiting for the ball instead of No-Neck Williams and his pea-shooter arm, it's doubtful the Bosox would have waved Fred Lynn home. But coach Don Zimmer gave him the green light—and probably suggested it wouldn't matter if he paused midtrip for a beer. Williams's tailing throw nailed Lynn, literally, twenty feet up the third-base line. Tie game.

An inning later, Boston put the winning run in scoring position. A healthy Bobby Bonds might have caught up to Bernie Carbo's drive to deep right center, but not one running at half-speed. Rick Burleson promptly doubled Carbo home. Moret held on to contain the Yankees for the eighth time in eleven tries, and now the Red Sox held the keys to first place. For good, it would turn out.

The Yankees staggered on to Milwaukee and Cleveland, where they dropped four heartbreakers in a row. Shea Stadium offered no respite. On the Fourth of July, Baltimore ambushed Catfish Hunter in the ninth, scoring three times. New York rallied for a run in its half, but fell short, 5–4.

Afterward, a frustrated Hunter dressed down his teammates for not playing aggressively. "After leaving Oakland, I wanted to be on another winner right away," he reflects. "The first year I came over, the Yankees knew how to win, but they didn't know how to be winners."

Rudy May, a steady 14–12, 3.06 ERA in 1975, says, "I remember Catfish saying, 'You fuckers aren't *playing*, man! This ain't the way a team that wants to win the pennant plays!'" At the time, says the left-hander, "I didn't see that. I'd never been where Catfish had been. But he was right. In '74 we'd gone the extra mile; in '75 we were just going through the motions."

The Yankees listened respectfully, but Hunter's words had little effect. As an 11–18 July unfolded, the ravaged team lagged further and further behind, so that when Boston arrived on the twenty-fifth for a quartet of games, New York was eight games back, its season on the line.

Game one went to the Yankees, despite feeble support from the bullpen—they had already squandered leads in the late innings twelve times this season. Sparky Lyle, the gravest offender, relieved Rudy May in the eighth with New York up 8–2. Five batters later, the Bosox had closed to within two, and Number 28 came out in favor of Felix "Tippy" Martinez, a rookie left-hander promoted from Syracuse in mid-July. Martinez hung on for his second of eight saves, tops on the club.

Lyle, though perfectly healthy, protected only six all year. The Count couldn't seem to paint the corners, something he blamed on inactivity. It was telling that when the Red Sox got to Pat Dobson for three runs in the ninth inning of Saturday's game, Bill Virdon called on Dick Tidrow (6–3, 5 SV, 3.13 ERA) to prevent further damage. Boston evened the series in a 4–2 final.

For the opener of Sunday's doubleheader, New York went with its best. Catfish Hunter and Bill Lee hurled scoreless ball into the ninth, an inning not for the squeamish.

Jim Mason turned up the thermostat in his personal hell by bobbling Fred Lynn's leadoff grounder. The rookie then stole second and one out later scored the game's lone tally on a Rick Miller single, only the third Boston safety Hunter allowed.

More Lynn heroics followed. In the bottom half, Graig Nettles smoked an apparent triple to the opposite field. Lynn galloped for the warning track and made a diving, somersaulting catch while Jim Rice hurdled over him to avoid a collision. The center fielder scrambled to his knees and triumphantly held up his glove, the ball peeking out of the webbing. "That was like the nail in the coffin for us," says Doc Medich.

The nightcap contained none of the first game's drama. Boston jumped out in front early and padded its lead to 6–0 by the seventh. As a rookie named Ron Guidry mopped up in his big-league debut, the near-capacity crowd began to entertain itself by brawling in the stands. "They'd been drinking all afternoon," Medich recalls.

Afterward the Yankees bravely tried to convince reporters, and themselves, that an August–September rebirth like last year's could put them right back in the running. But in their hearts they knew a ten-game deficit with sixty-two to go was insurmountable for a demoralized .500 ball club.

"I don't think there was any hope at that stage," says Fred Stanley—
"Chicken" to his teammates. "We knew we were missing three or four
big pieces of the puzzle. We were good enough to compete, but not
good enough to win."

IV

AROUND THE SAME time that New York City was running short of
money, George Steinbrenner was running out of patience.

Did the Yankees owner truly keep his hands off the team during his
suspension? According to sportswriter Maury Allen, "Everybody knew
George was meeting with Gabe Paul every day and telling him what
to do." Bowie Kuhn's restrictions did permit Steinbrenner to attend
games. From his box seat behind the home dugout, he roared his
disapproval when Bill Virdon let Stanley, a .222 hitter in 1975, come
to bat with the bases loaded and none out in the first game of Sunday's
Yankees-Bosox twin bill.

Virdon's low-key style did not sit well with The Boss, who preferred
a man more like himself—specifically, Texas's effusive Billy Martin.
The *Daily News*'s Phil Pepe recalls a conversation he had with Steinbrenner while in Arlington for a mid-July series between the Yankees
and the Rangers.

Describing a field general who sounded an awful lot like Virdon,
Steinbrenner told the reporter, "I don't like a manager who walks out
to the mound with his hands in his back pocket and his chin on his
chest, like the weight of the world is on his shoulders and he doesn't
know what to do. I like a guy to race out to the mound and—with a
flourish!—point to the bullpen, like he knows exactly what the problem is and what the solution is. *That's* the kind of manager I want!"

Pepe recalls thinking, "My God, Billy Martin's going to be the next
manager of the Yankees."

Three days after Virdon's squad moved on to Minnesota, Martin
suddenly became available, fired for the third time in six seasons.
While a brilliant strategist, he was a difficult, complex man whose
rapport with his bosses always began promisingly, only to end in
acrimony.

As a rookie manager in 1969, Martin lifted the Minnesota Twins
from seventh place to a division title, but lost his job over disputes
about the farm system. While there he mixed it up with the club's
traveling secretary in a hotel lobby one night and also used his fists
against twenty-game winner Dave Boswell outside a bar. Martin, a

concave five-foot-eleven 160-pounder, knocked the six-foot-three pitcher unconscious.

Detroit took a chance on him in 1971. The Tigers placed second, then muscled their way to the AL East flag in 1972. But the following year, Martin's penchant for publicly second-guessing players and hogging the headlines alienated his predominately veteran team. General manager Jim Campbell dismissed him in September.

"Billy had a way of wearing out his welcome after a couple of years in one place," concedes ex-Yankee Duke Sims, who played contentedly for Martin both in Detroit and in Texas, his next stop.

The Rangers had yet to escape the cellar since emigrating from Washington. But under their feisty new manager they tailgated Oakland all year and finished five games back in second. Martin, named 1974 AL Manager of the Year by the Associated Press, even managed to keep out of trouble (except, that is, for an incident in which he slapped the Rangers' sixty-year-old traveling secretary during an argument over whether or not the team should form a wives' auxiliary). In the Lone Star State that year, only Tom Landry surpassed Martin in popularity.

Nineteen seventy-five conformed to Martin's earlier pattern. The Rangers, verging on anarchy, backslid below .500. After polling his unhappy players, owner Brad Corbett discharged Martin on Monday, July 21.

The following Monday, with the Yankees still woozy from their lost weekend versus Boston, Gabe Paul received orders to lure Billy Martin to New York. (*Shhhhh*, don't tell Commissioner Kuhn.) First he had to find him. Martin was off fishing somewhere in the Colorado mountains with his wife and young son. Paul finally located him outside Denver and hopped a plane there immediately. Two days of discussions yielded nothing concrete; Paul returned to New York while Martin mulled over the Yankees' terms. As the week progressed, the rumors built to a crescendo.

"There was a general feeling around the ball club that Bill Virdon might be let go and Billy Martin might be coming on board," says Doc Medich. Virdon himself sensed that his days were numbered. On Friday, August 1, two hours before game time, Martin phoned Paul with his acceptance.

Steinbrenner instantly leaked word of the imminent signing to Phil Pepe. "At about four in the afternoon he called me and said, 'I think I'm going to make a change,'" the sportswriter recalls. "And he gave me the story." Pepe got the scoop into the evening edition. "One of the printers at the *Daily News* read it, went to a bar, and started talking about it," he recalls. "Well, somebody from UPI was there, so the news actually came out on the wire service before our paper hit the stands at about eight. Then all the papers started sending reinforcements to Shea Stadium."

The Yankees won their third straight, 5–4 over Cleveland. Dick Tidrow earned the save in relief of Catfish Hunter, although Fred Stanley deserved a share. With two outs and the tying run on second, George Hendrick looped a dying quail toward left. Number 11 scampered back and made a diving, tumbling grab. "It was probably the best catch of my life," says Stanley.

"I'm running off the field with the ball, and there are all these cameras all over the place. So I'm thinking, *All right! Man, they got down here quick!*" But the media detachment ignored the game's hero and trailed Bill Virdon down the runway and into his cramped office. "Nobody ever talked to me," Stanley adds, laughing.

The gentlemanly Virdon conducted himself with typical aplomb. Honest to a fault, he told the reporters he didn't know anything about his impending ouster. And he truly didn't. "It was the best situation I could have been in," he remarks. "Since I wasn't aware of it yet, I didn't have to answer any questions, and they stopped asking."

It wasn't until the clubhouse had emptied that Gabe Paul summoned Virdon to the team's executive offices and informed him of the change at the top, which, the Yankees president emphasized, he personally opposed. "I did not think Virdon should go at that time," Paul confirms. "But with ownership goes a proprietary right, and George felt he should be replaced."

Virdon seemed to vanish as abruptly as Jimmy Hoffa, who'd been reported missing three days before. He cleaned out his office early the next morning and left without ever getting to deliver a formal goodbye to his players.

But Virdon wasn't idle long. August wasn't even out before he touched down in Houston as manager of the Astros. His seven-year hitch there would deliver the franchise its first division flag, in 1980. Later, in 1983, he would move on to Montreal for two seasons.

With a few twists of fate in 1975—specifically, a few less twisted knees—Number 21 undoubtedly would have stayed on to direct the Yankees dynasty that from 1976 through 1981 generated two World Championships, four league pennants, and five division titles. "I think we could have won it," says Virdon, now back in the Pittsburgh organization as a roving batting and outfield instructor. "We were subject to more than our share of things that you just don't plan on. But that's baseball."

Virdon's firing saddened most Yankees. "I thought it was a shame," says Lou Piniella, "and it surprised me he was let go, because I thought he was doing a good job. I think the only thing that derailed Bill Virdon was the fact that Martin had become available, and George had this fascination with Billy."

Piniella, himself axed (twice) as Yankees pilot by Steinbrenner in the 1980s, chuckles and adds, "You can see from what's happened over the years that George is very spontaneous. Otherwise I think Bill would have remained in New York for quite a while."

The Yankees wrung every ounce of drama from the coincidence of Martin's return falling on Old Timers' Day. After Joe DiMaggio, Mickey Mantle, and Whitey Ford had all been introduced to a crowd of 43,968, the twenty-first manager in club history dashed out into the ninety-seven-degree heat. Ironically, Martin hadn't originally been invited, and just a few weeks earlier he'd damned New York management for not including him in this year's festivities, which showcased stars from its championship squads of the 1950s.

Though not particularly gifted, Martin played on six of those teams. He compensated for his modest abilities with bravado and fierce determination. Manager Casey Stengel, whom Martin idolized, referred to him affectionately as "that little punk—how I love 'im!"

The one season he amassed more than 500 at-bats, 1953, Martin posted a .257, the same as his lifetime batting average (with 15 home runs and 75 RBIs). In the Fall Classic, the scrappy second baseman's 12-for-24, 2 HR, 8 RBI performance won him the World Series MVP Award as the Yankees foiled the Dodgers in seven for their fifth consecutive crown.

Martin reveled in wearing the pinstripes, but a fracas at Manhattan's Copacabana Club on the occasion of his twenty-ninth birthday was the beginning of the end for him with the organization he loved. A half-dozen Yankees, among them Mickey Mantle, Whitey Ford, Yogi Berra, and the guest of honor, got into a scuffle with a Bronx bowling team and put one of them in the hospital.

Although Hank Bauer was charged with the assault, Martin absorbed most of the blame, probably because he was the most dispensable of the group. General manager George Weiss, who'd long considered Martin a negative influence on the impressionable Mantle, soon packed him off to Kansas City on June 15, 1957. Martin, believing Stengel hadn't stood up for him, refused to speak to his beloved mentor for years afterward.

Now Martin was back in pinstripes, wearing the number 1 that Pete Sheehy claimed to have handed him in 1950 because a wider number wouldn't have fit on the skinny kid's back. He also sported a sleek mustache that lent his boyish face a dark, brooding cast. The Yankees received a taste of Martin's alert, hands-on style midway through his debut.

In the top of the sixth, Cleveland got to starter Pat Dobson for three runs and had men at the corners when Martin waved in Sparky Lyle. Martin, anticipating a double steal, instructed the struggling reliever to throw over to first. Lyle promptly picked off Buddy Bell, ending the inning. He held the Indians scoreless the rest of the way while New York put two on the board in the sixth and three more in the eighth to pull out a 5–3 win.

Dobson, known as "Snake," had been elated by Virdon's removal—until he discovered his replacement's identity.

"I wasn't particularly fond of Billy Martin," he says. "We'd had run-ins before, when he was managing Detroit and I was with Baltimore. It all started in 1972, when I was pitching against Tom Timmerman." Timmerman, a friend of Dobson's from the minors, had once saved 27 games for the Tigers, yet Martin turned him into a starter. Dobson commented to a reporter that he felt Timmerman was better suited to relief. After the game, which Dobson won 1–0, the reporter repeated the remark to Martin.

"Well, Billy got all upset and said, 'Who does he think he is, my pitching coach?' " says Dobson, later a highly regarded pitching tutor for the Brewers and the Royals. "He made a statement that the next time I faced them, I was gonna have Tiger-itis, and balls would be rattling off the upper deck."

Dobson laughs wickedly. "I went to Detroit and beat them again. There were some words exchanged after the game; I think I flipped Billy the bird. And that was the end of it."

Not quite. Within two weeks of assuming command, Martin stashed Dobson in the bullpen without explanation. "Obviously Billy had a mind like an elephant," says the right-hander. "I knew when he came over I was gone." His premonition came true that winter, when he went to Cleveland for outfielder Oscar Gamble.

Dobson wasn't the only Yankee suddenly concerned about his future in New York. Elliott Maddox and Larry Gura had clashed with Martin his first spring in Texas—and each had soon found himself property of the Yankees. For Maddox, that was the second time Martin had deemed him expendable. In his first week as Tigers pilot he approved a trade sending the promising rookie to Washington in a multiplayer deal.

Maddox and Gura's leading roles in the Yankees' bid for the 1974 pennant raised questions about Martin's ability to judge talent. Maddox, unable to refrain from gloating, openly criticized his ex-manager in the papers. Martin returned fire, not only verbally but by having pitchers Jim Bibby and Stan Thomas throw at Maddox during a 1975 exhibition game. Yankees reliever Mike Wallace retaliated with a pair of brush-back pitches, sparking a bench-clearing skirmish.

The feud spilled over into the regular season. In the warring clubs' first confrontation, Thomas plunked Maddox on the elbow, forcing him out of the game. When Catfish Hunter sent a message by dusting off reserve catcher Bill Fahey, Martin expressed outrage and took another jab at Maddox, calling him a crybaby. Throughout it all, he denied ordering the beanballs.

As the Yankees front office still considered the injured center fielder a vital cog for 1976 and beyond, Gabe Paul saw to it that one of Martin's first tasks was to reconcile with Maddox. The new manager apologized by phone for having underestimated Maddox's hitting, an admission he later made to reporters in his first press conference. Maddox, who had heard similar sentiments upon Martin's arrival in Texas, remained understandably skeptical.

Martin's sincerity in this matter is hard to gauge, since Maddox's damaged knee limited him to fewer than two dozen games before New York swapped him to Baltimore in 1977. But if Larry Gura's experience is any indication, Martin was more concerned with appeasing his new bosses than actually mending relations with Maddox.

"When Billy first took over," the pitcher recalls, "I went into his office and told him, 'Hey, what happened in Texas is in the past, and this is a new start.' We both shook hands, and everything was fine. Then his first move was to go from a five-man rotation to a four-man rotation, which knocked me out." Gura frequently went eight, even eleven days between starts and wound up the year 7–8 (3.51 ERA).

"Next spring, as soon as Billy shook my hand, he said I was his fourth starter. I thought, *Great! This is what I've always wanted.* Well, I didn't pitch at all for six weeks. Then I got traded." Anytime Number 39 asked the manager why he wasn't pitching, "He'd find something to say just to get me out of the office.

"I was so sure I wasn't going to be with the team much longer," says Gura, "my wife and I didn't even rent furniture for our apartment in New Jersey. We slept on the floor." May 16 brought the welcome news he'd been expecting: a trade, to Kansas City, for backup catcher Fran Healy. "It was all uphill from there," he says.

Gura anchored the Royals' starting rotation for ten seasons before retiring at age thirty-eight. A .578 winning percentage, higher than contemporaries such as Frank Tanana, Vida Blue, Phil Niekro, and Dennis Eckersley during that period, placed him among the league's most dependable pitchers. Martin never did concede that he'd under-estimated the soft-spoken lefty.

It was his most glaring flaw that Martin at times let personalities blind him to players' talents. He preferred to surround himself with mirror images of his younger self. "Billy was always a hard-drinking, hard-living, very aggressive guy," says Maury Allen of the *New York Post*. "Hard-drinking, aggressive tough guys like Munson and Nettles were his favorites. People like Larry Gura he tended to beat up on."

Gura's fondness for tennis—a "pussy sport" in Martin's eyes—further soured the manager on him. He and Rich Coggins, another benchwarmer in 1975, used to take to the courts to keep in shape.

"One morning in Cleveland, Rich and I returned from playing tennis," Gura recalls. "Martin saw us come through the lobby. That night in the dugout, Billy sits down next to me and asks, 'How's your tennis?'

" 'It's fine.'

" 'You think it's good for you?' "

Gura told him, "Yeah, I do. I play right-handed, so I don't hurt my arm, and I don't play the day I pitch or the day before. I think it's great conditioning." Martin nodded and walked off.

A few innings later, players' rep Ed Herrmann collared Gura.

"Did you know Martin almost fined you and Coggins two grand each?" he asked.

"For what?"

"For playing tennis."

When Coggins heard that, he marched down the tunnel to the visitors' clubhouse, where Martin stood sneaking a cigarette.

"Okay, that's enough!" he shouted. "Let's go at it right now!"

"Of course," Gura says dryly, "nothing happened, because there wasn't anybody between him and Billy, and Billy never fought unless someone was around to 'restrain' him.

"I get back from the road trip," he continues, "and Gabe Paul calls me into the office and proceeds to tear me apart, asking me if I want to be a professional tennis player or a professional baseball player."

The pitcher retorted bitterly, "What would you rather have me do? Go to bed early and get up early and stay in shape by playing tennis, or do you want me to stay out drinking till two, three in the morning like a lot of guys do?"

Says Gura, "That night in the locker room I asked Billy, 'Hey, did you say anything to Gabe Paul?'

" 'No, I didn't say anything.' "

Gura scoffs, "It was quite interesting how Gabe Paul knew about me playing tennis." To no one's surprise, Coggins followed him out of town days later as part of a multiplayer swap with the White Sox.

Fran Healy quickly replaced Gura in the manager's doghouse. A Yankee close to Martin explains the manager's custom of picking one player for his whipping boy, to intimidate the others.

"Billy would find one guy and ride him unmercifully. If that guy did anything wrong, he was ridiculed, screamed at. And it worked rather well, really. *You didn't want to be that guy.* You understand? He had a few guys like that through the years." The "shit bums." "They were usually players who weren't the nucleus of the club, guys that were really expendable. He would chew them up and spit them out whenever he got the chance. Maybe that would keep the rest of the guys in line."

Overall, little of the turmoil many Yankees had anticipated materialized during Martin's first season. "The surprising thing about him was that he had this real tough-guy reputation, yet in the clubhouse he let the players alone," Lou Piniella recalls. "You heard about Martin punching out this guy and that guy, but I didn't see that side of him at all." Oddly, despite their similar temperaments, "I honestly never felt that Billy liked me all that much," says Piniella, sounding puzzled. "I didn't really have much of a rapport with him."

Martin's sometimes bilious personality may have drawn mixed reviews, but not his aggressive, unpredictable brand of baseball, which he wasted no time in implementing. In 56 games with Martin at the helm, New York pilfered 55 bases, as compared to just 47 steals in Bill Virdon's 104 games.

"I didn't think Martin was that good a manager when I played against him," Catfish Hunter admits. "But after having played under him, I think he was probably one of the smartest managers I ever played under. He didn't hesitate to make a move. He always knew what he was going to do."

Nevertheless, Martin was no more able to spur the Yankees back into contention than his predecessor. They plodded to a third-place finish, 83–77, .519, twelve games behind Boston. Over the last month, "Billy just laid back, watched us play, and evaluated the talent we had," says Fred Stanley, Martin's number one shortstop by season's end.

Two players who were assured jobs next year included former Indians Graig Nettles and Chris Chambliss, both of whom achieved belated success as Yankees. Nettles, disheartened by four years of toiling in deserted Cleveland Municipal Stadium, had rejoiced upon being traded with Jerry Moses to New York in 1972. "He felt like he'd been let out of prison," says Moses.

New Yorkers were slow to embrace Nettles, however, expecting him to evoke Roger Maris and other left-handed sluggers from teams past. Periodically he did: eleven home runs the first month of 1974 set an American League mark for four-baggers in April. But Nettles connected only eleven more times all year. "Graig was always a real streak hitter," says Doc Medich. "He'd carry us for a couple of weeks, then go into a slump for a while."

Meanwhile, Cleveland's Charlie Spikes and John Ellis, the two other principals in the six-man deal, each outperformed Nettles again. A New York sportswriter hyperbolically proclaimed the trade the best in Tribe history. Time quickly overturned that verdict.

In 1975, the thirty-year-old Nettles batted .267 BA, 21 HR, 91 RBI—more RBIs than any Yankees third baseman in history. He later added to his own record with totals of 93 in 1976 and 107 the following year. In all, Number 9 powdered 250 home runs for New York before a feud with George Steinbrenner got him banished to San Diego in 1984. As for Spikes and Ellis, while Nettles was winning election to the 1975 AL All-Star Team, their careers were already going into decline.

"It seemed like the longer Graig was in New York, the better he got," says Medich. "I think the fans' initial reaction bothered him, but Graig has a real wry sense of humor, and it got him through. Then after he'd been there for a while and had some success, he felt comfortable. But it did take him a few years to adjust."

If the years proved unkind to Gabe Paul on the Nettles swap—his last as Cleveland's GM—they thoroughly vindicated him on the controversial trade involving Chris Chambliss. The twenty-six-year-old first baseman hit .304 BA, 9 HR, 72 RBI in 1975, a season that Chambliss had feared he would end wearing another uniform.

"When I got to spring training," he says, "I really felt like I was going to be traded again." Virdon, still unconvinced that Number 10 could hit lefties, had both Roy White and Lou Piniella work out at first base in Fort Lauderdale. "Roy used my glove," Chambliss says, laughing. "I don't know if Bill didn't like me or what, but at that point I just knew that he was planning on either platooning me or maybe not playing me at all."

"I wasn't happy about it either," White says of Virdon's experiment, "but I didn't have much choice in the matter except to try making a go of it. After being in the outfield for so many years, it was scary to go back to the infield at a new position. But as it turned out, I played only about ten games at first."

The last week in spring training, White fractured his left thumb diving for a grounder and missed the first seven games of the season.

Chambliss made the most of his reprieve, shredding the ball so that Virdon couldn't budge him from the lineup. "The next thing you knew," says White, "I was back in left field, and Chris was a regular at first." In a reversal of 1974, Lou Piniella became odd man out.

On August 22, Chambliss's eighth home run helped Catfish Hunter to his seventeenth victory. New York's million-dollar man, a mere 13–10 through July, racked up 10 of 14 decisions to finish 23–14, 2.58 ERA, and joined Hall of Famers Walter Johnson and Lefty Grove as the only AL pitchers ever to string together five consecutive twenty-victory seasons.

Bobby Bonds also entered the record books in 1975, becoming the first player to stroke 30 home runs and steal 30 bases in the same season three times. His propensity for striking out (137 times) somewhat diluted a .270 BA, 32 HR, 85 RBI, 93 R, 30 SB record, but given that he'd played much of the year "on one leg," to quote Rudy May, it had to be considered a splendid season. Nevertheless, Bonds went home to San Carlos, California, that winter assuming he wouldn't be back.

"When Billy Martin took over," he explains, "we got into a couple of arguments because he had no concept of how bad I was hurt. I'd hit a ball in the hole and the shortstop would throw me out, which would have been impossible prior to the injury.

"And Billy thought, *He ain't hustling.* He put the steal on a couple of times, and I just couldn't make it because my knee was terrible. 'How can you get thrown out like that?' I thought, *Man, I'm hurt!* For him not to understand the true picture and then to judge me on that was probably the biggest injustice ever done to me in baseball.

"Then Billy got a grudge against me," Bonds continues. "He kept screaming at me. So I told him that if he kept doing it, I'd kick his little ass. I went into his office when there was nobody around, and I said, 'If you think you can whup me, fine. I'll beat the shit out of you, plain and simple. There's nobody to grab me and nobody to grab you. If you want to fight, let's do it.' "

After that, "I knew I was going to be traded," sighs Bonds, father of three-time MVP Barry Bonds, and now a San Francisco Giants coach. "I didn't want to be traded. Because I knew if we stayed healthy, there was no team in the American League that could beat us."

V

BONDS'S FEARS WERE realized on December 11, as Gabe Paul executed a pair of blockbuster trades that stole the spotlight at the winter meetings in Hollywood, Florida. First Bonds went to the California Angels for fleet center fielder Mickey Rivers, the AL's leading base stealer, and right-handed pitcher Ed Figueroa, 16–13, 2.91 ERA on a last-place club.

Paul's other deal sent Doc Medich to the Pirates for pitchers Dock Ellis and Ken Brett and a twenty-one-year-old rookie second baseman named Willie Randolph. "This is the jackpot!" Paul exulted, but Yankees such as Thurman Munson—and even Billy Martin—were more guarded. Some questioned the wisdom of giving up Bonds, the team's only right-handed power hitter. What's more, Ellis brought with him an 8–9 record and a history of stirring up trouble; Brett's elbow was suspect, shelving him twice in 1975; and Randolph, the most coveted of the three, had played only thirty games in the majors.

In fact, New York would profit so enormously from both trades, that were this Wall Street they would have merited the scrutiny of the SEC. But at the time, the Yankees' latest machinations provoked more questions than answers. Only a year ago, Bonds and Catfish Hunter had been hailed as the franchise's deliverers. The result? An eleventh fruitless season in a row, leaving the Yankees with the sad testimony of 885 wins and 884 losses since 1964.

PART V

Redemption

1976

STARTERS
Catfish Hunter
Ed Figueroa
Dock Ellis
Ken Holtzman
Doyle Alexander

Chris Chambliss (1B)
Willie Randolph (2B)
Fred Stanley/Jim Mason
(SS)
Graig Nettles (3B)
Roy White (LF)
Mickey Rivers (CF)
Oscar Gamble/Lou
Piniella (RF)
Thurman Munson (C)
Carlos May/Lou Piniella
(DH)

RELIEVERS
Sparky Lyle
Dick Tidrow
Grant Jackson

I

FOR THOSE WHO believe in omens, the second game of 1976 provided one as portentous as rain on a wedding day.

Billy Martin's team was three outs away from its first win of the season when Brewers third baseman Don Money obliterated a 9–6 New York lead by swatting a game-winning grand slam off Dave Pagan. The Yankees' hearts sank as they watched the ball disappear over the left-field wall at Milwaukee County Stadium, for they'd staged a magnificent late-inning comeback from a 6–0 deficit. All for naught—or so it seemed.

Suddenly Martin bolted out of the visitors' dugout, neck veins bulging. Pagan, who'd yo-yoed between New York and the minors since 1973, backed off the mound in fear. "I thought he was after me!" recalls the Canadian right-hander. "But he went shooting by me and over to the first-base umpire."

Martin, wearing a black armband in memory of recently deceased

Casey Stengel, gestured wildly at arbiter Jim McKean, who stared at him, puzzled, as if in a game of charades.

"I seen it! I seen it!" Martin shrieked. "You called time, and you got to back it up!"

Chris Chambliss joined in the argument. "It was really pretty strange," he recalls. "Dave was ready to go into a stretch with the bases loaded, and Billy was trying to call time to tell him he should be pitching from the windup. I saw him waving, so I turned around to the umpire and asked for time. Just as he raised his arms and called time out, Dave went into the stretch and threw the pitch.

"Both Billy and I were trying to get McKean to fess up to what happened," Chambliss continues. "Sure enough, the umpires met, he told the truth, and they had to bring the Brewers back onto the field. They were already up in the tunnel to the clubhouse to celebrate the victory. They were going crazy."

Pagan, given a reprieve, got Money to fly out. The Yankees escaped with a 9–7 conquest, setting the tone for a golden season in which the club returned to both prominence and the Bronx.

On April 15, the Yankees dedicated Mike Burke's dream home with an 11–4 pasting of the Twins. The refurbished Yankee Stadium ultimately cost New York City approximately $100 million, *four times* the original estimate.

A thousand protestors gathered across the street to decry the expense and the resulting cuts in city services. As has been borne out since, the refurbishing of Yankee Stadium has done little to stem the rising tide of poverty and urban decay in the South Bronx. To the Yankees, however, the overhaul was worth every penny of taxpayers' money ("The House That *You* Built," *New York Times* columnist Red Smith puckishly referred to it). "The park was beautiful," says Roy White. "We were all excited about being back in Yankee Stadium."

Shortstop Fred Stanley's first impressions were less favorable. "They changed a lot of it," he says. "There were some things about it that were the same, but it wasn't the old Yankee Stadium." Seating capacity had been scaled down, from 65,010 to 54,200, as had the distance to straightaway center, formerly 457 feet away. To put one over the wall now required a 417-foot wallop.

The left- and right-field foul poles, once 301 and 296 feet from home plate, now stood 312 and 310 feet away, yet the ballpark still retained its distinctive asymmetrical shape and much of its character. The decorative white façade no longer wrapped around the grandstand but hung from the bleachers.

The galaxy of retired Yankees stars attending the christening included Mickey Mantle, Joe DiMaggio, and ex-Mets skipper Yogi

Berra, now back in his familiar number 8 as one of Martin's coaches. Bobby Richardson delivered a pregame prayer. And present for his first home opener since 1973: George Steinbrenner. On March 2, Bowie Kuhn lopped nine months off his suspension. Perhaps coincidentally, the previous summer Steinbrenner's swing vote in a polling of major-league owners had prevented the commissioner's ouster.

The largest Opening Day crowd since 1946, 54,010, was still streaming into the ballpark when Minnesota's Dan Ford rode Rudy May's fifth pitch of the game over the 430-foot sign in left-center for a 2–0 Twins lead. Catfish Hunter turned to Ed Figueroa and drawled, "Forget what I told you yesterday."

New York's top two starters had been out surveying the revised dimensions the day before. "Catfish told me, 'Eddie, you see how big it is? We're not gonna give up that many home runs here,' " Figueroa recalls. Ford's blast forced Hunter to reconsider. He said, "Eddie, better keep the ball low, because in this park anybody can hit it out."

Both staffs kept the ball inside the stadium the rest of the way, but New York pushed across one run in the third, four in the fourth, and then added six more in the eighth. Dick Tidrow, recovered from a broken wrist that sidelined him the last six weeks of 1975, bagged the first win in the Yankees' new home with five innings of scoreless middle relief, while Sparky Lyle pocketed the first save there.

New additions Mickey Rivers, Oscar Gamble, and Willie Randolph made Gabe Paul look like a genius, as the trio accounted for eight hits, five runs, and five RBIs. Randolph, the recipient of that spring's James P. Dawson Award, singled twice, stole a base, and hustled down the right-field line to haul in a twisting foul pop in the eighth.

As the Yankees would see, the graduate of Brooklyn's Tilden High School could do it all. In him New York found its starting second baseman of the next thirteen years, the longest duty at that post of anyone in franchise history. Although Randolph hit only .164 in 61 at-bats for Pittsburgh in 1975, "Our scouts were very, very high on him," remembers Paul. "There was a general feeling in the organization that he had the possibilities of being a great ballplayer."

Randolph, who wore Mel Stottlemyre's old number 30, kept his average above .300 into June, finishing at .267 BA, 1 HR, 40 RBI, with 37 SB. Like Stottlemyre in his rookie season, the quiet twenty-one-year-old displayed unusual poise.

"Willie had an excellent eye at the plate, even for a young guy," double-play partner Fred Stanley recalls. "He stayed in there in the heat. Kept to himself, but he had good work habits. His on-base percentage was good, his stolen-base percentage was good, and he made few mistakes for a kid. I was impressed."

II

MARTIN'S TEAM CRUISED through a 10–3 April, silencing critics like *Newsday*'s sportswriters, none of whom picked the Yankees for higher than third. "Our ball club was refreshed and energized," reflects Lou Piniella, .281 BA, 3 HR, 38 RBI as a part-time right fielder and designated hitter. "We had an excellent spring training, worked hard to get into shape, and got out of the gate pretty good."

On May 20, the 19–10, .655 Yankees prepared to cross swords with Boston for the first time. The defending league champions floundered six games back, in fourth place, 13–16, .448. Nevertheless, says Figueroa, the opening-game starter, "They were the club to beat."

The Puerto Rican right-hander had K.O.'d Darrell Johnson's team three times in 1975. Through the first six innings he continued his dominance, fooling Red Sox batters with his tricky curve and sinker. Opponent Bill Lee, a seventeen-game winner in each of the last three seasons, was nearly as effective. New York held a 1–0 advantage in the bottom of the sixth when reserve outfielder-infielder Otto Velez lashed a two-out, two-on single to right. Lou Piniella dug around third as Dwight Evans scooped up the ball and bulleted a throw home, well ahead of the runner.

Number 14, accepting his fate, bore down on Carlton Fisk like a kamikaze pilot. His right shoulder caught the catcher in the chest, knocking him to the ground. When that failed to jar the ball loose, Piniella tried kicking it away. Suddenly the two were wrestling in the dirt.

"It was probably a little frustration on my part," admits Piniella. "Evans had already thrown out one runner at the plate in the game, and here I was in a similar situation. I went into Fisk pretty good, and we got into a scuffle. Before you knew it, there were a few more fist-fights."

In the Yankees dugout, rookie Willie Randolph grabbed a bat. "Put it back!" Billy Martin yelled. "Then they all charged," recalls former batboy Joe D'Ambrosio. "I wasn't at Iwo Jima, but this was *thrilling*." The entire New York and Boston squads converged on home plate. Even the teams' batboys eyed each other menacingly. "But our trainer said, 'Don't even think about it!' " says D'Ambrosio.

Spaceman Lee tried to pull Velez off Fisk and lived to regret it. First Mickey Rivers clocked him in the face, then Graig Nettles lifted him up and hurled him down on his pitching shoulder.

"You son of a bitch!" Lee screamed. "How could you be such an asshole?"

Nettles's response was to deck him a second time. One fan, inspired by the violence, climbed onto the field and also tried to assault Lee, who ended up missing nearly two months with torn shoulder ligaments. "I don't think he was ever the same after that," comments Dick Tidrow. He may have a point. The left-hander exceeded ten wins only once more through 1982, his final season.

The Yankees also suffered casualties. Rivers hurt his toe and had to sit out the rest of the series. "And I messed up my damn thumb pretty good," says Piniella. "I missed only a few games, but I lost a lot of strength in it for the rest of the year. Hell, I couldn't even open a door knob with my right hand.

"But hey," he says of the brawl, "it gave us some impetus."

Though the Red Sox finally solved Figueroa in the seventh, going on to an easy 8–2 victory, "It proved to us that we weren't going to be intimidated," says Fred Stanley. From then on, "Our club felt we were the one to beat, not Boston."

May 31 took the Yankees to Beantown, where bloodthirsty Red Sox fans were demanding revenge. "They said there were going to be problems in Boston," Joe D'Ambrosio remembers. "It was scary." In Detroit, on the eve of the four-game set, Billy Martin gathered his players together in the Tiger Stadium clubhouse. *Newsday* sportswriter Joe Donnelly sat in on the meeting.

"I couldn't believe what I was hearing," he says. "Billy told them, 'If any fans come over the top of the dugout, pick up your bats and be ready to take them apart. I'll be right with you.' Martin was supposedly a Civil War buff? Well, he seriously believed baseball was a battlefield."

In the opener, Fenway Park's largest crowd in twenty years directed its wrath mostly at Rivers. Coins, batteries, golf balls, rocks, cherry bombs, and signs taunting CHEAP SHOT ARTIST rained down on the Yankees center fielder, who had to wear a batting helmet for protection the entire game. When a third firecracker exploded near Rivers's feet in the eighth, fans were warned that one more missile would force a Red Sox forfeit. But by then Catfish Hunter held a commanding lead on his way to an 8–3 win.

New York banged out thirteen hits, among them Thurman Munson's seventh home run and thirty-fifth RBI. The twenty-nine-year-old receiver finished with 105, second in the league to Baltimore's Lee May, the older brother of recent Yankees pickup Carlos May.

Nineteen seventy-six brought Munson the level of acclaim he'd long sought. One week into the season Martin named him the franchise's first captain since Lou Gehrig retired in 1939. According to his teammates, no one was more deserving.

"Thurman was the heart and soul of the ball club, the guy who set the tone," attests Doc Medich. "When I was a rookie he took me out to dinner before a game and explained things to me. And he played hurt." Munson's knees ached all year, yet he donned shin guards for 121 games.

In July, Munson started his second consecutive All-Star Game. Making the honor sweeter than the year before was the fact that Carlton Fisk stayed healthy in 1976. Recognition also came from the Baseball Writers' Association of America, which voted him AL MVP based on a .302 BA, 17 HR, 105 RBI and a surprising 14 SB.

Despite these accolades, the season contained its unhappy moments, too. In the ninth inning of a 6–6 tie against Oakland on June 5, Munson pegged wildly past second on a stolen-base attempt, enabling Don Baylor to dust himself off and scamper all the way around the diamond. The Yankee Stadium crowd booed loudly.

More boos followed Number 15 to the plate in the bottom of the frame, intensifying after he struck out. On the way back to the dugout Munson thrust an index finger at the stands. Afterward, in the locker room, he was disconsolate.

"I'm not appreciated," he grumbled to anyone who would listen. If Munson seemed overly sensitive, it was partially because he'd worked hard to correct a two-year defensive slump. His twenty-two errors in 1974 and twenty-three errors in 1975, many of them coming on errant throws, led the league. Nevertheless, he won a Gold Glove award each season.

Reserve catcher Fran Healy competed against Munson in the minors and calls him the best defensive receiver he'd ever seen down there. But by 1976, he observes, "Thurman had lost his confidence throwing the ball to second, and struggled with that." Munson committed just fourteen miscues his MVP year, despite a broken index finger on his throwing hand.

One aspect of his game that remained constant was Munson's ability to know the hitters and call pitches. "The Brain," pitcher Dock Ellis called him. "Billy Martin was tough on catchers," says Healy, who ought to know, "but Thurman wouldn't listen to any bullshit." He put down the signs without so much as a glance at his manager, who had a reputation for controlling games from the bench.

"He made you feel so relaxed out there," praises Dick Tidrow, 4–5, 10 SV, 2.63 ERA. "There were a few times when he didn't even give me a signal. He'd wave his hand, like, 'C'mon, just throw it.' It was like you were dissecting the hitters, and he would take the thought process away from you, so you could get into a groove. After pitching to Thurman, I didn't want to throw to anybody else. He made it too easy and too much fun."

Playing baseball in New York wasn't always fun for Munson. He sometimes longed for the simplicity of baseball minus the demands of the media, the fickle fans, the pressure. His manager at Syracuse, Frank Verdi, remembers running into the Yankees at an airport during Munson's Rookie of the Year season.

"Skip," the twenty-three-year-old sighed, "I really wish I could be back at Syracuse."

"What are you, crazy?"

Verdi recalls: "He said, 'I'll tell you something: I'm not having any fun up here at all. Up here it's *all business.*' "

Most of all, Munson missed his wife and three children back in Canton, Ohio. He'd grown up distant from his own father, Darrell, a tenant farmer and long-distance trucker who rarely showed affection and who criticized his youngest son harshly. In a rare revealing moment, Munson told an interviewer, "To my face he'd tear me down, but to others he'd praise me to the sky."

According to Gene Michael, who was back with the Yankees in 1976 as an infield coach, "They'd always had some arguments, some differences. I think it had some bearing on Thurman. It made him a stronger family man. Because he was the opposite, very close to his children."

As early as 1973 he began hinting that he wanted to be traded to Cleveland. "I told him, 'Thurman, that would be the dumbest thing you ever did,' " says Bernie Allen. " 'You go there, you can be the greatest catcher around, and nobody's going to know you exist. You're better off right here.' "

To make playing in New York more bearable, Munson earned a private pilot's license in 1978. He began flying home, not only on off-days but following night games. "The club knew about it," says Phil Pepe of the *Daily News.* "He confided in me that he would leave the game, drive to Teterboro Airport in New Jersey, get in his plane, and be home by midnight." After seeing the kids off to school in the morning, Munson would tend to his real-estate holdings, which he oversaw as efficiently as he called a game. "Then he'd leave there around three in the afternoon and be at the ballpark by five.

"He asked me not to write about it," Pepe adds, "because they had insurance problems."

On August 1, 1979, Munson flew home from Chicago in his brand-new Cessna Citation jet, lettered NY15. The next afternoon, an off-day, he was practicing takeoffs and landings at Canton-Akron Regional Airport. He'd logged only thirty-four hours in the $1.4 million craft, an insufficient amount of time, authorities later concluded, to master jet flying.

Munson came in too slowly and at too steep an angle. He tried to recover by throttling up the twin engines, but didn't react quickly enough. The Cessna crashed short of the runway and burst into flames. His copilot and passenger, both of whom escaped the wreck with burns, tried to pull Munson from the plane, but the fire beat them back. He died in the wreckage, just thirty-two years old.

III

WERE IT NOT for a shoulder injury that kept him out of the lineup for much of September, Munson's teammate Mickey Rivers might well have walked off with the MVP award for 1976. The twenty-seven-year-old speed merchant immediately established himself as the team's offensive catalyst, batting a team-high .312.

"Every time we have Mickey at first, starting the inning, we always score," Ed Figueroa says in lightly accented English. "He always stole second, and with Roy White, Thurman, and all those other guys coming up behind him, we know we have a run for sure." Rivers scored 95 times. He didn't receive the green light from Martin as much as he would have liked, but still stole 43 bases in 50 attempts. Though reed-thin at five-foot-ten, 165 pounds, he showed surprising pop with the bat too, putting 8 balls over the fence and driving in 67 runs from the leadoff position.

The Yankees players enjoyed watching Number 17 as much as the fans did: the way he'd shuffle pigeon-toed to the plate, twirling his bat like a baton, then put the ball in play and dash to first base in 3.4 seconds. However, Rivers also confounded those around him with his mercurial behavior. Heads shook up and down the Yankees dugout whenever he loafed after a ball in the outfield or removed himself from the lineup with some mysterious ailment. Martin once fined him for arriving late to a doubleheader, but because Rivers was so valuable, he tended to coddle him.

"Mickey is a strange guy," Dick Tidrow says affectionately. "He can go on the road, get his meal money one day, and be out of money on day two." A fondness for racetracks accounted for Rivers's perpetually empty pockets. "Billy bent over backward for Mickey," Tidrow continues. "He did a lot of nice things for him, like sending his wife flowers and giving him extra money."

His personal problems aside, "Everybody on the team just loved Mickey," says sportswriter Phil Pepe. "He kept the clubhouse loose." Rivers, a product of the Miami ghetto, cracked up teammates with his peculiar brand of logic and his largely indecipherable lexicon of insults, such as "gozzle head" and "warple head." He and Carlos May used to engage in mock arguments over who was more intelligent.

One day in the Milwaukee locker room Rivers taunted May, "I'll bet you a hundred bucks I have a higher I.Q. than you."

May's retort: "You don't even know how to *spell* I.Q."

In game two at Fenway Park on June 2, Rivers went 2-for-5 with an RBI as Figueroa stopped the Red Sox 7–2. A rainout the night before helped to defuse the Boston fans. Somewhat. "They were all over us, booing, saying lots of bad words," says the pitcher. "We didn't worry about it, we just played to beat Boston, and we did it.

"Of course," he adds with a laugh, "we had a lot of memos from George saying that we had to beat them."

Dock Ellis, winner of his first four decisions in pinstripes, bowed to Luis Tiant in the finale, 8–2. Ellis, Figueroa, and Hunter comprised a solid starting threesome, but the rotation's fourth and fifth slots remained question marks, though through no fault of Gabe Paul. Martin, for reasons known only to him, chose to squander three reliable arms in Larry Gura, Ken Brett, and Rudy May.

Gura spent the first six weeks of the season in bullpen oblivion, then went to Kansas City in the May 16 trade for Fran Healy. Brett, a steady 35–23 for Pittsburgh the previous three seasons, left town two days later. "Kenny was an outstanding guy," says Healy, "but Billy just didn't like him, for whatever the hell reason it was." And May landed on Martin's wrong side by questioning the manager's decision to remove him from a 5–3 loss in Cleveland on May 27.

After the game, May ducked his head into Martin's office and remarked innocently, "Gee, Skip, I sure would have liked to have stayed in that game."

The temperamental Martin blew up at him. *"You motherfucker, you'll never pitch for me again!"* he railed. *"You son of a bitch, get the fuck out of here or I'll kick your fuckin' ass!"*

"What did I say?" May asked, perplexed. "I just want to talk to you about this."

"I'll never talk to your fuckin' ass again," Martin snarled.

Three nights later in Detroit, scheduled starter Dave Pagan had to be scrubbed at the last minute due to a virus. May, sitting in the dugout, heard Martin yell, "Hey!"

"I turned around," he recalls, "and Billy threw a baseball at me and hit me with it. He said, 'You're pitching tonight. And I'll tell you when the fuck you're coming out of the game. You got that?' "

The left-hander went all the way in blanking the Tigers 4–0, one of several brilliant displays he put on despite pitching irregularly. In his previous start against Ralph Houk's club, Number 43 had held Detroit scoreless for seven innings. Ten days earlier, in Kansas City, he no-hit the Royals through eight, but came away with no decision, as New York lost in extra innings 2–1. On May 19, May carried a shutout into the ninth in Cleveland to beat the Tribe 3–2.

Following his four-hitter at Tiger Stadium, the Yankees flew on to Boston for their crucial four-game set. May's wife drove up from New York to surprise him. The couple went out for a late-night bite to eat. When they returned to the team's hotel, Martin joined them in the elevator, "so drunk he couldn't even stand up," says May.

"He just wrung me out in front of my wife; called me everything. Then he took a swing at me, missed, and fell down. The elevator stopped at his floor. I dragged him off and left him lying there. My wife and I went on up to our room.

"I felt pretty bad about it," he goes on, "so I went back down, picked him up, got his keys out of his pocket, carried him into his room, and put him on his bed. The next day I confronted him about it. Billy didn't remember anything about it. He wouldn't even talk to me."

May's problems with Martin went far deeper than disagreements over his place in the rotation. The black pitcher bitterly resented Martin's stream of racial slurs. "I couldn't hide my feelings," he says. "I guess Billy sensed that or found that out, and boy, we went round and round.

"He was a racist," May says bluntly. "I heard him refer to Ron Blomberg as a 'fuckin' Jew.' 'Spics.' 'Niggers.' I didn't like the fact that he separated our team that way. Because we as ballplayers never thought about that. I might be black, and Sandy Alomar might be Puerto Rican, but I'm not a 'fuckin' nigger,' and he's not a 'fuckin' Puerto Rican'! That's why I had my problems with Billy."

Martin seemed incapable of seeing beyond a person's ethnicity. He routinely referred to himself as a dago, a reference to his Portuguese-Italian ancestry. Perhaps because he used racial epithets so casually, he didn't realize how hurtful they were.

His embattled relationship with Elliott Maddox harks back to a comment he made in 1970. Upon replacing Mayo Smith as the Tigers' pilot, Martin told reporters he didn't think he wanted the young outfielder on his club. Why not? "Because," he replied cryptically, "he's a downtown Detroit nigger." Apparently the remark wasn't a slip of the tongue. Joe Donnelly says he also heard him say it on another occasion.

But the *Newsday* sportswriter insists Martin possessed another side. He recalls how the Yankees manager quietly doled out money to ex-players down on their luck, many of them black and Hispanic. "Players would look him up for handouts, and Billy would give them three hundred or four hundred dollars," says Donnelly. "He was a soft touch for guys who'd given him what he wanted on the ballfield. He remembered them. That was his idea of loyalty."

When Martin went on to manage Oakland in 1980, he arranged a scouting position for Sandy Alomar. "Billy was always taking care of guys who he thought needed it," says Alomar, since 1991 a minor-league scout and instructor for the Chicago Cubs. "He was a great guy to all the Latin players; always treated us well. I loved playing for Billy."

Not May, who didn't start again for ten days. This time he went the distance against California, but lost to Frank Tanana 2–0. The next time he pitched it was in an Orioles uniform.

On June 15, trading deadline day, New York roosted atop the AL East with a four-and-a-half-game margin. Gabe Paul, not content to stand pat, conducted a blockbuster ten-player swap with Baltimore. In exchange for May, Rick Dempsey, Dave Pagan, Tippy Martinez, and prospect Scott McGregor, the Yankees received starters Ken Holtzman and Doyle Alexander, reliever Grant Jackson, reserve catcher Elrod Hendricks, and minor-league pitcher Jimmy Freeman. So many players were involved, Dock Ellis jokes, "It wasn't until they joined us that I started to figure out who was who—which guys had left, who came over, and what positions they played."

Paul's other announcement of the day was even more stunning. The Yankees had just purchased Vida Blue, a 22-game winner in 1975, from the A's for $1.5 million, the largest sum ever doled out for a single player. The transactions reunited the starting trio of Oakland's 1972–74 dynasty: Hunter, Holtzman, and Blue.

"I thought, *Heck, when they get over here, we might win it four, five years in a row!*" Hunter recalls. But Bowie Kuhn swooped down to nix the Blue deal, as well as Charlie Finley's sales of stars Joe Rudi and Rollie Fingers to Boston for $1 million apiece.

Why would the A's owner dismantle his Rolls-Royce of a franchise? As a preemptive strike against impending free agency. Just four weeks later, the owners and players agreed to a pact that permitted players with six years' big-league service to place themselves on the market, introducing true free enterprise to the national pastime at long last. Neither Blue, Rudi, nor Fingers had inked contracts for 1976 and were therefore eligible for free agency after the season. Likewise, just before Opening Day, Oakland had traded Holtzman and outfielder Reggie Jackson, both unsigned, to Baltimore for pitchers Mike Torrez and Paul Mitchell. Had Finley lost them in the upcoming free-agent draft, two draft choices would have been his only compensation.

"Mr. Finley was probably one of the smarter owners," observes Hunter. "He was going to beat free agency. He was going to sell them, because now they could get rid of *him*. The players weren't making the money they are today, and this way he could sell them, then build his team back up. But they wouldn't let him do it."

The commissioner ordered the three players to stay put pending a hearing. His position made unlikely allies of the Yankees and their longtime antagonist. Even league president Lee MacPhail was firmly in Finley's corner.

"I defended Charlie's right to deal the players," he says. "But Kuhn took the position that he was running the franchise down and shouldn't be allowed to do it." On June 18, Kuhn voided both deals "in the interests of baseball." His fear—not entirely unfounded, either—was that to allow the sales would ruin the sport by enabling only monied teams to prosper. Memories of how the Yankees of the 1920s had benefited so grandly at the expense of impoverished Red Sox owner Harry Frazee undoubtedly influenced the commissioner.

While Billy Martin and George Steinbrenner roared in protest, the decision may have actually worked to their advantage. With the additions of Holtzman and Alexander, New York's need for Blue wasn't nearly as great as Boston's for Fingers to improve its meager bullpen. And Rudi, a clutch hitter and defensive standout, would have proved a tremendous asset in Fenway Park, a right-handed hitter's paradise.

The night of the trading frenzy, New York took off on a week-long winning streak against Minnesota, Chicago, and Cleveland that put eight games' distance between it and the second-place Tribe. Ed Figueroa extended the roll to seven with a 6–0 three-hitter against the Indians on June 21.

"From that winning streak we got a lot of confidence that we were for real," Figueroa reflects, "and we started playing like champions." Although in 1977 the Yankees clubhouse would become a magnet for strife among the game's most talented—and unhappiest—assemblage of athletes, in 1976 this team that had been patched together largely through trades melded as a unit, both on and off the field.

"I had more fun in one year with the Yankees than in all my years with the Pirates," says Dock Ellis. "There were no cliques. We played together, partied together, fought together. Everything."

Fran Healy attributes the camaraderie to "the newness of winning. It was all new and exciting to everybody on that ball club, even to George," says Healy. "People didn't get caught up in the stuff they ended up getting into."

IV

GERALD FORD'S REFUSAL to bail out financially ailing New York City in 1975 prompted the now legendary *Daily News* headline FORD TO CITY: DROP DEAD. Which in turn inspired an up-and-coming Long Island singer named Billy Joel to imagine, in his song "Miami 2017 (Seen the Lights Go Down on Broadway)," a future in which the bankrupt, abandoned metropolis's lights were extinguished forever and its assets either destroyed or transferred elsewhere—including the Bronx Bombers, shipped by carrier to Norfolk, Virginia. During that dismal summer, such a scenario did not seem altogether implausible.

Just a year later the city was undergoing a renaissance. As part of America's Bicentennial celebration, millions lined New York Harbor and the banks of the Palisades to watch an armada of tall sailing ships from around the world glide up the Hudson River. At night a mammoth fireworks display lit up the skies around the Statue of Liberty. The thirty-eighth president of the United States wisely chose to observe the afternoon ceremonies offshore, aboard the aircraft carrier *Forrestal*.

A week later the Democrats came to Madison Square Garden. As that party plotted to take back the White House with its ticket of former Georgia governor Jimmy Carter and Minnesota senator Walter Mondale, the 50–31, .617 Yankees were sending six delegates to Philadelphia for the All-Star Game: Catfish Hunter, Sparky Lyle, Chris Chambliss, Mickey Rivers, Thurman Munson, and Willie Randolph. Graig Nettles, the AL home-run king of 1976 (.254 BA, 32 HR, 93 RBI), deserved inclusion too, as did Ed Figueroa and Dock Ellis, each with ten wins at midseason.

On the weekend of July 23, New York put away Boston for good, taking three straight in the Bronx. The stumbling fifth-place Red Sox had changed managers only days before, but not their luck.

In the Friday-night opener, Doyle Alexander kept the crowd of

43,252 on its feet as he no-hit Don Zimmer's club through eight innings. Boston's Bill Lee, making his first start since damaging his shoulder in the May 20 brawl, had to come out after four, trailing 7–0. The tag team of Nettles and Rivers inflicted injury with their bats this time, each touching Lee for a home run.

In the ninth, shortstop Rick Burleson dumped Alexander's first pitch into right field. Two more hits fashioned Boston's only run of the game, a 9–1 Yankees rout. The twenty-five-year-old junkballer proved to be the surprise of the ten-man Baltimore deal. In his next two starts he again flirted with no-hitters past the fifth inning. Earlier, on June 24, he'd taken a perfect game into the eighth against Cleveland.

A fearsome competitor, Number 52 forced his catchers to change signals more times than a traffic light. Fran Healy caught Alexander's August 2 two-hit shutout of Detroit, in which the first twenty Tigers went down without a hit. "Doyle could have had Bill Dickey, Roy Campanella, and Yogi Berra on a conference call about what pitch to throw, and he would have shaken them off," Healy jokes. "Thurman didn't want to catch him because of that. I didn't care. Doyle could pitch." The right-hander put up a 10–5, 3.29 ERA for New York.

On Saturday, Fred Stanley stepped to the fore. The batting order's ninth man knocked home two runs in Ed Figueroa's 4–1 win. Friday night he'd collected three RBIs with a pair of singles. Stanley, then going on twenty-nine, calls 1976 "my most enjoyable season,"

He and Jim Mason (.180 BA, 1 HR, 14 RBI) started off platooning, but gradually Stanley began playing almost every day. The career .216 hitter got his average up to .275 by mid-August, eventually settling at .238 BA, 1 HR, 20 RBI. His .983 fielding percentage was the best among AL shortstops and set a club record.

Chris Chambliss starred in Sunday's finale, witnessed by 49,723. In the bottom of the ninth, the Yankees' cleanup man came up with two on, two out, and Boston ahead 5–3. Zimmer brought in southpaw Tom House.

The former Braves reliever, best remembered for having caught Hank Aaron's historic 715th home run in the Atlanta bullpen, served up a fastball, and Number 10 seared it into the right-field stands. Yankees 6, Boston 5. The fans, once indifferent to the quiet first baseman, chanted his name—"We want Chambliss!"—refusing to stop until he came back out of the clubhouse for a curtain call.

A moment of vindication? No, he says. "I didn't really look back on where I'd come from. I never was that way. I was real proud of what I was doing. I knew I could hit, and I guess the confidence was just building as I went along. But I didn't have the attitude that I had to prove to anybody I was a good player," says Chambliss, .293 BA, 17 HR, 96 RBI. "I felt like I was a good player before I came there."

Having effectively eliminated Boston, the Yankees flew to Baltimore all primed to do the same to Earl Weaver's Birds, then fourteen and a half games back, in second. The Orioles, however, had other ideas and swept the series by scores of 3–1, 4–1, and 4–3.

Game two turned into a beanball war between Dock Ellis and Jim Palmer. Ellis freely admits to being the instigator, explaining, "I was into drugs and alcohol then. Reggie Jackson said something to me from the dugout, and Thurman Munson came out to the mound and asked, 'What are you gonna do?' "

Ellis replied, "Just sit behind the plate and watch me."

"So I tried to kill him," he says matter-of-factly. "It was a dangerous point in my career."

His next time up, Jackson took a fastball in the face that shattered his glasses. Palmer sent a message to the Yankees by plunking Mickey Rivers on the shoulder. "The big joke," says Ellis, "is that I tried to kill Reggie and Palmer hit our guy with a change-up. So there was no real retaliation."

Two years before, umpires ejected Ellis from a game for intentionally hitting the first three Cincinnati Reds to face him: Pete Rose, Joe Morgan, and Dan Driessen. His brain amped on speed, Ellis had intended to send the entire lineup to the emergency room.

At the time of the December 1975 trade with Pittsburgh, many observers felt that New York was asking for trouble in landing the quirky, rebellious right-hander, who had caused a stir in 1973 by wearing pink hair curlers in the outfield. Much ado about nothing, insists Ellis.

"I forgot I had the curlers on, and I went onto the field before batting practice and leaned up against the outfield wall at Wrigley Field. That's when I realized I had them in my hair. By the time I got back to the dugout to take them out," he explains, "UPI and AP had shot pictures—*click, click, click!* So it went all over the country and all over the world. I had people sending me articles from Ireland and Israel for me to autograph and send back!"

Says Ellis, "In New York, I doubt very seriously if people would have even paid attention." But in a conservative, blue-collar city like Pittsburgh, oh, how they paid attention. Fran Healy, a Yankees announcer from 1978 to 1984, and since then the voice of the Mets on cable TV, recalls, "A few years back I was going to Three Rivers Stadium in a cab. I like to quiz the drivers about what's going on with the ball club, so I asked, 'How come the Pirates can't draw fans?' He said, 'I'll tell you what hurt this team: *It was when Dock Ellis showed up with curlers in his hair!*'

"It's a shame he's going to be remembered for hair curlers," Healy adds. "Dock was a battler, a good pitcher. Bringing him over turned out to be an excellent trade for the Yankees." A 17–8 record and 3.19 ERA won Ellis the Comeback Player of the Year Award over Lou Piniella. What's more, he evolved into a team leader, cajoling Mickey Rivers whenever the moody outfielder got into one of his funks.

By his own admission, Ellis floated through the season in a drug-induced haze. "I was usually down in the corner of the dugout, high, messing with the camera guy or something," he says. "I was in another world."

Certainly drugs are readily obtainable in any baseball city, but in the Big Apple, says Ellis, "Kids threw me drugs on the field, because they'd heard I was a head, a get-high, a doper. That was a big, beautiful playpen for me, New York. I had all the drugs I wanted."

Before starts, "I'd take fifteen Dexamyls [an amphetamine] just to get ready to start thinking about pitching. Then, after the game, I'd want to go do some cocaine, smoke some weed, and drink some Courvoisier. Because I loved the high. I loved the feeling." Ellis claims Yankees management knew of his habit—and that others on the club indulged in cocaine and marijuana too—but never intervened, even though his drug use was heavy enough for teammates to notice.

The fireworks predicted between him and Billy Martin never went off. In fact, the two got along famously. The manager merely demanded that Ellis tone down his inflammatory rhetoric to the media. "That was our agreement," says the pitcher. "I wouldn't get into any controversial issues and he'd keep the press off my back. They knew when I was loaded and knew how to rile me. A couple of times I got ready to go on a roll, and Billy would pass by and say, 'Leave him alone.' He'd wink at me and I'd follow right behind him. We had respect for each other."

Ellis's relationship with the front office was another matter. The next spring, he essentially talked his way out of pinstripes. A holdout, Number 36 made his dissatisfaction with New York's offer highly public. "I was pissed off," he says. "Gabe Paul was tight with the money, and I told him to kiss my ass."

It was a remark he *didn't* make, however, that got Ellis traded. When New York stumbled out of the gate in '77, its impatient owner began issuing threats. *What's he worried about?* the Yankees grumbled. *It's the second week of the season.* Graig Nettles quipped to a reporter, "The more we lose, the more Steinbrenner will fly in. And the more he flies, the better the chances of the plane crashing." The

Boss imputed the anonymous quote to Ellis, who swiftly went to Oakland for right-hander Mike Torrez. "Gabe Paul was the one behind it," he says. "I didn't talk to Steinbrenner again until 1980, when I was out of baseball. He told me, 'I know you didn't say what they said you did.' "

Ellis exited the game prematurely at age thirty-four, his skills dulled by years of abuse. "Toward the end, I had no desire to really compete," he concedes. "It was just something that I had to do because I'd signed a three-year contract. The drugs had taken me to a point where I lived to get high."

Fortunately, Ellis realized he needed help. "There's a little cliché," he says. "I got sick and tired of being sick and tired." He checked into an Arizona treatment facility and claims he has remained clean ever since. Ellis later became a substance-abuse counselor in Los Angeles, his home town, and consulted for the Yankees through 1990. He now works for a sports talent agency in Arizona.

V

THE SIX-FOOT-THREE right-hander might have won twenty in 1976 had he not slowed down during New York's 18–11 August, a month that saw the Yankees put on some offensive spectacles reminiscent of Ralph Houk's 1961 arsenal, baseball's most awesome strike force of all time.

On August 18, at Yankee Stadium, Texas jumped out to an early 5–0 lead against Ken Holtzman. Roy White got New York on the board in the third with his twelfth circuit clout, then doubled home Willie Randolph and Fred Stanley as part of a five-run fifth. Rangers catcher Jim Sundberg took Sparky Lyle over the wall in the eighth, however, tying the game at six each.

In the bottom of the ninth, White, batting left-handed this time, ripped a clothesline into the stands for an 8–6 victory. The thirty-two-year-old switch-hitter excelled in the number-two spot between Mickey Rivers and Thurman Munson, batting .286 BA, 14 HR, 65 RBI. He could still turn on the speed too. White stole 31 bases and scored a league-high 104 runs. "A great, fun season," he calls his twelfth campaign.

"All the guys would probably tell you that," says Chris Chambliss. Of New York's three consecutive pennant winners, he cites the 1976 team as his favorite for its multifaceted attack: .269 BA (tied for second in the league), 730 R (second), 120 HR (second), 163 SB (third). "We probably had more power when Reggie Jackson came to us," Chambliss notes, "but in '76 we could do a lot of things."

Late-inning eruptions came to be expected. Four days after beating Texas in the ninth, an anticipated Sunday-afternoon pitchers' duel between Catfish Hunter and California's Frank Tanana dissolved as the Angels built up an 8–0 lead. Just two outs away from defeat, the Bronx Bombers strung together seven hits and a walk:

Piniella, a single to right; Chambliss, a double to right-center; Nettles, a bloop single, 8–1; Velez, a walk; Healy, a single to center, 8–2; Randolph, a double to right, 8–4; pinch-hitter Carlos May, a bad-hop single through the right side, 8–6. Up stepped Wednesday night's hero, Roy White.

Number 6 tore reliever John Verhoeven's first offering into the right-center bleachers for runs seven and eight. In an uncharacteristic display of emotion, he jumped on home plate with both feet as 52,864 thundered their approval. That California went on to take back the contest 11–8 in overtime was almost irrelevant. "To come back against Tanana, this scary left-hander?" asks Chambliss. "That's unbelievable."

Just as unbelievable was Hunter's 14–12 record and 3.53 ERA three quarters through the season. When lifted in the seventh, boos filled the ballpark. Number 29 doffed his cap as he walked to the dugout. "I'd have booed myself," he says of his performance.

The crowd's reaction didn't upset him, but a pitchers' meeting that George Steinbrenner called the next day left Hunter feeling hurt and insulted. "I'm paying you guys too much money," Steinbrenner began, looking directly at his $3.75 million ace.

"I always tried to give one hundred percent out there," reflects Hunter, who missed only one start all year. "If he didn't feel like I was doing it, he could do whatever he wanted." In May, the Yankees owner had angered Hunter by criticizing him in the papers for filming a Red Man chewing-tobacco TV commercial at Yankee Stadium the day he was scheduled to pitch. The Orioles shelled him for six runs in six innings. Hunter seemed most annoyed that Steinbrenner hadn't confronted him directly. "Why doesn't he call me like a man?" the normally easygoing pitcher grumbled to reporters.

Hunter absorbed Steinbrenner's private scolding without a word, just as he'd kept silent about the adhesions in his aching right shoulder. He first felt it stiffen after going all the way in a dazzling eleven-inning 1–0 win over Boston on May 22—his first start, incidentally, after The Boss's public condemnation.

"It kind of locked up, so I couldn't throw," says Hunter, 17–15,

3.53 ERA for 1976. The following year he missed nearly half the season, splitting 18 decisions and averaging 4.72 runs per nine innings.

"I thought, *Heck, I've got to do something*," he recalls. "Besides just playing out my career, I wanted to be able to throw to my kids when they got older. In 1978 I told the doctor, 'You've got to cut on it. Do something.' And so they put me to sleep and manipulated my shoulder, bent my arm back. The doctor said it popped so loud, he was sure he broke it. Ever since then, my shoulder's never hurt.' "

Hunter rebounded dramatically that year (12–6, 3.58 ERA), then suffered through a horrendous 1979 (2–9, 5.31) before retiring at age thirty-three. Weary of the travel, the father of three had vowed to quit baseball once his five-year contract expired. Today he still attends Yankees training camp as a pitching instructor, but otherwise lists his occupation as a part-time farmer. He rents some of his acreage to a high-school friend, he explains, and "If he gets in a bind, I still help him plant and harvest the crops."

Whispers of "What's wrong with Catfish?" followed Hunter throughout 1976. It wasn't until the eve of the October play-offs that New York announced his condition. Did Steinbrenner ever apologize for insinuating he wasn't giving his all? "No," says Hunter, sounding amused rather than bitter, "he never did."

Number 29 could barely comb his hair without pain, yet he compiled 299 innings, after having amassed 328 frames the year before. "I can still pitch," he explained to Billy Martin, "but there's something wrong with my shoulder." The manager appeared to have heard only the first half of what Hunter said.

On August 27, four days after Steinbrenner took the pitchers to task, Hunter again took out his resentment on the opposition. He and Frank Tanana hooked up for thirteen scoreless innings at Anaheim Stadium. "I might not have been throwing as hard as I did before," he recalls, "but I had real good control, and that's what kept me in the game." Reliever Grant Jackson, 6–0, 1.69 ERA in twenty-one appearances for New York, got the win when the Yankees scored five times in the fifteenth.

With an outstanding bullpen of Jackson, Tidrow, and Lyle—and an eleven-and-a-half-game lead over Baltimore—many questioned the wisdom of letting Hunter stay in so long. But that had been Martin's pattern all year. From mid-May through mid-June, Catfish logged 82 innings while going 4–3:

May 9: eleven and two thirds innings against Oakland; loses 4–3 in bottom of the twelfth.

May 14: six frames; bows 6–2 to Baltimore.

May 18: nine innings in Cleveland, despite trailing 6–1 after eight. New York rallies for five runs in the ninth, then scores five more in the sixteenth to win 11–6.

May 22: eleven-inning shutout against Boston, 1–0.

May 26: complete-game 4–3 win over Oakland.

May 31: complete-game 8–3 victory at Fenway Park.

June 4: pitches nine innings of a 4–4 tie that Oakland wins 6–4 in the eleventh.

June 9: hurls 8⅓ innings to hang 4–3 loss on California.

June 13: goes the distance in a 7–1 loss to Texas.

Hunter didn't complain then of feeling overworked, nor does he now. "I'd pitch twenty innings if they'd ask me to," he says. "I would never be a guy to say 'Take me out.'" While it isn't his nature to accuse Martin of exhausting an arm that had already racked up plenty of mileage, that was the opinion circulating among the Yankees. "There was a lot of talk in the clubhouse that Billy wore out Catfish," says Fran Healy. "He had a history of doing that."

Indeed, Martin's sixteen years show an inclination to sacrifice his pitchers' futures for the present. In 1980, his first year managing the A's, Oakland's young starting fivesome of Rick Langford, Mike Norris, Matt Keough, Steve McCatty, and Brian Kingman averaged over 250 innings apiece while totaling 79 wins; in strike-shortened 1981, over 159 innings each.

But in 1982, Martin's last season there, the quintet, en masse, was troubled by sore arms and fell from a combined 51–38 (.573) to 39–60 (.394). Two years later, only McCatty and Langford remained in the majors.

Martin's recklessness can be attributed to his abbreviated stays in most cities, none longer than the three full seasons he spent in Oakland. Since clashes between the pugnacious manager and the front office were inevitable, why not gun the engine and leave the repairs for your successor?

Martin, the product of an impoverished childhood in Berkeley, California, had the insecurity of many from the Depression era: *it can all be taken away.* Even as the Yankees waltzed to the division title, he feared he might lose the job he'd always coveted—especially when California fired Dick Williams in late July. After New York returned home from a 1–6 road trip on August 2, Williams joined Steinbrenner in his personal box behind the home dugout the next two nights, fueling Martin's paranoia.

Nineteen seventy-six's AL Manager of the Year was livid and embarrassed that his return should even be in question. "Billy was managing great," Dick Tidrow observes. Number 1 also bitterly resented the owner's interference.

Steinbrenner followed the example of his strong-willed, perfectionist father. Teenage George once lost a race at a school track meet. Henry Steinbrenner hurried down from the bleachers and demanded, "What the hell happened? How'd you let that guy beat you?" Similarly, after tough defeats, The Boss used to phone Martin's office or hotel room and grill him. *How could you let Mason hit for himself? Why'd you bring in Jackson and not Lyle?* He also thought nothing of questioning—or proposing—tactics in the middle of a game.

"George was always calling the dugout," says Ed Figueroa. "He wanted to tell Billy what to do. But Billy always said that he's the manager and he's going to do whatever he wants." One time the ringing phone so infuriated Martin, "He tore it out of the wall and fired it down," says Fran Healy. "It was comical." The Boss, undaunted, rang for him in the trainer's office instead.

Was he calling to discuss strategy, or had he spotted a Yankee in need of a trim? Steinbrenner revived his short-hair edict in spring training, an especially distressing development for newcomer Oscar Gamble. The valuable left-handed power hitter (.232 BA, 17 HR, 57 RBI in 340 AB) had to submit his shrublike Afro to a pair of scissors. Martin, an observant manager, sometimes had to break his intense concentration to field calls from the owner ordering him to tell so-and-so to see a barber or to tell so-and-so to put his cap back on.

"I remember we had a Sunday game in New York, and I asked Billy, 'Can I stay in the bullpen and take in a little sun?' " says Figueroa, the Yankees' top starter in 1976 (19–10, 3.02 ERA). "It was an off-day for me, so he told me to go ahead.

"I don't know how George found out—maybe somebody told him, or he had binoculars—but in the third inning he called Billy and told him to tell me I have to move back to the dugout. They had an argument. Billy asked him, 'Why? He won last night. Why not?' " Martin lost. "I had to run all the way from the bullpen in center field to the dugout in the middle of the game.

"A lot of things like that happened," the pitcher says with a sardonic chuckle. "Things that don't bother nobody, only George. It bothered us, because we are grown-up guys. We know what we have to do. He was like a father looking after his kids, to see if they were doing the right thing."

The Yankees could abide these relatively minor infringements of their personal freedom. But Steinbrenner overstepped his bounds by hiring private investigators to monitor his flock. "George had detectives after the players," says Sandy Alomar, "just to see what they were doing, whether they were behaving."

When the Yankees' rough patch extended to 4–11 through August 9, Martin showed signs of panicking. "Because Steinbrenner was beating on him," explains Dock Ellis, "Billy wanted us to pitch on three days' rest instead of four. I told him, 'I've never done that and never will.' The pitchers, we all looked at Catfish," who nodded they should comply. "Then we said, 'Okay, we'll do it.' "

Although 1976 was an oasis of calm compared to subsequent seasons in the Bronx, Martin's health suffered. He shed twenty pounds from an already thin frame, making him appear tired and drawn. The stress of managing also increased his alcohol intake, which in later years contributed to five firings at Steinbrenner's hands.

The Yankees began to feel the brunt of Martin's frustrations over his stalled contract talks. Sparky Lyle, 7–8, with a 2.26 ERA and a league-high 23 saves, appeared in more than half of New York's first 120 games. After California roughed him up on August 22, the game featuring the Bombers' eight-run, ninth-inning outburst, Martin sat down Number 28 down without explanation. Lyle pitched just once in the next eighteen games, despite repeated assurances from the manager that he would use him soon.

Following an 8–0 shutout of Milwaukee on September 8, the reliever made his unhappiness known to reporters. "Whatever he says to you, you can count on it being the exact opposite," he said, adding, "I liked him until I saw some of the stuff that was going on."

By that Lyle meant the deceit and divisiveness that later came to characterize Martin's clubhouse. "Billy tended to lie to people a lot about their position on the team," sportswriter Maury Allen observes. "He was a guy who played favorites and often would use one player against another. He spread a lot of venom in the clubhouse. The 1976 season was no different than any other. They just had great talent."

Newsday's Steve Jacobson flatly labels Martin a pathological liar. "You could not believe him about anything," he says. "Goodness, he was a wonderful storyteller on occasion. He would tell you about his grandmother going from San Francisco to Oakland on a raft with her household possessions because they didn't have a bridge in those days.

"But there were things Billy just couldn't bring himself to tell the truth about. He didn't *know* what was true. I talked to Phil Rizzuto once. He said he used to sit down next to Billy on the plane. Billy would be raving about things, and Rizzuto would be saying, 'Billy, *it didn't happen that way.*' "

The front office kept Martin squirming until mid-September, then

finally rewarded him with a $300,000 three-year pact and the praise
Number 1 had sought all year. George Steinbrenner could be capable
of great generosity. On September 25, he hosted a dinner party for
his team at Detroit's Caucus Club. Midway through, word arrived that
second-place Baltimore had just bowed to Boston 1–0, clinching for
New York its first title since 1964.

Champagne flowed, and Yankees shouted and hugged one another.
"A helluva party," Lou Piniella calls the celebration. "It was the first
time that any of us had experienced winning, and it was a great
feeling."

VI

BAD BLOOD BOILED between the Yankees and their play-off opponents, Kansas City. Batting titlist George Brett resented Billy Martin's
shabby treatment of his older brother, pitcher Ken Brett, early in the
year. The Western Division champs also rallied behind Larry Gura,
whose own problems with Martin were well documented.

Gura, disabled much of the summer by a groin-muscle pull, returned in September to lift the flagging Royals as much as anyone.
Down the stretch he won twice in relief, then shut out Oakland in
only his second start all year. Skipper Whitey Herzog tapped the quiet
lefty to start the October 9 opener at Royals Stadium, trusting that
Gura's determination to prove himself to his ex-manager might provide
a psychological edge. "I wanted to throw a perfect game," Gura recalls.

He was far from perfect, allowing twelve hits, but kept the ball
game against Catfish Hunter close: 2–1 through eight. In the ninth, a
Roy White double bought two insurance runs. Hunter didn't need
them. He spotted his pitches skillfully, walking none and limiting
Kansas City to five hits in a tidy 4–1 victory.

The next night Ed Figueroa, 1–6 lifetime against the Royals, took
the hill. "Even when I pitch good to them, the bullpen blow the game,
and I always lose," he says. Figueroa came out in the sixth trailing
4–3, and, sure enough, Dick Tidrow let the game slip out of reach.
The Royals piled on three more runs in the eighth, and the series
moved to New York tied at 1–1.

As Dock Ellis relaxed in the clubhouse TV room, preparing to go
up against left-hander Andy Hassler, a nervous George Steinbrenner
barreled inside. "Dock! Dock!" he repeated. "We've gotta have this
game. We've *got* to have this game."

In a paternal voice, Ellis told him, "George, I'm in here trying to get ready to pitch." He glanced at The Boss's stylish suit and cracked, "I've got to win the game if I want to wear suits like *you* got on there."

Steinbrenner brightened. "You win the game," he promised, "and I'll get you three suits! I'll get you three suits just like this!"

"Not just a suit for me," replied Ellis, "suits for everybody."

Two outs into the game and the Yankees were already bloodied, 3–0. For the first three innings, says Ellis, his middle finger twitched mysteriously, making it hard to grip the ball. "I didn't know what was going on," he says. "It could have been because of the fact that I was full of drugs. But I think it was a nerve, because my fingers still spasm."

He settled down, though, and muzzled the Royals the rest of the way. Chris Chambliss scorched a two-run homer in the fourth. And then, as Herzog carted in no fewer than four relievers, New York assembled a three-run sixth, capped by forgotten man Elliott Maddox's RBI double. A scoreless ninth from Sparky Lyle locked up the 5–3 win.

Directly after the game, Ellis flew off to attend the funeral of former Pirates pitching mate Bob Moose, who had died several days earlier in a car accident. When he returned the following day, a smiling Mickey Rivers ambled up to him in the clubhouse.

"Thanks for that suit, man!"

"Man, what you talking about?"

Ellis recalls, "George had put three-hundred-dollar gift certificates from Barney's in everyone's locker."

Hoping to wrap up the best-of-five series in four, Martin brought back Catfish Hunter on three days' rest. The Royals jumped on him for three runs in the second; two more tallies in the fourth sent Number 29 to the showers. The Yankees manager drew scathing criticism from the press for taxing Catfish's shoulder when he had Ken Holtzman ready. Following the 7–4 loss, Hunter himself commented that with a 2–1 edge, he'd assumed the Yankees would use the six-foot-two left-hander, winner of 19, 21, 19, and 18 games the last four seasons with the Oakland A's and an author of two no-hitters for the Chicago Cubs.

Holtzman, thirty, had tapered off to 14–11 in 1976 (9–7, 4.17 ERA as a Yankee). But he was a veteran of four consecutive AL championship series and was certainly well rested, having last pitched on the season's next-to-last day, a 4–3 win over Cleveland.

Yet Number 53 sat, not only through the play-offs, but the World Series as well. "I wish *I* had Holtzman," Whitey Herzog remarked before game five. "I'd sure use him." A host of managers would gladly have given him the ball every fourth day as he wished. Bizarrely, beginning the next spring, Martin stashed Holtzman in the bullpen, where he wasted away while collecting $165,000 annually. The pitcher the Yankees had hustled to sign to a five-year deal through 1980 started only fourteen games in 1977 and 1978 before returning to the Cubs that June in exchange for minor-league reliever Ron Davis.

"That was a tragedy," says Fran Healy. "Kenny Holtzman could still pitch. But for some reason, Billy didn't want to use him. This guy was the consummate professional. I caught him in a couple of ball games, and he still threw very well."

Theories are plentiful as to why Martin kept Holtzman in solitary confinement. Some say he disapproved of Gabe Paul's ten-man trade with Baltimore and spitefully wanted to ensure its failure. "If Billy wasn't involved in a trade," says sportswriter Phil Pepe, "the trade was no good.

"Also, Holtzman had something of a superior attitude, like he was better than most of the other players. He was a bit of an intellectual, not a typical jock and beer drinker." That Martin sneeringly referred to Holtzman on occasion as "The Jew" indicates that his feelings toward the pitcher went beyond a mere personality conflict. Then there were differences over pitching philosophy. "They wanted him to be a curveball pitcher instead of a fastball pitcher," explains Catfish Hunter. "And Holtzman was a fastball pitcher all the way."

Things reached a head during a game against Detroit in July 1977. "In the first inning," says catcher Fran Healy, "the Tigers were breaking bats all over the place, but balls were falling into the outfield, and they scored three runs. Instead of taking into account that these guys were getting jammed and Holtzman was making good pitches, Billy went out to the mound the next inning and said, 'I want you to throw curveballs every pitch from here on out,' because Billy liked the breaking ball. Thurman once told him, 'The reason you like the breaking ball is you couldn't hit it!'

"When Holtzman did get out of the inning, he told Billy, 'I'm leaving,' went into the clubhouse, and left.

"He had some real good years left," Healy continues, "and I think he just said the hell with this. I think not pitching might have played with his confidence, too. Kenny could have won a lot of games for that ball club." Two years of inactivity, however, all but ruined Holtzman. He retired following the 1979 season, at age thirty-four.

By bypassing Holtzman in favor of Hunter in game four, Martin left the Yankees without their ace for Thursday night's fifth and deciding contest. Rather than use Holtzman or Doyle Alexander, another fresh arm, he went with Figueroa—now 1–7 lifetime against Kansas City— also on three days' rest. "My arm was getting tired," admits the right-hander, who racked up 257 innings that year.

Figueroa turned twenty-eight on game day, October 14. It was a nip-and-tuck battle from the start. Royals first baseman John Mayberry jolted a two-run homer in the top of the first. But the Yankees quickly countered in their half. Mickey Rivers, a disappointing 4-for-18 thus far in the series, had received a private pep talk from George Steinbrenner the night before. He drilled a leadoff triple to left, then raced home on Roy White's infield single. White promptly swiped second and advanced to third on the first of Thurman Munson's three hits. Whitey Herzog wasted no time in going to his bullpen. Chris Chambliss greeted Paul Splittorff with a game-tying sacrifice fly.

The Royals forged a run in the second; the Yankees struck for two in the fourth. Rivers, 4-for-5 on the night, laced a single. The threat of Number 17 taking off so unnerved Splittorff that he walked White on five pitches. Both runners scored: one on a Munson single, the other on a grounder off Chambliss's bat.

The top four of the batting order collected all eleven Yankees hits that day. In the sixth they again combined for a pair of tallies: Rivers reached safely on a bunt; White sacrificed him to second; Munson followed with an RBI single. The catcher alertly tried to take an extra base, but a strong throw cut him down in the dirt.

Given the high stakes, some managers would have adopted a more conservative game plan, but not the unpredictable Billy Martin. Chambliss singled to keep the inning alive. Though the big man had stolen only one base all season, Martin sent him. For the second time in the play-offs, Number 10 slid into second ahead of the throw. The gamble paid off when third baseman Brett threw away Carlos May's rudimentary grounder. Chambliss loped across the plate for a 6–3 Yankees lead.

New York fans began their countdown to the pennant—nine outs, eight outs, seven—but encountered a setback at six.

Al Cowens singled to lead off the eighth. Out came Martin, signaling to the pen.

"Give me another hitter," pleaded Figueroa.

"No," the manager said firmly. "We're gonna bring in Grant Jackson. You pitched good." Figueroa jogged into the dugout serenaded by chants of "Ed-die! Ed-die! Ed-die!"

"When I left the game," he remembers, "I said, 'Well, that's a big gift I'm getting today for my birthday.'" Jackson sent it right back.

Jim Wohlford pinch-hit a single. Brett then stunned the sellout crowd of 56,821 into silence. Jackson, who'd allowed only one home run in fifty-eight and two thirds innings for the Yankees, dished up a pitch that the Royals' third baseman wrapped around the right-field foul pole. As he watched Brett chug around the bases with the tying run, "I got sick to my stomach," says Fred Stanley, 5-for-15 in the series.

Figueroa, icing his arm in the trainer's room, blew a circuit. "I was so mad," he recalls, "I grabbed my bucket of ice and threw it all over the place."

Jackson escaped the inning without further damage. Dick Tidrow then contained the Royals during a heart-stopping ninth. "I got the first two outs," he recalls, "but I threw a fastball down the middle, and Buck Martinez singled to center." Facing Cowens, a right-handed hitter capable of driving the ball to the opposite field, Tidrow tried working the inside of the plate. He pitched too carefully and ended up walking him. As Wohlford stepped into the batter's box, the sight of Brett in the on-deck circle sent tremors through the crowd.

Wohlford bounced a high chopper to Graig Nettles. First base was the easier play, but Number 9 whipped the ball to Willie Randolph, nipping the speedy Cowens in a photo finish.

Leading off for New York: Chris Chambliss. "He's gonna hit it out," Sandy Alomar predicted to batboy Joe D'Ambrosio. "He's got to hit one out, because if he doesn't do it, *I'm* on deck." Alomar, a .239 hitter in 1976, then pointed to his beloved, ancient mitt, lying on the bench. "My glove," he told the batboy. "Make sure you get my glove."

The crowd, which had behaved itself up to now, hurled bottles, beer cans, firecrackers, and toilet-paper rolls onto the field, forcing the umpires to call time. While the grounds crew cleared the debris from the outfield, Chambliss waited by the bat rack, annoyed at the delay. "I was a little anxious," he says. "It was cold too. That was a trying little time there."

Even more so for Royals reliever Mark Littell, 8–4, 16 SV, 2.04 ERA on the season. "That hurt Mark," says Larry Gura. "He was in a rhythm, and then that caused him to have to wait." The twenty-three-year-old righty possessed a live fastball and a wicked slider. "Maybe the delay changed his decision on the pitch he was going to throw," Gura suggests.

"Play ball!" shouted home-plate umpire Art Frantz.

Chambliss, 10-for-20 with 7 RBIs in the play-offs, took several tentative practice swings, then settled into his stance and narrowed his eyes. "I knew Littell was going to throw a fastball," he says. The crowd fell silent, drawing in its collective breath until there seemed to be no oxygen left in Yankee Stadium.

Littell, gaze fixed on the catcher, nodded at the sign, rocked his arms back and forth, cocked his right arm, and delivered a high inside fastball toward the small target some sixty feet away. Chambliss reared back, then stepped into the pitch, whipping the bat around in a smooth arc. The big electric clock in right field glowed 11:13.

Thurman Munson, perched on the dugout steps in his catcher's gear, didn't bother tracking the ball. From the resounding *crack!* he knew it was destined for the right-field seats and bounded out onto the field as if wearing springs, pumping both fists. Chambliss, though, wasn't sure. The white sphere sailed high and deep through the misty air.

"The whole stadium was pushing the ball out of the park," says Joe D'Ambrosio.

Right fielder Hal McRae leaped, waved his glove, and watched his team's dreams disappear on the other side of the wall. New York 7, Kansas City 6. The Yankees had won the pennant.

But not until Chambliss reached home plate, a task suddenly made as difficult as crossing Lenox Avenue at rush hour. Bedlam erupted. Before Number 10 broke into his home-run trot, fans came soaring over the tops of both dugouts, vaulted the walls, and swarmed onto the field. "We were outnumbered in about five seconds," says Tidrow.

D'Ambrosio ripped open his jersey and began stuffing players' gloves inside. He turned to grab Alomar's but someone had already made off with it. "Sandy was so hurt," he recalls.

By the time Chambliss got to second base, the bag was in the grasp of a celebrant. Chambliss gamely stabbed at it with his hand. Zigzagging to third, he fell, regained his footing, and resumed his perilous trip around the diamond. "I was worried about getting trampled," he recalls. "From that point on, I wasn't even worried about touching bases anymore."

He circled wide around third, then made a beeline for the dugout, slamming into one poor fellow just before making it inside. "I gave him a pretty good forearm," Chambliss says, laughing.

Roy White was still out on the field, where fans had taken up the chant "We're Number One!" "They picked me up on their shoulders and started carrying me around," he recalls. "It got kinda scary then. I thought I'd better get the hell out of there, because it was pandemonium." When the fans let him down, "I just bolted for the clubhouse."

For White, who witnessed the Yankees' collapse firsthand as a twenty-one-year-old rookie in 1965, the moment had special meaning. "When that ball went out of the park, I thought, *That just culminated ten years of frustration, of not getting that brass ring, of not having that pennant*," he says.

White, a Yankees coach and member of the front office in the mid-1980s, now works with youngsters and runs baseball camps. "We had some years there where the Yankees were kind of a laughingstock," he reflects. "So I think maybe I appreciated it a lot more than the guys who came along later and didn't have to go through the suffering that I did."

The Kansas City players listened in silence to the commotion outside. "It was depressing," says Larry Gura. "That series could have gone either way. Nobody said a word. We just sat." By contrast, the Yankees locker room resembled Times Square on New Year's Eve.

"People were crying," says Ed Figueroa. "People were kissing each other. Unbelievable." Mayor Abe Beame, actor Cary Grant, George Steinbrenner, and Gabe Paul all milled around the locker room. "I was up to the sky," says Paul. "I was very high." He had every right to be. The game's heroes—Chambliss, winning pitcher Tidrow, starter Figueroa, Rivers—all came to New York in his trades.

Amid the celebration, Graig Nettles cornered Chambliss, who was still gasping for breath. "Did you touch the plate?" he asked. Couldn't find it, the first baseman replied. "And it wasn't there, anyway," he says. Umpire Art Frantz was waiting on the field for him to make the home run official.

"I was trying to be unassuming, because there was still a mob of people out there," says Chambliss, today a coach for the St. Louis Cardinals. "So I put a jacket over my pinstriped jersey. I held on to two cops by the arm and we walked through the crowd and touched the area where home plate had been."

The New York Yankees' twelve-year odyssey was over.

A Lot of Guys Got Old at Once (Again)

BEFORE THEIR CHAMPAGNE-SOAKED uniforms had even dried, the Yankees were flying to Cincinnati the next morning for an abbreviated workout in a cold drizzle at Riverfront Stadium. Twenty-four hours later the World Series was underway.

The Reds, the previous year's World Champions, had swept Philadelphia in three, and so Sparky Anderson's squad was well rested, its starting rotation in order. Billy Martin had to open with Doyle Alexander, who hadn't pitched in three weeks. The Big Red Machine rolled over the dazed Yankees in four straight: 5–1, 4–3, 6–2, and 7–2.

"We never really came down from winning that play-off," admits Roy White. "We didn't have a chance to gather ourselves and say, 'Okay, let's get ready for the World Series.' The next thing you knew, it was over."

"For our club," Dick Tidrow observes, "the play-offs *were* our World Series that year."

Nonetheless, the Yankees believed they'd be back, and that a genuine dynasty was rising in the Bronx. "I thought so," says White. "I felt we had a good, solid nucleus. There was no doubt that we were going to be a force in the league."

Especially once the club further strengthened itself by dipping into baseball's first free-agent pool. On November 18, the Yankees partly avenged their World Series defeat and snagged Cincinnati's top pitcher, southpaw Don Gullet, for $2 million. In seven seasons, the twenty-five-year-old prodigy had compiled an extraordinary 91–44, .674 record. "I thought Gullet was going to make our pitching staff unbeatable," says Tidrow, today a Yankees scout.

Two weeks later, New York waved $2.93 million of George Steinbrenner's money at Reggie Jackson, the 1973 AL MVP. The same day, the front office announced its purchase of veteran outfielder Jimmy Wynn from Atlanta for a mere pittance: $250,000.

The three transactions were to exemplify the advantages and drawbacks of free agency and freewheeling spending, which hasn't had nearly the cataclysmic effect on the game that owners initially feared. The deals' ratio of successes to failures is fairly representative of what has transpired in the years since.

Gullet's 14–4 mark in 1977 raised his career winning percentage, the best of the decade, but a torn rotator cuff limited him to eight games the following season. He never pitched again after July 10, 1978. New York's return on its $2 million investment: a total of 30 starts and 203 innings.

Wynn, a once formidable player known as "The Toy Cannon," misfired in pinstripes, batting .143 in thirty games before receiving his release at midseason.

Jackson, thirty, powdered home runs as expected: 144 in five seasons. His left-handed bat also freed Gabe Paul to trade Oscar Gamble to the White Sox for all-star shortstop Bucky Dent, the finishing piece in the Yankees' pennant puzzle. But no one had anticipated the disruptive effect Jackson's disproportionately huge ego and salary would have on the team's chemistry.

Whining and grousing permeated the Yankees' 1977 spring camp. Thurman Munson demanded management upgrade his contract to fulfill George Steinbrenner's promise that he would always be the team's highest-paid player other than Catfish Hunter. Graig Nettles jumped the club briefly in protest over *his* wages. And both Sparky Lyle and Mickey Rivers screamed to be traded.

Jackson inflamed the situation by declaring haughtily at his introductory press conference, "I didn't come to New York to become a star. I brought my star with me." Any chance of finding acceptance among his new teammates was dashed that May when *Sport* magazine published an article in which Jackson defamed Munson, earning him a deep-seated animosity that took a good season or two to fade. Strain gripped the clubhouse, as players sniped at one another anonymously in the papers—and occasionally face to face.

From the outset, probably no one resented Jackson more than Billy Martin. Jackson found himself a pawn in the stormy marriage between Martin and Steinbrenner, the Liz and Dick of professional sports. The manager regarded Jackson as an unwelcome intruder foisted upon him by the owner and seemed bent on embarrassing him, batting the two-time home-run king as low as seventh.

The tension between them erupted on national television one Saturday in June when the two nearly came to blows in the visitors' dugout at Fenway Park after Martin had angrily called in Number 44 from right field for playing a bloop hit too casually for his taste. Coach Elston Howard had to separate them as cameras recorded the ugly affair: Martin jawing and pointing, and Jackson holding out his arms, as if to say "What did I do?"

Steinbrenner very nearly fired Martin then, and again a month later. His enthusiasm over an employee can chill quicker than a youngster's interest in a Christmas toy. "When the Yankees lost the World Series to Cincinnati," sportswriter Phil Pepe says, "George was really pissed and started questioning some of Martin's moves." A clubhouse confrontation in Florida set the tone for the next dozen years, with Steinbrenner threatening, "I ought to get rid of you!" and Martin shouting back, "Why don't you fire me right now?"

Despite these incessant distractions, the 1977 Bronx Bombers won 100 games, fending off Baltimore and Boston for the division title. In the play-offs they overcame a 2–1 deficit to stun Kansas City a second time, then handily beat Los Angeles four games to two in the World Series.

"We didn't particularly get along too well," understates Fred Stanley, now the director of player development for the Milwaukee Brewers. "But you don't have to be such buddy-buddies to the point where you're a big family. We didn't have that. We had twenty-five guys who knew how to play and knew how to beat somebody."

Bedeviled by injuries, the Yankees fussed and feuded again in 1978, yet Steinbrenner professed little concern. "A ship that sails on a calm sea gets nowhere," he declared. The Boss didn't appreciate how the increasingly unstable atmosphere ate away at a player like Thurman Munson, now more determined than ever to escape to Cleveland.

Shortly before his death, the Yankees captain reminisced wistfully with Fritz Peterson, then retired from the game and living near Chicago. "He said, 'You know, I'd give up all this to go back to the old days, when it was fun,' " Peterson recalls. "To him the old days were '70, '71, '72. Thurman loved those days."

Martin, as addicted to conflict and melodrama as Steinbrenner, kept reigniting the fuse that seemed to hiss perpetually in the New York locker room. "I respected Billy and thought he was an outstanding manager," Lou Piniella says. "But there were some headaches that he created that weren't needed." It didn't help that the manager's drinking was out of control.

"When Billy got drunk," says Maury Allen of the *New York Post*, "incredible things would come out of his mouth. Racial things, anti-Semitic things. He was simply a drunk. That's all there was to it." In Chicago in July 1978, Martin had late-night cocktails with White Sox owner Bill Veeck, who revealed that weeks before, he and Steinbrenner had discussed switching managers: Martin for Bob Lemon, who had served as New York's pitching coach the year before. The idea was league president Lee MacPhail's.

"Steinbrenner was mad at Billy, the White Sox were having trouble, and it looked like it could have been a very good deal for both teams," McPhail explains. "But the Yankees won a few ball games, and George backed away from it."

Martin did not react kindly to the news. At O'Hare Airport the following night, preparing to fly on to Kansas City, he launched into a tirade against Steinbrenner and Jackson in the presence of two reporters.

"One's a liar, the other's convicted," he muttered. The quote was splashed all over the morning papers, leading to his tearful resignation that afternoon. Lemon, whom Veeck let go shortly after the proposed managerial swap collapsed, took over a team eleven and a half games down in the standings. That Steinbrenner went and rehired Martin for 1980 just days later should have been fair warning of the pathological behavior going on at Yankee Stadium.

Under Lemon's calm hand, the 1978 Yankees pulled off one of the most miraculous recoveries in sports history, culminating in a dramatic 5–4 divisional play-off game at Fenway Park. From there the Bombers again dropped the Royals and the Dodgers for their first back-to-back flags since 1961 and 1962. In Steinbrenner's mind, his recipe for winning—talent and turbulence—had once again paid off.

For 1979 the Yankees added free agents Tommy John and Luis Tiant to twenty-game winners Ron Guidry and Ed Figueroa. The procession of superstars eager to play in the Bronx seemed unending. New York had the personnel to repeat, but no longer the fortitude. When the new season brought yet more upheaval—locker-room horseplay that disabled star reliever Goose Gossage in April; Lemon's firing in June; Munson's plane crash in August—the team could no longer revive itself. With Billy Martin back at the wheel, New York stumbled home in fourth, dispirited and dismantled.

Sparky Lyle now pitched for Texas, traded there the previous winter. Mickey Rivers joined him in August, in a deal that sent Oscar Gamble back to New York. During the off-season, the Yankees traded Chris Chambliss, still productive at thirty, to Toronto. Roy White got his walking papers and played two years in Japan, where his company-man sensibility fit in well.

Dick Tidrow left town on Steinbrenner's orders in May after the Yankees owner watched the Tigers shell him for three runs in one and two thirds innings. "Get rid of him," he told Yankees president Al Rosen, who complied. Tidrow won 11 of 16 decisions for the Chicago Cubs in 1979 and topped the National League in appearances the following year. Ray Burris, the pitcher New York received in return, went 1–3 and was sold to the Mets in August. By then Rosen had quit.

Gabe Paul would have prevented Steinbrenner from acting on impulse like that. In 1977, The Boss had wanted to close the deal for Bucky Dent by throwing in Guidry, about whom he'd once sneered, "He'll never be more than a triple-A pitcher." Paul, recognizing Guidry's potential, put his foot down, and minor-leaguer Bob Polinksy went to the White Sox instead. Guidry won 16 games for New York that year and the Cy Young Award the next with a sparkling 25–3, 1.74 ERA season.

But the man who'd sculpted the Yankees dynasty was no longer around to protect Steinbrenner from his own self-destructive impetuousness, having returned to Cleveland as president and general manager in December 1977. "I was thinking of retiring," he says. "But I was a great friend of Steve O'Neill's"—one of the Yankees' limited partners—"and he said he wouldn't take over the Indians if I didn't go with him. That's the only reason I went. I don't know what I would have done otherwise, but I certainly would have left the Yankees."

The arrival of free agency has distorted Paul's legacy, leaving the impression that he and Steinbrenner simply plucked players from a display case and dashed off checks. "What really built the ball club was good solid trading by Gabe," praises Lou Piniella, himself a Yankees general manager the first half of 1988. "It wasn't really free agency.

"Here's a club that went out and traded for a whole infield: Nettles, Dent, Randolph, Chambliss. They had their catcher in Munson, they had Roy White, and they traded for me and Rivers. Almost the whole club was trades, even the pitching. You look back at it and you marvel.

Some pretty good ideas reshaped that ball club," Piniella adds, "and Gabe Paul should get the credit for it."

To hear Steinbrenner tell it on occasion, *he* was the brains behind the Yankees' return to glory. "I made all those trades," he once said. Paul responds generously, "Who cares who gets credit? The big thing is what happened." Retired since 1987, he resides in Tampa, Florida, the corporate headquarters of the American Ship Building Company.

"I see George every now and then," Paul says. "We're good friends. I don't get in his hair," he adds, chuckling, "but we have a good relationship. We got along all right."

Steinbrenner is the archetypal modern millionaire: a high-profile personality as obsessed with publicity as profit. Ironically, his antics over the years have overshadowed his role in the Yankees' late 1970s rise. At first the club's principal owner conducted himself like the savvy executive who'd salvaged his father's carrier fleet and multiplied American Ship's revenues in the 1960s. He hired top-notch people, relied on their baseball expertise, and didn't shy away from taking out his bankroll.

"You've got to give him credit," says Piniella. "He took over a floundering franchise and within four years this club was back on top. He energized the team. He wouldn't take no for an answer as far as winning was concerned. Hell yes, he deserves a lot of credit.

"Over a period of eight or nine years"—beginning in 1974—"the Yankees put as good a product on the field as you could have in baseball. Then mistakes started coming into the equation," says Piniella, "and the team started going backward. Success probably spoiled George a little bit."

A division title and an American League flag at the start of the 1980s were largely illusory. The 1980 roster, though it lacked depth in the starting rotation and outfield, nevertheless won 103 games. Freshman manager Dick Howser received standout seasons from Reggie Jackson, Tommy John, Willie Randolph, and new catcher Rick Cerone, and could rely on an exceptional bullpen of Gossage, Ron Davis, and free-agent pickup Rudy May, not to mention a veteran bench (Oscar Gamble, Jim Spencer, Eric Soderholm, and returnee Bobby Murcer) that accounted for 51 home runs.

The addition of two San Diego Padres outfielders, superstar free-agent Dave Winfield and fleet-footed Jerry Mumphrey, couldn't compensate for deficiencies all over the diamond in 1981. Except for Winfield (.294) and Mumphrey (.307), no Yankees starter hit above .244. Overall, New York finished third, two games behind Milwaukee. But a two-month players' strike forced the season to be played in two halves, with an additional five-game play-off to determine the divisional winners. The Yankees, riding atop the AL East the day the national pastime suspended operation in June, slogged through the second half 25–26, already assured of a play-off berth.

Manager Gene Michael, like Howser before him, lost his job for standing up to the increasingly meddlesome and abusive Yankees owner. With Bob Lemon back on board in September, the Yankees fought off Milwaukee, three games to two, swept Billy Martin's Oakland A's in the league championship series, and appeared on the verge of capturing their twenty-third World Series, pinning losses on Tommy Lasorda's Dodgers in games one and two.

But New York's six-year dynasty came to an abrupt end in Los Angeles. The Dodgers scratched out three straight one-run victories, then crushed the Yankees 9–2 at The House That Ruth Built while their owner fumed. Graciousness and good sportsmanship were never Steinbrenner hallmarks. Afterward he issued an apology to all New Yorkers for his club's dismal showing. Like so many of The Boss's self-serving public-relations schemes, this one backfired, eliciting sympathy for the ballplayers and solidifying his growing image as the Simon Legree of baseball.

"And then," says Lou Piniella, sounding a refrain reminiscent of 1964, "the team got old."

When the Yankees went to refurbish themselves in the off-season, they discovered that top free agents were no longer queuing up in droves for a chance at the Steinbrenner sweepstakes. Cleveland pitcher John Denny chose to re-sign with the Indians—*the Indians! for less money!*—rather than perform under the big tent in the Bronx. "I didn't want to subject myself to how he runs the ball club," Denny sniffed.

The best the Yankees could do was to overpay grievously for a capable Cincinnati Reds outfielder named Dave Collins. Having let Reggie Jackson go to the California Angels, a move Steinbrenner would publicly admit regretting, the Yankees decided to revamp their offense around Collins, a base-stealing singles hitter.

Ironically, in the decade of greed, instant gratification, and a mounting national debt, the Yankees repeated the same mistakes that had plunged them into decline in the 1960s. "George seemed like he was building up the minor leagues," observes former Yankee Ron Swoboda. "Then when the results started showing up, he completely lost his patience with that process."

As Dan Topping and Del Webb had before him, Steinbrenner repeatedly mortgaged the future for the present, depleting the farm system in exchange for over-the-hill veterans or players who for various reasons provided little or no service:

Take, for example, Steve Trout, 0–4 in 1987. Inexplicably unable to get the ball over the plate as a Yankee, he was then quietly jettisoned that winter. He had cost New York a young pitcher named Bob Tewksbury, who would go 16–5, 2.16 ERA for St. Louis in 1992 and 17–10, 3.83 ERA in 1993.

Or Bill Gullickson, a defector to Japan after pitching one month in the Big Apple in 1987, leaving the Yankees with nothing to show for Dennis Rasmussen, their eighteen-game winner of a year before.

Or Rick Reuschel, a thirty-two-year-old National League veteran who split eight decisions in 1981, then damaged his shoulder and never pitched for New York again. Given his release, he later materialized back in the senior circuit, and from 1985 through 1989 won 72 games for Pittsburgh and San Francisco. The minor-leaguer New York had given up for Reuschel, versatile infielder-outfielder Pat Tabler, evolved into a consistent .280s hitter.

The roll call of promising youngsters who prospered in other teams' uniforms is endless, but the December 1982 trade for Dale Murray, a thirty-two-year-old Toronto Blue Jays relief pitcher, is a particular beauty. The Yankees gave up Dave Collins, pitcher Mike Morgan, and a little-known minor-league first baseman named Fred McGriff. Murray's totals as a Yankee: 3–6, 1 SV. Meanwhile, McGriff developed into one of the game's premier long-ball hitters, averaging 35 home runs per year from 1988 through 1993.

The grand experiment with Collins was scrapped midway through 1982, a year that saw the Yankees finish four games under .500 and cast aside not one but two managers. Bob Lemon, whom Steinbrenner promised a full season "no matter what," survived only fourteen games. Gene Michael got in the middle eighty-six before his head rolled (again), and Clyde King warmed the bench for the remaining sixty-two.

In 1983, Steinbrenner brought Martin back a third time. Then a fourth time, in 1985, during which the 97–64, .602 Yankees chased the Toronto Blue Jays down to the season's next-to-last day. In between, the club elevated coach Yogi Berra to pilot. His second managerial experience in the Bronx proved no happier than his first. Berra narrowly averted dismissal in 1984 for the team's third-place finish. The following spring, Steinbrenner again pledged, "Yogi will be the manager the entire season, win or lose." After a 6–10 start, the ax fell, and Number 1 replaced Number 8.

Steinbrenner's rationale for rehiring men he'd previously deemed incompetent remains a mystery. "You don't just get fired and cut loose there, you change jobs," chuckles Stan Williams, a three-time New York pitching coach in the 1980s. Four managers have served more than one tenure: Martin, five (1976–78, 1979, 1983, 1985, 1988); Lemon, two (1978–79, 1981–82); Michael, two (1981, 1982); and Piniella, two (1986–87, 1988).

Martin served for the last time in 1988. Buoyed by four .300 hitters—Dave Winfield, Ricky Henderson, Claudell Washington, and superstar first baseman Don Mattingly, one of the team's rare homegrown players of the 1980s—the Yankees roared off to their strongest start in a decade. But Martin's alcoholism cost him his job once again. In May he got into a fight in the men's room at a topless bar in Texas. Once the Yankees faltered, in June, Steinbrenner ditched Martin in favor of Piniella, then on his second tour of duty.

Martin died on Christmas Day 1989 following an afternoon of heavy drinking at a tavern with his longtime friend William Reedy. Reedy unsteadily took the wheel of Martin's pickup truck and skidded off the road, down a 300-foot embankment and into a concrete culvert, killing Martin instantly. At the time, rumors persisted that the sixty-one-year-old Martin would return to the Yankees dugout a sixth time in 1990 should the Yankees start sluggishly.

Never was the failure of Steinbrenner's policies more evident than that year, during which Commissioner Fay Vincent banned The Boss from the game for consorting with a known gambler. Under two managers, Bucky Dent and Stump Merrill, the Yankees slipped into last place in May and stayed there, finishing 67–95, .414. It was the franchise's most disastrous season in eighty-seven years.

Meanwhile, that year's Cy Young Award–winner in the NL was former Yankee Doug Drabek, who had been swapped to Pittsburgh after the 1986 season for a declining thirty-three-year-old pitcher, Rick Rhoden. The NL batting titlist: onetime Yankees farmhand Willie McGee, traded to St. Louis in 1981 for a pitcher who never even suited up in pinstripes. The World Series's Most Valuable Player? Yet another erstwhile Yankees prospect: Cincinnati hurler Jose Rijo.

And the 1990 World Champion Reds' skipper was none other than Lou Piniella.

The constant chaos and instability took its toll not only on the players but on disillusioned Yankees fans, who no longer felt as deep a kinship with this ever-changing collection of strangers, through whom the egomaniacal owner acted out his neuroses. New Yorkers reacted to Vincent's July 30, 1990, announcement outlining Steinbrenner's lifetime suspension (later amended to two and a half years) as if celebrating the end of a world war.

The Yankees entered the 1991 season much like the 1967 team had: saddled with a bankrupt farm system and an enthusiastic but still-developing front-office brain trust. Progress in the 1990s came slowly at first: a fifth-place finish in 1991 and a fourth-place tie in 1992. But at least New Yorkers were spared the lunacy that had gripped the franchise in recent years. Despite a dreary 1992, the team's talented rookie manager, Buck Showalter, was allowed to retain his job for 1993, a season in which the Yankees kept the Toronto Blue Jays in their sights through mid-September.

Even more surprising than the second-place finish, George Steinbrenner, reinstated in the spring, kept out of the team's business as promised. GM Gene Michael, who has occupied enough chairs in the organization to fill a section of the bleachers, prevented The Boss from firing him, as was widely rumored upon Steinbrenner's return, by rebuilding the club through trades and free agency with an acumen reminiscent of Gabe Paul. The black clouds in the Bronx suddenly lifted that year—and drifted over to Shea Stadium, home to the last-place Mets.

One day the Yankees' losing era of the 1960s and seventies won't mean much to baseball fans or historians, as the national pastime will almost certainly never see the likes of the Bronx Bombers' five-decade supremacy again. Already the Yankees of the 1980s and '90s have endured more barren seasons, twelve, than the squads of Horace Clarke, Bobby Murcer, and Fritz Peterson. But as the club entered the 1994 season, it appeared that at long last pinstripes might cease to resemble prison stripes.

APPENDIX
Final Standings and Batting and Pitching Records (by Year)

1964

Final Standings

Team	W	L	PCT	GB
New York	99	63	.611	——
Chicago	98	64	.605	1
Baltimore	97	65	.599	2
Detroit	85	77	.525	14
Los Angeles	82	80	.506	17
Cleveland	79	83	.488	20
Minnesota	79	83	.488	20
Boston	72	90	.444	27
Washington	62	100	.383	37
Kansas City	57	105	.352	42

Manager: Yogi Berra (No. 8)
Coaches: Frank Crosetti (No. 2), Whitey Ford (No. 16), Jim Gleeson (No. 31), Jim Hegan (No. 44)

Batting Records

(200 at-bats or more)

No.	Player, Position	AB	H	HR	R	RBI	AVG
32	Elston Howard, C	550	172	15	63	84	.313
7	Mickey Mantle, OF	465	141	35	92	111	.303
9	Roger Maris, OF	513	144	26	86	71	.281
1	Bobby Richardson, 2B, SS	679	181	4	90	50	.267
11	Hector Lopez, OF, 3B	285	74	10	34	34	.260
25	Joe Pepitone, 1B, OF	613	154	28	71	100	.251
34	Phil Linz, SS, 3B, 2B, OF	368	92	5	63	25	.250
15	Tom Tresh, OF	533	131	16	75	73	.246

No.	Player, Position	AB	H	HR	R	RBI	AVG
10	Tony Kubek, SS	415	95	8	46	31	.229
6	Clete Boyer, 3B, SS	510	111	8	43	52	.218

(under 200 at-bats)

No.	Player, Position	AB	H	HR	R	RBI	AVG
48	Elvio Jiminez, OF	6	2	0	0	0	.333
42	Pedro Gonzalez, 1B, OF, 3B, 2B	112	31	0	18	5	.277
38	John Blanchard, C, OF, 1B	161	41	7	18	28	.255
14	Harry Bright, 1B	5	1	0	0	0	.200
26	Archie Moore, OF, 1B	23	4	0	4	1	.174
41	Jake Gibbs, C	6	1	0	1	0	.167
12	Mike Hegan, 1B	5	0	0	0	0	.000
43	Roger Repoz, OF	1	0	0	1	0	.000

Team Leaders (Batting)

At-Bats:	679	Richardson
Batting Average:	.313	Howard
Hits:	181	Richardson
Doubles:	25	Mantle, Richardson, Tresh
Triples:	5	Tresh, Boyer
Home Runs:	35	Mantle
Runs:	92	Mantle
RBI:	111	Mantle
Stolen Bases:	13	Tresh

Pitching Records

(50 innings or more)

No.	Player	G	IP	W	L	SV	SO	BB	ERA
30	Mel Stottlemyre	13	96	9	3	0	49	35	2.06
16	Whitey Ford	39	245	17	6	1	172	57	2.13
22	Bill Stafford	31	61	5	0	4	39	22	2.67
56	Jim Bouton	38	271	18	13	0	125	60	3.02
18	Hal Reniff	41	69	6	4	9	38	30	3.12
39	Steve Hamilton	30	60	7	2	3	49	15	3.28
24	Al Downing	37	244	13	8	2	217	120	3.47
51	Pete Mikkelsen	50	86	7	4	12	63	41	3.56
45	Rollie Sheldon	19	102	5	2	1	57	18	3.61
19	Stan Williams	21	82	1	5	0	54	38	3.84

No.	Player	G	IP	W	L	SV	SO	BB	ERA
49	Bob Meyer *with Yankees (0–3 in 7 games), Los Angeles Angels (1–1 in 6 games), Kansas City (1–4 in 9 games); traded on 6/12/64, for cash*	22	78	2	8	0	55	58	4.37
23	Ralph Terry	27	115	7	11	4	77	31	4.54
14	Pedro Ramos *with Cleveland (7–10 in 36 games), Yankees (1–0 in 13 games); acquired on 9/5/64, for cash and two players to be named later: Ralph Terry and Buddy Daley*	49	155	8	10	8	119	26	4.60

(under 50 innings)

No.	Player	G	IP	W	L	SV	SO	BB	ERA
28	Buddy Daley	13	35	3	2	1	16	25	4.63

Team Leaders (Pitching)

Games:	50	Mikkelsen
Innings:	271	Bouton
Wins:	18	Bouton
Complete Games:	12	Ford
Shutouts:	8	Ford
Saves:	12	Mikkelsen
Strikeouts:	217	Downing
ERA (more than 100 innings):	2.13	Ford

1965

Final Standings

Team	W	L	PCT	GB
Minnesota	102	60	.630	———
Chicago	95	67	.586	7
Baltimore	94	68	.580	8

Team	W	L	PCT	GB
Detroit	89	73	.549	13
Cleveland	87	75	.537	15
New York	**77**	**85**	**.475**	**25**
California	75	87	.463	27
Washington	70	92	.432	32
Boston	62	100	.383	40
Kansas City	59	103	.364	43

Manager: Johnny Keane (No. 21)
Coaches: Frank Crosetti (No. 2), Cot Deal (No. 31), Vern Benson (No. 35), Jim Hegan (No. 44)

Batting Records

(200 at-bats or more)

No.	Player, Position	AB	H	HR	R	RBI	AVG
15	Tom Tresh, OF	602	168	26	94	74	.279
11	Hector Lopez, OF, 1B	283	74	7	25	39	.261
7	Mickey Mantle, OF	361	92	19	44	46	.255
42	Pedro Gonzalez, 2B, OF, 3B *with Yankees (.400 in 7 games) and Cleveland (.253 in 116 games); traded on 5/10/65, for Ray Barker*	405	103	5	38	39	.254
6	Clete Boyer, 3B, SS	514	129	18	69	58	.251
25	Joe Pepitone, 1B, OF	531	131	18	51	62	.247
1	Bobby Richardson, 2B	664	164	6	76	47	.247
42	Ray Barker, 1B, 3B *with Cleveland (.000 in 11 games), Yankees (.254 in 98 games); acquired on 5/10/65, for Pedro Gonzalez*	211	52	7	21	31	.246
32	Elston Howard, C, 1B, OF	391	91	9	38	45	.233
43	Roger Repoz, OF	218	48	12	34	28	.220
10	Tony Kubek, SS, OF, 1B	339	74	5	26	35	.218
12	Phil Linz, SS, OF, 3B, 2B	285	59	2	37	16	.207

(under 200 at-bats)

No.	Player, Position	AB	H	HR	R	RBI	AVG
26	Archie Moore, OF, 1B	17	7	1	1	4	.412
48	Roy White, OF, 2B	42	14	0	7	3	.333
20	Horace Clarke, 3B, 2B, SS	108	28	1	13	9	.259
47	Bob Schmidt, C	40	10	1	4	3	.250
52	Bobby Murcer, SS	37	9	1	2	4	.243
9	Roger Maris, OF	155	37	8	22	27	.239
41	Jake Gibbs, C	68	15	2	6	7	.221
53	Ross Moschitto, OF	27	5	1	12	3	.185

No.	Player, Position	AB	H	HR	R	RBI	AVG
38	John Blanchard, C, OF *with Yankees (.147 in 12 games), Kansas City (.200 in 52 games), Milwaukee (.100 in 10 games); traded with Rollie Sheldon to Kansas City on 5/3/65, for Doc Edwards*	164	30	4	12	16	.183
38	Doc Edwards, C *with Kansas City (.150 in 6 games), Yankees (.190 in 45 games); acquired on 5/3/65, for John Blanchard and Rollie Sheldon*	120	22	1	4	9	.183
57	Arturo Lopez, OF	49	7	0	5	0	.143
27	Duke Carmel, 1B	8	0	0	0	0	.000

Team Leaders (Batting)

At-Bats:	664	Richardson
Batting Average:	.279	Tresh
Hits:	168	Tresh
Doubles:	29	Tresh
Triples:	6	Tresh, Boyer, Richardson
Home Runs:	26	Tresh
Runs:	94	Tresh
RBI:	74	Tresh
Stolen Bases:	7	Richardson

Pitching Records

(50 innings or more)

No.	Player	G	IP	W	L	SV	SO	BB	ERA
39	Steve Hamilton	46	58	3	1	5	51	16	1.39
30	Mel Stottlemyre	37	291	20	9	0	155	88	2.63
14	Pedro Ramos	65	92	5	5	19	68	27	2.92
45	Jack Cullen	12	59	3	4	0	25	21	3.05
16	Whitey Ford	37	244	16	13	1	162	50	3.24
51	Pete Mikkelsen	41	82	4	9	1	69	36	3.28
24	Al Downing	35	212	12	14	0	179	105	3.40
22	Bill Stafford	22	111	3	8	0	71	31	3.56
18	Hal Reniff	51	85	3	4	3	74	48	3.80

No.	Player	G	IP	W	L	SV	SO	BB	ERA
45	Rollie Sheldon	35	193	10	8	0	112	57	3.86
	with Yankees (0–0								
	in 3 games), Kansas								
	City (10–8 in 32								
	games); traded with								
	John Blanchard on								
	5/3/65, for Doc								
	Edwards								
29	Bobby Tiefenauer	31	50	1	7	6	35	18	4.71
	with Milwaukee								
	(0–1 in 6 games),								
	Yankees (1–1 in 10								
	games), Cleveland								
	(0–5 in 15 games);								
	acquired from Milwaukee								
	on 6/16/65,								
	for cash; traded								
	to Cleveland on								
	8/11/65, for cash								
56	Jim Bouton	30	151	4	15	0	97	60	4.82

(under 50 innings)

No.	Player	G	IP	W	L	SV	SO	BB	ERA
23	Rich Beck	3	21	2	1	0	10	7	2.14
28	Gil Blanco	17	20	1	1	0	14	12	3.98
29	Mike Jurewicz	2	2	0	0	0	2	1	7.71
23	Jim Brenneman	3	2	0	0	0	2	3	18.00

Team Leaders (Pitching)

Games:	65	Ramos
Innings:	291	Stottlemyre
Wins:	20	Stottlemyre
Complete Games:	18	Stottlemyre
Shutouts:	4	Stottlemyre
Saves:	19	Ramos
Strikeouts:	179	Downing
ERA (more than 100 innings):	2.63	Stottlemyre

1966

Final Standings

Team	W	L	PCT	GB
Baltimore	97	63	.606	——
Minnesota	89	73	.549	9
Detroit	88	74	.543	10
Chicago	83	79	.512	15
Cleveland	81	81	.500	17

Team	W	L	PCT	GB
California	80	82	.494	18
Kansas City	74	86	.463	23
Washington	71	88	.447	25½
Boston	72	90	.444	26
New York	**70**	**89**	**.440**	**26½**

Managers: Johnny Keane (4–16; No. 21), Ralph Houk (66–73; No. 35)
Coaches: Frank Crosetti (No. 2), Jim Turner (No. 31), Vern Benson (No. 35), Wally Moses (No. 36), Jim Hegan (No. 44)

Batting Records

(200 at-bats or more)

No.	Player, Position	AB	H	HR	R	RBI	AVG
7	Mickey Mantle, OF	333	96	23	40	56	.288
20	Horace Clarke, SS, 2B, 3B	312	83	6	37	28	.266
32	Elston Howard, C, 1B	410	105	6	38	35	.256
25	Joe Pepitone, 1B, OF	585	149	31	85	83	.255
1	Bobby Richardson, 2B, 3B	610	153	7	71	42	.251
6	Clete Boyer, 3B, SS	500	120	14	59	57	.240
9	Roger Maris, OF	348	81	13	37	43	.233
15	Tom Tresh, OF, 3B	537	125	27	76	68	.233
43	Roger Repoz, OF, 1B *with Yankees (.349 in 37 games), Kansas City (.216 in 101 games); traded with Bill Stafford and Gil Blanco on 6/10/66, for Fred Talbot and Billy Bryan*	362	84	11	44	43	.232
48	Roy White, OF, 2B	316	71	7	39	20	.225

(under 200 at-bats)

No.	Player, Position	AB	H	HR	R	RBI	AVG
41	Jake Gibbs, C	182	47	3	19	20	.258
28	Steve Whitaker, OF	114	28	7	15	15	.246
40	Lou Clinton, OF	159	35	5	18	21	.220
12	Ruben Amaro, SS	23	5	0	0	3	.217
11	Hector Lopez, OF	117	25	4	14	16	.214
18	Mike Hegan, 1B	39	8	0	7	2	.205
27	Dick Schofield, SS, 3B *with San Francisco (.063 in 11 games), Yankees (.155 in 25 games), Los Angeles (.257 in 20 games); acquired from San Francisco on 5/11/66, for cash; traded to Los Angeles on 9/10/66, for Thad Tillotson and cash*	144	28	0	19	6	.194

No.	Player, Position	AB	H	HR	R	RBI	AVG
42	Ray Barker, 1B	75	14	3	11	13	.187
43	Mike Ferraro, 3B	28	5	0	4	0	.179
17	Bobby Murcer, SS	69	12	0	3	5	.174
23	Billy Bryan, C, 1B	145	25	4	5	12	.172

with Kansas City (.132 in 32 games), Yankees (.217 in 27 games); acquired with Fred Talbot on 6/10/66, for Roger Repoz, Bill Stafford, and Gil Blanco

No.	Player, Position	AB	H	HR	R	RBI	AVG
26	John Miller, OF, 1B	23	2	1	1	2	.087

Team Leaders (Batting)

At-Bats:	610	Richardson
Batting Average:	.288	Mantle
Hits:	153	Richardson
Doubles:	22	Boyer
Triples:	4	Boyer, Pepitone, Tresh, Clarke
Home Runs:	31	Pepitone
Runs:	85	Pepitone
RBI:	83	Pepitone
Stolen Bases:	14	White

Pitching Records

(50 innings or more)

No.	Player	G	IP	W	L	SV	SO	BB	ERA
16	Whitey Ford	22	73	2	5	0	43	24	2.47
58	Dooley Womack	42	75	7	3	4	50	23	2.64
56	Jim Bouton	24	120	3	8	1	65	38	2.69
39	Steve Hamilton	44	90	8	3	3	57	22	3.00
18	Hal Reniff	56	95	3	7	9	79	49	3.21
52 & 19	Fritz Peterson	34	215	12	11	0	96	40	3.31
24	Al Downing	30	200	10	11	0	152	79	3.56
14	Pedro Ramos	52	90	3	9	13	58	18	3.61
30	Mel Stottlemyre	37	251	12	20	1	146	82	3.80
22	Fred Talbot	34	192	11	11	0	85	73	4.36

with Kansas City (4–4 in 11 games), Yankees (7–7 in 23 games); acquired with Billy Bryan on

No.	Player	G	IP	W	L	SV	SO	BB	ERA
	6/10/66, for Roger Repoz, Bill Stafford, and Gil Blanco								
19	Bob Friend *with Yankees (1–4 in 12 games), New York Mets (5–8 in 22 games); traded on 6/15/66, for cash*	34	131	6	12	1	52	25	4.55

(under 50 innings)

No.	Player	G	IP	W	L	SV	SO	BB	ERA
29	Bill Henry	2	3	0	0	0	3	2	0.00
45	Stan Bahnsen	4	23	1	1	1	16	7	3.52
45	Jack Cullen	5	11	1	0	0	7	5	3.97

Team Leaders (Pitching)

Games:	56	Reniff
Innings:	251	Stottlemyre
Wins:	12	Stottlemyre, Peterson
Complete Games:	11	Peterson
Shutouts:	3	Stottlemyre
Saves:	13	Ramos
Strikeouts:	152	Downing
ERA (more than 100 innings):	2.69	Bouton

1967

Final Standings

Team	W	L	PCT	GB
Boston	92	70	.568	——
Detroit	91	71	.562	1
Minnesota	91	71	.562	1
Chicago	89	73	.549	3
California	84	77	.522	7½
Baltimore	76	85	.472	15½
Washington	76	85	.472	15½
Cleveland	75	87	.463	17
New York	**72**	**90**	**.444**	**20**
Kansas City	62	99	.385	29½

Manager: Ralph Houk (No. 35)
Coaches: Frank Crosetti (No. 2), Jim Turner (No. 31), Loren Babe (No. 36), Jim Hegan (No. 44)

Batting Records

(200 at-bats or more)

No.	Player, Position	AB	H	HR	R	RBI	AVG
20	Horace Clarke, 2B	588	160	3	74	29	.272
25	Joe Pepitone, OF, 1B	501	126	13	45	64	.251
7	Mickey Mantle, 1B	440	108	22	63	55	.245
28	Steve Whitaker, OF	441	107	11	37	50	.243
41	Jake Gibbs, C	374	87	4	33	25	.233
6	Charley Smith, 3B	425	95	9	38	38	.224
48	Roy White, OF, 3B	214	48	2	22	18	.224
12	Ruben Amaro, SS, 3B, 1B	417	93	1	31	17	.223
15	Tom Tresh, OF	448	98	14	45	53	.219
11	Bill Robinson, OF	342	67	7	31	29	.196

(under 200 at-bats)

No.	Player, Position	AB	H	HR	R	RBI	AVG
40	Lou Clinton, OF	4	2	0	1	2	.500
47	Frank Tepedino, 1B	5	2	0	0	0	.400
14	Jerry Kenney, SS	58	18	1	4	5	.310
27	Tom Shopay, OF	27	8	2	2	6	.296
10	Dick Howser, 2B, 3B, SS	149	40	0	18	10	.268
23	Bob Tillman, C *with Boston (.188 in 30 games), Yankees (.254 in 22 games); acquired on 8/8/67, for cash*	127	28	3	9	13	.220
38	Frank Fernandez, C, OF	28	6	1	1	4	.214
26	John Kennedy, SS, 3B, 2B	179	35	1	22	17	.196
32	Elston Howard, C, 1B *with Yankees (.196 in 66 games), Boston (.147 in 42 games); traded on 8/3/67, for Ron Klimkowski and Pete Magrini*	199	56	4	22	28	.178
23 & 50	Billy Bryan, C	12	2	1	1	2	.167
18	Mike Hegan, 1B, OF	118	16	1	12	3	.136
53	Ross Moschitto, OF	9	1	0	1	0	.111
42	Ray Barker, 1B	26	2	0	2	0	.077
68	Charlie Sands, C	1	0	0	0	0	.000

Team Leaders (Batting)

At-Bats:	588	Clarke
Batting Average:	.272	Clarke

Hits:	160	Clarke	
Doubles:	23	Tresh	
Triples:	3	Tresh, Smith, Pepitone, Whitaker	
Home Runs:	22	Mantle	
Runs:	74	Clarke	
RBI:	64	Pepitone	
Stolen Bases:	21	Clarke	

Pitching Records

(50 innings or more)

No.	Player	G	IP	W	L	SV	SO	BB	ERA
40	Bill Monbouquette *with Detroit (0–0 in 2 games), Yankees (6–5 in 33 games); acquired as free agent on 6/2/67)*	35	135	6	5	1	55	17	2.33
58	Dooley Womack	65	97	5	6	18	57	35	2.41
24	Al Downing	31	202	14	10	0	171	61	2.63
52	Joe Verbanic	28	80	4	3	2	39	21	2.80
30	Mel Stottlemyre	36	255	15	15	0	151	88	2.96
19	Fritz Peterson	36	181	8	14	0	102	43	3.47
39	Steve Hamilton	44	62	2	4	4	55	23	3.48
18	Hal Reniff *with Yankees (0–2 in 24 games), New York Mets (3–3 in 29 games); traded on 6/29/67, for cash*	53	83	3	5	4	45	37	3.80
54	Thad Tillotson	43	98	3	9	2	62	39	4.03
18	Steve Barber *with Baltimore (4–9 in 15 games), Yankees (6–9 in 17 games); acquired on 7/5/67, for Ray Barker, Chet Trail, Joe Brady, and cash*	32	172	10	18	0	118	115	4.07
22	Fred Talbot	29	139	6	8	0	61	54	4.22

(under 50 innings)

No.	Player	G	IP	W	L	SV	SO	BB	ERA
16	Whitey Ford	7	44	2	4	0	21	9	1.64
56	Jim Bouton	17	44	1	0	0	31	18	4.67
43	Dale Roberts	2	2	0	0	0	0	2	9.00
48	Cecil Perkins	2	5	0	1	0	1	2	9.00

Team Leaders (Pitching)

Games:	65	Womack
Innings:	255	Stottlemyre
Wins:	15	Stottlemyre
Complete Games:	10	Stottlemyre, Downing
Shutouts:	4	Stottlemyre, Downing
Saves:	18	Womack
Strikeouts:	171	Downing
ERA (more than 100 innings):	2.33	Monbouquette

1968

Final Standings

Team	W	L	PCT	GB
Detroit	103	59	.636	——
Baltimore	91	71	.562	12
Cleveland	86	75	.534	16½
Boston	86	76	.531	17
New York	**83**	**79**	**.512**	**20**
Oakland	82	80	.506	21
Minnesota	79	83	.488	24
California	67	95	.414	36
Chicago	67	95	.414	36
Washington	65	96	.404	37½

Manager: Ralph Houk (No. 35)
Coaches: Frank Crosetti (No. 2), Whitey Ford (No. 16), Jim Turner (No. 31), Jim Hegan (No. 44)

Batting Records

(200 at-bats or more)

No.	Player, Position	AB	H	HR	R	RBI	AVG
48 & 21	Roy White, OF	577	154	17	89	62	.267
25	Joe Pepitone, OF, 1B	380	93	15	41	56	.245
18	Andy Kosco, OF, 1B	466	112	15	47	59	.240
11	Bill Robinson, OF	342	82	6	34	40	.240
7	Mickey Mantle, 1B	435	103	18	57	54	.237
20	Horace Clarke, 2B	579	133	2	52	26	.230
14	Bobby Cox, 3B	437	100	7	33	41	.229

No.	Player, Position	AB	H	HR	R	RBI	AVG
41	Jake Gibbs, C	423	90	3	31	29	.213
29	Rocky Colavito, OF, P *with Los Angeles (.204 in 40 games), Yankees (.220 in 39 games); acquired as free agent on 7/15/68*	204	43	8	21	24	.211
15	Tom Tresh, SS, OF	507	99	11	60	52	.195

(under 200 at-bats)

No.	Player, Position	AB	H	HR	R	RBI	AVG
6	Charley Smith, 3B	70	16	1	2	7	.229
23	Ellie Rodriguez, C	24	5	0	1	1	.208
17	Gene Michael, SS, P	116	23	1	8	8	.198
38	Frank Fernandez, C, OF	135	23	7	15	30	.170
26	Mike Ferraro, 3B	87	14	0	5	1	.161
10	Dick Howser, 2B, 3B, SS	150	23	0	24	3	.153
12	Ruben Amaro, SS, 1B	41	5	0	3	0	.122
9	Steve Whitaker, OF	60	7	0	3	3	.117
51	Tony Solaita, 1B	1	0	0	0	0	.000

Team Leaders (Batting)

At-Bats:	579	Clarke
Batting Average:	.267	White
Hits:	154	White
Doubles:	20	White
Triples:	7	White, Robinson
Home Runs:	18	Mantle
Runs:	89	White
RBI:	62	White
Stolen Bases:	21	White, Clarke

Pitching Records

(50 innings or more)

No.	Player	G	IP	W	L	SV	SO	BB	ERA
45	Stan Bahnsen	37	267	17	12	0	162	68	2.05
39	Steve Hamilton	40	51	2	2	11	42	13	2.13
30	Mel Stottlemyre	36	279	21	12	0	140	65	2.45
19	Fritz Peterson	36	212	12	11	0	115	29	2.63
52	Joe Verbanic	40	97	6	7	4	40	41	3.15
58	Dooley Womack	45	62	3	7	2	27	29	3.21
18	Steve Barber	20	128	6	5	0	87	64	3.23

No.	Player	G	IP	W	L	SV	SO	BB	ERA
40	Lindy McDaniel *with San Francisco (0–0 in 12 games), Yankees (4–1 in 24 games); acquired on 7/12/68, for Bill Monbouquette*	36	71	4	1	10	52	17	3.31
22	Fred Talbot	29	99	1	9	0	67	42	3.36
24	Al Downing	15	61	3	3	0	40	20	3.52
40	Bill Monbouquette *with Yankees (5–7 in 17 games), San Francisco (0–1 in 7 games); traded on 7/12/68, for Lindy McDaniel*	24	101	5	8	1	37	15	4.35

(under 50 innings)

No.	Player	G	IP	W	L	SV	SO	BB	ERA
29	Rocky Colavito	1	3	1	0	0	1	2	0.00
17	Gene Michael	1	3	0	0	0	3	0	0.00
51	John Wyatt *with Boston (1–2 in 8 games), Yankees (0–2 in 7 games), Detroit (1–0 in 22 games); acquired on 5/18/68, for cash; traded on 6/15/68, for cash*	37	49	2	4	2	42	26	2.74
56	Jim Bouton	12	44	1	1	0	24	9	3.68
54	Thad Tillotson	7	10	1	0	0	1	7	4.35
56	John Cumberland	1	2	0	0	0	1	1	9.00

Team Leaders (Pitching)

Games:	45	Womack
Innings:	279	Stottlemyre
Wins:	21	Stottlemyre
Complete Games:	19	Stottlemyre
Shutouts:	6	Stottlemyre
Saves:	11	Hamilton
Strikeouts:	162	Bahnsen
ERA (more than 100 innings):	2.05	Bahnsen

1969

Final Standings

Team	W	L	PCT	GB
East Div.				
Baltimore	109	53	.673	——
Detroit	90	72	.556	19
Boston	87	75	.537	22
Washington	86	76	.531	23
New York	**80**	**81**	**.497**	**28½**
Cleveland	62	99	.385	46½
West Div.				
Minnesota	97	65	.599	——
Oakland	88	74	.543	9
California	71	91	.438	26
Kansas City	69	93	.426	28
Chicago	68	94	.420	29
Seattle	64	98	.395	33

Manager: Ralph Houk (No. 35)
Coaches: Jim Turner (No. 31), Elston Howard (No. 32), Dick Howser (No. 34), Jim Hegan (No. 44)

Batting Records

(200 at-bats or more)

No.	Player, Position	AB	H	HR	R	RBI	AVG
6	Roy White, OF	448	130	7	55	74	.290
20	Horace Clarke, 2B	641	183	4	82	48	.285
17	Gene Michael, SS	412	112	2	41	31	.272
1	Bobby Murcer, OF, 3B	564	146	26	82	82	.259
2	Jerry Kenney, 3B, OF, SS	447	115	2	49	34	.257
25	Joe Pepitone, 1B	513	124	27	49	70	.242
41	Jake Gibbs, C	219	49	0	18	18	.224
26	Jimmie Hall, OF, 1B	246	55	3	23	27	.224
	with Cleveland (.000 in 4 games), *Yankees (.236 in 80 games),* *Chicago Cubs (.208 in 11 games);* *acquired on 4/14/69, for cash;* *traded on 9/11/69, for Terry* *Bongiovanni and cash*						
10	Frank Fernandez, C, OF	229	51	12	34	29	.223

No.	Player, Position	AB	H	HR	R	RBI	AVG
15	Tom Tresh, SS, OF, 3B *with Yankees (.182 in 45 games), Detroit (.224 in 94 games); traded on 6/14/69, for Ron Woods*	474	100	14	59	46	.211
11	Bill Robinson, OF, 1B	222	38	3	23	21	.171

(under 200 at-bats)

No.	Player, Position	AB	H	HR	R	RBI	AVG
12	Ron Blomberg, OF	6	3	0	0	0	.500
23	John Ellis, C	62	18	1	2	8	.290
15	Thurman Munson, C	86	22	1	6	9	.256
12	Billy Cowan, OF, 1B *with Yankees (.167 in 32 games), California (.304 in 28 games); traded on 7/26/69, for cash*	104	25	5	15	13	.240
46	Frank Tepedino, OF	39	9	0	6	4	.231
55	Dave McDonald, 1B	23	5	0	0	2	.217
14	Bobby Cox, 3B, 2B	191	41	2	17	17	.215
9	Dick Simpson, OF *with Yankees (.273 in 6 games), Seattle (.176 in 26 games); traded on 5/19/69, for Jose Vidal*	62	12	2	10	9	.194
9	Ron Woods, OF *with Detroit (.267 in 17 games), Yankees (.175 in 72 games); acquired on 6/14/69, for Tom Tresh*	186	34	2	21	10	.183
21	Jim Lyttle, OF	83	15	0	7	4	.181
38	Len Boehmer, 1B, 3B, SS, 2B	108	19	0	5	7	.176
21	Nate Oliver, 2B *with Yankees (.000 in 1 game), Chicago Cubs (.159 in 44 games); traded on 4/19/69, for Lee Elia*	45	7	1	15	4	.156
27	Tom Shopay, OF	48	4	0	2	0	.083

Team Leaders (Batting)

At-Bats:	641	Clarke
Batting Average:	.290	White
Hits:	183	Clarke
Doubles:	30	White
Triples:	7	Clarke
Home Runs:	27	Pepitone
Runs:	82	Clarke, Murcer
RBI:	82	Murcer
Stolen Bases:	33	Clarke

Pitching Records

(50 innings or more)

No.	Player	G	IP	W	L	SV	SO	BB	ERA
19	Fritz Peterson	37	272	17	16	0	150	43	2.55
30	Mel Stottlemyre	39	303	20	14	0	113	97	2.82
22	Jack Aker	53	82	8	6	14	47	35	3.17
	with Seattle (0–2 in 15 games), Yankees (8–4 in 38 games); acquired on 5/20/69, for Fred Talbot								
39	Steve Hamilton	38	57	3	4	2	39	21	3.32
24	Al Downing	30	131	7	5	0	85	49	3.38
40	Lindy McDaniel	51	84	5	6	5	60	23	3.55
50	Bill Burbach	31	141	6	8	0	82	102	3.65
45	Stan Bahnsen	40	221	9	16	1	130	90	3.83
54	Ken Johnson	30	74	2	5	2	59	33	3.89
	with Atlanta (0–1 in 9 games), Yankees (1–2 in 12 games), Chicago Cubs (1–2 in 9 games); acquired on 6/10/69, for cash; traded on 8/11/69, for cash								
22	Fred Talbot	45	146	6	10	1	83	54	4.38
	with Yankees (0–0 in 8 games), Seattle (5–8 in 25 games), Oakland (1–2 in 12 games); traded to Seattle on 5/20/69, for Jack Aker								
18	Mike Kekich	28	105	4	6	1	66	49	4.54

(under 50 innings)

No.	Player	G	IP	W	L	SV	SO	BB	ERA
26	Ron Klimkowski	3	14	0	0	0	3	5	0.64
56	John Cumberland	2	4	0	0	0	0	4	4.50
23	Don Nottebart	20	24	1	1	0	13	7	6.38
	with Yankees (0–0 in 4 games), Chicago Cubs (1–1 in 16 games); returned to Cincinnati on 4/26/69								

Team Leaders (Pitching)

Games:	51	McDaniel
Innings:	303	Stottlemyre
Wins:	20	Stottlemyre
Complete Games:	24	Stottlemyre
Shutouts:	4	Peterson
Saves:	11	Aker
Strikeouts:	150	Peterson
ERA (more than 100 innings):	2.55	Peterson

1970

Final Standings

Team	W	L	PCT	GB
East Div.				
Baltimore	108	54	.667	——
New York	**93**	**69**	**.574**	**15**
Boston	87	75	.537	21
Detroit	79	83	.488	29
Cleveland	76	86	.469	32
Washington	70	92	.432	38
West Div.				
Minnesota	98	64	.605	——
Oakland	89	73	.549	9
California	86	76	.531	12
Kansas City	65	97	.401	33
Milwaukee	65	97	.401	33
Chicago	56	106	.346	42

Manager: Ralph Houk (No. 35)
Coaches: Mickey Mantle (No. 7), Jim Turner (No. 31), Elston Howard (No. 32), Dick Howser (No. 34), Jim Hegan (No. 44)

Batting Records

(200 at-bats or more)

No.	Player, Position	AB	H	HR	R	RBI	AVG
15	Thurman Munson, C	453	137	6	59	53	.302
10	Danny Cater, 1B, 3B, OF	582	175	6	64	76	.301
6	Roy White, OF	609	180	22	109	94	.296
20	Horace Clarke, 2B	686	172	4	81	46	.251

No.	Player, Position	AB	H	HR	R	RBI	AVG
1	Bobby Murcer, OF	581	146	23	95	78	.251
23	John Ellis, 1B, 3B, C	226	56	7	24	29	.248
9	Ron Woods, OF	225	51	8	30	27	.227
17	Gene Michael, SS, 3B, 2B	435	93	2	42	38	.214
13	Curt Blefary, OF, 1B	269	57	9	34	37	.212
2	Jerry Kenney, 3B, 2B	404	78	4	46	35	.193

(under 200 at-bats)

No.	Player, Position	AB	H	HR	R	RBI	AVG
21	Frank Tepedino, OF, 1B	19	6	0	2	2	.316
27	Jim Lyttle, OF	126	39	3	20	14	.310
41	Jake Gibbs, C	153	46	8	23	26	.301
28	Ron Hansen, SS, 3B, 2B	91	27	4	13	14	.297
25	Pete Ward, 1B	77	20	1	5	18	.260
26	Frank Baker, SS	117	27	0	6	11	.231
46	Bobby Mitchell, OF	22	5	0	1	4	.227

Team Leaders (Batting)

At-Bats:	686	Clarke
Batting Average:	.302	Munson
Hits:	180	White
Doubles:	30	White
Triples:	7	Kenney
Home Runs:	23	Murcer
Runs:	109	White
RBI:	94	White
Stolen Bases:	24	White

Pitching Records

(50 innings or more)

No.	Player	G	IP	W	L	SV	SO	BB	ERA
40	Lindy McDaniel	62	112	9	5	29	81	23	2.01
22	Jack Aker	41	70	4	2	16	36	20	2.06
24	Ron Klimkowski	45	98	6	7	1	40	33	2.66
19	Fritz Peterson	39	260	20	11	0	127	40	2.91
30	Mel Stottlemyre	37	271	15	13	0	126	84	3.09
45	Stan Bahnsen	26	233	14	11	0	116	75	3.32
38	Steve Kline	16	100	6	6	0	49	24	3.42
56	John Cumberland	22	75	5	4	0	44	19	3.48

with Yankees (3–4 in 15 games), San Francisco (2–0 in 7 games); traded on 7/20/70, for Mike McCormick

No.	Player	G	IP	W	L	SV	SO	BB	ERA
54	Gary Waslewski *with Montreal (0–2 in 6 games), Yankees (2–2 in 26 games); acquired on 5/15/70, for Dave McDonald*	32	80	2	4	0	46	42	3.71
18	Mike Kekich	26	99	6	3	0	63	55	4.82
29 & 56	Mike McCormick *with San Francisco (3–4 in 23 games), Yankees (2–0 in 9 games); acquired on 7/20/70, for John Cumberland*	32	99	5	4	2	49	49	6.18

(under 50 innings)

No.	Player	G	IP	W	L	SV	SO	BB	ERA
39	Gary Jones	2	2	0	0	0	2	1	0.00
39	Steve Hamilton *with Yankees (4–3 in 35 games), Chicago White Sox (0–0 in 3 games); traded on 9/9/70, for cash*	38	48	4	3	3	36	17	2.98
49	Lloyd Colson	1	2	0	0	0	3	0	4.50
52	Joe Verbanic	7	16	1	0	0	8	12	4.50
43	Rob Gardner	1	7	1	0	0	6	4	5.14
50	Bill Burbach	4	17	0	2	0	10	9	10.06

Team Leaders (Pitching)

Games:	62	McDaniel
Innings:	271	Stottlemyre
Wins:	20	Peterson
Complete Games:	14	Stottlemyre
Shutouts:	2	Peterson, Bahnsen
Saves:	29	McDaniel
Strikeouts:	127	Peterson
ERA (more than 100 innings):	2.01	McDaniel

1971

Final Standings

Team	W	L	PCT	GB
East Div.				
Baltimore	101	57	.639	——
Detroit	91	71	.562	12
Boston	85	77	.525	18
New York	**82**	**80**	**.506**	**21**
Washington	63	96	.396	38½
Cleveland	60	102	.370	43
West Div.				
Oakland	101	60	.627	——
Kansas City	85	76	.528	16
Chicago	79	83	.488	22½
California	76	86	.469	25½
Minnesota	74	86	.463	26½
Milwaukee	69	92	.429	32

Manager: Ralph Houk (No. 35)
Coaches: Jim Turner (No. 31), Elston Howard (No. 32), Dick Howser (No. 34), Jim Hegan (No. 44)

Batting Records

(200 at-bats or more)

No.	Player, Position	AB	H	HR	R	RBI	AVG
1	Bobby Murcer, OF	529	175	25	94	94	.331
6	Roy White, OF	524	153	19	86	84	.292
24	Felipe Alou, OF, 1B	469	135	8	52	69	.288
	with Oakland (.250 in 2 games), Yankees (.289 in 131 games); acquired on 4/9/71, for Ron Klimkowski and Rob Gardner						
10	Danny Cater, 1B, 3B	428	118	4	39	50	.276
2	Jerry Kenney, 3B, SS, 1B	325	85	0	50	20	.262
14	Ron Swoboda, OF	213	55	2	24	26	.258
	with Montreal (.253 in 39 games), Yankees (.261 in 54 games); acquired on 6/25/71, for Ron Woods						
15	Thurman Munson, C	451	113	10	71	42	.251
20	Horace Clarke, 2B	625	156	2	76	41	.250
23	John Ellis, C, 1B	238	58	3	16	34	.244
17	Gene Michael, SS	456	102	3	36	35	.224
41	Jake Gibbs, C	206	45	5	23	21	.218

No.	Player, Position	AB	H	HR	R	RBI	AVG

(under 200 at-bats)

No.	Player, Position	AB	H	HR	R	RBI	AVG
21	Rusty Torres, OF	26	10	2	5	3	.385
12	Ron Blomberg, OF	199	64	7	30	31	.322
9	Ron Woods, OF *with Yankees (.250 in 25 games), Montreal (.297 in 51 games); traded on 6/25/71, for Ron Swoboda*	170	49	2	30	19	.288
13	Curt Blefary, OF, C, 3B, 1B, 2B *with Yankees (.194 in 21 games), Oakland (.218 in 50 games); traded on 5/26/71, for Rob Gardner*	137	29	6	19	14	.212
28	Ron Hansen, 3B, 2B, SS	145	30	2	6	20	.207
27	Jim Lyttle, OF	86	17	1	7	7	.198
11	Danny Walton, OF, 3B *with Milwaukee (.203 in 30 games), Yankees (.143 in 5 games); acquired on 6/7/71, for Frank Tepedino and Bobby Mitchell*	83	16	3	6	11	.193
21	Frank Tepedino, 1B, OF *with Yankees (.000 in 6 games), Milwaukee (.198 in 53 games); traded with Bobby Mitchell on 6/7/71, for Danny Walton*	112	21	2	11	7	.188
26	Frank Baker, SS	79	11	0	9	2	.139
25	Len Boehmer, 3B	5	0	0	0	0	.000

Team Leaders (Batting)

At-Bats:	625	Clarke
Batting Average:	.331	Murcer
Hits:	175	Murcer
Doubles:	25	Murcer
Triples:	7	White, Clarke
Home Runs:	25	Murcer
Runs:	94	Murcer
RBI:	94	Murcer
Stolen Bases:	17	Clarke

Pitching Records

(50 innings or more)

No.	Player	G	IP	W	L	SV	SO	BB	ERA
22	Jack Aker	41	56	4	4	4	24	26	2.57
30	Mel Stottlemyre	35	270	16	12	0	132	69	2.87
38	Steve Kline	31	222	12	13	0	81	37	2.96
19	Fritz Peterson	37	274	15	13	1	139	42	3.05

No.	Player	G	IP	W	L	SV	SO	BB	ERA
45	Stan Bahnsen	36	242	14	12	0	110	72	3.35
18	Mike Kekich	37	170	10	9	0	93	82	4.08
40	Lindy McDaniel	44	70	5	10	4	39	24	5.01

(under 50 innings)

No.	Player	G	IP	W	L	SV	SO	BB	ERA
39	Rob Gardner *with Oakland (0–0 in 4 games), Yankees (0–0 in 2 games); traded with Ron Klimkowski on 4/9/71, for Felipe Alou; reacquired on 5/26/71, for Curt Blefary*	6	11	0	0	0	7	5	2.53
54	Gary Waslewski	24	36	0	1	1	17	16	3.25
46	Roger Hambright	18	27	3	1	2	14	10	4.33
43	Terry Ley	6	9	0	0	0	7	9	5.00
29	Jim Hardin *with Baltimore (0–0 in 6 games), Yankees (0–2 in 12 games); acquired on 5/28/71, for Bill Burbach*	18	34	0	2	0	17	12	5.03
50	Al Closter	14	28	2	2	0	22	13	5.14
39	Gary Jones	12	14	0	0	0	10	7	9.00
50	Bill Burbach	2	3	0	1	0	3	5	12.00

Team Leaders (Pitching)

Games:	44	McDaniel
Innings:	274	Peterson
Wins:	16	Stottlemyre
Complete Games:	19	Stottlemyre
Shutouts:	7	Stottlemyre
Saves:	4	McDaniel, Aker
Strikeouts:	139	Peterson
ERA (more than 100 innings):	2.87	Stottlemyre

1972

Final Standings

Team	W	L	PCT	GB
East Div.				
Detroit	86	70	.551	——
Boston	85	70	.548	½
Baltimore	80	74	.519	5
New York	**79**	**76**	**.510**	**6½**
Cleveland	72	84	.462	14
Milwaukee	65	91	.417	21
West Div.				
Oakland	93	62	.600	——
Chicago	87	67	.565	5½
Minnesota	77	77	.500	15½
Kansas City	76	78	.494	16½
California	75	80	.484	18
Texas	54	100	.351	38½

Manager: Ralph Houk (No. 35)
Coaches: Jim Turner (No. 31), Elston Howard (No. 32), Dick Howser (No. 34), Jim Hegan (No. 44)

Batting Records

(200 at-bats or more)

No.	Player, Position	AB	H	HR	R	RBI	AVG
1	Bobby Murcer, OF	585	171	33	102	96	.292
15	Thurman Munson, C	511	143	7	54	46	.280
24	Felipe Alou, 1B, OF	324	90	6	33	37	.278
6	Roy White, OF	556	150	10	76	54	.270
12	Ron Blomberg, 1B	299	80	14	36	49	.268
25	Johnny Callison, OF	275	71	9	28	34	.258
10	Celerino Sanchez, 3B	250	62	0	18	22	.248
20	Horace Clarke, 2B	547	132	3	65	37	.241
17	Gene Michael, SS	391	91	1	29	32	.233
11	Bernie Allen, 3B, 2B	220	50	9	26	21	.227

(under 200 at-bats)

No.	Player, Position	AB	H	HR	R	RBI	AVG
23	John Ellis, C, 1B	136	40	5	13	25	.294
14	Ron Swoboda, OF, 1B	113	28	1	9	12	.248
27	Rich McKinney, 3B	121	26	1	10	7	.215
36	Hal Lanier, 3B, SS, 2B	103	22	0	5	6	.214

No.	Player, Position	AB	H	HR	R	RBI	AVG
21	Rusty Torres, OF	199	42	3	15	13	.211
2	Jerry Kenney, SS, 3B	119	25	0	16	7	.210
42	Charlie Spikes, OF	34	5	0	2	3	.147
41	Frank Tepedino, PH	8	0	0	0	0	.000

Team Leaders (Batting)

At-Bats:	585	Murcer
Batting Average:	.292	Murcer
Hits:	171	Murcer
Doubles:	30	Murcer
Triples:	7	Murcer
Home Runs:	33	Murcer
Runs:	102	Murcer
RBI:	96	Murcer
Stolen Bases:	23	White

Pitching Records

(50 innings or more)

No.	Player	G	IP	W	L	SV	SO	BB	ERA
28	Sparky Lyle	59	108	9	5	35	75	29	1.91
40	Lindy McDaniel	37	68	3	1	0	47	25	2.25
47	Fred Beene	29	58	1	3	3	37	24	2.33
38	Steve Kline	32	236	16	9	0	58	44	2.40
22	Jack Aker *with Yankees (0–0 in 4 games), Chicago Cubs (6–6 in 48 games); traded on 5/17/72, as player-to-be-named-later in 1/20/72, trade for Johnny Callison*	52	73	6	6	17	37	26	2.96
39	Rob Gardner	20	97	8	5	0	58	28	3.06
30	Mel Stottlemyre	36	260	14	18	0	110	85	3.22
19	Fritz Peterson	35	250	17	15	0	100	44	3.24
18	Mike Kekich	29	175	10	13	0	78	76	3.70
29	Casey Cox *with Texas (3–5 in 35 games), Yankees (0–1 in 5 games); acquired on 8/30/72, for Jim Roland*	40	77	3	6	4	31	29	4.44

No.	Player	G	IP	W	L	SV	SO	BB	ERA
(under 50 innings)									
54	Steve Blateric	1	4	0	0	0	4	0	0.00
45	Larry Gowell	2	7	0	1	0	7	2	1.29
45	Rich Hinton *with Yankees (1–0 in 7 games), Texas (0–1 in 5 games); traded on 9/6/72, for cash*	12	28	1	1	0	17	18	3.86
22	Ron Klimkowski	16	31	0	3	1	11	15	4.06
54	Jim Roland *with Oakland (0–0 in 2 games), Yankees (0–1 in 16 games), Texas (0–0 in 5 games); acquired from Oakland on 4/28/72, for cash; traded to Texas on 8/30/72, for Casey Cox*	23	31	0	1	0	17	18	5.28
29	Wade Blasingame *with Houston (0–0 in 10 games), Yankees (0–1 in 12 games); acquired on 6/6/72, for cash*	22	25	0	1	0	16	19	5.76
50	Al Closter	2	2	0	0	0	2	4	13.50
50	Doc Medich	1	——	0	0	0	0	2	——

Team Leaders (*Pitching*)

Games:	59	Lyle
Innings:	260	Stottlemyre
Wins:	17	Peterson
Complete Games:	12	Peterson
Shutouts:	7	Stottlemyre
Saves:	35	Lyle
Strikeouts:	110	Stottlemyre
ERA (more than 100 innings):	1.91	Lyle

1973

Final Standings

Team	W	L	PCT	GB
East Div.				
Baltimore	97	65	.599	——
Boston	89	73	.549	8
Detroit	85	77	.525	12
New York	**80**	**82**	**.494**	**17**
Milwaukee	74	88	.457	23
Cleveland	71	91	.438	26
West Div.				
Oakland	94	68	.580	——
Kansas City	88	74	.543	6
Minnesota	81	81	.500	13
California	79	83	.488	15
Chicago	77	85	.475	17
Texas	57	105	.352	37

Manager: Ralph Houk (No. 35)
Coaches: Jim Turner (No. 31), Elston Howard (No. 32), Dick Howser (No. 34), Jim Hegan (No. 44)

Batting Records

(200 at-bats or more)

No.	Player, Position	AB	H	HR	R	RBI	AVG
12	Ron Blomberg, DH, 1B	301	99	12	45	57	.329
1	Bobby Murcer, OF	616	187	22	83	95	.304
15	Thurman Munson, C	519	156	20	80	74	.301
2	Matty Alou, OF, 1B, DII *with Yankees (.296 in 123 games), St. Louis (.273 in 11 games); traded on 9/6/73, for cash*	508	150	2	60	29	.295
20	Horace Clarke, 2B	590	155	2	60	35	.263
43	Jim Ray Hart, DH, 1B *with San Francisco (.000 in 5 games), Yankees (.254 in 114 games); acquired on 4/17/73, for cash*	342	86	13	29	53	.251
6	Roy White, OF	639	157	18	88	60	.246
50	Duke Sims, C, OF, DH *with Detroit (.242 in 80 games), Yankees (.333 in 4 games); acquired on 9/24/73, for cash)*	261	64	9	34	31	.245

No.	Player, Position	AB	H	HR	R	RBI	AVG
18	Mike Hegan, 1B, DH, OF *with Oakland (.183 in 75 games),* *Yankees (.275 in 37 games); acquired* *on 8/18/73, for cash*	202	49	7	20	19	.243
9	Graig Nettles, 3B, DH	552	129	22	65	81	.234
24	Felipe Alou, 1B, OF *with Yankees (.236 in 93 games),* *Montreal (.208 in 19 games); traded on* *9/6/73, for cash*	328	76	5	29	31	.232
17	Gene Michael, 2B, SS, 3B	418	94	3	30	47	.225

(under 200 at-bats)

No.	Player, Position	AB	H	HR	R	RBI	AVG
23	Jerry Moses, C, DH	59	15	0	5	3	.254
10	Celerino Sanchez, DH, 3B, OF, SS	64	14	1	12	9	.219
11	Fred Stanley, SS, 2B	66	14	1	6	5	.212
22	Hal Lanier, SS, 2B, 3B	86	18	0	9	5	.209
11	Bernie Allen, 2B, 3B, DH *with Yankees (.228 in 17 games),* *Montreal (.180 in 16 games); traded on* *8/13/73, for cash*	107	22	2	10	13	.206
41	Otto Velez, OF	77	15	2	9	7	.195
46	Rick Dempsey, C	11	2	0	0	0	.182
25	Johnny Callison, OF, DH	136	24	1	10	10	.176
14	Ron Swoboda, OF, DH	43	5	1	6	2	.116

Team Leaders (Batting)

At-Bats:	639	White
Batting Average:	.329	Blomberg
Hits:	187	Murcer
Doubles:	29	Murcer, Munson
Triples:	4	Munson
Home Runs:	22	Murcer, Nettles
Runs:	88	White
RBI:	95	Murcer
Stolen Bases:	16	White

Pitching Records

(50 innings or more)

No.	Player	G	IP	W	L	SV	SO	BB	ERA
47	Fred Beene	19	91	6	0	1	49	27	1.68
28	Sparky Lyle	51	82	5	9	27	63	18	2.51
40	Lindy McDaniel	47	160	12	6	10	93	49	2.86
42	Doc Medich	34	235	14	9	0	145	74	2.95
30	Mel Stottlemyre	38	273	16	16	0	95	79	3.07

No.	Player	G	IP	W	L	SV	SO	BB	ERA
39	Wayne Granger *with St. Louis (2–4 in 33 games), Yankees (0–1 in 7 games); acquired on 8/7/73, for Ken Crosby and cash*	40	62	2	5	5	24	24	3.63
19	Fritz Peterson	31	184	8	15	0	59	49	3.95
38	Steve Kline	14	74	4	7	0	19	31	4.01
48	Sam McDowell *with San Francisco (1–2 in 18 games), Yankees (5–8 in 16 games); acquired on 6/7/73, for cash*	34	136	6	10	3	110	93	4.11
36	Pat Dobson *with Atlanta (3–7 in 12 games), Yankees (9–8 in 22 games); acquired on 6/7/73, for Frank Tepedino, Wayne Nordhagen, Al Closter, and Dave Cheadle*	34	200	12	15	0	93	53	4.40
18	Mike Kekich *with Yankees (1–1 in 5 games), Cleveland (1–4 in 16 games); traded on 6/12/73, for Lowell Palmer*	21	65	2	5	0	30	49	7.52

(under 50 innings)

No.	Player	G	IP	W	L	SV	SO	BB	ERA
50	Dave Pagan	4	13	0	0	0	9	1	2.84
39	Jim Magnuson	8	27	0	1	0	9	9	4.28
29	Tom Buskey	8	17	0	1	1	8	4	5.40
29	Casey Cox	1	3	0	0	0	0	1	6.00

Team Leaders (*Pitching*)

Games:	51	Lyle
Innings:	273	Stottlemyre
Wins:	16	Stottlemyre
Complete Games:	19	Stottlemyre
Shutouts:	4	Stottlemyre

Saves: 27   Lyle
Strikeouts: 145   Medich
ERA (more than 100 innings):   2.86   McDaniel

1974

Final Standings

Team	W	L	PCT	GB
East Div.				
Baltimore	91	71	.562	——
New York	89	73	.549	2
Boston	84	78	.519	7
Cleveland	77	85	.475	14
Milwaukee	76	86	.469	15
Detroit	72	90	.444	19
West Div.				
Oakland	90	72	.556	——
Texas	84	76	.525	5
Minnesota	82	80	.506	8
Chicago	80	80	.500	9
Kansas City	77	85	.475	13
California	68	94	.420	22

Manager: Bill Virdon (No. 21)
Coaches: Whitey Ford (No. 16), Mel Wright (No. 31), Elston Howard
(No. 32), Dick Howser (No. 34)

Batting Records

(200 at-bats or more)

No.	Player, Position	AB	H	HR	R	RBI	AVG
12	Ron Blomberg, DH, OF	264	82	10	39	48	.311
14	Lou Piniella, OF, DH, 1B	518	158	9	71	70	.305
27	Elliott Maddox, OF, 2B, 3B	466	141	3	75	45	.303
23	Alex Johnson, OF, DH *with Texas (.291 in 114 games), Yankees (.214 in 10 games); acquired on 9/9/74, for cash*	481	138	5	60	43	.287
6	Roy White, OF, DH	473	130	7	68	43	.275
1	Bobby Murcer, OF	606	166	10	69	88	.274
2	Sandy Alomar, 2B, SS, 3B, DH, OF	333	87	1	47	28	.261

No.	Player, Position	AB	H	HR	R	RBI	AVG
	with California (.222 in 46 games), *Yankees (.269 in 76 games);* *acquired on 7/8/74, for cash*						
15	Thurman Munson, C, DH	517	135	13	64	60	.261
10	Chris Chambliss, 1B	467	119	6	46	50	.255
	with Cleveland (.328 in 17 games), *Yankees (.243 in 110 games);* *acquired with Dick Tidrow and* *Cecil Upshaw on 4/26/74, for Fritz* *Peterson, Steve Kline, Fred Beene,* *and Tom Buskey*						
22	Jim Mason, SS	440	110	5	41	37	.250
9	Graig Nettles, 3B, DH	566	139	22	74	75	.246
18	Mike Hegan, DH, 1B, OF	243	57	9	24	41	.235
	with Yankees (.226 in 18 games), *Milwaukee (.237 in 89 games);* *traded on 5/13/74, for cash*						
44	Bill Sudakis, DH, 1B, 3B, C	259	60	7	26	39	.232

(under 200 at-bats)

No.	Player, Position	AB	H	HR	R	RBI	AVG
17	Gene Michael, 2B, SS, 3B	177	46	0	19	13	.260
46	Rick Dempsey, C, OF, DH	109	26	2	12	12	.239
24	Otto Velez, 1B, OF, 3B	67	14	2	9	10	.209
20	Horace Clarke, 2B, DH	137	28	0	8	5	.204
	with Yankees (.234 in 24 games), *San Diego (.189 in 42 games);* *traded on* *5/31/74, for cash*						
26	Fernando Gonzalez, 2B, SS, 3B, DH	142	29	1	12	9	.204
	with Kansas City (.143 in 9 games), *Yankees (.215 in 51 games);* *acquired on 5/5/74, for cash*						
51	Terry Whitfield, OF	5	1	0	0	0	.200
41	Duke Sims, C, DH, OF	121	24	3	8	8	.198
	with Yankees (.133 in 5 games), *Texas (.208 in 39 games); traded on* *5/8/74, for Larry Gura*						
11	Fred Stanley, SS, 2B	38	7	0	2	3	.184
13	Walt Williams, OF, DH	53	6	0	5	3	.113
43	Jim Ray Hart, DH	19	1	0	1	0	.053
43	Jim Deidel, C	2	0	0	0	0	.000
52	Larry Murray, OF	1	0	0	1	0	.000

Team Leaders (Batting)

At-Bats: 606   Murcer
Batting Average: .311   Blomberg

Hits:	166	Murcer
Doubles:	26	Piniella, Maddox
Triples:	8	White
Home Runs:	22	Nettles
Runs:	75	Maddox
RBI:	88	Murcer
Stolen Bases:	15	White

Pitching Records

(50 innings or more)

No.	Player	G	IP	W	L	SV	SO	BB	ERA
28	Sparky Lyle	66	114	9	3	15	89	43	1.66
39	Larry Gura	8	56	5	1	0	17	12	2.41
41	Mike Wallace *with Philadelphia (1–0 in 8 games), Yankees (6–0 in 23 games); acquired on 5/3/74, for Ken Wright*	31	60	7	0	0	35	37	2.85
38	Cecil Upshaw *with Cleveland (0–1 in 7 games), Yankees (1–5 in 36 games); acquired with Chris Chambliss and Dick Tidrow on 4/26/74, for Fritz Peterson, Steve Kline, Fred Beene, and Tom Buskey*	43	68	1	6	6	34	28	3.04
36	Pat Dobson	39	281	19	15	0	157	75	3.07
43	Rudy May *with California (0–1 in 18 games), Yankees (8–4 in 17 games); acquired on 6/15/74, for cash*	35	141	8	5	2	102	58	3.19
29	Tom Buskey *with Yankees (0–1 in 4 games), Cleveland (2–6 in 51 games); traded with Fritz Peterson, Steve Kline, and Fred*	55	99	2	7	18	43	36	3.38

No.	Player	G	IP	W	L	SV	SO	BB	ERA
	Beene on 4/26/74, for Chris Chambliss, Dick Tidrow, and Cecil Upshaw								
30	Mel Stottlemyre	16	113	6	7	0	40	37	3.58
33	Doc Medich	38	280	19	15	0	154	91	3.60
19	Dick Tidrow *with Cleveland (1–3 in 4 games), Yankees (11–9 in 33 games); acquired with Chris Chambliss and Cecil Upshaw on 4/26/74, for Fritz Peterson, Steve Kline, Fred Beene, and Tom Buskey*	37	210	12	12	1	108	66	4.16
19	Fritz Peterson *with Yankees (0–0 in 3 games), Cleveland (9–14 in 29 games); traded with Steve Kline, Fred Beene, and Tom Buskey on 4/26/74, for Chris Chambliss, Dick Tidrow, and Cecil Upshaw*	32	161	9	14	0	57	39	4.36
38	Steve Kline *with Yankees (2–2 in 4 games), Cleveland (3–8 in 16 games); traded with Fritz Peterson, Fred Beene, and Tom Buskey on 4/26/74, for Chris Chambliss, Dick Tidrow, and Cecil Upshaw*	20	97	5	10	0	23	36	4.64
47	Fred Beene *with Yankees (0–0 in 6 games), Cleveland (4–4 in 32 games); traded with Fritz Peterson, Steve*	38	83	4	4	3	45	28	4.66

No.	Player	G	IP	W	L	SV	SO	BB	ERA
	Kline, and Tom Buskey on 4/26/74, for Chris Chambliss, Dick Tidrow, and Cecil Upshaw								
29	Dick Woodson *with Minnesota (1–1 in 5 games), Yankees (1–2 in 8 games); acquired on 5/4/74, for Mike Pazik*	13	55	2	3	0	24	16	5.07

(under 50 innings)

No.	Player	G	IP	W	L	SV	SO	BB	ERA
42	Ken Wright	3	6	0	0	0	2	7	3.00
40	Tippy Martinez	10	13	0	0	0	10	9	4.15
48	Sam McDowell	13	48	1	6	0	33	41	4.69
53	Dave Pagan	16	49	1	3	0	39	28	5.14
40	Rick Sawyer	1	2	0	0	0	1	1	9.00

Team Leaders (Pitching)

Games:	66	Lyle
Innings:	281	Dobson
Wins:	19	Dobson, Medich
Complete Games:	17	Medich
Shutouts:	4	Medich
Saves:	15	Lyle
Strikeouts:	157	Dobson
ERA (more than 100 innings):	1.66	Lyle

1975

Final Standings

Team	W	L	PCT	GB
East Div.				
Boston	95	65	.594	——
Baltimore	90	69	.566	4½
New York	**83**	**77**	**.519**	**12**
Cleveland	79	80	.497	15½
Milwaukee	68	94	.420	28
Detroit	57	102	.358	37½

Team	W	L	PCT	GB
West Div.				
Oakland	98	64	.605	——
Kansas City	91	71	.562	7
Texas	79	83	.488	19
Minnesota	76	83	.478	20½
Chicago	75	86	.466	22½
California	72	89	.447	25½

Managers: Bill Virdon (53–51; No. 21), Billy Martin (30–26; No. 1)
Coaches: Whitey Ford (No. 16), Cloyd Boyer (No. 21), Mel Wright (No. 31), Elston Howard (No. 32), Dick Howser (No. 34), Art Fowler (No. 42)

Batting Records

(200 at-bats or more)

No.	Player, Position	AB	H	HR	R	RBI	AVG
15	Thurman Munson, C, DH, OF, 1B, 3B	597	190	12	83	102	.318
27	Elliott Maddox, OF, 2B	218	67	1	36	23	.307
10	Chris Chambliss, 1B	562	171	9	66	72	.304
6	Roy White, OF, 1B, DH	556	161	12	81	59	.290
25	Bobby Bonds, OF, DH	529	143	32	93	85	.270
9	Graig Nettles, 3B	581	155	21	71	91	.267
45	Ed Herrmann, DH, C	200	51	6	16	30	.255
2	Sandy Alomar, 2B, SS	489	117	2	61	39	.239
11	Fred Stanley, SS, 2B, 3B	252	56	0	34	15	.222
22	Jim Mason, SS, 2B	223	34	2	17	16	.152

(under 200 at-bats)

No.	Player, Position	AB	H	HR	R	RBI	AVG
49	Kerry Dineen, OF	22	8	0	3	1	.364
13	Walt Williams, OF, DH, 2B	185	52	5	27	16	.281
44	Terry Whitfield, OF, DH	81	22	0	9	7	.272
46	Rick Dempsey, C, DH, OF, 3B	145	38	1	18	11	.262
23	Alex Johnson, DH, OF	119	31	1	15	15	.261
12	Ron Blomberg, DH, OF	106	27	4	18	17	.255
52	Otto Velez, DH, 1B	8	2	0	0	1	.250
26	Rich Coggins, OF, DH *with Montreal (.270 in 13 games), Yankees (.224 in 51 games); acquired on 6/20/75, for cash*	144	34	1	8	10	.236
24	Rick Bladt, OF	117	26	1	13	11	.222
20	Eddie Brinkman, SS, 3B, 2B *with St. Louis (.240 in 28 games), Texas (.000 in 1 game), Yankees (.175 in 44 games); acquired from*	140	29	1	8	8	.207

No.	Player, Position	AB	H	HR	R	RBI	AVG
	Texas on 6/13/75, for cash						
14	Lou Piniella, OF, DH	199	39	0	7	22	.196
42	Bob Oliver, 1B, DH, 3B	38	5	0	3	1	.132
54	Dave Bergman, OF	17	0	0	0	0	.000
52	Larry Murray, OF	1	0	0	1	0	.000
20	Eddie Leon, SS	0	0	0	0	0	——

Team Leaders (Batting)

At-Bats:	597	Munson
Batting Average:	.318	Munson
Hits:	190	Munson
Doubles:	38	Chambliss
Triples:	5	White
Home Runs:	32	Bonds
Runs:	93	Bonds
RBI:	102	Munson
Stolen Bases:	30	Bonds

Pitching Records

(50 innings or more)

No.	Player	G	IP	W	L	SV	SO	BB	ERA
29	Catfish Hunter	39	328	23	14	0	177	83	2.58
43	Rudy May	32	212	14	12	0	145	99	3.06
28	Sparky Lyle	49	89	5	7	6	65	36	3.12
19	Dick Tidrow	37	69	6	3	5	38	31	3.13
33	Doc Medich	38	272	16	16	0	132	72	3.50
39	Larry Gura	26	151	7	8	0	65	41	3.51
36	Pat Dobson	33	208	11	14	0	129	83	4.07

(under 50 innings)

No.	Player	G	IP	W	L	SV	SO	BB	ERA
40	Tippy Martinez	23	37	1	2	8	20	32	2.68
41	Rick Sawyer	4	6	0	0	0	3	2	3.00
49	Ron Guidry	10	16	0	1	0	15	9	3.45
53	Dave Pagan	13	31	0	0	1	18	13	4.06
41	Mike Wallace	12	13	0	0	0	8	6	6.23

with Yankees (0–0 in 3 games), St. Louis (0–0 in 9 games); traded on 6/13/75, for cash

Team Leaders (Pitching)

Games:	49	Lyle
Innings:	328	Hunter
Wins:	23	Hunter
Complete Games:	30	Hunter
Shutouts:	7	Hunter
Saves:	8	Martinez
Strikeouts:	177	Hunter
ERA (more than 100 innings):	2.58	Hunter

1976

Final Standings

Team	W	L	PCT	GB
East Div.				
New York	97	62	.610	——
Baltimore	88	74	.543	10½
Boston	83	79	.512	15½
Cleveland	81	78	.509	16
Detroit	74	87	.460	24
Milwaukee	66	95	.410	32
West Div.				
Kansas City	90	72	.556	——
Oakland	87	74	.540	2½
Minnesota	85	77	.525	5
California	76	86	.469	14
Texas	76	86	.469	14
Chicago	64	97	.398	25½

Manager: Billy Martin (No. 1)
Coaches: Yogi Berra (No. 8), Bob Lemon (Nos. 21 & 33), Elston Howard (No. 32), Dick Howser (No. 34), Art Fowler (No. 42)

Batting Records

(200 at-bats or more)

No.	Player, Position	AB	H	HR	R	RBI	AVG
17	Mickey Rivers, OF	590	184	8	95	67	.312
15	Thurman Munson, C, DH, OF	616	186	17	79	105	.302
10	Chris Chambliss, 1B, DH	641	188	17	79	96	.293
6	Roy White, OF	626	179	14	104	65	.286

No.	Player, Position	AB	H	HR	R	RBI	AVG
14	Lou Piniella, OF, DH	327	92	3	36	38	.281
38	Carlos May, DH, OF, 1B	351	91	3	45	43	.271
	with Chicago White Sox (.175 in 20 games), Yankees (.278 in 87 games); acquired on 5/18/76, for Ken Brett and Rich Coggins						
20	Willie Randolph, 2B	430	115	1	59	40	.267
9	Graig Nettles, 3B, SS	583	148	32	88	93	.254
11	Fred Stanley, SS, 2B	260	62	1	32	20	.238
23	Oscar Gamble, OF, DH	340	79	17	43	57	.232
46	Rick Dempsey, C, OF	216	42	0	12	12	.194
	with Yankees (.119 in 21 games), Baltimore (.213 in 59 games); traded with Rudy May, Tippy Martinez, Dave Pagan, and Scott McGregor on 6/15/76, for Ken Holtzman, Doyle Alexander, Grant Jackson, Ellie Hendricks, and Jimmy Freeman						
22	Jim Mason, SS	217	39	1	17	14	.180

(under 200 at-bats)

No.	Player, Position	AB	H	HR	R	RBI	AVG
47	Kerry Dineen, OF	7	2	0	0	1	.286
24	Otto Velez, OF, DH	94	25	2	11	10	.266
40	Fran Healy, C, DH	144	35	0	12	10	.243
	with Kansas City (.125 in 8 games), Yankees (.267 in 46 games); acquired on 5/16/76, for Larry Gura						
2	Sandy Alomar, 2B, DH, SS, 3B, OF, 1B	163	39	1	20	10	.239
46	Gene Locklear, OF, DH	99	22	0	11	9	.222
	with San Diego (.224 in 43 games), Yankees (.219 in 13 games); acquired on 7/10/76, for Rick Sawyer						
27	Elliott Maddox, OF, DH	46	10	0	4	3	.217
26	Juan Bernhardt, OF, DH, 3B	21	4	0	1	1	.190
18	Ellie Hendricks, C	132	23	4	8	9	.174
	with Baltimore (.139 in 28 games), Yankees (.226 in 26 games); acquired with Ken Holtzman, Doyle Alexander, Grant Jackson, and Jimmy Freeman on 6/15/76, for Rudy May, Tippy Martinez, Scott McGregor, Dave Pagan, and Rick Dempsey						
26	Cesar Tovar, OF, DH, 2B	84	14	0	3	6	.167
	with Oakland (.178 in 29 games),						

No.	Player, Position	AB	H	HR	R	RBI	AVG
	Yankees (.154 in 13 games); acquired on 9/1/76, for cash						
26	Rich Coggins, OF, DH	100	16	0	5	6	.160
	with Yankees (.250 in 7 games), Chicago White Sox (.156 in 32 games); traded with Ken Brett on 5/18/76, for Carlos May						
47	Larry Murray, OF	10	1	0	2	2	.100
20	Mickey Klutts, SS	3	0	0	0	0	.000
12	Ron Blomberg, DH	2	0	0	0	0	.000
44	Terry Whitfield, OF	0	0	0	0	0	——

Team Leaders (Batting)

At-Bats:	641	Chambliss
Batting Average:	.312	Rivers
Hits:	188	Chambliss
Doubles:	32	Chambliss
Triples:	8	Rivers
Home Runs:	32	Nettles
Runs:	104	White
RBI:	105	Munson
Stolen Bases:	43	Rivers

Pitching Records

(50 innings or more)

No.	Player	G	IP	W	L	SV	SO	BB	ERA
28	Sparky Lyle	64	104	7	8	23	61	42	2.26
40 & 18	Tippy Martinez	39	70	5	1	10	45	42	2.33
	with Yankees (2–0 in 11 games), Baltimore (3–1 in 28 games); traded with Rudy May, Rick Dempsey, Dave Pagan, and Scott McGregor on 6/15/76, for Doyle Alexander, Ken Holtzman, Grant Jackson, Ellie Hendricks, and Jimmy Freeman									

No.	Player	G	IP	W	L	SV	SO	BB	ERA
25	Grant Jackson	34	78	7	1	4	39	25	2.54

*with Baltimore
(1–1 in 13 games),
Yankees (6–0 in
21 games);
acquired with
Doyle Alexander,
Ken Holtzman,
Ellie Hendricks,
and Jimmy
Freeman on 6/15/76,
for Rudy May,
Tippy Martinez,
Rick Dempsey,
Dave Pagan, and
Scott McGregor*

No.	Player	G	IP	W	L	SV	SO	BB	ERA
19	Dick Tidrow	47	92	4	5	10	65	24	2.63
31	Ed Figueroa	34	257	19	10	0	119	94	3.02
36	Dock Ellis	32	212	17	8	0	65	76	3.19
38	Ken Brett	29	203	10	12	2	92	76	3.28

*with Yankees (0–0
in 2 games),
Chicago White
Sox (10–12 in 27
games); traded
with Rich Coggins
on 5/18/76, for
Carlos May*

No.	Player	G	IP	W	L	SV	SO	BB	ERA
52	Doyle Alexander	30	201	13	9	0	58	63	3.36

*with Baltimore
(3–4 in 11 games),
Yankees (10–5 in
19 games);
acquired with Ken
Holtzman, Grant
Jackson, Ellie
Hendricks, and
Jimmy Freeman
on 6/15/76, for
Rudy May, Tippy
Martinez, Rick
Dempsey, Dave
Pagan, and Scott
McGregor*

No.	Player	G	IP	W	L	SV	SO	BB	ERA
29	Catfish Hunter	36	299	17	15	0	173	68	3.53
53	Ken Holtzman	34	247	14	11	0	66	70	3.65

*with Baltimore
(5–4 in 13 games),
Yankees (9–7 in
21 games);
acquired with
Doyle Alexander,*

No.	Player	G	IP	W	L	SV	SO	BB	ERA
	Grant Jackson, Ellie Hendricks, and Jimmy Freeman on 6/15/76, for Rudy May, Tippy Martinez, Rick Dempsey, Dave Pagan, and Scott McGregor								
43	Rudy May	35	220	15	10	0	109	70	3.72
	with Yankees (4–3 in 11 games), Baltimore (11–7 in 24 games); traded with Tippy Martinez, Rick Dempsey, Dave Pagan, and Scott McGregor on 6/15/76, for Doyle Alexander, Ken Holtzman, Grant Jackson, Ellie Hendricks, and Jimmy Freeman								
53	Dave Pagan	27	70	2	5	1	47	27	4.73
	with Yankees (1–1 in 7 games), Baltimore (1–4 in 20 games); traded with Rudy May, Tippy Martinez, Rick Dempsey, and Scott McGregor on 6/15/76, for Doyle Alexander, Ken Holtzman, Grant Jackson, Ellie Hendricks, and Jimmy Freeman								

(under 50 innings)

No.	Player	G	IP	W	L	SV	SO	BB	ERA
43	Jim York	3	10	1	0	0	6	4	5.59
49	Ron Guidry	7	16	0	0	0	12	4	5.63

Team Leaders (Pitching)

Games:	64	Lyle
Innings:	299	Hunter

Wins:	19	Figueroa
Complete Games:	21	Hunter
Shutouts:	4	Figueroa
Saves:	23	Lyle
Strikeouts:	173	Hunter
ERA (more than 100 innings):	2.26	Lyle

Parts of this appendix have been adapted from *Yankees by the Number*, compiled and published by George D. Wolf (see Bibliography).

BIBLIOGRAPHY

Allen, Maury. *Roger Maris: A Man for All Seasons*. New York: Donald I. Fine, 1986.

Berra, Yogi, with Tom Horton. *It Ain't Over . . .* New York: McGraw-Hill, 1989.

Bouton, Jim, *Ball Four*. New York: World Publishing, 1970.

Dickson, Paul. *The Dickson Baseball Dictionary*. New York: Facts on File, 1989.

Duren, Ryne. *The Comeback*. Dayton, Ohio: Lorenz Press, 1978.

Ford, Whitey, with Phil Pepe. *Slick*. New York: William Morrow, 1987.

Ford, Whitey, Mickey Mantle, and Joseph Durso. *Whitey and Mickey*. New York: Viking, 1977.

Gallagher, Mark. *Explosion! Mickey Mantle's Legendary Home Runs*. New York: Arbor House, 1987.

———. *Day by Day in New York Yankees History*. New York: Leisure Press, 1983.

Golenbock, Peter. *Dynasty: The New York Yankees, 1949–1964*. Englewood Cliffs, New Jersey: Prentice-Hall, 1975.

Guidry, Ron, and Peter Golenbock. *Guidry*. Englewood Cliffs, New Jersey: Prentice-Hall, 1980.

Gutman, Dan. *Baseball Babylon*. New York: Penguin, 1992.

Heat Moon, William Least. *Blue Highways: A Journey Into America*. New York: Atlantic Monthly Press, 1982.

Honig, Donald. *The New York Yankees: An Illustrated History*. New York: Crown, 1981.

Hunter, Catfish, and Armen Keteyian. *Catfish: My Life in Baseball*. New York: McGraw-Hill, 1988.

Jacobson, Steve. *The Best Team Money Could Buy.* New York: Atheneum, 1978.

Kubek, Tony, and Terry Pluto. *Sixty-One.* New York: Macmillan, 1987.

Lally, Dick. *Pinstriped Summers.* New York: Arbor House, 1985.

Lee, Bill, with Dick Lally. *The Wrong Stuff.* New York: Viking, 1984.

Lyle, Sparky, and Peter Golenbock. *The Bronx Zoo.* New York: Crown, 1979.

Madden, Bill, and Moss Klein. *Damned Yankees.* New York: Warner Books, 1990.

Mann, Jack. *The Decline and Fall of the New York Yankees.* New York: Simon and Schuster, 1967.

Mantle, Mickey, with Herb Gluck. *The Mick.* New York: Doubleday, 1985.

Martin, Billy, with Phil Pepe. *Billyball.* New York: Doubleday, 1987.

McCarver, Tim, with Ray Robinson. *Oh, Baby, I Love It!* New York: Villard, 1987.

Miller, Marvin. *A Whole Different Ball Game.* New York: Birch Lane Press, 1991.

Munson, Thurman, with Martin Appel. *Thurman Munson.* New York: Coward, McCann and Geoghegan, 1978.

Nettles, Graig, and Peter Golenbock. *Balls.* New York: G. P. Putnam's Sons, 1984.

Okrent, Daniel, and Harris Lewine, eds. *The Ultimate Baseball Book.* Boston: Houghton Mifflin, 1984.

Pepe, Phil. *The Wit and Wisdom of Yogi Berra*, second edition. Westport, Connecticut: Meckler Books, 1988.

Piniella, Lou, and Maury Allen. *Sweet Lou.* New York: G. P. Putnam's Sons, 1986.

Schaap, Dick. *Steinbrenner!* New York: G. P. Putnam's Sons, 1982.

Shatzkin, Mike, ed. *The Ballplayers.* New York: William Morrow, 1990.

Smith, Myron J., Jr. *Baseball: A Comprehensive Bibliography.* New York: McFarland, 1986.

Smith, Norman Lewis. *The Return of Billy the Kid.* New York: Coward, McCann and Geoghegan, 1977.

Sugar, Bert, ed. *Baseballistics*. New York: St. Martin's, 1990.

Tullius, John. *I'd Rather Be a Yankee*. New York: Macmillan, 1986.

Veeck, Bill. *The Hustler's Handbook*. New York: G. P. Putnam's Sons, 1965.

Wolf, George D. *Yankees by the Number* (1986 and 1991 editions). Privately published (available from George D. Wolf, 2323 Delanoy Avenue, Bronx, New York, 10469-6305).

In addition, the author drew on the sports reporting of the newspapers *Newsday, The New York Times*, the New York *Daily News*, and the *New York Post*, and *Sports Illustrated*.

ABOUT THE AUTHOR

PHILIP BASHE is the author or coauthor of *Preventing Cancer, Teenage Idol, Travelin' Man: The Complete Biography of Rick Nelson, You Don't Have to Die: One Family's Guide to Surviving Childhood Cancer, When Saying No Isn't Enough: How to Keep the Children You Love off Drugs, That's Not All Folks!, Dee Snider's Teenage Survival Guide, Heavy Metal Thunder*, the *Rolling Stone Rock Almanac*, and the forthcoming *Patients' Guide to Tests and Procedures*.

A former magazine editor and radio announcer whose work has appeared in the *New York Times Book Review*, the *Buffalo Evening News, Reader's Digest, Parade Magazine, Billboard*, and other publications, Bashe lives with his wife, author Patty Romanowski, and son, Justin, in Baldwin, New York. He is also a scrappy singles hitter for the Dharma Bums team of the Huntington Softball League.